D1554814

"I think that the saving of 530 children is, I imagine, t
ence a man can have. You say in Hebrew: The one w
the one that saved the life of the whole world.

But when you save 530 children it's really unforgettable. I want to express,
on behalf of our people, our nation, our recognition of your courage, your
wisdom, of your determination under extremely difficult conditions at a
time when our connections were extremely weak."

—President Shimon Peres

"David Littman was an extraordinary figure, tall, commanding, elegant,
self-confident, and enormously courageous, physically and politically. This
book is the story of part of that courage, which he self-depreciated as play-
ing a role, almost as in a film, in the remarkable clandestine rescue of 530
Jewish children from Casablanca. But his role there was more important
and required more daring than that of the character played by Humphrey
Bogart in the celebrated film, Casablanca. Fortuitously he played his heroic
role a year before the first James Bond film appeared in 1962."

—Prof. Michael Curtis
Distinguished Professor Emeritus
of political science at Rutgers University

"In the case of rescue operations, very often the people who were recruited
for these operations were not members of the Mossad, very often [they were]
volunteers. The risk in operating such an operation was very great, but it
was also a very, very grave risk taken by the people who volunteered and one
such volunteer was David Gerald Littman, who had no experience at all in
intelligence activities."

—Efraim Halevy
Chairman of the MLM/I ICC
Head of the Mossad 1998–2002

DAVID G. LITTMAN

OPERATION MURAL

AN ENGLISHMAN AND THE MOSSAD IN CASABLANCA

THE CLANDESTINE EMIGRATION OF
530 MOROCCAN JEWISH CHILDREN TO ISRAEL

RVP Press
New York

RVP Publishers Inc.
41 East 11th Street, 11th Floor
New York, NY 10003

© 2015 David Littman / RVP Publishers Inc., New York

Edited by Ariane Littman

"Fragments of Memory" and "The Story of David Bar-Sheshat" (in "A Thousand and One Nights") translated from the Hebrew by Amos Riesel.

All rights reserved. No part of this book may be reproduced in any form or by any electronic or mechanical means, including information storage and retrieval systems, without permission in writing from the publisher, except by a reviewer who may quote brief passages in a review.

RVP Press™ is an imprint of RVP Publishers Inc., New York.
The RVP Publishers logo is a registered trademark of RVP Publishers Inc., New York.

The publication of this book was supported by International Center for Western Values, Amsterdam.

Library of Congress Control Number: 2015930080

ISBN 978 1 61861 340 0

www.rvppress.com

Table of Contents

Acknowledgments

On July 2011, I started working with my father on the present book and although he was seriously ill at the time, he was determined to see it printed with all its numerous documents, pictures and testimonies. He felt that this would ultimately "put the historical record right."

It had been inherent for him to resonate the voices of the 530 children who had left Morocco in 1961 through Operation Mural. Yossi Shahar, aged 12 when he left, consented in March 2012 to write his "Fragments of Memory" whilst his mother, Rachel Sabbah, recounted in a touching interview the painful separation from her first-born son. There are still many untold stories hence Yossi and Rachel's distinctive and unique contribution to this book is exceptionally valuable. I would like to express my deep gratitude to both of them for providing us with their personal stories.

I extend my gratitude to Zvi Gilat, whom I contacted in August 2013 and who kindly agreed we translate the significant testimony of David Bar-Sheshat which first appeared in the Israeli newspaper *Hadashot* on May 9, 1986 in his detailed article, "A Thousand and One Nights." I would also like to thank Amos Riesel for the excellent job he did in translating both testimonies into English.

As I pursued my editorial work I realized that the book would not be complete without the compiling accounts from the Mossad agents. Such an undertaking was only made possible thanks to the generosity of Gad

Shahar, Carmit Gattmon and Pinhas Katsir who shared with me their fascinating recollections as Mossad agents in Morocco together with their fond and lively memories of the tall and young "British subject of his Majesty the Queen." I would like to express my profound appreciation to Shmuel Toledano for his warm words during our interview in 2013, a year after my father passed away, and likewise for his continuous support and tireless efforts so that Mural's role be acknowledged both by President Shimon Peres in 2008 and by the Mossad in 2009. Profound appreciation is extended as well to Professor Michael Curtis, Distinguished Professor Emeritus of Political Science at Rutgers University in Princeton, for adding in his preface another dimension to the role played by my father at the UN Human Rights Council in Geneva.

I would also like to thank The Swiss Federal Archives (SFA) in Bern for providing File (G.65.40.sd) that throws a new and crucial light on the conciliatory policy of the Swiss authorities in Bern during Operation Mural, a copy of which was first handed to my father in 2008 by the Swiss Ambassador in Tel Aviv, Walter Haffner. I thank Mrs. Erika Katz for translating the German documents of this file. Furthermore, I would like to thank the Dorot Jewish Division of the New York Public Library for providing in digital format some of documents from the David Littman and Bat Yeor Archives.

Most of the pictures from Morocco in 1961 were shot by my father, an enthusiastic photographer, with the exception of those at OSSEAN's office in Casablanca and those of the children aboard the ship S.S. *Ionia* which were taken by Dr. Claude Dreyfus. I would like to thank his son Freddy Dreyfus for donating years ago these unique pictures. Much appreciation also goes to Raphael Rebibo for recounting his role in the operation and for providing the exclusive image of the children at the Home de la Forêt in Switzerland together with the Israeli officials.

I would like to thank as well Carlos Gonzalez for digitalizing the hundreds of documents and photographs from my father's files, Udi Katzman for his work on the black and white pictures and documents for the current edition and Dyanne Fowler for kindly typing out the names of the children in the appropriate format. Likewise I would like to express my deep gratitude to Michal Yehezkel who has proofread the manuscript with great meticulousness and to René van Praag and Astrid Bosch for making this book a reality, posthumously fulfilling my father's wish of having the story of Operation Mural published with all its documents and pictures. Ultimately, I would like to thank my dear father for granting me the opportunity of working together with him on this important historical document and for entrusting me with the completion of his book. I thank both my mother and him for having taught me, through their actions during this mission in particular but also through their writings and their deeds in general, the higher value of courage and determination for the sake of others.

Ariane Littman
Jerusalem, March 2015

Starting a Married Life
with a Common Commitment

Gisèle Littman

In 1961, my husband David Gerald Littman, being part of a fierce network of courageous men and women, succeeded in smuggling out of Morocco over 530 Jewish children in order to bring them to Israel. When this clandestine affair took place, we had just been married for eighteen months. The covert Moroccan operation, which had been under the supervision of the Mossad, was only disclosed to the general public after decades.

David Littman, the man who provided bold leadership to crucial elements of this mission, documented a detailed record of the entire endeavor in order to supply his supervisors at Mossad with information on how "their" mission had been executed. Common to the Modus Operandi of a secret service, the Mossad ordered Littman to destroy any record of the operation. Littman, however, did not obey. Subsequent to Littman's reluctance to destroy the written account of this covert operation, we can ascertain, today, in great detail how Operation Mural was implemented.

Littman's main duty was to take care of the complex logistics of the mission and to provide a camouflage cover for the illegal operation. During this period of time, Jews were not allowed to emigrate from Morocco. Operation Mural granted Jewish families a secured way to send some of their youngsters to Israel and to fulfill the Zionist ideal. Although many were thrilled to be offered this opportunity, it meant splitting up families. Needless to say, this was not easy for either parents or siblings.

David Gerald Littman, code-name "Mural," with his wife Gisèle
and their baby-daughter Diana in the office 105 Dumont d'Urville, June 24, 1961

David Gerald Littman wrote this book during the last two years of his life. For over three decades he had been a very active and forceful promoter of human rights and defender of Israel at the United Nations Commission/ Council of Human Rights in Geneva. In 2010, David Littman and Paul Fenton published a compendium of documents on the Jews of the Maghreb, a work on which he had researched for many decades. The same year, in November, on our return from Paris where we both had launched our respective books, we learned that David had acute myeloid leukemia (AML). Doctors gave him a few weeks of life expectancy. He died in May 2012.

David's greatest cherished dream was to publish one of the most intensive and extensive milestones of his life, however brief it may have been: the clandestine aliya of 530 Jewish children smuggled out of Morocco in 1961. His souvenirs were untarnished and all the documents, reports, correspondences and photographs relating to this event of our life were preciously safeguarded in drawers with drafts of manuscripts. The suddenness of his illness provided the tragic impetus for completing this work. From

December 2010, David underwent intense and cumbersome chemotherapy treatments at a clinic in Genolier (VD, Switzerland), but most of the time he could work at home. When his condition began to deteriorate, I requested from our second daughter, Ariane, who resided in Israel, to return. She subsequently assisted her father, providing him with advice and computerizing the data, a task which he couldn't do on his own anymore. Till the last days of his life, David worked on his manuscript, remembering with precision the events of the mission to which he dedicated his utmost self.

David and I met as young students at the Institute of Archaeology, University College London (UCL), in December 1958, a year after my family's dramatic departure from Egypt. We were both idealists, sharing a love for art and archaeology. David was a young man with a deep faith and a spontaneous and generous inclination to help others. He was well versed in biblical history and liked to quote from the bible, never concealing his Jewishness. His genuine and frank conduct concerning his identity, under any circumstances and till his dying day, has always surprised me. He proudly manifested his fidelity to Israel even in the most racist and antisemitic arenas such as the United Nations Commission/Council of Human Rights in Geneva. Whilst serving at the Commission/Council on Human Rights, he was not only battling antisemistism in the United Nations arena, but was also denouncing the oppression of Christians in Islamic societies and supporting with great passion other related courses.

In 1961, when David proposed the Moroccan mission to me, I immediately understood its inherent dangers: death sanctions for Zionism in any Arab country. Memories of sleepless nights in Egypt, of repressed anxiety, and this ominous feeling that death could grapple you at any moment, flashed back in my mind. Would I accept? Would I refuse? On the one hand I would be transferred back to this darkness from which perhaps I would never return; on the other hand I would be abandoning a mitzvah which was requested of me. I was aware of the priceless freedom these children would be gaining in Israel. Moreover, by accompanying my husband to Morocco, I would not be failing him. Furthermore, what would we do with our three month old baby-girl? Would we bring her into a dangerous mission? This concern weighted heavily upon my decision to go with David.

However, since I was unable to separate from either her or from David, we took the baby with us.

Different reasons motivated our participation in a dangerous mission to Morocco. From his aspect, my husband asked to participate since he was eager to help persecuted Jews. When I met him as a young man of twenty-five, I was astonished by his profound feeling of gratitude, even of guilt, for having enjoyed an easy life. One of seven children, he had a privileged upbringing and education thanks to a protective, self-made and successful father. David was very tall and an expert in boxing and numerous sports, self-assured and indifferent to danger.

My childhood and background had been quite the contrary. Born in Cairo to a Sephardic wealthy family, I felt from early childhood the strains of World War II. The British Commonwealth Forces occupied Cairo while the German Nazi and Italian Fascist armies were advancing from Libya to Alexandria. Nearly every night we rushed to the shelter with the other terrified tenants of our building. The traumatic noise from the anti-aircraft guns filled the surrounding darkness and was compounded by imposed blackouts. Blue paint covered our windows, strewn with large scotch paper, to prevent the glass from blowing up into pieces during the German bombardments of the city. British military police controlled the strict implementation of its security orders.

For my siblings and I, the war reverberated a strange ambiguity, mixing fear and folly. Naturally, we often saw my mother crying over her Parisian family who were forced to wear the yellow star or run into hiding. However, we also enjoyed the precipitous arrival of our young cousins into our home, fleeing Rommel's advance toward Alexandria. Subsequently, it was our turn to leave Cairo and go into hiding with other Jewish families within the Egyptian countryside. When we were disobedient, our Yugoslavian governess threatened us, warning us of the impending arrival of the Germans who would kill us all just as they were doing with European Jews.

For Jews in Arab countries, the war didn't end in 1945. The British army, stationed in Cairo, directed its operations against Palestinian Jewry while the Muslim Brotherhood hordes pillaged, destroyed, burned Jewish commercial establishments, hospitals, schools, houses, raping and killing the unfortunate that fell under their clasp. In 1947, several Arab countries, including Egypt, prepared for war against Palestinian Jewry. In a few years, oppressive, Nazi-type laws against Jews in Egypt, coupled with a regime of threats, insecurity and spoliations, succeeded in annihilating a community more than two thousand years old.

Swept away with the tide of a million Jewish refugees fleeing the Arab Muslim countries, I found myself in London in 1957, with my family ruined and stateless. In Egypt, my family belonged to the wealthy notables that contributed to Jewish charitable organizations. In England, we became the beneficiaries of Jewish generosity who helped the refugees from Egypt. In London, I discovered the Ashkenazim, a Jewish population quite different from the meek, intimidated, persecuted Sephardic Jews living among hostile Muslim populace, unprotected by the law. I also met young Israeli students who were not like me, conditioned by fear and a feeling of being an anonymous object, subject to a series of chaotic events. However, the most amazing discovery which filled me up with admiration was the discovery of British society. This background contributed to my reluctance and yet my desire to help the Moroccan Jews.

During Operation Mural I acted as David's assistant. However, shortly after arriving in Morocco, I discovered that I was pregnant again. This happy news complicated our situation. I had a critical decision to take. I could have left David and returned to London with the baby. But no! I decided to stay by my husband's side and continue to help him. At the time, David was suffering from a stomach-ulcer and during this period of crisis I had to be with him.

On page 167–175, I described my few encounters with the Moroccan Jews. David and I empathized with them, being moved by the same solidarity that had kept alive the Jewish people for over 3,000 years, in spite of persecutions. I, in turn, stretched out, to the Moroccan Jews, the same helping hand which the British Jews had extended to me. David totally immersed himself into this mission, carrying on heavy responsibilities for such a young man and in difficult circumstances. He was dedicated and fearless. He discovered his extraordinary capacities that he would have been ignored had he refused the mission. True, we were collaborating with people with superior gifts of abnegation, courage and generosity; they directed and advised David brilliantly. Although we didn't know them, we felt supported by their intelligence and solidarity toward the same goal: to help these captive Jews to reach freedom in Israel.

After we each left Morocco separately, it took us time to adjust to our new life: a family of soon to be four, for which David took care to secure a comfortable flat in Geneva. We had prosaic problems to solve which absorbed us; however we both inscribed at the University of Geneva, David in the Archaeology section and I in the Faculty of Social Science.

Soon, Ariane, a gorgeous curious and blue eyed baby, came into the world, requiring all my attention. Morocco was behind us, forging one more link that bounded us together, David and me, with the feeling of having accomplished the mission for which we both volunteered.

Jerusalem, March 2015

Homage to My Friend David Littman

Prof. Michael Curtis

Distingished Professor Emeritus of Political Science

at Rutgers University

David Littman was an extraordinary figure, tall, commanding, elegant, self-confident, and enormously courageous, physically and politically. This book is the story of part of that courage, which he self-depreciated as playing a role, almost as in a film, in the remarkable clandestine rescue of 530 Jewish children from Casablanca. But his role there was more important and required more daring than that of the character played by Humphrey Bogart in the celebrated film, *Casablanca*. Fortuitously he played his heroic role a year before the first James Bond film appeared in 1962.

David, the son of Polish Jews who had immigrated to Britain, had an elitist education, at an English Anglican public school, and at Trinity College, Dublin. At his public school, Canford, in Dorset he took part in Sunday morning services, acquiring knowledge of Anglican rituals that would later be helpful in Morocco. At the daily evening school prayer meetings the maverick David always chose passages from the Old Testament of the Bible to recite. This was the prelude for his constant reference to Biblical passages during his political speeches later on.

That education combined with his native character gave him confidence to face the world. This self-confidence sprang from the authority he acquired as a result of his skill and his leadership in a variety of school sports, cricket, tennis, rugby, and boxing. He was trained in political science, history, and archaeology, but became an activist, not an academic specializing

David G. Littman in the early 50s

in archaeology, though he earned a university degree with honors. Littman had spent World War II years in the U.S., was concerned with the business heritage of his father, and seemed set to lead a peaceful and prosperous life. However, while living in Switzerland, first in Lausanne and then in Geneva, he read William Shirer's book, *The Rise and Fall of the Third Reich,* which profoundly influenced him and led him to ponder both the complexity of international affairs and what Jews living in Switzerland could have done during the war. He then saw his future as an activist, as an individual aiding Jews and the state of Israel in the postwar period.

David, at the time somewhat eccentric and naïve, was eager to help fellow Jews, but was rebuffed by organizations in Switzerland to which he had applied. However, at the age of twenty-seven he was drawn, through his solicitation to the OSE (Oeuvre de Secours aux Enfants), the Jewish international organization for children, into the drama of going to Morocco for Youth Aliyah, supposedly on a humanitarian mission to bring Jewish children for holidays in Switzerland. David was always quoting from Shakespeare and the lines from Julius Caesar were appropriate to his decision to engage in this drama: "There is a tide in the affairs of men which, taken at the flood, leads on to fortune." This was his moment.

The setting for the drama was that after 1956 Moroccan Jews were not allowed to leave the country, though the Israeli Mossad evacuated some people by secret channels. In January 1961, a ship, *L'Egoz,* transporting Moroccan Jewish refugees capsized near Gibraltar with 44 deaths, half of whom were children. The Mossad realized it had to change its strategy to get Jews out of North Africa. This would mean an operation supposedly of a humanitarian nature to give poor children a holiday abroad, but the real objective of which was to get the children to Israel.

By chance Littman asked OSE if he could help in anything at exactly the moment an emissary was needed to carry out the Mossad plan, and he was chosen. On March 16, 1961, David, latter joined by his wife Gisèle Orebi, arrived in Casablanca, and Operation Mural, the code name given to David, began. Gisèle, the petite pregnant wife who had lived under terror as a Jew in Egypt and fled to London in 1957 where she met David at the London Institute of Archaeology a year later, was also anxious to do something for the Jewish people. David had been

Gisèle and David G. Littman in Morocco

sent by a number of Jewish organizations, and worked under the guidance of the Israeli controlled Misgueret (framework) group.

Littman rose to the occasion with his ability to make contacts with people of various kinds. The handsome, proud Jewish David became the English gentleman "Gerald" (Littman's middle name) and purported to be an Anglican, playing the role with distinction, singing hymns with which he was familiar from school days, at the Anglican Church in Casablanca. Gisèle, carrying a baby several months old, bravely masqueraded as a French Catholic.

The complex account of how he persuaded Jewish families to make the difficult decision to allow their children to be sent to Israel, under the pretense of going on a holiday for non-Jews as well as Jewish children in Switzerland, unfolds in the following pages; the story concludes with the transport of the 530 children in five convoys, two by boat and three by air. In retrospective Littman saw himself as a mixture of naivete and boldness, an unconscious but willing tool of the Israeli Mossad.

Littman understated his courage and his resourcefulness in devising ways to succeed, including the use of a collective passport system for the

Children from the first convoy waiting to board
the *S.S. Ionia*, June 26, 1961

children. Herein, his striking personality was a key factor. It was his elitist demeanor, seen by some as snobbish, his skill at forming social and cordial relations with local Moroccan officials, his participation as the gifted tennis player with an air of grandeur, and his associations with the British consul, his tennis partner, the Swiss Red Cross delegate and Swiss Consul in Casablanca, as well as with the Moroccan head of security, who invited David and Gisèle to dinner, that led the Moroccan authorities to grant passports for the Jewish children. The Swiss authorities, it is now realized, acted with diplomatic discretion, allowing David to continue his activities, though probably aware of its nature, and in a sense compensating for their indifference to the fate of Jews during the World War II.

David had succeeded in his mission of rescue beyond all expectations, He prevailed despite the genuine threat of being caught and tortured for his and Gisèle's activity. His success had wider implications. Operation Mural led to a larger Jewish emigration of about 100,000 Jews from Morocco

David G. Littman at the UN

through Operation Yakhin between 1961 and 1964, implementing the same technique of collective passports for Jews which Littman had employed. Today less than 3,000 Jews remain in Morocco.

On a number of occasions David quoted from the prophet Jeremiah: "Behold I will bring them from the north country and gather them from the coasts of the earth . . . the (Jewish) children shall come again to their own border." David had helped return the children to Israel and would persist in his objective to combat antagonism against Jews and the state of Israel. He did so in two ways, first, by being the representative of several Non-Governmental Organizations at the UN; second, by being the relentless, and often very loud, champion of Gisèle's brilliant books, written under the pseudonym of Bat Ye'or (Daughter of the Nile), on the subject of *dhimmitude*, the status of Jews in Muslim countries, a concept she made universally familiar, and on the increasing prominence of Muslims in European countries.

David did not go gently into the night. In Casablanca, he had displayed impressive physical courage. In Geneva, particularly at meetings of the UN Human Rights Council he demonstrated equally formidable political courage. In a witty literary allusion he pointed out that the UN Emperor, strutting in his palace, was naked. The Emperor leading the "international community" was descending incontinently and recklessly the staircase which led to a dark gulf. He was tireless in denouncing the hypocrisy of that "international community."

He challenged the Islamic game, installing Sharia law, to replace the dominant paradigms of international relations, and the 1948 Universal Declaration of Human Rights which was aimed at creating a framework for the world in need of universal codes based on mutual consent. As a representative of the Association for World Education (AWE) and of the World Union for Progressive Judaism (WUPJ) he was the spokesman for sanity, for fairness against the continual onslaughts against Israel, and the defender of human rights.

Regardless of the attempts in the international bodies to stop him from delivering his short statements he was often a lonely voice, persisting in castigating the abuse of international bodies which largely centered on denouncing Israel. He stressed the persistence of antisemitism or Judeo-phobia, under the guise of "anti-Zionism," in the Arab and Muslim world, the calls for jihad in the name of Allah, the racism and culture of hatred taught in Arab schools, and the efforts of Muslim organizations to prevent any criticism of Islam. David was fond of quoting Karl Popper: "We should therefore claim in the name of tolerance, the right not to tolerate the intolerant."

David was an ebullient personality, passionate in his beliefs, a joy to be with, and a delightful companion with whom to share food, drinks, and conversation whether in New York, London, Paris, or Geneva. This book is a worthy tribute and will endear him to those who did not know him personally.

Princeton, February 2015

My Father's Last Mission

(July 2011–May 2012)

Ariane Littman

On July 2011, fifty years after my father played "his real-life exit" from his risky mission in Morocco and while he was being treated for leukemia in the hospital, courageously fighting his last battle and in an effort to lift his spirits, I proposed to help him with a project I knew he still aspired to accomplish. During the remaining ten months of his life *Operation Mural: An Englishman and the Mossad in Casablanca*, became his priority; we worked together on it even as he was being treated in the intensive care unit. Until his very last day, he found solace seeing me working by his side, asking with concern whether all the pictures and documents had been incorporated in the book. After his death in May 2012, I continued with the mission which he had bestowed upon me; *Operation Mural* transcended his earthly departure leaving instead the memory of his vivid and forceful presence.

The story was not new to me since some of its protagonists had crossed my childhood. I recall an elderly man, Professor Bloch, as well as Doctor Claude Dreyfus, a renowned chiropractor, both living in Geneva. I recollect a certain Naphtali Bargiora who lived with his wife, Yaffa, in the Old City of Jerusalem, and more particularly, I recall Gad and Ruth Shahar, dear friends of my parents who lived in Kibbutz Regavim. Now and then, when my father drove us, my brother Daniel and I to our Hebrew lessons in Geneva, he would relate puzzling stories of a lost wallet, secret lists of children, Swiss watches and police interrogations in far-away mysterious Morocco.

David G. Littman and his daughter Ariane during the filming of the documentary *Operation Mural*, Ouzoud Waterfalls, Morocco, 2006

However, it was only in 1984 while reading Shmuel Segev's article in *Maariv* that I fully comprehended my parents' daring role in this clandestine mission; at the time, my father, aged twenty-seven, and my mother, pregnant again and with a five-month baby, volunteered to go to Morocco. In 1986, I was also present, together with my brother, when they received a special certificate of gratitude by Prime Minister Shimon Peres during the Mimouna festivities in Jerusalem. Twenty years later, in 2006, my father asked me to join him and his contacts Gad (Georges) and Pinhas (Jacques) on a supposed tourist trip to Morocco during the making of the documentary film *Operation Mural*. One day, while strolling together in the shuk of Casablanca we were followed and stopped by a policeman in civilian clothes who asked to see the official permit for my professional cameras. I felt a sudden apprehension but my father kept his calm, explaining to the policeman that we were a group of tourists and that he could contact our guide. That day I got a lively hint of the way he must have handled things back in

1961. Through my camera lenses, I captured Morocco's colorful landscapes as they blended with his narration, I watched him gather memories with meticulous and painful care as he walked backward on the paths of time. The trip to Morocco linked me in a strong yet subtle way to a story that took place while I was just a faint presence in my mother's womb. Subsequently, I would feel this connection again during the moving ceremonies at the Presidential Residence (2008) and the Intelligence Center (2009) which I documented at his request.

David G. Littman choosing the pictures for the book, Switzerland 2011

With my father in hospital, I started reading his narrative based on *The 1961 Report* and then went through the files of original documents he had kept with great care. I could feel the pulse of the story unfolding through the missives he sent the fictive N. Lehmann, at times being slightly sarcastic when facing "obstruction" from his contacts nicknamed "Leoni and Berger."

Always profuse with details and in a refined English, when his epistles were dismissed as too long, he once ironically wrote back: "If my grammar and prolixity still cause concern may it also cause reflection." I was particularly moved when looking through the slides of anonymous smiling children I found the lists with the names and the addresses of the 530 children who had left behind their families to embark on their adventurous journey in the summer of 1961. I did wonder if their journey echoed the memory of my father's own journey across Europe, when in the spring of 1940, aged seven, he embarked for America on the *S.S. Conti di Savoia* with his parents and four of his siblings, Roama, Peter and Barbara (the twins), and his youngest sister, Shirley. The two eldest boys, Louis and Allan were already in New York.

This clandestine rescue story of Jewish Moroccan children from Morocco to Israel via Switzerland was revealed to the public in 1984. The journalist, Shmuel Segev, while openly naming my parents, had given false names to the other protagonists involved in Operation Mural, due to security reasons and following instructions by the Mossad. This discrepancy perpetuated itself over time in the press and elsewhere, and was heightened by incorrect facts recounted by people whom, as my father often mentioned, were "sitting in an office thousand kilometers away."

I felt, and he agreed with me, that the inclusion of genuine documents and photographs to his narrative would ultimately "put the historical record right," a battle which my father had endeavored with since the beginning.

In the book, the documents were summarized in English in order to make them more accessible to the readers, yet this doesn't liken the liveliness and the stylishness of the original, and a diligent reader will be duly rewarded reading the genuine letters.

As I read his letters, it occurred to me that it was not only his courage but also his independent mind that had allowed him to achieve this mission "beyond all our expectations," as per the words of Alex Gattmon. It was certainly that same independent mind that led him to disobey the orders from Naphtali Bargiora, his contact in Paris, to destroy all the spare copies of *The 1961 Report* he sent him in March 1962. A *Report* as he wrote to Moshe Kol, Head of the Youth Aliyah Department, he had "hasten to finish so that 'historical' record is preserved if it is truly wanted." Seven months later, in July 1962, he dispatched the *Report* to Mr. Kol together with some additional documents, in a sealed envelope via the Israel Ambassador in Bern. That same *Report* allowed Shmuel Segev to add a new chapter in his book *Operation "Yakhin" The Secret Immigration of Moroccan Jews to Israel*, published in 1984.

However, more than recognition—which he sought as a natural token of appreciation for the risks he took with my mother and my sister Diana in order to achieve his mission—"truth" was at the core of his battle. Perhaps this derived from his acute perception, as an historian by formation, of the importance of facts in the construction of historical narratives. Such facts being often distorted by "unfortunate falsification by omission," the perpetuation of which remaining unchallenged, as he once wrote Gershom Shoken, the editor in chief of *Haaretz*.

In January 1962, in his letter to Moshe Kol, he added a long postscript on Bruno Kern, a non-Jew, who had volunteered to accompany the fourth convoy and was accidently omitted by Prof. Bloch from the list of those who had contributed to the mission. Twenty-two years later it was his turn to be omitted, becoming instead the "Jew with a British passport" in Moshe Kol's article published in *Haaretz* in May 1984, one month after Segev's article on Mural. Subsequently, he sent two letters to the editor in chief of *Haaretz*, clarifying Moshe Kol's inexactitudes regarding Operation Milhar (Mural's fictive name). Although he had hoped "the columns of *Haaretz* are open to those who wish to put the historical record right," his first letter was returned claiming to be too long for publication and the second letter which was much shorter, was never published. Again in 1986, he wrote to the editor of *The Jerusalem Post*, correcting inaccuracies in two articles published on the occasion of the meetings with the "children" organized by the *Beyahad* organization, the ideological movement of Jews of North African Origin. But inaccuracies persisted over the years whether in Hebrew or English publications. Likewise in 1991, in the important book by the renowned reporter and writer, Tad Szulc, Naphtali Bargiora becomes the chief organizer for the Swiss rescue operation and the one who sets up the office in Casablanca.

His profound sense of veracity also guided him to categorically refuse to change the record of the "scandalous and irresponsible July 9th incident" in which eighty-five children from the first convoy were sent to Israel in the midst of the operation. His refusal impaired his twenty year-long friendship with Moshe Kol, the only Israeli personality to have officially thanked him for his role in Operation Mural.

The missives he submitted to OSSEAN and to Moroccan officials are genuine historical documents as to what actually happened during the summer of 1961. The facts and details in his prolific correspondence vividly bear witness to the evolution of the rescue mission under his direction. Reading them, one can follow step by step how my father organized and made possible the actual departure of 530 children. His autonomy of mind and creativity is visible in the way he developed his nexus of contacts with Moroccan officials from various ministers, negotiating until the very end with Mr. Ghomari from the Entr'Aide, the possible arrival of a separate group of Moslem children to the consternation of his contacts abroad. Similarly, at a very early stage he favored collective passports, defying orders from Naphtali Bargiora and likewise later on and in agreement with "Georges" his contact from the Misgeret, he ignored demands for "selection" with regard to the "psychological" suitability of the children sent to Switzerland.

The incident involving Si Alaoui Tajjedine, Khalifa of the first district of Casablanca, who accused him of being implicated in "an exodus" of Jewish children, is well detailed in his letters. He cunningly writes N. Lehmann that she must "also find such accusations extremely strange," adding: "In our second year in Morocco we must do our utmost to attract the Moslem youth so that such absurd aspersions cannot be levied against the Oeuvre and its reputation."

He handled with astuteness and resourcefulness this incident that could have brought about the exposure of the whole operation. Getting in touch with Mr. D'khissi and Mr. Hajjaj, important connections he cultivated, he wrote a letter to Mr. Cheradi, Director of the Cabinet of Casablanca's Governor, stressing that while it is not in the habit of the Oeuvre to ask the religion of the children, he would be glad to organize a convoy of exclusively Moslem children, emphasizing that it would be deplorable should the Oeuvre fail to bring youths of different countries together due to this unfortunate incident.

For obvious reasons all events related to "Georges" and the Misgeret do not appear in my father's letters to N. Lehmann but are described in his 1961 Report, posterior letters and speeches. In this present book he pays tribute at length to all the brave men and women who took part in the mission and made it possible.

As part of his cover as a British Anglican my father was also busy weaving his social connections with the British Consul. He played with him tennis, celebrating at his house Queen Elisabeth's official birthday and as he wrote N. Lehmann "happy to say that there is a Church of England here, so our spirituals needs will not be neglected."

As to his Swiss contacts, in his letters to N. Lehmann, he consistently followed up the possible transfer to France of the *Haemophiliac*, a boy he promised Mr. Reinhard, the chief delegate of the League of the Red Cross, to assist.

Waiting impatiently for the key letter from Mr. Maeder of the Federal Police for Foreigners, he met the Swiss Consul in Casablanca and the Swiss Ambassador in Rabat as soon as the letter arrived. He hoped for a personal recommendation from the Ambassador, Mr. Bernath, who had meanwhile received a letter from Prof. Bloch (signed Prof. Aberson) to be forwarded to Princess Lalla Aïcha of Morocco. My father wished for an interview with the Princess who was the president of the Entr'Aide Nationale and could facilitate obtaining documents for the children's journey. The Swiss officials were astonished by his rather "improper ways of proceeding" as perceptible in their own confidential correspondence and even Miss Lehmann wrote him to refrain from asking documents other than visas as "we Swiss are quite formalists and fantasy is not our strong point."

The letter to Princess Lalla Aïcha was not in my father's files but among the documents of file G.65.sd.* entitled: "Oeuvre Suisse de Secours aux Enfants de l'Afrique du Nord, Colonies de Vacances Organisées par M. Littman."

This secret file about my father and OSSEAN throws an important light on the policy of Switzerland during Operation Mural. It contains the confidential correspondence between the Department of Foreign Affairs at the Federal Political Department (EPD) in Bern on the one hand and the Ambassador and Consul of Switzerland in Morocco on the other hand. In the spring of 2008, my father received photocopies of the file from the Federal Archives in Bern thanks to the initiative of the Swiss Embassy in Tel Aviv. This allowed him to pay tribute during the reception at the Presidential Residence to "the diplomatic discretion of the Swiss authorities, who turned a blind eye to what might have become a potential exodus of Jewish children from Morocco to Israel via Switzerland, and implicitly accepted mass collective passports and Swiss visa facilities."

In April 2012, just before being hospitalized once more, he left me the file that had gone astray. Reading this confidential correspondence, I realized its important historical value and contacted at once the Swiss Federal Archives from the Federal Department of Home Affairs (FDHA) in Bern. I soon received by email all the original documents of file G.65.sd.* and a significant chapter on Swiss conciliatory policy was added, just a month before his decease.

I can not find the words to express my grief, knowing my father will never hold in his hands *Operation Mural, An Englishman and the Mossad in Casablanca.* Yet it is my hope that the present book with its photographs, original letters, newspaper articles, lists of children and moving testimonies will ultimately "put the historical record right," a battle my father fought for relentlessly during his lifetime. Hopefully, this book might also provide an incentive to research the stories of those children sent by their brave families, for the love of Zion, on a journey whose final destination was full of qualms.

Jerusalem, 2015

Preface

On July 1, 2009, just three days before my 76th birthday, a special event took place at the Israel Intelligence Heritage and Commemoration Center (IIHC) at Glilot, Tel Aviv, when Israel's deputy Mossad chief conferred on me the Hero of Silence Order (the ninth person to receive it since 1985): "An order of highest esteem and appreciation awarded to David Gerald Littman: A clandestine warrior, who risked his life and who served a sacred cause of the People and of the State of Israel."[1]

This was preceded by the screening of a few sequences from the 2007 documentary film, *Operation Mural: Casablanca 1961*[2] and a very moving presentation by IICC Chairman Efraim Halevy (Mossad chief between 1998–2002), to an audience of over two hundred persons in their packed assembly hall with family, friends and members of the Israeli intelligence communities.[3]

During this moving event, when going up to the podium to receive the award, I vividly recalled the words of the Mossad chief in Casablanca, Alex Gattmon, when we met secretively for the first and only time on the eve of my July 24, 1961 departure from Casablanca—a moment in my life that I shall never forget: "*I wanted to see you personally before you leave tomorrow to tell you that your mission has succeeded beyond all our expectations. I thank you. We all thank you.*"

Part I
The Mission 1961

CHAPTER 1

In Search for a Mission

On November 30, 1960, aged twenty-seven, installed in a fine flat with a small garden at 55 Chemin de la Cigale, above Lausanne, and envisaging a new life in Switzerland with a beautiful wife and new-born baby, I began reading William L. Shirer's *The Rise and Fall of the Third Reich*. I had read much on the Second World War, but this magnum opus acted as a catalyst and I kept asking myself, while pushing Diana's pram overlooking the Alps, what could a Jew have done then in Switzerland, a neutral country—and what could I do *now* for the Jewish people and Israel?

Soon I was knocking at the door of every international Jewish organization in Geneva with a simple request: "What can I do to help?" I made it clear that I did not require a salary. Very little interest was shown by those who were greatly surprised by such an unusual offer—it was even suggested that I might organize receptions to raise funds for Israel.

A Fatal Meeting

In mid-January, I came to what I had decided would be my last door at 11 rue du Mont Blanc, opposite the main post office, close to the Geneva railway station. The director of OSE (Oeuvre de Secours aux Enfants, an organization that cared for Jewish children), welcomed me. A few days before Professor Jacques Bloch had received a visitor who had asked him if he knew a young man willing to accept a humanitarian mission for Jewish children in Morocco. The Jewish Agency and the Youth Aliyah, Israeli children's organization, were seeking to bring Jewish children from Morocco to Israel. Moshe Kol—its president, who was later to become Israel's Minister of Tourism—had been successful in persuading Mrs. Eleanor Roosevelt to write a letter to the newly-restored Sultan Muhammad V on this matter, but there had been no reaction.

Jacques Bloch couldn't believe his ears on hearing my offer and welcomed me warmly. A few days later, Naphtali Bar-Giora of the Jewish Agency's immigration department returned to interview me and explained the proposed mission. Much later I learned from him that it was his idea for the Jewish Agency and Youth Aliyah to collaborate with OSE in a "Swiss holidays" system for Jewish children to reach Morocco. There was never

Prof. Jacques Bloch at the Littman's home in Switzerland, 1963

Gisèle Orebi's grandfather:

Aslan Levy Orebi Bey (1860–1915)

any mention to me at any time of the Mossad being involved.

I discussed it with Gisèle for several days. Born in Cairo, she had experienced the war tension and turmoil since the 1940s. After the Arab League's refusal of the November 29, 1947, UN General Assembly Partition Plan for Mandated Palestine, and then the 1948–1949 Arab-Israel war, over 1300 Egyptian Jews had been jailed under King Farouk, and 500 more by Nasser in 1956, while hundreds of thousands had either been expelled, fled or had left Egypt and other Arab countries, as it was extremely difficult for Jews to lead a normal life there. Faced with this impossible situation under Nasser's regime, having had their property sequestrated and stripped of their Egyptian citizenship, the Orebi family decided to seek refuge abroad soon after the Suez Crisis.

Gisèle Orebi, touring Upper Egypt, 1954

Now, barely three years later, Gisèle found herself living a normal life in Switzerland—a life free of fear, with a protective husband and a lovely new-born baby, endeavouring to forget the past. Yet, in spite of the anguish felt at the thought of returning to an Arab country and its inherent danger—a danger she understood far better than I did—she had agreed to such a

Gisèle Orebi (sitting on a camel, second left) guiding an Italian group of tourists at the Memphis Pyramids, 1954

clandestine and risky mission for her own specific reason. Happily married and in gratitude for the birth of our blue-eyed, blond haired Diana, she felt a great desire to do a good deed—a *mitzvah* in Hebrew.

My case was different. I was still undecided about my professional future, but over-confident that I could deal with any problem that might arise. Greatly inspired by Shirer's book, I wished to undertake something that I

Gisèle Orebi (standing on the right) with a group of tourists
at the Mokattam overlooking Old Cairo, 1955

felt others couldn't do. My elitist education at Canford School and Trinity
College Dublin had rendered me oblivious to risks. Being young, naive, as
well as adventurous and with financial independence, I was fortified in my
illusion that there would be no possible risks in such a mission.

Having persuaded Gisèle to join me, eventually with Diana, I waited three
weeks for Bar-Giora's confirmation. I was totally unaware of the *Piscès (Egoz)*
tragedy of January 10–11, 1961 when forty-four Jews had died (amongst them
twenty-four children) after their dilapidated, clandestine boat had capsized
in a storm off the Moroccan coast. I knew little then about the history and
current situation of Moroccan Jews.

I flew to London to alert my eldest brother Louis of my departure. He
tried very strongly to dissuade me from accepting, warning me: "The Israelis
won't do anything to help if you're imprisoned in Casablanca." But I didn't
waiver, even renouncing my American citizenship at the U.S. Consulate in
London on March 10. I obtained a British passport, like Gisèle, with Diana
inscribed in both, so as not to arouse suspicions in Morocco. Gisèle and
Diana had been refused U.S. citizenship, although I had lived in the USA for

five years as a dual Anglo-American citizen before I was twelve, but not after.

I then dealt with outstanding family business matters, made arrangements for Diana and our Italian nanny to reside at the Orebi home in Ealing after Gisèle would join me in Morocco a fortnight later. Returning to Switzerland two days later, I arranged for Gisèle's departure to London, vacated our Lausanne apartment and then flew to Paris on March 14, where I was fully "briefed" and checked by Alex Korani, who felt that even my British passport could cause some problem because of Diana's second Hebrew name.[4]

On her arrival in London, Gisèle was strongly influenced by her parents and by Louis, and when I called her just before leaving for Casablanca she tried to dissuade me from going by saying she had decided not to go after all, to which I replied without hesitation: "I'm very sorry but I have decided to go as was agreed." Instantly, she replied: "I'm joining you in two weeks—take care of yourself." I left Paris early on March 16 for Casablanca.

Thirty years later, I learned from an old friend, archaeologist Prof. Amnon Ben Tor, that he had been asked to keep an eye on me during the Hazor "dig," in the summer of 1958, and had been questioned in February 1961 about my reliability, to which he had simply replied: "He's OK!"

Family background

My great grandfather, Zanvel Shmuel (Reb Zawel) Littman, was born in 1812 in Radomsk, Poland, then part of the Russian Empire. He died in 1906, aged ninety-four. He was one of the thousands of Jewish teenagers forcibly conscripted into the imperial army as a Cantonist ("Nicolai") soldier for twenty-five years during the nightmarish reign of Czar Nicholas I (1825-55), who had initiated the system, by a 1827 statute, and aimed at facilitating the conversion of Jews to Orthodox Christianity. In 1855, a year before the statute was reduced to a five year period by Czar Alexander II—called by Benjamin Disraeli: "the kindliest prince who ever ruled Russia"—Regimental Quartermaster Sergeant Littman was honourably discharged. His twenty-five years of military service and a medal allowed him to settle anywhere

David Gerald's great grandfather:
Zanvel Shmuel Littman (1810–1906)

in Russia. He married Esther in Moscow and they had four sons and two daughters; on her premature death, he returned to Radomsk in the Jewish Pale where he married a widow with whom he had a fifth son, Morris.

After the Czar's assassination in 1881, the modest liberalism of his reign resulted in a wave of pogroms. All but one of Shmuel's children immigrated to America in the 1880s and only the eldest son, Meyer Jonah, remained in Poland; Morris, the youngest reached New York in 1893. When I met Morris in New York in 1958, he related a few memorable stories his father had told him about life in the Russian army, including the siege of Sebastopol in 1855.

My grandfather, Meyer Jonah, was born in Moscow in 1860 and moved to Czestochowa in 1890 where he joined the Chassidic movement. A respected *shamas* of his synagogue, close to Rabbi Avigdor Shapiro, he became a lover of the poor people who came to tell their stories in time of trouble. Immigrating to America in 1920, he joined the Young Men's Hebrew Association Synagogue in the Bronx. As a *shamas*, he was beloved and respected by everyone—supporting dozens of rabbinical families in America and in Poland and founding an interest-free loan fund that helped businessmen and

David Gerald's grandfather:
Meyer Jonah Littman (1860–1942)

workers alike. Until his last breath, quietly, without asking for recognition, he raised money and collected clothes which he sent in small packages to the poor people who remained in Czestochowa.[5]

Meyer's second son, Joseph Aaron, my father, was born in 1898 and reached New York in 1913 with a ticket sent by his uncle Morris. On obtaining U.S. citizenship, Joe finally persuaded his parents as well as his siblings to join him—just before the gates of freedom in America were closed in 1921.

Travelling to London on business in the early 1920s, Joe Littman met Evelyn Hetty Gold whom he married in February 1925. My mother, her parents and siblings had arrived in England from Sosnowiec, Poland after the bloody pogrom of 1909. Two years later, father began his successful career as a London real estate investor and property developer—just before the 1930s Depression. He became a British citizen after the birth of his seventh child in December 1935. I was the sixth, the youngest of four boys, born on the 4th of July 1933. We all had dual Anglo-American nationality from our father.

After the outbreak of the Second World War father decided to send us to America with our mother at a time when the government—due to expected food shortage—was assisting with the departure of thousands of children to the Commonwealth and encouraging those who had the means to send their children abroad for holidays since the war was not expected to last long. I was not yet seven years old when the five of us: Roama, Peter and Barbara

Joseph and Evelyn Littman with their seven children on Friday evening, London, 1939
(left to right: Father Joseph Aaron Littman, Shirley, Barbara, Roama, Mother Evelyn,
Louis, Allan, Peter and David)

(twins), Shirley and I crossed Europe by train with our parents in the spring
of 1940—during the "phoney war" period, just before the collapse of France.

From Genoa we embarked on the *S.S. Conti di Savoia* for a week's journey
to America (Louis and Allan had preceded us to New York in autumn 1939,
staying with parents). Father continued his journey to British Mandatory
Palestine where, ever optimistic, he made a real estate investment before
returning to London. As he was over 41—the military age—and with seven
children to support, he was not drafted into the British army. Since only merchandise could be transferred during wartime, not money, mother managed
to clothe and feed us all for five long years by selling British textiles based
on the "samples" sent by Dad. We first lived in a small rented house in Long
Beach, Long Island, an hour by train from New York, but soon moved to a
larger apartment on the promenade facing the sea. We returned to England
five years later in August 1945, a month after my twelfth birthday.

Growing up: 1946-1959

On our return in August 1945 we were surprised to find ourselves living in a very nice house in Bournemouth, a coastal resort town, where father soon acquired the Cumberland Hotel on the East Cliff and then the prestigious Palace Court Hotel facing the Pavilion. The next year we moved to a spacious new home, with a tennis court, in Winnington Road, Hampstead, London.

Although my father was not strictly observant, I remember often crossing the adjacent golf club with him on foot to reach the synagogue. Once he told me, and I have never forgotten his words: "I have succeeded in life and you will be able to do anything you want, even become a diplomat."

He wanted his children to have the best education: Louis studied law at Trinity College Cambridge; Roama at the Royal College of Music (in 1949 she sang at the Royal Albert Hall with Sir Malcolm Sargent conducting the Royal Philharmonic Orchestra); Allan graduated from Harvard; and Barbara later from Pennsylvania State University.

In spring 1946, my brother Peter was accepted at Canford School, Wimborne, Dorset, and I followed him in May, not yet thirteen—the

The Littmans' house in North London (Winnington Road, Hampstead) from 1946

Canford School cricket match with David G. Littman as captain and wicket-keeper, 1951

David G. Littman, Head of Wimborne House, Canford School, June 1951.

In a black jacket as a school prefect, sitting next to House Tutor Michael

Rathbone and Housemaster Michael Frewer.

Wimborne House cricket team with David G. Littman
wearing his school cricket-team captain's jacket, 1950

David G. Littman Captain of Wimborne House Hockey Team, 1950

Trinity College Dublin 1st tennis team with David G. Littman in the center standing, 1952

youngest boy in the school. As I stammered badly, I could not perform a traditional *Bar-Mitzvah* at the age of thirteen. About four years later my father arranged for me to be treated by Lionel George Logue, King George VI's speech therapist, who put me on the long road to healing. At Canford (founded in 1923), we experienced a typical English elitist "public school" education, attending church on Sunday morning as father had failed to persuade the headmaster, the Reverend Canning, that we should be excused; Catholics had the same obligation at the six boarding "houses." Only those boys in the non-boarding "day-house" were exempt from attending the compulsory Anglican church service on Sunday mornings.

I was good at sports, playing in the second school rugby and hockey teams, throwing the javelin in the Athletes' team and became captain of tennis in 1949 (Junior Wimbledon 1950), captain of boxing, and in 1951 captain of the first cricket team, where I excelled as Canford's best wicket-keeper ever.

From September 1950, I was the head of Wimborne House and one of seven "school prefects" in a school of more than 450 boys. We had many obligations, supervising the boys in our House—guided by the housemaster and the house tutor—and arranging all the house sports activities. There were also special privileges such as strolling across the finely cut lawns of Lord Wimborne's former magnificent nineteenth century domain, with one or both hands in trouser pockets—just like the masters. House prefects used the ordinary pebbled paths, with one hand allowed in a jacket pocket. Often, as the senior boy, I would be expected to pronounce the one sentence prayer ("grace") at meals, either in English or in Latin, thereby allowing 200 boys in the main dining room to start their meal. And there was also lunch at the

David G. Littman
holding his B.A. degree
with honors at Trinity
College Dublin, 1956

headmaster's table, with my school prefect colleagues and distinguished guests. Being constantly engaged in sports and playing either at Canford or other schools on Tuesday, Thursday and Saturday afternoons, I was less active in science studies, but had a good memory and excelled in history.

After passing my school certificate examinations in summer 1951, father took me to Ireland, hoping that I would be accepted to Trinity College, Dublin (T.C.D.), as Peter had been in 1949. My poor Latin was a problem, but private lessons helped and I managed to pass the entrance exams.

Father died of cancer two years later in August 1953. More than half a century later, Joseph Aaron Littman was named—in a comparison with current billionaires—as *"a top property developer"* of his time and *"the only self-made man to make the top ten in the first half of the 1950s."*[6] He left an important estate with heavy mortgages as well as much tax (91% of income then) still owed and death duties to be paid (70%). It was not even certain, according to Louis, that there would be available funds for me to complete my studies at T.C.D. but we all assumed that everything would somehow sort itself out—and providentially it did a few years later with the inflation of sterling after the 1956 Suez War.

During the 1954 Christmas holidays I went on my first European tour (Belgium, France and Italy). In October 1955, having obtained a *Moderatores* in Modern History and Political Science (B.A. with Honors) at T.C.D, I began a five-month tour of the eastern Mediterranean, visiting Greece, Turkey, Egypt (as far south as Aswan), Lebanon, Syria, Jordan, and staying six weeks in Israel before returning to London in late March 1956 via Italy and Switzerland.

At that time a non-Muslim foreigner could not obtain a tourist visa for either Jordan or Syria unless the request was accompanied by a copy of a baptism certificate or a consular letter stating that the person was not a Jew; on discovering this on the journey from Alexandria to Beirut, I described myself—when asked the purpose of my trip—as *"a Christian Baptist wishing to visit the holy sites in Palestine during the Christmas holiday."* I was the only person to leave the ship in Beirut on December 23, at a time when tension was at its highest in the Middle East and bloody riots had broken out after the *Baghdad Pact* was signed a month earlier by Britain, Iraq, Iran, Turkey and Pakistan.

I was very lucky in obtaining a Jordanian visa at their consulate in Beirut, the day before Christmas, without a baptismal or consular certificate—by simply stating that the American consulate had closed. No one bothered to check. I was even luckier in obtaining my Syrian visa at the border on arrival by the regular Beirut-Damascus bus, because of the Jordanian visa stamped into my passport. An American Baptist pilgrim, educated in Europe, was then an "open sesame" in the Holy Land.

Thanks to the help of Yusuf Yassir, a young Arab refugee from Jaffa whom I met in Amman and who found me inexpensive lodging in Ramallah, I was able to visit most holy sites during the Christmas holiday period, even the Tombs of the Hebrew Patriarchs and Matriarchs at Hebron's Machpela Cave. There, on reaching the seventh step before entering the impressive Herodian Tomb, a mosque, the guide declared "*No Jew has ever gone beyond this step!*"[7]

David G. Littman holding a lamb, Kibbutz Beit Hashita, 1956

Crossing into Israel on January 4, 1956, at Jerusalem's Mandelbaum Gate, the Israeli security official, on seeing "Littman" in my passport greeted me with a surprised "*Shalom.*" Thirty years later I learned that I had been put under surveillance during my six-week visit—and again on my return to Israel during the summer of 1958 to excavate at Hazor, an archaeological site in Upper

Galilee. Apart from the strangeness of a Jew entering Israel from Jordan at that time, this special "security measure" probably resulted from the fact that Yusuf had asked me to send him photographs of their family house in Jaffa, near Tel Aviv. In trying to find it, I soon realised that the house numbers had been changed, so I took photos from every angle. This could well have been considered strange as a large military base was nearby.

I remained in Israel for two months, touring the country "from Dan to Beersheba"—going south to Eilat on the Red Sea with its small population, then being built as a port—and staying with relatives, especially the Buchman family at Kibbutz Beit Hashita near Bet Sh'ean in the fertile Jezreel Valley. Although feeling more British than American, and more Jewish than Zionist, I felt at home in Israel, albeit very much of an outsider as a result of my "public school," elitist English upbringing.

Since the nineteenth century, this education system had nourished confident empire builders. It may well have inspired me to become a "Baptist pilgrim" in Syria and Jordan—and five years later it provided me with a natural eccentricity that enabled me to play the role of an Anglican working for OSE, a Geneva-based international non-government organization in Casablanca.

Arriving back in London in mid-March 1956, Louis thought that I should learn more about real estate through experience, becoming an assistant to the senior partner at the reputable firm of Goddard and Smith, opposite Christie's in King Street. He persuaded both Peter and me to join him in his new home that he had rented in Addison Road, Kensington.

After two months of real estate training, I had little enthusiasm for property business and soon enrolled for postgraduate studies in Palestinian Archaeology under Kathleen Kenyon at the Institute of Archaeology, London University, situated in Regents Park, with courses given in Mesopotamian archaeology by the famous Prof. Max Mallowan, Agatha Christie's husband.

In November 1957, still uncertain of my professional future, I made another hasty decision and left for America "to teach history," but changed my mind five months later and returned to London and to archaeology in the spring. Dr. Kenyon, who could not enroll a British Jew for the annual Jericho "dig" in Jordan, recommended me to Prof. Yigal Yadin of the Hebrew University. During the summer of 1958 I was back in Israel, participating in his success-

Archeological Excavations at Hazor (Israel), summer 1958. David G. Littman (third right) next to Amnon Ben Tor (second right) with Yigal Yadin (second left).

ful excavations at Hazor in the Galilee alongside Amnon Ben Tor and David Ussishkin, two friends who became later well-known archaeologists for their excavations, at the sites of Hazor and Lachish respectively.

On returning home—via Rome after witnessing Pope John XXIII's election in St. Peter's Square—I was reluctant to continue my archaeological studies, but nonetheless returned for "a last fling." Soon after, at the Institute of Archaeology, I met a new French-speaking student, Gisèle Orebi, a stateless Jewish refugee from Egypt. She and her parents, from a well-known Cairo Jewish family—her grandfather, Aslan Levy Orebi, had been made a *Bey* by the Ottoman Sultan before the First World War—were obliged to leave Egypt the previous year just after the Suez war. She obtained a modest grant from the London Jewish Refugee Committee, established to help thousands of Jews who were then fleeing Egypt and Hungary. During the summer of 1959, we excavated together in a "dig" near Salisbury and decided to marry on August 31. Gisèle became a British citizen after our marriage, receiving her passport after only two days. Our religious marriage followed on September 6, 1959.

We left on a frugal, extended, six-week honeymoon through Belgium, France and Italy, having managed to get an extra "honeymoon" credit on my bank overdraft. On our return to London, we moved into a small flat near Marble Arch owned by my mother, but Gisèle's health problems, resulting from London's damp and cold climate, convinced me to drop archaeology altogether. In early March and on doctor's advice—Gisèle was then pregnant—we headed for a warm climate, driving to Sicily, including a brief visit to Tunis. We settled at Torvaianica, near Ostia on the coast, an hour's drive from Rome

Gisèle Orebi, Cairo 1945

where we watched some of the 1960 Olympic Games. In September, we headed north to Lausanne, following the advice of Gisèle's elderly grand-aunt, who lived there and who had recommended a fine maternity clinic. I

David G. Littman and Gisèle Orebi at their wedding
at the New West End Synagogue in London, September 1959

then left for London to attend Louis' wedding to Gisèle's elder sister Colette, and soon after my return Gisèle gave birth to Diana on November 24, 1960 at the Clinique Montchoisi overlooking Lake Geneva.

All this only became possible after I was appointed one of four family administrators of the Estate in January 1960, supervised by Louis and father's lawyer, Leonard Tobin. Unexpected inflation in the late 1950s, the first in decades, allowed us to float a public company. By offering 30% of the shares on the stock market, we were able to pay off the large, accumulated income taxes and estate duty. We were then informed that a fixed income would soon be available—and even a small capital sum to repay our bank debts that had accumulated in the 1950s with Barclays Bank's acceptance.

CHAPTER 2

The First Phase of Operation Mural
(March to May 1961)

In early March 1961, Professor Bloch had obtained official letters of introduction for my future mission from key Swiss organizations. He took me with him to Bern and introduced me to several officials as the delegate of the newly created Oeuvre Suisse de Secours aux Enfants de l'Afrique du Nord (OSSEAN).[8] Its task was to arrange for Moroccan children to be brought for holidays or convalescence to OSE's Home de la Forêt, situated in the mountainous village of Morgins.

OSE's "Home de la Forêt" in
Morgins-Valais, Switzerland, 1961

Essential Letters of Recommendation

These personal recommendations, which were indispensable for my work included a letter dated March 8, 1961 from René Steiner, Secretary-General of the Swiss Red Cross (Children's section), addressed to A.E. Reinhard, the chief delegate of the League of Red Cross Societies in Morocco regarding Algerian refugees and victims of the Franco-Algerian war.[9] Reinhard was also covering the tragic consequences of the 1960 earthquake at Agadir. Professor Bloch also obtained a letter, dated March 2, 1961, and another (March 7) from Dr. M. Tromp, President of the Commission for hospitalizing foreigners in Switzerland.[10] He received another one from Mr. Maeder of the Federal Department of Justice and Police, promising him that a note would be sent to the Swiss ambassador in Rabat and the consul in Casablanca, authorizing visas of up to three months for Moroccan children with a valid passport to remain in Switzerland under OSSEAN's auspices.[11]

OSE, founded in Russia in 1912, accredited to the UN Federation of Non-Governmental Organizations, had a good reputation for its efficiency, particularly during the war years when actively rescuing up to 3000 Jewish children in Nazi-occupied France. Professor Bloch was well-known to the director of the children's section of the Swiss Red Cross and other Swiss organizations. A former professor of English literature at the University of St. Petersburg before the revolution and then publisher of Russian classical literature in Berlin (1924–1939), he and his wife worked in France with OSE before finding refuge in Switzerland at the last moment in summer 1943.

Professor Bloch and his wife were lucky to have been among the 27,000 Jewish men, women and children allowed into Switzerland during the Second World War—about 40,000 were turned back, whereas a total 285,000 other refugees were accepted. Tragically, Professor Bloch's sister had been barred entry by a frontier-guard, although carrying a letter of introduction from a distinguished Swiss professor, inviting her to lecture on Slavic literature, in which she was expert, at the University of Basle. This recommendation and the legal visa were inscribed in her real name—different from the name on the papers she was using to travel safely; she was turned back and killed by the Nazis.

At sixty-nine, nearly twenty years after his arrival in Switzerland, Bloch's relationship with various authorities in Bern was both friendly—especially with René Steiner at the Swiss Red Cross—as well as constructive. As an affiliated member of Switzerland's Aide Suisse à l'étranger (Swiss Aid for foreign countries), OSE was well-placed to offer its aid to the 1961 campaign; and Dr. Fischer, its head, had been informed of my mission to Morocco but not, to my knowledge, of the true purpose—children's immigration to Israel via Switzerland.

It is possible that OSE's real intentions were understood later in Bern, but this was neither discussed nor mentioned then. When it later became known later, there would have been those who, remembering the war period, simply decided to turn a blind eye. Just as long as the groups of children left Switzerland within three months, no difficulties were anticipated by OSE from the authorities.

The letters of introduction and recommendation represented the *sine qua non* for the start of the mission. One of them actually referred to me as the delegate of the Oeuvre Suisse de Secours aux Enfants Nord-Africains; another as the collaborator of the Oeuvre de Secours aux Enfants en Afrique

Prof. Bloch and his wife together with David G. Littman in Switzerland after the Operation, 1962

du Nord et au Maroc. In order to obtain these letters of recommendation, as well as official Swiss co-operation, OSSEAN's link with OSE, via Prof. Bloch, was essential.

However, on the Moroccan side any suspected connection with OSE would have proved disastrous as OSE had worked in Morocco under the French Protectorate, being labelled a "Zionist" organization. Thus, the choice of the name "OSSEAN" because of its similarity to the name "OSE" was later to cause me problems, but it is difficult to imagine how the Swiss authorities would have reacted to an unknown organization.

I opened a POB address in the name of OSSEAN at the main Geneva post office opposite OSE's office. Official notepaper mentioning this address was printed for use in Geneva and in Casablanca. Letters were signed by the fictive "N. Lehmann" OSSEAN's regular secretary-general (Miss Aïda Schirmann). The director of OSSEAN was referred to as "Professor Aberson" (such a person actually lived in Geneva and accepted that his name be used)—in reality, Prof. Jacques Bloch.

Geneva—Paris—Casablanca

On March 15, 1961, Gisèle flew to London with Diana, and I to Paris. There, I was briefed for security by "Alex Korany", the Mossad's N° 2, in his attractive apartment, formerly the residence of the recently-deceased famous French actor Gérard Philippe. Alex was perturbed to see Diana's third name, "Avivah" (a Hebrew name meaning "spring"—actually the "h" was unnecessary), inscribed in my British passport and this he skillfully had changed to "Avivar" (with a South American resonance like "Bolivar").

The next day, I arrived in Casablanca at midday and booked a room at the modest Hotel de Cernay. That very same afternoon I met Mr. Reinhard and gave him Dr. Steiner's letter of introduction. We had a friendly discussion in his office, which continued after a second meeting the following morning. He was most sympathetic and helpful and I believe he had no idea of our real intentions at that stage, and maybe not for subsequent weeks afterwards.

Mr. Reinhard was anxious to have OSSEAN's collaboration regarding the transfer to France of a young Moroccan boy suffering from haemophilia who required special care. Dr. Steiner's letter of recommendation had specifically referred to this possibility. He mentioned that there might be a travel obstacle since the boy was Jewish; passport procedures were particularly long and difficult, and for Jews almost an impossibility. He told me of his first-hand experience of their humiliating situation, and added that it was scarcely possible for him to even employ Moroccan Jews, although they were usually more efficient than their Muslim compatriots.

Mr. Reinhard felt that our "mountain-cure project" for Moroccan children would prove successful and was willing to take me with him to Rabat to introduce me to a high-level official in the Health Ministry with whom he had an appointment on Monday. Once again he returned to the Jewish question, advising me strongly not to heed those who might wish to ban them from eventual list of applicants.

Then, and on later occasions, he explained how frequently misunderstandings and petty quarrels arose between his collaborators and various Moroccan officials with whom they were in contact regarding Algerian refugees—he added that he had preferred his earlier post in the Congo.[12]

Jews in Morocco: a Historical Background

After the Second World War, the Jewish population in all of Morocco (French and Spanish Protectorates and Tangiers) numbered slightly under 300,000. In the eight years between Israel's independence in May 1948 and Morocco's independence in March 1956, approximately 100,000 Jews had been able to leave for Israel—the first Moroccan "Aliyah"—and about 20,000 others settled elsewhere, mainly in France and Canada.[13]

The initial attitude of King Muhammad V and his government toward Moroccan Jewry after the country's independence in 1956 was positive, however all emigration to Israel was forbidden on the insistence of the Arab League, especially due to President Gamal Abdel Nasser's pressure. The postal service between Morocco and Israel was cut. It became very difficult for Moroccan Jews to obtain a passport and a Jewish businessman could not travel to France with his wife or children on his passport.

By 1958 the situation had greatly deteriorated and much apprehension for the future had replaced earlier optimism. Some Jewish youths were arrested for "Zionism," Jewish girls were frequently raped and minors abducted and forcibly converted to Islam. This policy was institutionalized when the head of the Istiklal Party, Allal El Fassi, became Minister of Islamic Affairs, after which there was an almost daily announcement of Jews converting to Islam.

Clandestine activities were soon developed by Israel's secret service (Mossad), in cooperation with local Jewish groups, to hasten the departure of as many families as possible. However, this was a hazardous operation and after independence, from November 1956 till May 1961, more than 10,000 Jews left Morocco secretly for Israel.

Two events occurred in early January 1961 which proved to be a watershed for Moroccan Jewry. Firstly, President Nasser was received with great pomp when he arrived in Casablanca for a special meeting of the Arab League. Jewish Moroccan children who had gathered in the streets, like their Muslim compatriots, to welcome the president were harshly dispersed. The color of the youth's uniforms (blue and white) was not appreciated by the charismatic leader of the Arab world nor by the Moroccan populace. However, other groups of Jewish children, who were dressed in traditional Moroccan scout uniforms, were able to reach the coast unhindered and leave the country clandestinely by boat that same night.

Soon after, in the early morning of January 11, 1961, a week after the Arab Summit Meeting at Casablanca—hosted by King Muhammad V, with Egyptian President Gamal Abdel Nasser as the star—an old RAF motor boat, renamed the *Piscès* (*Egoz),* the "nut," as it became known in Hebrew), capsized in a storm on leaving the shore near Tangiers for Gibraltar. Forty-three Jewish Moroccan clandestine emigrants—twenty-four of them children—an Israeli and a Spaniard crewman drowned. The only survivors were the Spanish captain and his assistant.

The plight of Moroccan Jewry was brought to the world's attention. The Moroccan government found itself in an unenviable situation at a moment when it relied heavily on Western, particularly American, support and aid. The liberal Muhammad V was now discreetly pressured to intervene and he may well have initiated a slightly more flexible policy regarding the issuance of individual passports to Moroccan Jews just before he died in March when he was succeeded by his son King Hassan II.

The *Egoz* tragedy did not hinder the slow Jewish exodus, nor the courageous activities of the Misgueret ("network"). A new chief of operations, Lieutenant-Colonel Alex Gattmon and his wife, Carmite, (a Belgium Catholic), had arrived in Casablanca in December; he had left the Israeli Air Force to take up his new appointment. He was assisted by a dedicated team of local, as well as Israeli youth. Aside from clandestine departures of between 100 and 300 persons per month, the Mossad was looking for a breakthrough action, whereby the Moroccan government would feel obliged, through various pressures, to take a political decision which might lead to a mass legal exodus of Jews. They had misgivings about the Jewish Agency / Youth Aliyah / OSSEAN for holidays in Switzerland, particularly about my capacity to undertake it, nonetheless they agreed to collaborate. Isser Harel was still the head of the Mossad, having tracked down Adolf Eichmann in Buenos Aires in May and whose trial began in Jerusalem on April 2, 1961, being widely covered in the media.

Key Moroccan Connections in Rabat

Mr. Reinhard took me to Rabat on Monday March 20 and introduced me to Dr. Laraki in the Ministry of Health. The latter seemed interested in the idea of sending Moslem children to Switzerland for a cure or convalescence, but only if it would cost the Ministry nothing: "Not a penny, Mr. Littman, not a penny!" Mr. Mazzour, director of the official "Youth and Sports" organization of Rabat, was equally keen to send a group of thirty to forty children for a three weeks' holiday providing the cost was minimal. Mr. Layrak, in charge of the newly-created Red Crescent, had been delegated by Dr. Laraki to accompany me. He even sought my help for a ten-year-old boy suffering from myopathie-speedo-hypertrophied (a form of spastics) and even suggested I open my OSSEAN office in the Red Crescent's official building in

Rabat. Through him—either then or on my second visit to Rabat two days later—I met other officials, the head of the French community and a ladies committee responsible for Jewish children.

From the very friendly manner I had been received in Rabat—thanks to my Swiss letters of recommendation and Mr. Reinhard's initial intro-ductions—I soon realised the importance for my "cover" of widening my contacts with governmental and non-governmental organizations. However, this would not be possible if I rigidly maintained OSSEAN's rate of ten Swiss francs per child per day (the equivalent of fifty Swiss francs today or about fifty-five dollars), plus transport costs, which were my written instructions.[14] It seemed to me wiser to "enter into negotiations", on the basis that any final agreement was highly unlikely, as each organization's aim was to reduce its financial contribution to virtually nothing. This had recently been the case for a group of children, so I was informed, whose holidays had been entirely subsidized by the Belgium government. Had my evaluation proved wrong, I would have found myself with an inextricable financial and technical problem, for not only was I told not to offer a lower rate, but our ten Swiss francs was later raised to thirteen Swiss francs per day per child,[15] eliciting from me a sarcastic reply: "If there should be a definite disapproval of my actions from a distance of 2,000 kilometres and an attempt to tie my hands in advance, I would ask you, dear Madame [Lehmann], to arrange for my replacement by a more able colleague."[16]

These short-sighted considerations remained wholly disproportionate to the greater goal which it was hoped to achieve, although perfectly "normal" when viewed from my contacts in Paris and Geneva.

During my early conversations with Bar-Giora, I had argued strongly for bringing some Muslim children to Switzerland in order to demonstrate OSSEAN's good will to Moroccan children of all faiths. Unfortunately, this proposal had not been appreciated either by him or by Youth Aliyah's repre-sentative in Marseilles, Arieh Reiffler. They feared that the operation might be transformed into a holiday camp for Muslims and they were unable even to contemplate for even a moment the possibility of a 1,000 dollar budget (30,000 dollar equivalent today) to cover such an eventuality.

It soon became clear that the original plan for convalescent or mountain-cures was totally impractical and I decided to set our goal on "holidays" for perfectly healthy children. By March 23, I wrote to Lehmann that it would be "better to concentrate our resources and energy on the summer period, beginning towards the end of June."[17] This decision was not appreciated in Marseille or Paris. Miracles were expected and three months was considered too long to wait for results, especially for those in Jerusalem. At least four similar emissaries had already been sent to Morocco over the past few years since Morocco's independence, without any success and at considerable expense. The only Jewish child taken out of the country till then as a result of such schemes had been a baby born to the wife of a Jewish doctor-emissary, whose medical certificates for the Jewish candidates had been extremely meticulous, but who was unable to find a way of convincing the Moroccan authorities to provide them with any type of passports for "convalescence abroad."

In a similar vein Mr. Reinhard once related to me with much humour the visit of a lady to his Casablanca office—"a Mrs. Warburg, wife of a Belgian banker I think." She had asked for his help in trying to arrange for the reunion of Jewish children from Morocco with their parents and relatives in Israel and he informed her that this was outside of his competence. However, he casually asked her how many children she had in mind. When she mentioned a figure of 6,000 he was flabbergasted, for he had imagined that she was making a plea for a few children. He asked her why she hadn't raised the matter at the World Jewish Congress meeting in Rabat which she had attended. At this she became white and replied nervously that this was impossible. He added, with a broad grin: "Imagine, they are afraid to talk of mass emigration publicly in Rabat and yet they would like me to do it. Why, if I breathed a word of such an idea to any Moroccan person in authority I'd be obliged to leave the country within twenty-four hours!"

My "cover" was developing nicely. I arranged for 1,000 medical certificates[18] to be printed and also overprinted a part-Arabic text on OSSEAN's prospectuses that I had brought with me, showing a view of the Home de la Forêt in Morgins (Canton of Valais). On March 27 I was back in Rabat, and then several more times, making the rounds and prospecting. One of the more important meetings was with a Mr. Chaoui, Head of the Consular and Social Department of the Foreign Ministry, who offered sound advice and co-operation, proposing even to circularise the governors of the principal towns in which the eventual candidates were resident.[19]

First contact with "Georges"

It was ten days after my arrival (March 26) that I first met my secret contact whom I learned after my mission was a Mossad agent. "Georges"—his real name I only learned later was Gad Shahar, born in Tunisia, a founder-member of Kibbutz Regavim—later told me that he had been taken aback when he saw me coming to meet him at the prearranged Don Camillo Café. "You looked so tall and unmistakably "Jewish" that I asked myself how someone so conspicuous could have been chosen for such a job. And when I heard your French, I was even more in despair." Georges found me very naive and inexperienced for such an activity—indeed I was—but he realised that there was no alternative. He listened carefully to what I told him about my first contacts, which impressed him and then thoroughly briefed me, offering much advice and explaining how I was to contact him in the future—always from public phone booths, using a veiled but normal language. We arranged our four next meetings, so that we didn't need to communicate by phone. He advised me to find an office in Casablanca, not Rabat.

I had already moved from the modest Hotel de Cernay to the Hotel de Noailles and was advised by Mr. Reinhard to try to rent an apartment in the annex of the well-known Hotel Anfa, where Roosevelt and Churchill—at the January 1943 Casablanca Conference—made the historic declaration for the unconditional surrender of Germany at the January 1943 Casablanca Conference. It would be more suitable once my wife and baby daughter arrived. I was lucky to find one to be vacated on April 15; thus we became Mr. Reinhard's neighbour. I was just as fortunate regarding OSSEAN's office which I rented on the ground floor of 105 rue Dumont d'Urville: two rooms, modestly furnished, each having a separate entrance from the corridor.

I could not rely on public transport or taxis to get me from one end of Casablanca to the other, sometimes twice a day, or for my frequent trips to Rabat and elsewhere. A car was indispensable, yet it had not been

Gisèle Littman leaning on the Renault Dauphine car, outside Fez, May 1961

budgeted for me by my bosses. Apart for paying for my transport, hotel and office expenses, they had not accepted nor felt required to issue any other payments on my behalf. They were unhappy at the idea of having to underwrite such costs till the summer on a mission in which they were losing confidence, and the purchase of a car was the last straw. Once again my independent financial situation allowed me to act as I thought best. The day Gisèle arrived on March 31, I purchased a second-hand 1956 Renault Dauphine at only 300 dollars. We were united again and were able to collaborate on the difficult mission facing us, having decided that it would be appropriate to bring Diana to Morroco within a month.

Sightseeing in Southern Morocco

In conformity with the project of getting OSSEAN better known, we made a one-week tour, via Fez and Meknes to Ksar el Souk and Erfoud deep into the southern desert beyond the High Atlas mountains. It was planned that we would meet up with Mr. Reinhard and his assistants there, as they would be visiting some of the Red Cross centres for Algerian refugees.

Gisèle Littman with Mr. Reinhard on the roof of a desert building, April 1961

Gisèle Littman with Mr. Reinhard inside the house of a patient, April 1961

This goodwill tour was an ideal occasion for requesting, wherever possible, official letters of introduction—at Georges' suggestion. There were a few refusals as a circular letter had just been received on this subject, but luckily the Minister of Health provided me with a personal recommendation to state hospitals, and Mr. Ghomari, Secretary-General of the Entr'Aide Nationale, gave me another in both French and Arabic (both remained in my Casablanca office when I left hurriedly on July 24). These letters were of invaluable aid and strengthened our credentials whenever I presented them. He encouraged me to visit several of their establishments, especially re-education centres handling those who had been paralysed shortly before by absorbing airplane oil, which had been sold to them under the premise of being normal cooking oil. I had tried, through Mr. Ghomari, to arrange for us to be received by the king's sister, Princess Lalla Aïcha, the honorary president of the Entr'Aide, but she was abroad.[20]

We called on a few Jewish community leaders in some towns, but none seemed particularly interested in sending children to holiday-camps in Switzerland under our auspices. On one occasion I was asked whether OSE was related to OSSEAN, to which I replied in the negative. One reason for their lack of enthusiasm was our high cost; the other, their conviction, implicit in the conversation, that it would be a waste of time to consider the matter in view due to the unlikelihood of Jewish children receiving passports to travel.

The week was consumed solely with meetings and we greatly enjoyed visiting the towns and countryside. The official mourning period for Muhammad V was over and in nearly every city we found ourselves watching spectacular fantasias in honour of the new king. We even encountered several unusual adventures. In one case, having been late for a rendez-vous in the south with Mr. Reinhard and his colleagues, we endeavoured to find them on the desert road, along uncertain tracks which had been indicated to us—all to no avail. After some hours we had given up all hope when suddenly a cloud of dust on the horizon indicated the arrival of a vehicle.

We expected disappointment again but soon noticed a jeep marked with a red cross. As both our vehicles halted in the middle of nowhere, I couldn't resist the urge of calmly stepping out of my Renault and extending my hand to Mr. Reinhard, solemnly asking: "Dr. Livingstone, I presume!"

Fantasia event in Fez (and throughout Morocco) for King Hassan II, April 1961

King Hassan II waiving to the public, Casablanca, April 1961

David G. and Gisèle Littman in the desert by Mr. Rheinhard's ambulance, April 1961

He laughed heartily, and this lucky encounter enabled us to see, accompanied by him, a number of villages far off the beaten track where he was visiting the sick. It opened our eyes to the grandeur of Morocco and the great misery in which most of its inhabitants lived in that desert region. We drove southwards from Erfoud, into the Tafilalet, to Rissani, and even Taouz, not far from the Algerian border. It was strange to find, as far south as Erfoud—with its superb luxury hotel outside the town—the proverbial Jews, bustling around, often recognizable by their European-type clothes, each wearing a French black beret. This specific headgear signified their freedom from the inferior status and the obligatory discriminatory clothing that they had been forced to wear for centuries before the French arrival in 1912—and that many of them still continued to wear out of custom. If anyone wanted to buy gasoline or a soft-drink, or virtually anything in Erfoud, it was still the Jewish merchant to whom they turned, as it had been from time immemorial (and rarely the Berber), on whom the visitor depended.

On our return to Casablanca on April 16, we assumed the role of an

Gisèle Littman at an open market in the desert somewhere on the road to Erfoud, April 1961

A group of Jews in Casablanca, 1961

The Littman couple
strolling in a Moroccan
souk, summer 1961

affluent British couple, who had altruistically accepted to aid a Swiss international organization, as we happened to reside in Switzerland. Instead of
using my first name, David, I opted for "Gerald" (my middle name), as the
name "David" in Morocco was immediately linked to being a Jew. There
was a difficulty when I filled in Gisèle's arrival form at the central office of
the Sûreté Nationale when receiving her registration booklet authorising a
three month visit. To the question: "Mother's name?" I hesitated, and then
quickly inscribed: Renée Delmar. "Renée" was her first name, and "Delmar"
sounded much better than "Levy", her mother's maiden name. Her father's
name, "Marc Orebi," posed no problem, and it was in her passport. I had
done the same on arrival: instead of "Joseph", my father's first name, I wrote
"Mark" and for my mother's family name, I wrote "Jones", instead of her
real name "Gold."[21]

Social Connections in Casablanca

I had announced our arrival at the British consulate from the start and found the consul to be very friendly (Georges was not over-enthusiastic about this). The consul was an early morning tennis player and occasionally we had a game together. I was no longer the player I had been in 1950 at seventeen—winning several trophies, including the Bournemouth (Open) Boys Junior singles tournament against the French Casablanca champion, and finishing at the boys' Junior Wimbledon among the first 100 in the UK—but I was soon in reasonable form and a worthy partner for singles or doubles.

A few times I was to be seen at the Sunday morning Anglican Church service, joining in the hymn singing which I knew well from school. On June 10, more than two months later, I was present at the consul's house to celebrate Queen Elizabeth's official birthday. A Moroccan journalist who was also there—we had invited him to dinner on an earlier occasion—thoughtfully listed me the next day in *Le Petit Marocain*, as "among the personalities present. . ." It was important for our social credentials as much as my professional image.

Another breakthrough occurred a week after our return from our southern tour. Georges suggested I contact Mr. Cuny, a French journalist from *La Vigie Marocaine*. I invited him to lunch, mentioning that it was the Swiss consul in Casablanca who had given me his name as the man who might agree to write an article on OSSEAN's activities. He was pleased to hear it and reciprocated with a long article on April 25, introducing our organization by reproducing large sections of what appeared on our prospectus, as well as a photograph of the mountain chalet. The publicity value of this unpaid coverage was important and allowed the parents of our candidates to say that they had heard about OSSEAN through an article in the local press. Smaller adverts were placed in two newspapers (one Arabic) and in the *La Vigie Marocaine*.[22]

Our cover was nearing completion and I redoubled my efforts in Rabat to obtain a vague confirmation that the Entr'Aide and the Ministry of Education were willing to send groups of children to Switzerland under the auspices of OSSEAN. By then, about 150 Muslim children were considered as possible candidates, although it was abundantly clear that fifty would be a more feasible number, assuming financial matter could be agreed. The negotiations continued, as I dropped the price first to seven and then to five francs per day (one dollar and twenty cents, the equivalent of about thirty-five dollars today), but it wasn't low enough even though I was informed that the government might agree to provide free transport if our charges were reduced more. I lost no occasion in displaying the long article in *La Vigie Marocaine*, and presented a personal visiting card stressing our Swiss connection. Officials in the various ministries in Rabat had become used to my regular visits and were always friendly.[23]

Already on April 8, I had written to Lehmann that I planned to fly to London to bring back my daughter "within a fortnight," but my work increased greatly once our Casablanca office opened. However, Gisèle was not willing to be separated from Diana for much longer and I agreed with her, for it was now clear that the mission might continue for several months. I finally left on May 2 for London to fetch her, and decided to make a stopover in Paris to meet with Naphtali Bar-Giora (Youth Aliyah Department from the Jewish Agency in Paris) and Ariel Reiffler (Youth Aliyah in Marseille), as well as Prof. Jacques Bloch in Geneva.

Casablanca—Paris—Geneva—London—Casablanca

I was received coldly in Paris by Bar-Giora and Reiffler (I only met the latter briefly), both of whom showed no interest in hearing either my elaborate descriptions or the names of my various contacts. Even my letters to Geneva were considered much too long and they were clearly confused about my various initiatives. Their original hastily-conceived plan had provided for quick, tangible results and a steady follow-up. Its overall modifications by their maverick emissary—with the agreement of Georges and the Mossad chief in Morocco, Alex Gattmon—left them perplexed. Instead of being able to announce the arrival in Israel of a dozen or so Moroccan Jewish children before Passover, with more to follow, they found themselves hearing "new ideas" and propositions well after that holiday period had passed—propositions which seemed to imply an open-ended engagement to subsidise holidays for Muslims, as well as two more months of preparations before any real results could be expected for Jewish children. They felt they were no longer in control of their "man in Casablanca," but would bear the responsibility and expenses for his errors of appreciation and failure. This psychological brow-beating even included a suggestion that I seemed to be "having a good time" in Casablanca at their expense. This was the last straw for me and I sarcastically proposed, check-book in hand, to cover all the costs till then, even suggesting that perhaps they had a "better person" to replace me. Immediately, in a total reversal, Bar-Giora's tone changed, professing a reborn confidence in my capability of not losing sight of the trees as I entered the forest of intrigue. He even promised to seek a compromise solution on the question of subsidies for a small group of about 30 Muslim children.

Feeling myself once again firmly in the saddle, but angered over the initial lack of understanding encountered in Paris, I flew on to Geneva on May 4 to report to Prof. Bloch. A bond of friendship had grown up between us since our first meeting in January. Although a delayed summer arrival for Moroccan Jewish groups would seriously complicate OSE's regular summer camps for French and British Jewish children in Morgins, he readily accepted to seek additional chalets there and elsewhere, promising to handle the situation as it evolved, on the understanding that Bar-Giora and Reiffler agreed, as OSE depended on them for this Mission. Letters were soon drafted for H.R.H. Princess Lalla Aïcha and Mr. Nasser El Fassi, Head of the Department of Secondary Education. These letters were to be sent to the Swiss ambassador in Rabat, via the Swiss Foreign Ministry in Bern, who would, it was hoped, accept to forward them.[24]

I remember well that bright sunny day in Geneva, brimming with enthusiasm. Crossing the Rhône I stopped for a cold drink near the seated statue of Jean-Jacques Rousseau, who had left some rarely-quoted notes, on which he had scribbled: "Athens, Sparta and Rome have perished and all their peoples have vanished from the earth; though destroyed, Zion has not lost her children."[25]

Adolf Eichmann had been captured a year earlier (May 6, 1960) and his trial was then in progress in Jerusalem (April 2-August 14). When Eichmann had ruthlessly implemented the diabolical annihilation of European Jewry, "Zion" was not yet free and six millions perished (including a million and a half children) to the general indifference of war-torn Europe. Now, an independent Israel was endeavouring to gather in the remnant of Zion who desired to reach her shores. I was determined to make my small contribution to that historical, humanitarian cause.

My spirits uplifted by my brief stopover in Geneva during which I rented an apartment for our October return, I flew on to London. There followed two hectic days: my mother was ailing, two of my sisters were expecting babies; urgent family business matters required my attention; Diana's nanny, Pierra, had to return to Geneva where she would be employed at OSE's mountain home in Morgins until our return; and I had to reassure my parents-in-law, and brother Louis and Colette—the only members of my family who knew where I had been and what I was doing in Morocco.

Diana Littman, Anfa Hotel swimming pool, Casablanca, June 1961

And then there was delightful five-month Diana, with her little tuft of blond hair curled up, her wide clear-blue eyes, and her soft rose-tinted cheeks that required constant pressing and pinching.

The long journey back to Casablanca with a stopover in Paris was not a joy-ride for either of us. As Diana lay contented in her basket-carrier, encumbered on all sides by my books, cooing and crying and occasionally sleeping among all the usual baby-paraphernalia, I suddenly realized the seriousness of the risks ahead, and had a moment of doubt, quickly dismissed. The last lap of the journey proved the truth of Gisèle's point that I was totally lacking in the most elementary qualifications as a father. I managed the baby-feeding, but little else, and a stewardess was constantly rallying to my assistance. Even with her help, on arrival that evening there was no way of masking my embarrassment as I handed over a soaking, exhausted baby bundle to an enraptured mother, after a separation of five weeks.

The family was reunited and this most natural event had unwittingly

Gisèle and Diana Littman, Anfa Hotel swimming pool, Casablanca, June 1961

provided us with the perfect "cover." On reflection, I felt that no one would suspect a delegate from a Swiss organization—an English Anglican with his French-born Catholic wife and baby in the Anfa hotel—might be a secret Zionist emissary, whose aim was to send Moroccan Jewish children to Switzerland for holidays and then on to Israel—to encourage their parents who would follow later, clandestinely, by boat at night.

Gisèle and Diana and another happy event

Before I left for London, Gisèle had told me she was pregnant, but asked me not to tell her parents. This new situation added considerably to her psychological stress, since she felt a deep responsibility for the new life she was carrying, while becoming physically more vulnerable. Temperamentally, child-bearing made her happier and her maternal instinct now drove her to protect her future new-born (Ariane Yaël), although she was fully aware of the dangers she faced in Morocco. Nevertheless, she felt morally obliged to fulfill her commitment, redoubling her efforts to contribute to our success. There was another complication. Diana's health was affected by the stifling heat and Gisèle was obliged to prepare a special daily diet, taking meticulous care about cleanliness and infections.

In spite of all this, her collaboration never flagged and we discussed everything. She would translate my letters into French and often typed them on her frequent trips to the office in the

Gisèle and Diana Littman, Anfa Hotel swimming pool, Casablanca, June 1961

Gisèle Littman with Moroccan women in a public garden in Casablanca, 1961

afternoon to help me reply to the parents or take messages in my absence. She joined me at a few contacts with Georges, who once visited us at the Anfa apartment to see how we lived. Later he preferred that she not join me for our late night meetings, considering it unnecessarily risky. When our work greatly increased she would stay in the office till the early hours of the morning, or worked in the evening at Mrs. Tordjman's home, the head of the travel agency, SIRTAM. The lack of a phone in our apartment caused her much anxiety when I was obliged to work late in the office.

I took everything for granted in those tense months. I assumed Gisèle would always be there as wife, mother and collaborator. I was reluctant to see further or even attempt to analyse her problems and the considerable strain under which she was laboring. In spite of her general tiredness and a physical and psychological malaise—a young very pretty woman, now pregnant, born in Egypt, living an unusual drama—she remained steadfast till the end. She seemed to be a contented young mother, helping her husband whenever she could, whereas, in fact, her stress was constantly increased, particularly during the third month of her pregnancy in July. I was so obsessed with my task to get the children out of Morocco that I didn't realize the grief of both parents and children being separated. As a mother, Gisele felt this profoundly and wrote about it movingly twenty-five years later in the book *Roots in the Orient* (published in Hebrew in 1986).[26]

An Ideal Family Cover for a Humanitarian Mission

I have already referred to Diana's arrival in early May, aged five months and a week, but have hardly spoken about her as the very centre of our family life throughout the subsequent eleven weeks. Nothing could have been a more natural relaxant than playing with our adorable, roly poly baby daughter. True, once awakened late at night she could howl like the loudest, but in the morning before I left for the office she would placidly bleat: "ba-ba," intrigued by the foam on my chin as I shaved, to which I usually replied with a long "ba-a-ah" that often frightened her to easy tears. There were memorable moments by the swimming pool of the Hotel Anfa or at the Kon-Tiki beach. All in all, it would have been impossible to imagine me continuing my mission, month after month, without Gisèle and Diana together by my side, the perfect "cover." She was also a perfect comfort and inspiration to her parents during those anxious months of tension, in spite of all the dangers, and the difficulties for her mother. She was exactly eight months old when I left Casablanca on July 24 with the final group and her sister Ariane was due to "arrive" barely six months later when we reached Geneva safely.

CHAPTER 3

The Second Phase of Operation Mural
(June 26–July 10, 1961)

Retrospectively, the entire 130 day Operation Mural may be divided loosely into three phases: March 16 to May 22 / May 23 to June 25 / June 26 to July 24.

The first phase had required the laborious establishment of OSSEAN's credentials. This phase continued for a fortnight after my return to Casablanca with Diana on May 6, and overlapped with the second phase concerning the processing of the children and the formalities for passports. On May 11, I had a long interview in Rabat with both Mr. Omar Senoussi, a high official in the Ministry of Education and Mr. Skiredj, the director per interim at the Consular and Social Division of the Foreign Ministry (in the absence of Mr. Chaoui who was on a pilgrimage to Mecca). The latter requested me to address a formal letter to the Ministry of Foreign Affairs about our work, our intentions and our eventual requirements regarding travel documents. On May 17, I carefully prepared a three-page letter, relying on Gisèle for its formulation into correct French. It remained a key document, copies of which I showed whenever I was questioned by government officials. Several names were mentioned, including the Swiss ambassador in Rabat and the consul in Casablanca, both of whom had received confirmation from Bern the previous month of my *bona fide* mission on behalf of Moroccan youth.[27]

Conciliatory Policy of the Swiss Authorities

I had met Swiss Consul M. Birschler and his colleagues soon after my arrival and had also contacted the embassy twice. Ambassador E. Bernath had been on holiday in Switzerland, but on his return he received me most amicably. During the conversation, I asked his advice as to the policy I should adopt regarding eventual Jewish applicants, casually referring to Mr. Reinhard's evaluation on this subject. He confirmed his compatriot's viewpoint with another conclusive example. The Swiss government had proposed a comprehensive technical training course in Switzerland for thirty Moroccan children who had completed secondary education. The selection would be based on a competitive aptitude examination. To the Moroccan official's disappointment, ninety percent of the successful candidates were Jews, although at that time they represented under two percent of the population. The government decided to drop the generous Swiss offer altogether.

Mr. Bernath added—and this confirmed what Mr. Reinhard had already told me two months earlier—that Jews were to be found in large numbers in lower-echelon staff positions because of their efficiency as compared with their Muslim countrymen. He also told me that I should not allow Jewish applicants to be deleted by any government pressure. He wished me luck in my work and told me to contact his staff for any advice I might need. He even offered to give me a general letter of recommendation if I thought it might help.

Unfortunately, and unknown to me, the formal letter he had received from the highest police authority in Bern requesting him and the Casablanca consulate to facilitate all Swiss visas for the children also mentioned that OSSEAN would be entirely responsible for the financing of this action.[28] Of course this was true as far as Switzerland was concerned, and it was necessary for Prof. Bloch to give this guarantee, but mention of this in letters sent from Bern to Morocco was unfortunate. On taking my leave of the ambassador, I mentioned how "reasonable" our charges were. He showed his surprise, the Swiss consul in Casablanca had reacted similarly, for they had believed till then that the entire action was benevolent and this was its chief attraction.

The next day, May 14, I committed my first mistake by writing to thank the ambassador for our meeting and requested a letter of recommendation for the head of the Social and Consular Section of the Ministry of Foreign Affairs.[29] His secretary telephoned and arranged a second meeting with the ambassador. On May 18, I found him as pleasant as ever, but he was less free with his offers of help. He had received a letter from Bern and now had probably understood our real goal.[30] He didn't want Switzerland to be involved except for granting visas. He intimated that he could not provide the letter of recommendation which he had considered giving me five days earlier, as our work was not of a "diplomatic" nature. He spoke to me in the presence of his secretary, who later drew me aside and warned me that he had never known of passports being granted, either collectively or individually, in less than two or three months, and that he doubted very much if the Moroccan authorities would alter this policy to suit us. The implication seemed to be clear, although this was not stated explicitly "for Jewish children."

Mr. Bernath also informed me that Professor Aberson's letter addressed to Princess Lalla Aïcha just received via Bern, could not be transmitted by him through diplomatic channels, although this had been the method suggested by Mr. Ghomari in the hope that it might help the Entr'Aide Nationale to obtain a Moroccan government transport grant for Muslim children.[31]

Swiss suspicions were certainly aroused in the first week of June when Consul Birschler asked a bridge partner to make enquiries about our organization on a forthcoming visit to Geneva: "It's strange that a Swiss organization should send an English Jew as its delegate to Morocco!" Perhaps the word "Jew" was added by Hélène Tordjman in a later recapitulation of the story when she informed me of this much later in July.[32] In the letter to me of June 16 letter, Lehmann made it very clear that I should expect a quick delivery of the visas from the Swiss consulate but nothing more, which is what Ambassador Bernath had already told me on May 18.[33]

In spring 2008, I contacted Ambassador Walter Haffner from the Swiss Embassy in Tel Aviv and invited him to join us at President Shimon Peres' Residence in Jerusalem for the private reception in commemoration of Operation Mural on June 1.[34]

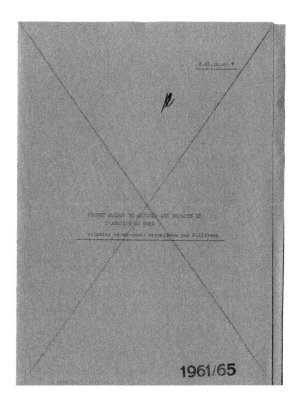

Photo of file (G.65.40.sd)
from Swiss Archives

I asked the Ambassador to look for possible information regarding my activities in Morocco in 1961 and to my surprise I received the copy of a file entitled: "Oeuvre Suisse de Secours aux Enfants de L'Afrique du Nord. Colonie de vacances organisées par M. Littman" from the Historical Department of the Swiss Federal Department of Foreign Affairs in Bern. This file (G.65.40.sd) throws a new light on the role of Switzerland in the Mural Affair as one reads the exchange of confidential letters between the Swiss Embassy in Rabat and the Federal Political Department in Bern (EPD). On May 18, the Federal Political Department in Bern sends a confidential letter to the Swiss ambassador in Rabat, Mr. E. Bernath, which mentions that "eighty percent of the children attending this summer holidays in Morgins are Jewish and that not all of them might come back," this information, writes the Minister, must remain confidential in order not to put "the families in danger."[35] The Ambassador having received a day earlier the order to limit himself to issuing visas and to refrain from any letters of recommendations to Mr. Littman, fears serious problems and asks the Federal Political Department to reconsider the whole matter.[36] Yet while the Swiss authorities did not want to be involved in a "mass exodus" which could jeopardize relations with Morocco, they decided to allow the three months visas as authorized by the Federal Police for Foreigners on March 21. A policy reiterated in a confidential letter dated June 3 in which Bern asks the Ambassador not to provide information on OSSEAN.[37] That same day, the Ambassador receives a letter from the Secretary-General of the Entr'Aide Nationale, Mr. Ghomari, asking his advice on the summer holidays organized by OSSEAN for Moroccan children.[38] Two days later, the Ambassador sends an express and confidential letter to Bern asking how to react to this "embarrassing demand."[39] In the short telegram of June 9, Bern refers to the instructions sent on June 3 and three days later the Ambassador writes to Mr. Ghomari that OSSEAN is a private organization unrelated to the Swiss Authorities.[40]

Such a conciliatory policy from the Swiss Authorities in Bern was an invaluable contribution to the success of Operation Mural with all the necessary visas issued by the Swiss Consulate in Casablanca, often at the last moment with much rapidity and understanding.[41]

Moroccan Jewish Parents Arriving at our Office

Our activities suddenly increased enormously, but it was important to continue negotiations with the Moroccan officials. But now Georges' Misgeret (the Hebrew word for "framework," the Mossad's network in Morocco) had been organized and parents started calling regularly at our office. With hindsight, it was well that this difficult phase had not started earlier for it would simply have given the authorities more time to investigate our activities. Until then no one had taken any notice of OSSEAN's activities. Even until June 8 there was no inkling of what was being prepared. When it was finally realized, it was too late to begin enquiries and stop everything without risking an international scandal which the Moroccan authorities did not want.

The Misgeret began contacting parents who wished to send their children to Israel; they were then processed at night in difficult circumstances with a general medical examination. It was decided to aid the poorest families, as it was felt that the lower middle-classes could decide for themselves later.

The parents came to our office at 105 Dumont d'Urville officially for information; on a second visit they signed (many with just a thumb-print) the passport demands and left the necessary documents, as well as a deposit of 200 dirhams which they had been given the previous evening by a member of the network. I would return the money to Georges the same night and it would then be made available to other parents, handing me 200 dirhams per child. They had been told that we were not Jewish and that they should agree to anything we might say regarding either the holiday-camps for their children or its cost. They came, lining up patiently with extraordinary faith, assured by the Misgeret that they would arrange for the children to go on from Switzerland to Israel. Any parent naive enough to ask whether we could send his or her child to Israel was firmly shown to the door and warned that a report would be sent to the prefecture if they returned—this harsh manner had an effective result.

A receipt was given to each parent who paid the 200 dirhams and a duplicate kept. The first allowed the network to know which parents had paid us the money given to them, whereas the second was "proof" that the parents had paid a deposit to OSSEAN for their child's holiday; it could be shown to any authority soliciting information.

The task of this special group from the Misgeret, in preparing all the necessary documents, especially in obtaining the school identity cards for 530 children, was enormous. With the departure of each convoy, the stream of parents coming to our office continued. A few members turned up casually to collect medical forms, but in particular I remember one young woman—pretending, skillfully, to be a "social worker"—who worked so determinedly and thoroughly that on July 16 and 17 she brought all the documents for the last 130 children, thus in effect helping us to include all the passports demands. Her efforts and those of her colleagues were justly rewarded since all but two of the children who had been cleared left on

July 22nd or on July 24th with me. It was only toward the last week of our mission that she actually realised—it could no longer be concealed from her—that we too were collaborating with the network. The secret had been well kept from her and her colleagues so as to avoid a chain of forced confessions in case of arrest. On Sunday July 17, "Celine"—as I knew her—was followed from the office by a car parked opposite, and soon after she was sent safely out of the country. Several members had been apprehended by the authorities, before, during, and after our mission, of whom some were brutalised and one—I was later told by Georges—died in hospital. A tribute is owed to "Celine" and to all those indigenous North African Jews—heroes of silence—who worked with such devotion under considerable danger.

Simplified Collective Passport Formalities

On May 23, I obtained an interview with Mr. Muhammad Hajjaj, head of the administrational division of the prefecture of the governor at Place Mirabeau, dealing with the issuing of passports. It was Mr. Hajjaj's signature which was then required for each passport delivered in Casablanca and his co-operation was therefore essential. I showed him my Swiss and Moroccan credentials and explained our ostensible aims. He knew of our coverage in *La Vigie Marocaine* from his assistant, a Mr. Zammit, of Maltese origin I think. My mention of Mr. Ghomari drew a smile; he mentioned that they had been at school together. I immediately suggested that he telephone him in Rabat for confirmation of my statement that the Entr'Aide would be sending a group of children to Switzerland in the summer under our auspices. I gave him the phone number and to my great relief Mr. Ghomari soon confirmed that "at least forty children" would be entrusted to us from among the sons of the "Martyrs of the Resistance" organization. The effect of Mr. Ghomari's statement was so salutary that, in my presence, speaking in French, he committed himself to a principle which he was unlikely to modify later. Mr. Hajjaj, of Berber origin, always struck me as a man of integrity and principles. He informed Mr. Ghomari that the passport formalities for the children living in the region of Casablanca would be simplified, enabling delivery within one week of the demands reaching him and that for collective passports there would be no charge. After this conversation Hajjaj became very friendly and, at my suggestion, authorised me to prepare the two green passport forms in my office. These were necessary requirements for each child—afterwards he accepted one form for any number of children coming from the same family—and I was even authorized to control the parents' signature in my office. This turned out to be a most unusual concession and he facilitated my task even more by dispensing me from the necessity of completing the forms in Arabic—French being sufficient. We discussed the type of passport that would be required and I showed no preference, acting as if individual passports would be issued, so that he should feel free to decide. I said that in Europe only a single sheet of paper, with the children's names inscribed, was required for collective youth-trips.

Notwithstanding these concessions, the formalities were still far from simple. As well as the passport forms, the following documents were officially required: an original (or duplicate) birth certificate of the child or "livret de famille" (family document); a certificate of residence; an official school identity-card, with the child's photograph, signed and stamped by the director of the school (this latter document was essential for collective passports).

Georges informed me the same evening that obtaining a certificate of residence was a long and complicated process. The next day Mr. Hajjaj accepted to drop this normal requirement, as only children groups were involved, not adults. He also authorized me to take all of the completed documents to the respective district in which the children lived for rapid processing by the office of each khalifa, as this would speed up the complicated process.

The idea of "collective passports"[42] had germinated in my mind following Mr. Reinhard's first suggestion of using a "feuille de route collective" (a "collective travel paper") to facilitate the formalities. Interestingly enough, the final decision for collective passports was probably motivated firstly by the desire of the Moroccan authorities to expedite matters for their official Muslim groups—at that time they were not aware of any Jewish candidates or other groups—and later, as a preventive measure, to avoid Jewish children eventually staying abroad at the end of the holiday period. This would have been impossible if collective passports were used, as they would only remain valid if all the persons listed travelled together. No one could have imagined that none of the children on each and every collective passport would return to Morocco.

My instructions had been to request individual passports, which would allow more flexibility, in case a child had to return to Morocco. It soon became evident that individual passports could not be obtained easily, whereas collective passports could. This reality was not however appreciated in Marseille, Paris and Jerusalem. I was again firmly instructed that individual passports were preferred.[43] I finally persuaded Georges that this short-sighted policy should be ignored—and he and his boss Alex Gattmon agreed with me and both supported my initiative.[44]

A Meeting with a Highly Placed Security Person

On May 31, I was called to the governor's office at the Prefecture of Casablanca, situated in the main square, to be interviewed by Muhammad D'khissy (pronounced *Dhrissy*), who had his office on the first floor, room no. 49. In charge of Social Affairs, he enquired into the past history and activities of OSSEAN and its present aims in Morocco. Our conversation lasted forty-five minutes and I was encouraged that he was satisfied with my explanations, adding that Mr. Ghomari had spoken to him about me and that, as there were other organizations interested in our holiday-camps, he had been asked to discuss these matters with me. He felt that we should have contacted the Moroccan embassy in Bern before launching our action so that our mountain-homes could have been visited by a Moroccan official, but otherwise he had no complaints. He wished us all success, promised to say a good word on our behalf to Mr. Hajjaj (a personal friend of his) and chatted amiably with me on the scenic beauties of Switzerland. He stated pertinently that it would be advisable for collective passports to be used so as not to allow any children to leave the group at any time.[45] Soon after, I learned from Mme Tordjman—confirmed by Georges—that Mr. D'khissy was a very important personality, probably the head of a the political security department of the governor.

On learning this, I decided that it would be wise to seek a closer relationship, rather than risk being questioned when I might least expect it. Georges also confirmed Muhammad D'khissy's key post and approved my suggestion. Then, three weeks later, on June 21, I recognized him at Casablanca airport. It was crowded with journalists, photographers and government officials welcoming the returning Algerian delegation from the first France-FLN Evian Conference, and Mr. D'khissy was walking arm in arm from the airplane, with the chief Algerian delegate.

A Suspicious Khalifa

By the end of the first week in June, all the appropriate documents had either been provided by the parents or completed in our office. Although no final written confirmation had been received concerning Muslim groups (they were scheduled to leave in August), this lack of "cover" was not serious as the fault did not lie with us, but with Mr. Ghomari who was awaiting free government transport. Reservations on ships leaving from Casablanca or Tangiers to Marseille in July for over a hundred were becoming more and more problematic, forcing me to make a provisional booking on June 26.

The moment had come to put my cards on the table, draw a deep breath, and pray for success. I fixed an appointment with Si Alaoui Tajjedine, the khalifa of the 1st district of Casablanca—the old Medina—in which at least sixty percent of our families resided. He received me cordially on June 8, assuring me that he would facilitate all formalities. The next day, in a letter of June 9 to Lehmann and in a subsequent complaint (June 11) to the governor of Casablanca, I described the scene in detail: Si Alaoui Tajjedine took one of the completed passport-forms, glanced at it casually, then a second, before snatching up a third. His expression underwent a change and by the time he had taken the fifth form he was shocked. Throwing them on his desk, he reacted strongly: "No! I will not sign—it's an emigration, an exodus, a political matter; you should not have become involved in this business, Mr.

Littman!" Affecting utter surprise, I asked him what he meant by this accusation as he could see that the children had been inscribed by their parents for holiday camps in Switzerland and I showed him a few deposit receipts. "What are you trying to imply, Sir?" I asked him indignantly, in my faulty French. "They are all Jews!" was his rejoinder, to which I replied: "How can I be expected to distinguish the religion of a Moroccan child from names like: Amar, Ifrah, Knafou, Chriqui and Malka—are you so sure they're all Jews?" He took another handful, glanced at them briefly and threw them down: "This is a political matter it is totally outside my responsibility!"[46]

I asked him to call Mr. Hajjaj for confirmation that the Entr'Aide Nationale was preparing a group under our auspices and that we were acting in good faith, but could not and would not refuse candidates on the basis of their religious faith. He called this "mere words", but phoned Mr. Hajjaj nonetheless, speaking in Arabic; it was clear that he did not agree with Tajjedine's attitude, who then calmed down, requesting me to leave him all the forms so that an official investigation could be carried out. I left his office crestfallen. All our plans, our work, our hopes, seemed to be dashed at that moment. Nothing seemed possible now, other than an international scandal, demonstrating that Morocco patently defied the right of a citizen to leave and return to his country of birth.

Liberal Attitudes by Senior Casablanca Officials

Yet it was Si Alaoui Tajjedine's explicit invective which was to benefit our cause immensely. His public outburst to an English delegate, representing a Swiss NGO organization, was in complete contradiction to Morocco's recent statement at the United Nations that Jews could have passports automatically like every other Moroccan citizen. Since the death of Muhammad V and the accession of his son, Hassan II, more than a cosmetic change of attitude had taken place. Tajjedine's behaviour was probably not appreciated either by liberal Moroccans in authority or by the king who wished to improve Morocco's image in the Western World and at the UN.

Georges quickly arranged for a liberal Muslim personality, favourably disposed to the Jewish community, to call Mr. Hajjaj and inform him of the gravity of the "incident" which had taken place and its possible repercussions. When I went to Mr. Hajjaj the next day to report he was very much affected by my detailed account of how Tajjedine had treated me. He advised me to "appeal to the governor", through Mr. Cheradi the director of his cabinet, and told me not to be discouraged or upset by what had happened.[47] Georges also contacted a municipal councillor of Casablanca, Max Loeub, a Jew of some importance in Morocco, who had a high reputation on account of his activity during the struggle for independence. I met him briefly and showed him a few deposit receipts—on hearing what had happened he became angry. He would see the governor himself about this matter and Tajjedine would undoubtedly be removed from his post after all the children had returned home from their holidays, thereby proving his error. I had a chance meeting with Mr. D'khissy at the Kontiki swimming pool who asked me how my work was progressing and repeated my story in details. He was shocked like Mr. Hajjaj and Mr. Loeub had been and touched his forehead with his forefinger, announcing that Tajjedine was crazy; he asked me not to take him seriously and promised that he would look into the matter personally. To all three, I explained that OSSEAN had never yet encountered such a deplorable reception and that we were not accustomed to asking the candidate's religion. Swiss organizations disliked intensely such scandals that might reach the international media. Would it not be better for me to close my office and simply send a report to Geneva? On no account must I do that, he replied. It was not my fault that the parents till now who had inscribed their children individually were all Jews. The important thing was that they were Moroccans and that my contacts with other governmental organizations were fruitful.

On my second meeting with Tajjedine on June 10 he was much more diplomatic, but continued to express doubt on our aims; he reiterated his threat to have me personally investigated. I communicated his words soon after to both Hajjaj and D'khissy, who reacted very strongly, even though the khalifa had finally accepted to process our forms officially.

I followed Mr. Hajjaj's June 10 advice and prepared an appeal to the governor of Casablanca, addressed to the director of his cabinet, Mr. Cheradi.

This three-page letter,[48] dated June 11 was very carefully drafted and Gisèle translated it into elegant French. It provided a summary of my activities and contacts in Morocco till then, referred to my letter of May 17[49] to the foreign ministry, copies of which I had left with Hajjaj, D'khissy and Tajjedine, and detailed the "Tajjedine" incident graphically. The governor's direct intervention was requested, particularly as transport reservations had already been made for June 26 "with the encouragement of Messrs. Hajjaj and D'khissy", yet the Moroccan candidates for OSSEAN's holiday-camps were apparently being refused passports solely on account of their religion. The appeal ended with an offer to organize immediately a private group, exclusively of Muslim children from Casablanca, "if the parents came forward to inscribe their children", as well as my deep regret that the deplorable "incident" of June 8 might put an end to OSSEAN's 1961 efforts in Morocco.

I handed this June 11 letter personally to Mr. Cheradi the next day; by coincidence, on the same day that I was listed in *Le Petit Marocain* as "among the personalities present" at the official British consular celebration of Queen Elizabeth's birthday two days earlier. Mr. Cheradi received me courteously, read carefully both my May 17 and June 11 letters and recommendations, and promised to bring the matter to the attention of the governor.

A Providential Passport Breakthrough

When I saw Tajjedine for the third time a few days afterwards he was somewhat less confident and his voice unsteady. He asked me why I hadn't told him on my first visit about my various contacts in Rabat: "I don't know who you have on your side Mr. Littman but this whole business has been thoroughly planned; every word I say to you reaches those in high places." Because of this, he had already decided to number the passport demands that I brought to him which would all be sent to Mr. Hajjaj to do with as he pleased. He would not sign them individually, but would provide Mr. Hajjaj with a general report. He told me there and then that he had emphasised a number of points: all the children were Jewish; they came from very modest families; he could not understand how they could pay what we were asking; OSSEAN should be entirely responsible if their parents defaulted on the payment, and that only collective passports should be delivered to these groups.[50]

During either our second or third meeting he confided: "Do you know that as much as 80,000 Jews used to live in this first khalifa district ("arrondissement") and now there are only 40,000 at most? With a look of astonishment, I asked him but where have they gone?"

"To Palestine," he spat out in disgust and explained how Jews were leaving clandestinely by open boats without passports. My face showed bewilderment and I asked him why they should go there of all places, now that independent Morocco had so much to offer them. He complained of Zionist propaganda, but added that the majority of those who left regretted having done so after their arrival in Palestine. We talked about the fate of these "unfortunates" and I suggested to him that the whole matter was probably merely a psychological reaction: it would appear that Jews cannot leave and return to Morocco as they wished and perhaps the propaganda you mention is more effective than would be the case if they had complete freedom of movement. I added that I was convinced that the desire of such poor parents to send their children to Switzerland under our care for a month's holiday stemmed from a wish that their children should benefit from this unique opportunity of having a holiday abroad. "Why not make it as easy for them to go abroad as to go to Rabat, and you'll see how few will wish to go", I concluded. He smiled at my suggestion.

Tajjedine may have guessed what was being prepared from the very beginning. In fact, I remember him making a rather noteworthy remark to the effect that, "we were expecting something like this to be conceived", or words to that effect. He knew the actual condition of the parents who were allegedly sending their children on a costly holiday to Switzerland and my statement that perhaps the parents might have used their "savings" for this occasion, or have been aided by a Moroccan Jewish charitable institution, did not convince him. "Come with me for a walk into the Medina and I'll show you how wretchedly they live" was his answer. I had to plead an urgent appointment to avoid him proving to me what I already knew. Perhaps he was not entirely sure of our motives, and when his superiors began to chide him, and then criticise his attitude severely, he decided angrily, to place the responsibility on their shoulders.

By thus washing his hands of the whole business, and declining even to make the nominal enquiry on each candidate, he facilitated the bureaucratic procedure beyond our wildest expectations. It was now possible to get the passport demands through his district's office within forty-eight hours, as his staff were instructed to accelerate the procedure. Later, with the help of a clerk from this same passport section, the formality was reduced to half an hour and, finally, to five minutes—no more than the time necessary to write the numbers on each form! Out of a final total of 530 children, more than 300 were from the Mellah (first khalifa district), but he kindly processed a dozen or two demands that had nothing to do with the first district, so that we might benefit from this facility after the staff of the second khalifa district deliberately slowed down the procedure.

The second khalifa district of Casablanca was of quite a different stripe. Whereas Tajjedine understood, opposed, and was overruled by his superiors, Si Berrode Abdellaoui took the forty passport forms from me on June 10 without reacting at all. He merely stated that he would make the customary enquiries in each case. He wore an ostentatious diamond set in a gold ring on his left little finger, but his non-committal manner did not inspire me with confidence. His policy was one of procrastination and he inevitably left me to kick my heels outside his door. I soon took the habit of arriving very early in the morning to pour out my complaints as he stepped out of his car. Si Berrode Abdellaoui remained a problem for me till the end. I hesitated however to try bribery, as I was advised to do, for fear of compromising myself. Instead, I distributed a supply of Swiss chocolates to members of both district passport sections in the most natural way, as well as at the Place Mirabeau préfecture—to those who were in a position to remove the inevitable "red tape" that was unavoidable in any administration. Once, a half bottle of whiskey was enough to persuade a French clerk in the préfecture to give our collective passports priority. Unconsciously, I was using my connections with the governor's aides (D'khissy and Hajjaj—both of Berber origin) in order to pressure the two khalifas (Tajjedine and Abdellaoui—of Arab origin), who were below them in rank.

Within a week of Tajjedine's tantrum, our whole position was miraculously changing. Instead of preparing an international scandal, I had merely to concentrate my friendly pressure on Mr. Hajjaj in the hope that the deadline of June 26 would find me in possession of both passports and Swiss visas. He was waiting for instructions as to what sort of passports to deliver and finally was told to provide collective passports. I am pretty certain that this was a policy-decision, as already explained above—to reduce the risk of any child leaving the group. This preference seemed to calm and reassure everyone, especially my automatic acceptance. Incidentally, this decision saved us over one thousand dollars (the equivalent of over thirty-thousand dollars today) as there was no charge in Morocco for collective passports, whereas the charge for individual passports was about two dollars each (about sixty dollars today).

Our First Convoy of 127 Children Leaves for Marseilles

On the June 25, the *S.S. Ionia*, a Greek ship returning from Mecca, was offering extremely reasonable fares from Casablanca to Marseilles. SIRTAM, the travel agency owned by Mr. and Mrs. Tordjman, was responsible for the booking. This is how I first met Hélène Tordjman, a courageous Swiss Jewess, married to a Moroccan Jew. At the beginning, knowing nothing about her, I was very aloof, but she was curious about me and on a visit to Geneva unfortunately learned far too much. On her return to Casablanca she astonished me with this knowledge, but when she conveyed me a private message from Mrs. Hélène Bloch, Prof. Bloch's wife, whom she knew well, I was obliged to acknowledge the true purpose of our mission. Fortunately, this was the only leak from Geneva. There seemed no reason for me not being in touch with her, since SIRTAM was well-known; soon it became our indispensable travel agency.[51]

In detailed letters of June 9 and 10,[52] I informed "Lehmann," first of my despair, and then of the turnabout in our fortunes; in that of June 12,[53] I stated that I had reserved 102 places aboard the boat *S.S. Ionia* sailing two weeks later. I outlined the possibility of sending "from 100 to 200 children in this convoy" and insisted that an adequate number of monitors should arrive in Casablanca to take care of the children on the boat and on the long bus journey from Marseilles to Morgins in the canton of Valais, Switzerland. The ages of the girls and boys were from eight to sixteen, but the average age range was from twelve to fifteen.

With only a fortnight left to organize everything in Casablanca and Geneva, much panic ensued. Complications soon arose: the head of the second Casablanca district, Si Abdellaoui refused his signature for twelve—later reduced to four—of the fifty-one children from his district on the grounds that they had already left school.

Many of the school identity-cards were unstamped or unsigned by the director and therefore invalid. Some of the addresses provided were incorrect. But the preparation of the collective passports had actually begun! On June 16, I cabled Geneva's OSE office:

COLLECTIVE PASSPORTS OFFICIALLY COMMENCED. HOPE LEAST 80 FROM FIRST LIST 110 COMPLETE WEDNESDAY NEXT. DOUBTFUL SECOND LIST READY DEPART IONIA 25. THEN 2 JULY PAQUET. TAI CONFIRM CASA–LYON 10 JULY 85 SEATS FORCED RELEASE SOME TOURIST ACCOMMODATION IONIA OTHERWISE OEUVRE RESPONSIBLE. ALWAYS PLACES DORMITORY.[54]

My letter of June 18[55] shows that the number of children already processed had reached eighty-five, the next day ninety-three; and I added, in my June 19 express letter: "As I said before, 'at least 80' all being well, and possibility up to 100; I am hammering away on all sides, but there are too many nails."[56] The big problem was the school identity-cards—a major stumbling block that required urgent improvisation! From that moment, the local Misgeret network did wonders, arranging that the children received adequate "school accommodation." Photographs were stuck on authentic-looking cards and correctly stamped. I learned the method myself a little later and became quite an expert. This helped us raise the numbers to 127 children for the first departure on June 26 aboard the S.S. Ionia.

The paperwork was taking on gigantic proportions and I stressed that

David G. Littman in his office, (105 Dumont d'Urville, Casablanca),
with Aïda Schirmann, alias N. Lehmann, OSSEAN's secretary-general, June 24, 1961

Dr. Claude Dreyfus, who left his medical practice in Geneva to volunteer,
is helping in the OSSEAN's office

Miss Schirmann's ("Lehmann") presence a few days before had become indispensable, as Gisèle and I could not handle the mountain of forms. The other collaborator required for the ship journey should also come as soon as possible.

On June 21, Schirmann arrived from Geneva. Two days later, Michel Steuermann, director of the Home de la Forêt, arrived with Dr. Claude Dreyfus, a chiropractician, who had left his medical practice for a week to help us. The three of them aided us considerably in completing the formalities, particularly Aïda Schirmann who worked non-stop. The crossing to Marseilles was no picnic for them.

The collective passports (four in all for the 127 children) were handed to me at the last possible moment—a precedent that was followed for the four other convoys—on Saturday, June 24 by Mr. Okbi, Mr. Hajjaj's assistant in charge of preparing all passports. It was only by extreme good-will that the Swiss consulate agreed to stamp in the visas on a Saturday afternoon.[57] We were in a position to reciprocate. As a result of our substantial bookings, Mrs. Tordjman had been able to obtain two first-class complimentary tickets for members of the consulate on the same ship. Thus OSSEAN's respectability was again enhanced by the presence of the Swiss consul and his wife at the port of Casablanca, coming to wave goodbye to their young son and the chancellor, both of whom boarded the ship at the same time as the Moroccan Jewish youngsters.

My express letter dated 4:30 p.m. Monday, June 26 began: "The S.S. Ionia steamed out from the 'Gare Delande' at about 12:20 p.m. this afternoon. She carries 127 children of Moroccan nationality who will be taking their month's holiday in Switzerland with the full collaboration and help of the Oeuvre, a good beginning I trust to the Oeuvre's efforts in North Africa. The ship is due in at Marseilles between 10:00 a.m. and 11:00 a.m. on Thursday the 29th June and the buses should be at the dockside as early as possible. At the latest count there were 66 boys and 61 girls."[58]

The miracle had begun. A political concession had been wrung from the Moroccan authorities. The port authorities ticked off the names of the happy holiday-dressed children, carrying Moroccan flags, and the ship departed. Now that the political objective had been achieved, it was to have a big effect

Children from the first convoy waiting
to board the *S.S. Ionia*, June 26, 1961

Young girl from the first convoy holding a piece of paper with her name,
the date and the hour of her departure, boarding the *S.S. Ionia*, June 26, 1961

Children from the first convoy on the deck
of the *S.S. Ionia*, June 26, 1961

S.S. Ionia leaving Casablanca, June 26, 1961

in every sphere for those who were working for the exodus of Jews, either legally or illegally. Henceforth, the vital question in our minds concerned the number of children that could be brought to Israel from Morocco via Switzerland in a month by using the special system of "collective passports."

Was our success merely an exceptional stroke of luck at a particularly auspicious moment? Would the authorities discover our aims and close the office? There were moments when this seemed possible and one of these occurred four days later during my meeting with Mr. Cheradi.

My Stolen Wallet

Arriving at the Anfa hotel in the early evening of June 16, I discovered that my wallet was no longer in my back pocket. Horrified, I drove frantically back to 105 Dumont d'Urville, and to the post office where I had shortly before sent the above mentioned cable. No trace of it in either place! I returned home in an agitated state and broke the news to Gisèle. The money was of no importance, my driving licence was replaceable—as were other papers—but that same morning I had typed the first list of over one hundred names for our *S.S. Ionia* convoy and had foolishly placed a copy in an inside pocket of my wallet. The list of Moroccan Jewish children with names, addresses and ages was typed out on a thin airmail sheet. Anonymous, it could have been damning evidence of my "Zionist activities" if it would have fallen into the hands of an unscrupulous person, or an attentive policeman.

Gisèle and I discussed the matter at length. There was no alternative other than to report the loss to the police; not to do so would be even more perilous. I acted immediately. That same evening, the police rang back for complementary information and Gisèle called me at a nearby cocktail party at which I had felt obliged to participate because of the likely presence of important officials and diplomats whom I hoped to meet. Later that night, I picked up Georges in my car as usual, and we drove along the silent coast. He was equally appalled and decided to prepare for the worst.

Gisèle and I spent a sleepless night discussing the likely outcome of it all. There seemed only three possibilities: nothing would ever be found; an empty wallet would be found with or without the incriminating list; the police would catch the thief in possession of an unopened wallet, although this latter chance seemed highly unlikely.

The next morning, Gisèle was resting with Diana in the garden of the Anfa hotel by the swimming pool when she was called to the phone. Once again it was the police, this time convoking me to the central police-station "as soon as possible." I had deliberately given only my hotel address. No other indication was made to Gisèle. Nervously, she called me at the office and I felt a pain in the pit of my stomach, not unusual for one suffering from a duodenal ulcer for the past seven years, dependent on pills, glasses of milk, as well as sandwiches, to calm these bouts of gnawing pains.

I drove straight to the station and was lead into a small room. There on the table in front of me were a number of wallets. Was one of them mine I was asked by the policeman in charge? I felt my heart pounding. "Yes," I replied, with much delight and gratitude, but showing no anxiety. "Please examine it carefully and tell me if anything is missing", he said, nonchalantly. The thought raced through my mind: they already have the list and

Gisèle Littman standing next to
the post office building where the
wallet was stolen

he is watching your reaction! I took my wallet, found there all the money
(Moroccan, Swiss, French) and papers, and then—half-turning at a moment
when one of his colleagues called him into another room—I hastily opened
the complicated, hidden, inside-flap and discovered that my thin piece of
paper with the list of children was in its place and had almost certainly not
been seen or touched by anyone. Only a photograph of Gisèle in a bikini
was missing. "Absolutely everything is here", I replied when he came back
into the room and repeated his question.

Well-known to the police, the skilful pickpocket had been caught as he
left the post office the evening before with both pockets bulging. It took me
a few moments to recover from my realization that the danger was past. He
refused any gift but finally did accept a generous donation for the police
fund that I placed in the public box. I regretted the loss of the beautiful
photograph of Gisèle, but rejoiced in the auspicious outcome.

I would hardly consider myself to be "religious", but as I left the police
building I mumbled a sincere prayer heavenward. I felt then—and still do

today—that such occurrences can be described in common language, either as "lucky", or "providential." I prefer the latter term with all that it might signify. This incident fortified me at a crucial moment and strengthened my resolution.

Later, on July 3, I was called to the very same building, also housing the Sûreté Régionale of Casablanca. My interrogator was acting on the instructions of a letter from the governor's office. It was dated June 17—the very day that I left with a prayer on my lips, clutching my wallet—but it took seventeen days to be acted upon.

Reinforcing my "Cover"

While awaiting Miss Schirmann ("Lehmann") at the airport on June 21, I had recognized Mr. D'khissy welcoming the FLN delegation and realised his importance. I decided that we should get to know him better—particularly as he had been so co-operative since we first met on May 31—as such a social relationship would reinforce my "cover" (in fact, this friendship became crucial at critical moments during my operation). Soon after, I rang and invited him and his wife to dine with us at the hotel Anfa on June 30; so successful was that evening together that within a week we were their guests at home for an extraordinary Moroccan meal. We were now on the very best of terms, and Georges told me that it was rare for someone in his position to invite us to their home for a family meal. Thereafter, we met almost daily, during the lunch break, at the select Kon-Tiki swimming pool by the sea. This break from the office was becoming more and more difficult, as I was then rushing to and from one office to another, but a constant contact with him was of too great an importance to neglect. When I couldn't go, Gisèle would go with Diana when Mme Loiselet our French nanny was not available to look after her. Mr. D'khissy was often at the Kon-Tiki with three of his children and I remember Mrs. D'khissy joining him twice. In the most natural way, we were becoming more than just mere acquaintances.

I even spoke to him casually of my family business affairs in England— and may even have invited him to our Palace Court Hotel in Bournemouth.

I explained my humanitarian decision to work for OSSEAN and for North African children. I told him that our president was surprised by the number of Jewish candidates from Casablanca and had instructed me to arrange with Moroccan authorities the formation of a convoy of thirty Muslim children for up to a month's holiday in one of our Homes. The only cost would be the transport, the rest would be covered entirely by OSSEAN.

Mr. D'khissy emphasised that we should in no way feel embarrassed by this social phenomenon, even if prejudiced men like Tajjedine, whom he obviously disliked, were highly critical of us. The importance was our aim to aid Moroccan children without distinction; the fact that all of the candidates were so far Jews was irrelevant—this was purely a social phenomenon, for Muslim parents hesitated to allow their children to travel abroad for holiday-camps.

My explanation created an excellent impression and Mr. D'khissy lost no time in introducing me, at the Kon-Tiki, to Mr. El Khamar ben Abdeslam (part owner of El-Khmar Fils, a large carpet shop in the Blvd. El Hansali) who was an organizer of holiday-camps for the sons of members of the Union of Moroccan Labour. On this and subsequent meetings—all at the Kon-Tiki—El Khamar asked for more information and was seriously considering sending a group in August. He probably did not finalize anything in the following fortnight in the hope that we would offer to pay the travel expenses, as the Austrian government had allegedly done the previous year. On that occasion, his welfare organization had received full credit at absolutely no financial cost. My intention in making such a generous offer at that particular moment was to cement our relationship with Mr. D'khissy, so that he would be convinced, beyond any doubt, of our good faith and would support me unhesitatingly.

Here was OSSEAN's official offer to take thirty Muslim children without charge to Switzeralnd, while all other children were paying ten Swiss francs per child per day (two dollars and forty cents—the equivalent of over seventy dollars today, for over sixty thousand dollars for thirty children during one month). I could no longer be accused of deliberately selecting or accepting only Jewish children.

A Police Interrogation

I was called to the Sûreté Régionale (SR) police station on July 3 and questioned on my work in Switzerland and Morocco. As usual, I backed up my answers by showing my panoply of credentials. Mention of this or that high-placed official seemed to impress my interrogator, who was not particularly astute. When I handed him the long letter addressed to the Foreign Ministry on May 17, he read it carefully and then proceeded to write it out in longhand, almost verbatim—evidently his report needed padding. While he was thus engaged, I managed to glance casually at the letter which he had negligently pushed aside and, reading it backwards, obtained a clear idea of its contents. Typed in French on official notepaper of the Casablanca préfecture it was dated June 17 and signed "Ibrahami." The SR was ordered to make a full enquiry on me and my activities just as Tajjedine had announced almost four weeks earlier!

When asked how many children were already inscribed for vacations in Switzerland and the proportion of Jews amongst them, I replied forcefully that no Swiss institution ever asked the religious faith of its candidates either in Morocco or elsewhere. However, I solemnly acknowledged that Mr. Hajjaj had told me that probably all the children were Jewish—and I added, as an afterthought, that it was an unexpected phenomenon which has been fully explained to me by Mr. D'khissy three days ago and that I hoped to find a satisfactory solution to it.

I could read the surprise in his eyes on learning from my lips, obviously for the first time, that one convoy of Jewish children had left for Switzerland a week earlier. He was quite unable to conceal his astonishment on being informed that it had consisted of 127 children, travelling on four collective passports, who had left from the port of Casablanca on the *S.S. Ionia* that had just arrived from Mecca with returning pilgrims—I couldn't resist adding this information. His amazement soon turned to embarrassment. It slowly dawned on him that the delay in implementing the instructions sent on June 17 had resulted in a *fait accompli* and that his interrogation was now irrelevant, especially as our project appeared to have official approval. A rubber stamp "report" might serve by avoiding awkward questions from his superiors, and would coincide with what appeared to be an official policy decision.

By a fortunate coincidence all municipal officials had good reason to be distracted at that time as a new governor had been nominated shortly before by the King Hassan II. On July 6, Colonel Driss Ben Omar, known for his liberal leanings, officially took up his duties. This was certainly not the moment to draw the attention of the prefecture to inefficiency on such a minor matter.

On that same day, while processing at the central passport office the names of the children scheduled to leave for Switzerland in four days time, I was unexpectedly left alone by Mr. Hajjaj's clerk when he was called urgently into the adjacent room; in his haste, he closed the door behind him. Within a tantalising arm's reach, on the desk between us, the official file concerning OSSEAN stared up at me, invitingly. The temptation was irresistible and, in an instant, I had switched it around and began turning the pages. The first letter in French which caught my eye looked familiar. It was dated June 17 and I recognized the signature of "Ibrahami." It referred to my having been in contact with the Foreign Ministry in Rabat, stated that OSSEAN was considered trustworthy and confirmed that full confidence could be placed in me as its delegate. Footsteps ended my indiscretion and the file found its rightful place instantaneously just as the door opened and the clerk reappeared.

I was now aware of the total picture. These two letters dated June 17 from Ibrahami were almost certainly due to Tajjedine's report a week earlier. The positive one sent to Mr. Hajjaj have been influenced by my complaint addressed to the governor, my long discussion with Mr. Cheradi on June 12, as well as a good word from Mr. D'khissy. This was clearly the official green light which had allowed Mr. Hajjaj to begin preparing the collective passports. The second letter sent to the police must have arrived the day after my wallet was handed back to me in that very same building, and was undoubtedly in response to Tajjedine's insistence that my activities be investigated—whereas one communication was acted upon immediately the other, fortunately for me, was delayed.

Later, I learned from Mrs. Tordjman that Mr. Ibrahami was generally considered to be the éminence grise of every governor of Casablanca, and his personal anti-Zionist feelings were well-known. Be that as it may, from that moment onwards I knew that my cover had passed the crucial test and not been found wanting; this knowledge encouraged me to redouble my efforts to process the maximum number of children for the holiday-camps before July 26, when the first "holiday group" was scheduled to return to Morocco.

CHAPTER 4

The Third and Final Phase
of Operation Mural
(July 11-July 24, 1961)

Meeting Georges two days later after the departure of the first convoy on the *S.S. Ionia*, we set our sights at a figure of 300 children, nearly 180 in the subsequent month. He acknowledged that the technical side of preparing all the various documents had caused tremendous, unforeseen problems and that a new Misgeret group had been formed specifically to deal with everything and speed up the work.

During this period, other activities were being organized that steadily increased the numbers of clandestine departures. Georges might find himself on the same night seeing off a small boat convoy from a deserted coast, just after meeting with me around midnight. He never spoke to us about his other activities until many years afterwards when we met at Kibbutz Regavim, his home in Israel.

Following the departure of the first convoy, my July 1 letter to "Mme Lehmann" was optimistic in tone. I referred to D'khissy's encouraging words of advice to us at dinner the night before and added: "Mr. D'khissy is most helpful and never fails to aid me in pushing in the right direction when it is necessary, and only yesterday he telephoned to the Khalifa of the II Arrondissement [Abdellaoui] to ask him to speed up his 'enquêtes'; the Khalifa of the I Arrondissement [Tajjedine] is now most courteous and returns the passport demands within two days. Our unfortunate first meeting is all but forgotten."

I confirmed the reservation of a TAI chartered airplane, "since I am fully confident that I can fill the eighty-five places." In trying to convey a clear message that a flood of children should be expected, thereby indicating the weight of the administrative burden, I explained: "formalities [now] take less time. However, I doubt if I can go on sleeping four hours a night for another month, and the work involved is taking its toll [. . .] Homes must be found to house all these children should your bookings from Europe and Morocco outnumber the space already available."[59]

Unexpected Problems at OSE's Swiss Holiday Home

Two letters arrived from "Lehmann" on July 5 and 6.[60] The first announced the arrival at Morgins and Champéry (Canton of Valais) in the early hours of June 29 of the 127 children transported in three buses from Marseilles. The "good administrative preparation" was appreciated, but the "choice of children was not carried out with enough perspicacity." "Undesirable elements" had burned mattresses, torn up sheets and broken locks on the *SS Ionia*. Grave problems were envisaged and I was instructed to undertake "serious psychological examinations"—not just a medical control—failing which OSSEAN's action in Morocco would be jeopardised. "Our friends in Bern" (Bar-Giora and Reiffler) insisted that this message be transmitted to me.

The second letter was in reply to mine of July 1, which arrived after the first had been mailed from Geneva. I was told not to confirm for another three days the chartered airplane on July 10. Moreover, the older children in the first convoy were causing chaos and there was constant danger from "obstinate smokers", apart from the more natural problems arising from adolescent girls and boys being mixed. An ingenious solution was approved: "It is necessary to bar from your list all the adolescents above the age of fifteen." The instructions contained in these two letters illustrate the concepts and mentalities prevailing then from afar, totally irreconcilable with those being pragmatically adapted on the spot, as a result of events.

On the one hand, the Jewish Agency's Youth Aliyah department (headed by Moshe Kol in Jerusalem and represented in Marseilles by Arieh Reiffler) were endeavouring to continue its task of bringing all Jewish children to Israel whose parents desired it. They were to be chosen, if possible, on the basis of an aptitude test determined both by a medical and a psychological examination—i.e., a form of selection, approved by the foreign ministry, whose head was then Moshe Sharrett (formerly Shertog), although this word was a taboo subject, and remained so for a long time after 1961.

The immigration department of the Jewish Agency, represented by Naphtali Bar-Giora in Paris, was basically interested—as was Alex Gatt-mon—in achieving a change in the government's policy towards Moroccan Jewish emigration subsequent to the *Egoz* tragedy. However, as only children were involved in this particular operation, it had been agreed that its cost was to be covered out of a special Youth Aliyah budget and therefore that department's various requirements became mandatory.

It was agreed that OSE-Switzerland (Prof. Jacques Bloch and Mlle Aïda Schirmann in Geneva), the vital cog in the machinery, would follow instruction received from "our friends in Bern" (Bar-Giora and Reiffler). In my letters to Geneva, I often referred to both of them, collectively, as "Herrn Berger and Leoni,"[61] humorous nicknames which neither of them appreciated—"Berger" for Bar-Giora, and "Leoni" for Reiffler, whose first name, Arieh, signified a "lion" in Hebrew. For OSE, organizing holiday-camps for hundreds of potential arrivals from Morocco caused considerable administrative problems. Firstly, their customary summer camps for Jewish children from France and England might have to be rearranged or cancelled at the last moment; secondly, improvisation in accommodating groups beyond the capacity of OSE's two chalets in Morgins (180 persons), including extra staff, posed insoluble problems, unless Youth Aliyah was willing to cover an eventual financial risk and provide a global guarantee for OSE. Later, after the arrival of the first convoy of 127 children, the question of order and discipline arose. OSE's reputation in the small villages of Morgins and Champéry (Canton of Valais) was no light matter, neither was the extra internal organization necessary to cope with the unruly "elements", one of whom had allegedly torn a stray cat to pieces with his bare hands! It was hardly surprising then that Youth Aliyah's insistence that psychological tests be carried out in Morocco was rapidly endorsed by OSE—neither organization realising that such an undertaking was completely unrealistic in the actual circumstances that prevailed in Morocco, with barely three weeks remaining.

On the other hand, those working on the spot had to deal with the everyday problems, as they arose, and their chief objective was to accelerate mass Jewish emigration to Israel in every way, and in the shortest possible time. Alex Gattmon and Georges soon realized that in cases where parents wished to make aliyah they obviously would not consider leaving behind one or more of their children—even with a close relative—yet it was no easy task to submit whole families to the hazards of clandestine sea-transport at night.

My own feelings had been clearly expressed on March 23 when I wrote that our goal should be concentrated "on the summer period, beginning towards the end of June." For three months I had continued hammering home this elementary truth, but to no avail. Either there was still little faith in my optimistic prognostications as the weeks advanced in May and June, or the financial consequences (difficult to explain in Jerusalem) in the case of failure were viewed with more anxiety than the administrative complications which might arise if the mission was overwhelmingly successful. I knew that we were faced with a deadline, for each OSSEAN candidate accepted by the Moroccan authorities on a collective passport reduced the number of those who had to leave clandestinely at great risk; and, on the other hand, the number of parents ready to emigrate to Israel was thereby increased. Also, the global cost of bringing a child to Switzerland was roughly one-half that required to transport an adult or child to Gibraltar only, illegally. The first convoy was supposed to return to Casablanca "after about a month." Because of heavy summer bookings, I had only been able to reserve with the "Paquet" line (through the SIRTAM agency) a block of one hundred return places on the August 1 Marseilles-Casablanca ferry, and had requested a further twenty-seven places. This unexpected transport problem had allowed me to request extensions on Swiss visas (to August 5) and on the validity of the collective passports (to August 15). Therefore, at the very latest, I would have to be out of Casablanca before August 14, and the children out of Switzerland ten days earlier. The official date of their return was announced for August 1 and any prolongation would only be feasible—as I envisaged it—if a "subsidised extension" (a trip to France for instance) was linked with a later convoy of Muslim children covered by "OSSEAN's generosity." I raised this matter once again in my July 1 letter but to no avail.[62] Looking back fifty years later, it is clear that, aside from anything else, an extra cost of 4,000 dollars (the equivalent of 120,000 dollars today) was a chief factor.

No arguments from afar would have modified my determination not to keep our machinery running, now that all was working so smoothly. Only instructions on the spot could have done that and they did not come. On July 4, I cabled Geneva that the contract with TAI for the July 10 chartered plane was signed, and in my letter of the same date[63] I mentioned that I was preparing a third convoy and had sixty children almost processed. I ended with kindest regards to "Herr Leoni" and: "Cordial greetings also to Herr Berger—it is my birthday today and I am in excellent spirits!" The next day was a public holiday in honour of Mr. Ferhat Abbas, the Algerian FLN leader, on an official visit to Morocco. My letter of that date (6:00 p.m.), only thirty hours after the previous one, mentioned "about one hundred children" for the third convoy—an increase of forty. But I had received that afternoon the first reply dated July 3 from Geneva and I ended mine ironically: "It is rather late in the date to ask for psychological examinations—the Lake of Geneva must look simply splendid! Here we are in the midst of a heat wave and we manage to struggle along as best we can."

The next evening, I met Georges, and as we drove along the coast and felt the warm sea-breeze I explained to him my latest discovery (Mr. Ibrahami's revealing communication to the passport department) and discussed the two letters from Geneva, as well as the amazing speed-up in the passport procedure. His group of course were indirectly responsible for this, in that the parents they were processing kept arriving at OSSEAN's office non-stop, and my wife and I had difficulty coping with such large numbers who waited patiently in line outside. Fortunately some of the parents inscribed as many as three, even four of their children! We laughed at the request for "psychological examinations." The hasty secret medical examination for each child was difficult enough to organize, but was essential to obtain a Swiss visa. An additional psychological examination simply proved how little was understood about the conditions under which we were all operating. Georges confirmed that under no circumstances should I cancel any reservations and that I should simply ignore all negative instructions from Geneva from whatever source. We agreed that on no account would any "selection" be implemented by us and that even cripples would be treated exactly as other candidates—so long as they passed a simple medical examination. We decided to raise our goal from 300 to 400 children, although a big obstacle was the lack of transport facilities during the second half of July.

Aïda Schirmann ("Lehmann") faithfully arrived on the July 8 TAI flight via Paris and was once again of great help to us in the last-minute preparation for the departure—I found time to take her to Rabat for a few hours of sightseeing which she appreciated. The three collective passports, containing ninety-three names, were finally signed by Mr. Hajjaj on the very morning of the flight—a very nervous moment for us all, particularly as the Swiss visas had to be stamped in within the hour, and again this was done with the maximum of speed and understanding.[64] Fortunately, our chartered plane arrived late and all went smoothly, especially TAI's agreement to accept ninety-three children and Schirmann, although the plane's full capacity was eighty-five adult passengers, but the younger children weighed much less than adults. Our second convoy left on July 10 from Casablanca to Lyon.

An Irresponsible Decision

In my 1961 report, I had described what follows "with certain regrets," but felt obliged to do so, as a warning against eventual repetition and the obvious risks for others. The event is essential to the narrative, because it provoked a "religious scandal" in Israel at that time and, more than any other reason, halted any prolongation of Operation Mural at a crucial moment. As for the ultimate responsibility, I can only record what I learned about it at that time. There seemed to be no good reason to conceal details neither in 1961, nor in 1984, and even less in 2011.[65]

In mid-June, Georges went to Geneva and Paris to prepare the ground for the arrival of the first convoy. At my request, he obtained further promises that, under no circumstances, would any of the children be sent out of Switzerland before the operation had ended—i.e., with the departure of Gisèle, Diana and me from Casablanca. There was no sense in sending some of the children to Israel a few weeks earlier, thereby increasing the risks for our safety if the Moroccan authorities had sent someone to check the numbers of children and for the successful continuation of the mission that such a decision would imply. The argument, later put forward, that there was a lack of available accommodation in Switzerland was flimsy because since March 23, I had emphasized that the crucial period would begin at the end of June.

Notwithstanding all the promises made and elementary common sense, on July 9, one day before the departure from Casablanca of the second convoy of ninety-three children, eighty-five children from the first convoy were driven by bus to Marseilles where they boarded a plane to Israel. Fortunately, I was not informed of this foolhardy act and the reasons for it till I met Mr. Reiffler in Switzerland a fortnight later. Then, he made no apologies and considered the whole incident as an administrative reaction to a difficult accommodation problem. He had not considered what might have happened if the Moroccan embassy in Bern, on instructions, had decided to visit the two homes where over 220 Moroccan Jewish children were supposed to be enjoying their Swiss holidays.

In retrospect, it is easy to understand what must have caused this decision. Youth Aliyah was unwilling or unable to guarantee OSE for any lost down payment concerning unused supplementary chalet reservations. OSE was in poor financial shape and could not take such risks alone. When 127 children arrived, on June 29, via the *S.S. Ionia* from Marseilles all the available accommodation was immediately filled. An attempt was made to stop the second convoy without a thought that our mission was limited in time. When these instructions were ignored in Casablanca something had to be improvised and the easiest way out was chosen in spite of potentially dire consequences. Obviously, this "plan" was acceptable to someone with authority in Jerusalem, otherwise an Israeli airplane could not have been sent to Marseilles to fly the eighty-five children to Israel. Nonetheless, whether the responsibility was single or joint, this act has always remained incomprehensible to me and to those directly involved in the operation with whom I discussed it at the time, or subsequently.

An Initial Change of Moroccan Policy

After the new governor of Casablanca, Colonel Driss ben Omar, took up his duties a wind of change was immediately felt, particularly by the Jews. Almost the first thing he did was to inform the khalifas of the various districts of Casablanca that "no Jew should be refused a passport, nor should its delivery be unnecessarily delayed." He did not want to hear that officials under his juridiction had refused a passport for any Jew who had made his request in the normal way. This policy-change, which affected only Casablanca at that time, came less than five months after the death of Muhammad V who had been pressured to adopt a more liberal attitude on this issue after the *Piscès (Ergoz)* scandal. It was nonetheless a complete volteface of policy towards the Jewish minority since Morocco's independence, a policy which was typified by Tajjedine's outburst to me exactly one month earlier. Our own success had preceded this declaration by ten days with the departure of the first convoy of Jewish children using collective passports.

The first reactions to these instructions were staggering. Jews came to their respective district offices to complete the forms in their thousands; many files virtually ignored at the first and second districts, sometimes for months or even years, were precipitately transferred to the Place Mirabeau préfecture. Mr. Hajjaj and his staff who had been instructed to issue passports held back at his office, could not cope with this flood even after receiving eight new clerks. On my regular visits to the inner rooms I was witness to the chaos prevailing. I saw one room, about five by five metres, literally covered with passports that were stacked in piles up to knee level; the desks of three other rooms were also covered and among the thirty odd names that I was able to read, all were clearly Jewish. It was a fine sight, but it had one serious drawback and I was soon made aware of that by Mr. Hajjaj himself. When he saw me arrive with the completed forms for yet another large group of children, he informed me that it would be impossible for him to return our collective passports before two weeks at the minimum, as he could not hold up the other work just for us. He was frank, but I knew that we could not afford to wait two weeks for the departure of the next convoy.

Without even reflecting on what I was saying, I asked him outright to let me be responsible for writing out the French part of each collective passport containing the rudimentary information on every child; I added, sympathetically, that it was not fair that the "préfecture" should spend so much time on us, whilst there was no charge for the collective passports. "Could I not help?" I pleaded. He was taken by surprise, remained pensive an instant, and then without any hesitation, turned to Mr. Okbi, his chief assistant in the passport section, a very friendly Algerian, and instructed him to give me the appropriate collective passport pages. The details of two children were to be completed on each sheet (individual passports were most probably being issued mainly to middle-class couples, who were anxious to make a holiday or business trip abroad). OSSEAN's activities were fortuitously becoming associated with this sudden "holiday urge" of Moroccan Jews, and a change of attitudes, even policy. The stars seemed to be tilting to our side, or could Mr. Hajjaj have understood and approved our intentions? Later, after my departure, it became clear to me exactly when and why the Moroccan government resigned itself to a mass exodus of its Jewish citizens in what became known as "Operation Yakhin."

At this point we had another stroke of good fortune: ever since Tajjed-dine had given his staff definite instructions to return our documents as quickly as possible to the préfecture, I had noticed a young Moroccan clerk in the first district (Sidi Bousmara), who used to greet me warmly. One day, finding myself alone with Muhammed Abdallah Lahraoui, I told him that Mr. Hajjaj would be happy if I could find someone capable of filling in the Arabic passport pages. Would he do it if I paid him for the work? Muhammed accepted immediately, happy at the thought of having his name brought to the attention of Mr. Hajjaj. On finishing his work at noon at Sidi Bousmara, he would come straight to my office, would lunch with me on sandwiches and soft drinks, working conscientiously and efficiently until 3:00 p.m. On some occasions he would even come in the evening at

7:00 p.m. and, staying until midnight, would complete in Arabic all the pages I had already completed in French. Thus he helped me to write out the passport pages for 310 children from July 13 to 21.

But that was not all; Muhammed was so eager to please me that, occasionally, when I would grumble that the second district office was taking too much time on their "enquiries," he would simply act as if the families actually lived in the first district, number the "green demand" accordingly at his passport office the next morning, and bring it back to me at noon to enable us to complete the passport page. There were at least twenty children whose documents were insufficient for the purpose of obtaining passport facilities; Muhammed simply winked, numbered them like the rest, thus giving himself more work. At three dollars an hour (the tariff I was advised to give him by "Jacques," who became my contact after Georges left for Paris on July 14), he was probably one of the best-paid clerks in Casablanca, and in one week probably received from me what he normally earned in two months (three dollars per hour, the equivalent of ninety dollars today).

Mr. Hajjaj's staff were so overworked by then that Mr. Okbi accepted the fact that OSSEAN's office was also writing out the Arabic portion of the passport sheets. I had also become the recognized courier for bringing the passport demands back from the two district offices to the préfecture. Nobody seemed to have noticed or minded that I had taken over virtually all the stages in obtaining the passports, especially those that concerned the first district. During the afternoon, parents would arrive, leave their documents, the ten percent deposit and sign the forms. In the night, with the help of Gisèle and even Muhammad (if we worked in the office), or Mme Tordjman (if we went to her house), the forms were completed for the fifty children—fifteen hours of work for one person (five for three persons). Early the next morning, I would carry them to the respective districts. If it was the 1st district—and by that stage seventy-five percent were from there—Muhammed would hand them back to me officially within ten minutes; I would then return to my office and prepare the passport sheets in French; at midday Muhammed would arrive and complete the Arabic part of the passport. I would then stagger round to the préfecture with a bulging briefcase and deposit everything with Mr. Okbi. All this could take place within twenty-four hours. It only remained for Mr. Okbi to staple the sheets together, add the official top page and check that they had been correctly filled in (this verification was never done) and put everything in front of Mr. Hajjaj for his magic signature. One major problem arose however: the Jewish schools had closed and no directors could be found to sign the school identity cards. The Misgeret network improvised: they collected scores of blank school identity cards, stamped them with official school stamps and just filled in any child's name who lacked such a card. When "Celine" (code-name for one of the members of the Misgeret) came to see me on the last days, and gave me the documents for 130 children, many of these were lacking the appropriate cards. With the blank ones already stamped which she gave me and the photographs of each child, I was able to "prepare" at least sixty school identity cards myself—all this in the back room of our office, while Muhammed was working away on the passports in the front room. "Celine", of course, came through to see me—as did the parents—by way of the corridor, so that Muhammed rarely saw who was coming or going. From July 10 to 24, 403 more children left Morocco under our auspices as a result of this special improvised "system."

Convenient Contracts with a Private Airline

L'Union de Transport Aérien, or UTA (also known as TAI), was not doing well on their Paris-Casablanca flights and after some negotiations we were able to agree on mutually convenient arrangements. This was solely due to the co-operation of Michel Friedmann, the head salesman, who took over the running of the Casablanca office after the director, Frederick Hawkins, had left for his holiday in late June. The Air Administration at Rabat, co-operating with Royal Air Morocco, refused UTA permission to fly direct to Geneva and we had to be satisfied with Lyon airport. Their flight from Casablanca to Paris was simply "de-commercialised" and chartered by us, the cost per person coming to a modest 200 dirhams. It became possible to clear a plane of all its passengers only a few days before the actual departure, as no more than from ten to twenty persons were usually booked on it. Mr. Friedmann trusted me and sometimes the deposit and the final payments were made by me on the very day of the departure, when the passports were already in my hands. At the end, he must have guessed what was happening. I thought that he might be of Jewish origin, but he did not refer to it. His wife was certainly not Jewish. He was friendly and co-operative, and readily agreed to de-commercialise two of UTA's flights (July 10 and 24) from Casablanca to Lyon.[66] Later, when our requirements increased beyond all expectations, he provided a third plane (July 19) on short notice. Without such facilities, it would have been impossible to overcome the serious transport problems, as our ever-increasing requirements coincided with the height of the summer vacation period.

In the end, nearly half the children travelled by air on three convoys (256 out of 530) from Casablanca to Lyon, at a cost of less than forty dollars each (the equivalent of 1200 dollars today). OSSEAN was not even charged for the nine supplementary passengers on the July 10 flight, nor for the five complimentary tickets provided to the accompaniers who arrived on UTA flights from Paris. Alternate dates were even discussed for the return flights, including the possibility that those who had left on June 26 would return by air "in early August." In such an eventuality, the obligation for UTA to use Lyon's Brion airport rather than Geneva would be a definite advantage, as the extended Swiss visas expired on August 5. The "special" all-Muslim group that I had proposed might then allow the first convoy to benefit from "a French camping excursion in the Ardèche region", thereby extending the period of the action for a week or two. I explained this to Aïda Schirmann before she left on July 10.[67] On the 12th, she wrote to me (signed "Lehmann"): "As for the special group, please inform us as quickly as possible about their departure date. As Miss Schirmann told you, we intend to rent another chalet, but we need to have a precise date."[68] But time was running out. On the 14th and 15th I received two cables from "Lehmann" asking me, as she had in her letter of the 12th, to exclude transport by boat and instead send the children by charter planes so as to reduce problems in controlling possible "undesirable elements" like those who had burned mattresses on the *S.S Ionia*; she also asked if there was a way to send the children directly to Geneva so that they would not have to undergo another tiring journey by bus from Lyons to Morgins.[69] Such a request indicates the total lack of understanding of the real dangers of the mission.

Devoted Monitors and Determined Adventurers

For the first convoy by ship on June 26, Prof. Bloch had been able to enlist—aside from Miss Schirmann—the help of a friend, the young Dr. Claude Dreyfus, and of Michel Steuermann, who directed, with his Israeli wife, the Home de la Forêt in Morgins. For the second convoy on July 10, Aïda Schirmann was once again available.

Although Prof. Bloch was well-known to the Jewish community leaders in Geneva, yet no volunteers could be found from the whole community (then about 3,000) to accompany any of the last three convoys. "Work," "holidays," a host of reasons were given to explain the lack of interest for a few days' collaboration—with no real risk involved, but no great fun either. Solidarity needed at a crucial moment was lacking.

Prof. Bloch's absence from Geneva for a brief period in mid-July did not help matters. When I unexpectedly announced the arrival of a third convoy on July 19, no-one was available to make a twenty-four hour journey and even the convoy of July 22 was still lacking adults to accompany the children. At the very last moment, four persons were hastily sent on the same UTA flight from Paris on July 19 which had been de-commercialised for the return journey to Lyon. They came to accompany the children for the third and fourth convoys.

I recognized the devoted Aïda Schirmann immediately as she disembarked but not the others. I had insisted that at least two men would be necessary on the ship, but there was only one. Bruno Kern, a non-Jewish friend of Dr. Claude Dreyfus, had accepted to take a week off from his job to help a Swiss organization in what he thought was a routine holiday-camp for Moroccan children. I was then introduced to Runia Laski, who happened to be passing through Geneva, described as active with Jewish organizations in Mexico. The fourth was Andrée Guggenheim, a young Swiss Jewish woman.

Parents with the children from the third convoy, and Gisèle Littman in white, overseeing the departure, Main Square by the post office, Casablanca, July 19, 1961

Parents with the children from the third convoy ready to board buses leaving for the airport, Main Square, Casablanca, July 19, 1961

After the preliminary welcome, a lively discussion ensued while the plane was being prepared, and my wife was occupied with the eighty children, all anxious to embark. Who was to accompany the children on this flight? Mr. Kern was needed for the convoy by ship, leaving in three days; Schirmann was indispensable for administrative tasks and for the fourth group: Mrs. Laski spoke no French, only English and Spanish; Miss Guggenheim was the obvious choice but she flatly refused to return. In the presence of police and customs officials and UTA representative, the heated discussion dragged on endlessly. It was soon clear that "wild horses" could not have dragged her back onto the plane! There was only one way to end it: Schirmann offered to leave immediately as there was no alternative.

Afterwards, the absurdity of the whole situation unravelled, hour by hour. Another man was clearly needed for the fourth ship convoy. Miss Guggenheim had taken care of this in Geneva; on July 21 a Dr. Burgos (not Jewish) arrived in Casablanca at OSE's full expense (UTA had no flight from Paris on that day). Fortunately, Miss Schirmann joined him—this was her fourth

Bus ready to leave for the airport,
Main Square, Casablanca, July 19, 1961

trip. Naturally enough, the doctor wanted to do some sightseeing, and his energetic girlfriend, who had been of no help to us in the office, joined him. She later came with him to the office and began to describe their visit to the mellah in the presence of my assistant, Muhammed. She managed to provoke preposterous quarrels, so that Gisèle and I had the feeling we were sitting on a powder keg. I was later informed that she had been helpful on the ship, once she had arranged a first-class cabin for herself and her friend—paid by OSE. Dr. Burgos, on the other hand, was not asked to help and did not offer to do so. Mrs. Laski proved to be willing and conscientious, but her qualifications in handling children with whom she could not communicate were limited. She also had an Israeli visa attached to her passport, on a separate piece of paper that had been crudely torn out, and this was to cause problems at Tangier before the departure, as was the fact that Miss Guggenheim had an Israeli visa stamped into her passport.

The role of Mr. Bruno Kern was in quite another category. He was superb, never resting, endlessly active in the office and at Mrs. Tordjman's home and—as I was informed—on the three day journey from Tangier to Marseilles. He had only one hand, but as I wrote: "without his assistance then, and on the ship, it would have been difficult to imagine the last convoy of 147 children, either leaving or arriving intact." On the night of July 21, he alone remained with Gisèle and me in the office and at Mrs. Tordjman's house, completing the hundreds of forms until two in the early morning. The departure, six hours later for the long bus journey to Tangier, found him as active as ever. Everyone acknowledged that without his presence the children would have caused havoc on the ship. It was only later that he understood the purpose of the holiday-camps. The biggest irony was that his name was omitted from the list sent to Jerusalem of those having contributed to the action.[70] Mr. Kern was thus forgotten for several months, albeit thanked warmly by Prof. Bloch. Miss Guggenheim, however, received warm official thanks from Mr. Kol, director of Youth Aliyah, as did Mrs. Laski, who felt suitably inspired by this attention to declare publicly in Mexico soon afterwards that she, representing "OSE-Mexico," had been one of those chiefly responsible for the aliyah of Jewish children from Morocco to Israel. Hers was neither the first nor was it to be the last such absurd claim, but the real injustice was that a man like Mr.

Kern should have been treated in such a cavalier manner. I later learned that his decision was a moral one, as he had—in the Swiss army, where he lost his hand from a grenade—recognised the crimes of the Nazis and the strict policy of the Swiss authorities to Jewish refugees during the War.

Gifts in Moderation

I had been extremely reluctant to use bribery, namely in the system of "backsheesh" in order to further our aims. Georges on the contrary, often emphasised its efficiency but I had always hesitated on the grounds that it was unnecessary and highly risky for me. Moreover, the integrity of the policeman who returned my wallet intact, refusing any remuneration other than that for the police fund, had impressed me. Yet, I was not loathe to handing out much-appreciated Swiss bars of chocolate on appropriate occasions, eventually distributing more than fifty in this way.

My reluctance to go further disappeared in July. Although Mr. Abdel-laoui, the khalifa of the second district, had received official instructions not to hold up passport requests, his chief assistant dealing with these formalities was determined to receive some form of gratuity, or "encouragement." Mr. Harajchi, a hunchback, was outwardly friendly to me, but fully aware of his key position. It was he who decided whether or not the mokhadam's "enquiry" was necessary before the passport request was signed by the khalifa. On offering timidly a twentieth bar of chocolate, I realised from his expression that gifts were likely to produce rapid effects.

After the first batch of children had been processed by his office—perhaps as a consequence of Mr. D'khissy's direct intervention—there was an unmistakable slow-down, perhaps due to the accrued demand for passports following the governor's announcement. This coincided with the considerable acceleration of our activities and the rapid processing of passports requests by Tajjedine's office. When Schirmann had left on the July 10 convoy, I asked that those arriving from Geneva bring an attractive Swiss watch, nicely packed. I suggested that they should glitter without being gold. Just before returning to Geneva on July 19, following the airport scene, there was hardly time for her to pass me the three watches. Each watch had cost only sixteen dollars (the equivalent of five hundred dollars today), but was worth three times more in Morocco. The watches had arrived at the last moment, just in time.

Early the next morning, July 20, I called on Mr. Harajchi at his office. As with Muhammad, I had once visited him at his home, a gesture which he had much appreciated. But something else was clearly required and now was the moment. I took out from my briefcase our gift, beautifully wrapped with coloured ribbons as only the Swiss know how to tie and presented it to him as if it was a medal, adding with solemn words, more or less: "On the occasion of the 50th anniversary of the founding of our organization, our president, Professor Aberson, asked me to convey to you this small souvenir. It is intended as a small token of appreciation for all your devoted work for us." I also mentioned that his nomination as one of the three supervisors, invited to accompany the groups leaving in August under the auspices of the Moroccan government had been confirmed. Harajchi carefully untied the ribbons, opened the attractive box and viewed the elegant watch with pleasure. He slipped it quickly into his desk, then turning to me with a confident smile thanked me warmly, adding: "Come back this evening or tomorrow morning for the remaining documents." I insisted that, because of the transport question, I needed them that night and offered to come to his home to collect them. He nodded his assent. When I called later in the evening, he handed me fifty-five out of the remaining sixty validated forms, all signed by Abdellaoui and told me that the remaining five would be ready the next morning at his office.

A Dangerous Moment at our OSSEAN Office

After receiving the forms from Harajchi, I met "Jacques" (my new contact since Georges' departure on July 14 for a three weeks' absence) and a Brit ("Johnny"). Jacques,[71] with whom I collaborated smoothly, confirmed that my mission was definitely ending soon and we discussed the plans for the last convoys and our family's departure.

I left them early, returned home and picked up Gisèle to help at the office that evening—with Diana in her cot. Muhammad joined us. I had not told Mr. Kern or the others that we would be working that night. It certainly would not have boosted their morale had they seen how our "passport office" functioned, and we could not afford indiscretions.

Towards midnight, I was still churning out brand new school identity cards in the back room. This necessitated gluing each child's photograph as close as possible to the director's stamp on the school card, or using, where appropriate, a newly-received official school rubber stamp in order to give the cards a more authentic finish. Gisèle was working in the front room with Muhammad. I occasionally came to ask a question, so that Muhammad would have no reason to come back to my room. As Gisèle was filling out the official passport pages in French, he completed them in Arabic. The comic touch was not lacking for a name: "Last name": BENCHABAT, "First name": CHALOM.

Suddenly, a bald head popped through my open window, almost like a jack-in-the-box, and called out "David!" and then disappeared. I felt as if I had been pole-axed, immediately recognising Johnny and realising in a flash the grave faux-pas he had made. Yet, at that stage in the game, nothing would have surprised me. I strolled down the corridor casually, calling to Gisèle: "It's all right, I'll see who's there." When I came face to face with Johnny, as we both hugged the wall of the office, he understood from my eyes that something very serious had occurred. "Guess who's in there?" I asked him, hardly controlling my anger. By this time, Muhammad was showing curiosity and I could hear Gisèle engaging him in conversation as he leaned out of the window, supposedly for a breath of air. I got Johnny to turn his back and walk to his car—fortunately it was on the same side of the street. By the time we were all sitting inside, out of Muhammad's sight and earshot, I had difficulty controlling my feelings. I reminded Jacques and Johnny that Muhammad had never heard me addressed as "David", but only as "Gerald", and that I feared the worst—unless I could invent a satisfactory explanation before returning to the office. I asked why they had come. Their voices betrayed their anxiety and apologies poured from their lips. Finally, one of them asked if I had found their car keys in my Dauphine.

The irony of it all struck me! For my wife, I was a proverbial loser of keys, glasses and umbrellas—I had even "lost" my wallet in Casablanca! Now, our fate seemed linked to "lost keys." I told them to wait in their car, went over to mine, searched it twice, found nothing and returned furious. We sat a few more moments together envisaging the consequences and then fixed a meeting for the next day. I advised them to dispose of their car, as Muhammad might have taken note of the number plate, and walked back to the office having regained my composure. A plausible story went through my mind. On entering the front room, I spoke to Gisèle more or less in these words: "Do you remember my old school friend Christopher, whom we ran into the other day at the hotel and took for a drive? He left something in my car. Strange, he insists on using my first name which I've hardly heard for over ten years. It reminds me of King Edward VIII, who always preferred his first name, David, rather than Edward, just as I've always preferred my second name Gerald." Then, turning to Muhammad, I asked him how the work was going and then went into the back room to continue my production of school identity cards, hoping that Muhammad had been convinced by my story, as he seemed to be.

The Joy of a Jewish Hunchback

The next morning, July 21, I collected the remaining five forms from Harajchi and prepared the last school identity cards and passports with Muhammad's vital help.

A very special incident occurred that morning. Two days earlier, an adolescent had brought to me all his documents unaided, which meant that he had not been screened by the Misgeret. He was a little surprised that I had accepted them, as he had brought no deposit money and seemed to be awaiting my refusal with despair and resignation—for he was a hunchback. The expression in his eyes spoke volumes, even if he had not dared to mention Israel by name. As I could now prepare virtually any passport for any child I wished, I decided then and there that I would facilitate his chances, and I gave him hope by mentioning that perhaps I could find a charitable organization willing to cover his Swiss holiday. I asked him to come back on the Friday and to be ready to leave the next day, July 22. There he was, standing in the doorway with a friend. Weighing my words, I informed him that he had been accepted for the holiday-camp, that the cost would be covered by a "social security" fund, and that he should come tomorrow at 6:00am to the main square ready for the departure by bus to Tangiers. "Moi," he asked with pride, "J'ai été accepté?" (Me? I have been accepted?) He stood for a moment dumbfounded, his face radiantly expressing joy and his dreams of redemption in Israel, while his friend gasped. I have never forgotten that very moving scene and the expression of pure joy on his face.

My appointment had been fixed at the prefecture for 5:00 pm. Neither Mr. Hajjaj nor Mr. Okbi, had any inkling of the number of candidates being processed by us during the last few days. The third convoy (July 19) had not been too much of a surprise, ten days after the second one, as I had already referred to a "waiting list"; but a fourth convoy only three days later, closely followed by a fifth was quite another matter. I hadn't dared mention numbers, and until the very last moment didn't even know whether the chartered UAT plane on the 24th would be half empty or not (The Paquet company's reservations for the 22nd had been settled through SIRTAM and I settled UAT's bill the same day).

All offices closed at 7:00 pm; once again I found myself waiting confidently for Mr. Hajjaj's magic signature. Mr. Okbi had earlier received his glittering present and was now even more co-operative, with hopes of a Swiss trip. He checked through the pages of the eight collective passports.

Mr. Hajjaj was flabbergasted when he perceived that a further 230 children were ready to leave so soon after the last convoy. He called me to his office and expressed his surprise. I reassured him, as plausibly as I could, that as there was no more transport facilities for another week, OSSEAN had therefore been encouraged by me to rent two more chalets and modify prior plans. The next convoy would probably not be leaving for two weeks— this would be the Moroccan Labour Union group, whose plans were almost finalized. I regretted my evident anxiety, but the Swiss consulate was closing shortly and if I did not receive the passports and the Swiss visas in time, no one could leave, the money for the tickets would be wasted and the loss to OSSEAN would be great. Finally, at 6:45pm, Hajjaj signed the top pages on each passport and handed them to me. I thanked him profusely and dashed to the Swiss consulate where I arrived just as it was closing.

Seated opposite the consular agent on duty and with his encouragement I stamped in the visas while he added the validity dates—on 115 pages! Half an hour later everything was done—a dream comes true! Supreme irony: for these 230 passport and visa formalities, I had been directly involved in the whole procedure from A to Z—even completing the Swiss formalities. This gesture was characteristic of the helpful Swiss attitude throughout. Their instructions were to facilitate the issuing of visas to OSSEAN. They had realized that the passports forms were likely to be signed at the very last moment and adopted an extremely flexible policy, without which our plan would have failed.

Fortunately, I was able to make a last small gesture in a discreet manner. The capacity of our chartered plane was eighty-six passengers and UAT was strict. We had only eighty-three children. At my suggestion, UAT accepted to include two Swiss who happened to be on their way home. They were charged only half the usual single fare. The last seat was left for an unnamed person, who was expected to arrive from Geneva so I explained. In fact it was left vacant for my precipitate departure.

A Vital and Indispensable Assistant

Gradually, Muhammad Abdullah Lahraoui became more and more indispensable. There was always the possibility that he had been asked by his superiors to keep his ears and eyes open, but this seemed more and more unlikely as I got to know him better. At first, he had been perplexed on discovering that all of OSSEAN's candidates for the holiday period were Jewish, but I stressed Mr. D'khissy's valid explanation, and he had seen for himself the brusqueness with which Gisèle and I treated those who came to the office, either without the necessary documents or deposit, or who made allusions to Israel. As I was persona grata with Messrs. D'khissy, Hajjaj and Tajjedine, that was quite sufficient for Muhammad. "How I long to be finished with all these Jews", I once declared, while referring enthusiastically on the planned August convoys under government auspices, when he would be one of the monitors in Morgins. At his home, he had even confided to me that OSSEAN's initiative was highly considered. He told me of a woman who had tried to sponsor holidays for twenty Moroccan children in Spain, but had been unmasked as representing a "Zionist" organization and permission was refused. I had noticed this lady once in Tajjedine's reception room and another time in Mr. Hajjaj's, and had kept my distance from her. She looked nervous and lacked confidence.

Miss Schirmann informed me that Muhammad was imitating my every gesture; it is probable that he was delighted at having an English boss who paid him well—and willingly neglected some obvious irregularities. From the moment I accepted his invitation to lunch at his home, while both his mother and sister served us in the customary manner, his appreciation knew no bounds. Following the incident over the keys and for practical reasons I decided to ask him to act as my personal assistant on July 22 when the fourth convoy would leave from Casablanca for Tangiers-Marseilles. He accepted with evident satisfaction, both for the evident financial advantages and for the obvious prestige involved.

The Courageous and Reliable Hélène Tordjman

In the last frantic fortnight, Gisèle and I had gone to Mrs. Tordjman's home on several occasions, always taking a circuitous route. After a pleasant dinner, we would all work together, sometimes with her secretary, on the mass of paperwork that we could not handle in the office without a secretary. She and Mr. Tordjman could not have been more hospitable and accepted without hesitation whatever risks this might entail. I learned much later that she had been active in Zionist activities since 1948, when Jewish emigration was authorised under the French Protectorate. A year later, in 1962, she became involved again, suffered arrest and imprisonment for ten days in 1965, and was only released when she refused all nourishment other than water.

We took Aïda Schirmann and Bruno Kern to Mrs. Tordjman's home on that Friday night. There was still a lot of work to do preparing the last two passenger lists. Mrs Tordjman realized that, as well as the difficult task of persuading the parents that their children must travel on a Saturday—no easy task for religious Jews, as the youngsters themselves would refuse to eat anything on the long five-hour bus journey to Tangiers unless they were assured by her that the food was kosher. In the morning, her servant cooked fifty chickens, and that evening—while Diana lay asleep in her straw basket nearby—she and Gisèle prepared a mountain of sandwiches for 150 persons, while the rest of us drew up the definitive transport lists from the stacks of collective passports just received. Indeed, there had been no alternative to the Saturday *Paquet* ship, as no other transport was available and by the time the July 19 and 24 UAT flights were offered our requirements had doubled. The July 22 crossing from Tangiers to Marseilles was the only ship on which places were available in the last two weeks of July. Thus, 147 children—raised from birth not to travel on the Sabbath—would be allowed, exceptionally, by their parents to travel by bus and then by ship on that day of rest, thereby breaking the sacred commandment which could traditionally only be avoided in order to "save a life."

A Traffic Incident, a Police Agent and More Luck

That same week, I had again experienced an anxious moment. Speeding from one khalifa's office to another in the early morning, a policeman flagged me down for a traffic offence and requested to see my driving license which I had left either at home or in the office. I had no intention of driving back to Anfa—on the outskirts of the town—as many parents were certain to be patiently awaiting me at the office in order to recover their precious "livrets de famille." I therefore told him that I had left my license in my office and promised to bring it personally to him or to the nearest police station that same day. To my dismay, he preferred to leave his traffic duties and come to my office then and there. As I drove off at a snail's pace, my thoughts were racing on—and my imagination too. What to do? My unexpected passenger showed too much interest in my work. Then to my great relief, it become clear why: his brother was looking for a job and maybe I could help him? I moved into third gear, becoming more outgoing. By the time we reached the junction before rue Dumont d'Urville I had given him a "next week" appointment for his brother, following which he showed little interest in checking my license. I parked on the corner so that he wouldn't realize that the long line of people—obviously Jews—began at my office. We stood talking for a moment by my car, before he stopped another vehicle to return to his daily task—another providential event, I felt.

Yet, this incident had unforeseen consequences. Unknown to me, a woman living above our office had observed the scene. She was Jewish, married to a Muslim, and had become curious as to what was attracting so many poor Jews to our office over the past two months. A day or so later, I arrived to find the inevitable line of parents, many wearing their jellabas and babouches, as well as two of our newly-arrived monitors who informed me that the woman had noticed a policeman questioning me the previous day and wouldn't be surprised if I had been apprehended as a Zionist agent and the office closed. Her remark caused consternation, but I wasn't too perturbed on being informed of it, probably because the intense activity of the last few days had left me no time or inclination to worry about such gossip. Yet this warning light, coming as it did at that time, was a clear confirmation that our activities would have to end soon despite the acceleration in the processing of collective passports.

However, this incident—coupled with a ludicrous situation that was developing in Israel—did finally convince those directly responsible for our safety (the Mossad), that Operation Mural should end with the fifth convoy on July 24 and that "their man in Casablanca" and his wife and daughter had to leave Morocco.

The unexpected arrival of eighty-five Moroccan children, on July 9, in Israel had sparked a typical Israeli "show" of burlesque proportions. The secret leaked out quickly after a group of ultra-orthodox Jews from Mea Shearim arrived at the Youth Aliyah center at Kiriat Yearim in order to "save" these Moroccan Sephardi children from spiritual contamination at the hand of a non-religious institution. Inevitable disputes ensued and were reported in the press and even on the radio. Georges was appalled on learning the news while listening to Kol Israel Lagola in Casablanca, a few days before leaving for Paris on July 14. He informed his boss, Alex, about it and it was decided that I had to leave as soon as possible. This Israeli imbroglio could have been anticipated by those responsible for it.

The Crucial Saturday July 22

The vast Place des Nations Unies of Casablanca slowly filled with parents and children early on Saturday morning. Aïda Schirmann, Bruno Kern and the others had joined Muhammad and me in organizing the youngsters into groups and checking them against the lists. It was soon realised that twenty children were missing. Perhaps their parents had not received the express letter of confirmation, or perhaps they had simply refused the suggestion that their children would travel on a Saturday? Whatever the reason, I knew that if they did not leave that day, they could not leave at all under our auspices—and perhaps never! A last effort had to be made to find them, but how? Some youngsters, members of the Misgeret—in Muhammad's eyes they might have been relatives of the youngsters—offered assistance. I arranged for a dozen of them to go by bicycle, car, or taxi to locate the families at their homes and joined one group. Muhammad and the other remained to check all the assembled children and to put them on the buses that were due to arrive at 7:30 am for the trip to Tangiers.

My guide took me rapidly to the mellah where I beheld an unforgettable and hallucinating scene. At the entrance to the humblest of dwellings, I perceived three generations of one family: the grandparents, parents and their children, including a new-born baby being fed by its mother. I counted eleven persons. Conscious of the absurdity of my words, I nonetheless explained in my poor French, tongue in cheek, that if their two children who were booked for the holidays were not allowed to leave, the money deposited for their holidays would be forfeited. My companion let me finish and then spoke in Arabic, making it clear that it was of vital importance that the two left very quickly. His arguments seemed more convincing than mine. Soon the children were dressed and ready to leave, each with his suitcase, while the whole family looked on bewildered. We returned to the main square an hour later with four children, and learned that seventeen out of the twenty missing children had joined the convoy.

Everything was ready for the departure. I called out the names of the three missing children as a last control—and one name was Fhima, Isaac. Suddenly, one of the adolescents who had come to see off a friend stepped forward spontaneously and said to me: "I'm Fhima, David, not Isaac." He was dressed simply. I glanced quickly at Muhammad five metres away and saw that he was occupied and had not heard anything. Without a moment's hesitation, I put my hand on the boy's back, pushed him into the bus: "Fhima, Isaac, present!" And so he left for Israel, with a smile on his face, a T-Shirt on his back, but without even a toothbrush or the opportunity to say goodbye to his family. They would all soon rejoice.

It was after 8:00am, we were behind schedule, and more and more cars were passing through the other end of the square, which was still fairly empty. Then pandemonium broke out. Someone was shouting in Arabic and French. I caught sight of a wild-looking young man in his middle twenties. He was highly excited and kept trying to climb on a bus while members of the Misgeret succeeded in throwing him off. I heard the word "Israel" and his angry shouts implying that he also was ready to go there. People were trying to stop him as he stood there, furious, bleeding from the scratches sustained in the struggles. Muhammad was concerned, spoke to him, and took down his name and address. For an instant I stared in disbelief, riveted to the spot, then waved to the drivers of the first four buses to leave. The poor fellow, in a last desperate effort, broke free from those holding him and managed to get half way through the back door of the fifth bus before I grabbed him and pulled with all my strength. He lost his hold and fell back on the ground as the doors snapped closed. I ran to the front of the bus, quickly jumped in next to Muhammad, who was faithfully holding my briefcase, and the bus screeched out of the square in pursuit of the other three. This time, I really lost my temper and did not hide my feelings. Such a "happening" was like a nightmare! I cursed, stating that I would never take another Jew! Muhammad promised that the madman ("le fou") would be convoked to the first district office on Monday to explain his unruly conduct. The next day I learned from Jacques that the man ran to the nearest police station and half an hour later returned in a police car. There was hardly anyone in the square by then for the parents had quickly dispersed. As his bizarre story of "Zionists" in the Place des Nations could not be substantiated, he was kept in prison for the weekend to cool his heels.

In our precipitate departure, Mrs. Tordjman had forgotten to hand me the boat tickets. It was necessary to stop somewhere to call her and this reminded me of something else. Three months earlier, I had ordered a few pieces of hand-wrought iron objects from an artisan on the outskirts of Rabat. A week earlier I had called him to have them packed. I remembered this only at that moment and ordered our bus—now leading the other four—to head for the man's modest workshop. An hour later, the convoy arrived and the buses parked at a distance. The children were able to stretch their legs and eat a kosher sandwich, while I called Mrs. Tordjman, paid for our merchandise and had the bulky packed ironwork mixed with the children's baggage. It was difficult to have been more nonchalant and the expressions of astonishment on the faces of the monitors testified to my eccentricity. For Muhammad, on the other hand, it was no more than what he would have expected from me, an eccentric Englishman. Certainly, a "Zionist" would never have acted in such an irresponsible manner!

Unforeseen Difficulties at the Port of Tangiers

The five buses drew up at the port of Tangiers at just after two in the afternoon, only half an hour before the ship's scheduled departure. Most of the children were exhausted from a long journey in the stifling heat. The supervisors had been made aware of the presence of unruly adolescents, inevitable in an outsize holiday-camp group of 147, who were later to cause them so much trouble on the three-day journey from Tangiers to Marseilles. My somewhat tough, no-nonsense, approach to this problem during the stopover was not approved, but order was restored. The ship's representative was awaiting us and informed me that he knew of our late arrival from Mrs. Tordjman and that the tickets were ready. Fortunately for us, the ship's departure had been delayed for an hour as it had docked late.

The police and customs formalities began, but my thoughts were elsewhere. Gisèle and Diana were then being driven to Casablanca airport by Mrs. Tordjman who had promised that she would see them safely on board an Air France Caravelle flight to Paris. As I was to learn later there was no hitch and Georges was at Paris-Orly airport to meet Gisèle as she awaited her London-bound connection, holding Diana in her arms. He reassured her that I would be out of Morocco by Monday, as planned.

Muhammad's presence was essential. He facilitated all the formalities. Fortunately, the new tickets were not examined carefully, for I noticed a grave mistake that had been made: they were single, not return, tickets! I handled over the four collective passports one at a time, waiting patiently for the official to compare each corresponding school identity card. After seventy-five pages, he was bored and less interested in the Swiss individual passports of our supervisors. He didn't even bother to open the fourth one, that of Miss Guggenheim, with its incriminating Israeli visa.

Mrs. Laski handed over her own Mexican passport from which her Israel visa—on a separate piece of paper—had been clumsily torn out. It was retained for a twenty minute meticulous examination. I explained that Mrs. Laski was unconnected with our organization, was merely a volunteer monitor and that the missing pages were, according to her, simply a customs receipt relating to purchases from one of the countries she had visited. It didn't help, her passport was declared "invalid," and this incongruous situation reflected on our bona fide position. I insisted strongly that Mrs. Laski's passport problems had nothing whatsoever to do with the Swiss holidays of 147 Moroccan children whose papers were perfectly in order, and pleaded that they be allowed to go on board before the ship lifted anchor. Muhammad backed me and pleaded in Arabic and eventually the children were allowed to embark with their monitors. Mrs. Laski's passport was finally stamped, returned and she too was allowed to leave. Probably, the technical difficulties of either contacting the Mexican embassy or consulate in Morocco over the weekend, or of holding Mrs. Laski in custody till Monday, were both considered disproportionate. We had all faced a disastrous situation through incredible incompetence—and been saved by pure providence! I bade farewell with some relief to our friendly

Mexican helper who, some months later, metamorphosed herself into the official "representative of the Mexican OSE", who had actively participated in the "rescue action in Morocco."

We were now ready to wave goodbye, but half an hour passed and the ship remained stuck to the quay. To my consternation, its departure was then announced for 8:00pm. There was little point in worrying for five hours; it was infinitely more relaxing to visit Tangiers, for I had decided that we would leave only when the ship did. We took a taxi and then walked about like tourists. However, my heart was not in it and to this day I have no recollection whatsoever of what we saw. By 8:00 pm we were installed in a nice restaurant on a balcony overlooking the harbour. The fish was tasty enough, the wine good, but the ship was still stuck in the port, idly reclining, as on a painted ocean.

Suddenly, at about 9:30 pm, the silence of the warm summer's night was shattered by the deliciously triumphant blast of the ship's siren. I have retained a fondness for such sounds, ever since as a boy of nearly seven I was taken by my mother, with five of my brothers and sisters on the *Conte di Savoia* from Genoa to New York, barely a few weeks before France's collapse in June 1940. This time, the resonance echoing over the water sounded more like the haunting strains of the shofar in the synagogue after Yom Kippur.

I watched the ship glide from its berth and, looking at Muhammed, raised my glass in a toast: "To our August convoys and to your first trip to Switzerland!" Another long blast drowned out my words as we clinked glasses, each of us lost in his own dreams.

We were soon in a taxi to Casablanca, arriving on Sunday morning at about 3:00 am. I bade Muhammad "au revoir," asked him to call me on Monday afternoon, and took a taxi to the Anfa hotel. Sadly, I found the flat empty, but Gisèle's cable was there announcing her safe arrival with Diana at her parents' home. My head hit the pillow like a log for a sound sleep of two hours.

When my alarm clock woke me, I felt a terrible stomach ulcerous pang, for I didn't know how I'd get through all that had to be done in one day. I drove straight to the office through deserted streets. First, there were the remaining school identity cards that needed to be fabricated. Then, there was the weary task of separating disposable material from essential things I preferred to keep and those that had to be destroyed. A plan came to mind as I sorted them out—maybe it wouldn't be so bad if the first policeman's search turned up copies of some of my key correspondence with high Moroccan officials, as well as the letter of introduction from the Minister of Health, in Arabic and French. This might result in some of them being consulted and the matter conveniently hushed up. I left the copies in my open drawer, adding a few receipts for hotels and the office.

There were still a few dozen "livrets de famille" awaiting collection from parents whose children had left on Saturday, or were leaving the next day. I put them into my car and gave them to Jacques that same night. A serious situation arose after my departure. These precious documents had to be returned to their owners. The network decided to mail them rather than deliver them personally, but the young woman whose job it was to take them to the post office got cold feet at the last moment and simply dumped them in a garbage bin without even telling her superiors. This panicky decision could be understood in the prevailing circumstances, as she had feared for her safety if she was questioned at the post office, but it became a disaster for all the families concerned, who were thus deprived of their only identity papers. The parents were thereby placed in an impossible situation, for they could not remain silent, but did not know how to explain the loss of their precious documents—and the responsibility for the loss fell on OSSEAN, which had evaporated overnight.[72]

I froze as the doorbell rang, dizzy from sorting out what to keep, what to destroy, and what to leave. Perhaps it was a parent who had come on the chance of finding me on a Sunday, I thought. When I found Muhammad at the door, I was flabbergasted. True, I had mentioned to him that I might work in the office for a few hours on Sunday, but I had also made it quite clear that I didn't need any help till Monday evening. There he was, dressed elegantly in a new sports outfit, wearing the glittering watch I had given him as gift "from our president." Was he, after all, the perfect agent? I need not have been anxious for a moment, he had simply come to greet me, proud of his new attire, probably lost in his reveries of snow-capped mountains in Switzerland. I too was dreaming of Geneva and praying that I would see it with my eyes tomorrow!

I returned to our Anfa apartment and started packing. I had explained to the receptionist that my wife and daughter's departure for a few weeks "because of the heat" had tempted me to move to a hotel nearer to my office till their return. This was most convenient as one of their clients desired to occupy an apartment for just that period. I left my new hotel address, paid my bill, announced my departure the next morning and made another reservation for the same apartment from August 15.

I was running behind time. An Englishman whom I had met at a cocktail party was seriously interested in purchasing my car. We had fixed an appointment that evening at 6.00 pm. I drove round to his place, he tested it to his satisfaction and we agreed to meet the next morning to exchange the car against his check in sterling, drawn on a London bank. I had managed to unload the Dauphine at the last possible moment, after four months intensive use, at a loss of only one hundred dollars (the equivalent of three thousand dollars today). This vital means of transport had been refused to me in March on orders from Jerusalem or Paris; without it I could not have functioned efficiently.

I sped back to the office with an inexpensive case, purchased for a special purpose. It was soon the right weight, crammed with OSSEAN's publicity material. I locked it, went around to the small hotel, booked in "for about three weeks," as of Monday, gave my office address and told the night clerk that I'd be back the next evening with the rest of my luggage. I took a receipt for the bag and, as an afterthought, left it in the office. I dumped more incriminating material in a suitable public garbage container, and for my last night in Casablanca went to dine at our favourite restaurant in the centre of town, La Reine Pedauque. It would soon be time for my final meeting with Jacques.

Clandestine Meeting with Head of the Mossad

I drove to the prearranged meeting place and Jacques got in beside me. He told me that the boss ("le patron") wished to meet me and suggested he drive my Renault Dauphine while I sat in the back. Such a meeting was highly risky and unusual and we had to be extremely vigilant. Jacques drove for a few minutes then circled a roundabout twice and more slowly a third time. The car stopped abruptly on a corner, a tall imposing man opened the back door on my left and sat down beside me. Jacques sped off along the wide boulevards, out to the coastal road.

I instantly recognized the newcomer's voice from his first words (we had spoken on the phone once), pronounced in an authoritative tone: "I wanted to see you personally before you leave tomorrow to tell you that your mission has succeeded beyond all our expectations. I thank you both. We all thank you." I was very tired, living daily on my nerves and was suffering from my chronic ulcer pains. His kind words warmed my heart and I cherished them then and ever since after we became friends in Israel from 1964.

I related to him all that had happened over the past two days. Alex Gattmon then informed me that the entire staff at the airport had been changed three days earlier, the day after our July 19 convoy. No one knew exactly why this had been done, but it was probably a security decision related to our two UAT charters with only Jewish children. I should be ready for a closer scrutiny of both passports and school identity cards, and perhaps even an attempt to question the younger children as to their holiday destination. I should act naturally, avoid panic or anger, and if I was stopped from leaving on the same plane—according to our prearranged plan—I should make no fuss, show no anxiety, stay to see the plane take off, leave the airport in a taxi and come on foot later at 6:00 pm to a well-known café without being followed. He insisted that it was highly unlikely that I would be barred from boarding the plane, but, if it did happen, his network would get me out of Morocco: "Leave that to us!" He asked me if I had any questions or any specific request. "Yes", I said, choosing my words carefully, almost maliciously, to fit the strange role that had been mine for over four months: "I'd rather not have to swim to Gibraltar—how do you propose to get me out of here, if necessary?" He smiled, tapping me on the shoulder, and answered firmly: "You'll leave from the same airport, within forty-eight hours—count on it!" I was duly impressed by his assurance and—as he confirmed to me much later in Israel—that's what counted more than anything else at such a moment. I didn't give the matter another thought after that. I thanked him heartily and we exchanged a long handshake. His face was enveloped by a warm smile that was characteristic of the man. We were now back in town; Jacques slowed the car and stopped on a corner as Alex left us as swiftly as he had entered. Jacques drove on, going over with me the last details before we parked near his car and I gave him the family documents which, as described, were to finish in a dustbin instead of at the post office. It was close to midnight. I headed for the Anfa hotel, finished packing, cleaned up, and took a nap.

CHAPTER 5

A Disenchanted Return to Europe

Two hours was all the sleep I had that night. The next ten hours required meticulous preparation. My official alibi for leaving was already available. A prearranged cable from Geneva to me explained the difficulty of finding monitors. It ended:

> PLEASE ACCOMPANY PLANE 24 YOURSELF. ORDER PREPARE
> HERE RETURN VOYAGE FIRST GROUP. YOUR PRESENCE BEING
> URGENT THIS PURPOSE. LEHMANN.[73]

I drove early to the Tordjman home and left her my personal belongings, toothbrush included. They would be brought to the downtown assembly point and mixed up with the children's suitcases before all were stacked on the buses. We went over the scenario to be enacted at the airport; by now, she was fully in the picture and would be present at the airport as director of SIRTAM.

I drove my Dauphine to its new owner, collected my cheque, left the apartment key at the hotel and took a taxi to the office. I found the concierge, gave her the office key with the request that she clean the office that afternoon or tomorrow. The next stop was at the Banque Franco-Suisse pour le Maroc where I withdrew almost the totality of the balance of my account. The initial deposits left with the telephone and electricity companies were in both cases sufficient to cover their respective invoices. A 500 dirham deposit had been made in April to the estate agent for the use of the office furniture. F.E.A.U.—Maroc was unlikely to worry too soon, as the rent had been paid till July 31 and the deposit guaranteed almost two months rent. (Actually, they only made enquiries ten days later and received an ambiguous reply dated August 15 that OSSEAN's new delegate would be returning shortly.)[74]

Farewell Casablanca

At the assembly point, the usual joyous faces of the youngsters contrasted with the rather uncertain expressions of their parents—all milling around, feverishly handing up suitcases, including mine. The agency had everything under control. Soon the buses were on the way to the airport, crammed with eighty-three children, much luggage, and me to accompany them.

The TAI plane from Paris was late in arriving and the various airport formalities could not start until it finally landed at about noon. Then there were surprises. Fortunately, no interest was shown in the mountain of luggage, but the police verification of travel documents was totally different from what it had been five days earlier. Then, and on July 10, I alone had presented the passports and given details of the holiday-camp in Switzerland. This time the children were all lined up, one behind the other, and questioned individually. Faces against photographs, first and last names in the collective passports against those on the identity cards! If they had expected to find an error in the Arabic transliteration, they badly underestimated my Arab assistant's efficiency. As for the rest, there was little chance of a snag, for the whole passport and school identity card process from A to Z had occurred under our aegis. Although about a dozen children living in the second district had been processed as if they had lived in the first, this could not easily be controlled. True, had they obtained a list of all the pupils in the various Jewish schools, discrepancies would have been discovered, but this was highly unlikely as the schools were private and had closed a month earlier for the summer holidays. Actually, this angle had obviously not been considered, otherwise each child would have been asked the name of his or her school and that would certainly have led to obvious contradictions between their answers and what was written on the school cards. Also, the children listed were only from two or three schools, from which blank forms had been provided by the Misgeret.

The only questions asked, in a friendly manner, related to the destination of the youngsters. Notwithstanding the fact that the parents had been told not to mention the final goal, even to their elder children, many of the adolescents had understood or overheard family conversations and had been sworn to secrecy. But how could the magic word of "Israel," in such a context, be hidden from their younger brothers and sisters who were a more vulnerable prey to questioners? Here was a real danger and I watched the progress of the queue with trepidation for about an hour. Suddenly, I noticed that it was the turn of a shy-looking, barely eight years old boy. Too much was at stake so I strode to the front and asked naively in my atrocious anglicized French why these same questions had to be put to each child. "Monsieur, vous savez leur destination: nos chalets de vacances sont en Suisse!" ("Sir, you know their destination, our holiday camps are in Switzerland!") "Is it necessary to ask the identical question eighty-three times, while our chartered plane is waiting? The children have a long voyage by air and land, can they not all board the plane while their documents are being examined to your complete satisfaction?" Strangely, my English-accented browbeating did not cause offence, rather the contrary; it was considered perfectly natural in the circumstances. Perhaps the role they had been given as child interrogators was not to their liking; perhaps an Englishman's public appeal to fair-play in a newly independent Morocco had an effect. Whatever the reason, a senior official came up, intervened abruptly and acceded to my request. The children were allowed to embark and all the baggage was loaded onto the aircraft.

The moment had finally come to play my role. Shakespeare's words came to mind: "One man in his time plays many parts." The Casablanca airport was the stage and the last part had to be played well as it was my real-life exit from an exotic adventure!

I had demonstrated outward concern two hours earlier when no super-

above and below: Children from the fifth convoy waiting to board UAT plane
at Casablanca airport, July 24, 1961

visor had descended from the TAI plane from Paris. The regular Royal
Air Maroc service from Paris, due in shortly, was the last possibility for a
passenger from Geneva to reach Casablanca. It landed without our monitor—as planned. I fumbled for the cable, envisaging such an eventuality—
"It looks like I shall have to bring the convoy to Switzerland myself after
all, the children can't possible go unaccompanied . . . but I don't even have
my pyjamas or a toothbrush with me, only my passport . . . see you in two,
maximum three days." I spoke loudly and naturally, in the direction of Helen
Tordjman and Michael Friedmann, and then shook hands with both of them.
She winked encouragingly and he—to my utter astonishment—whispered
two words of encouragement in English: "Good luck!"

All municipal and government offices closed between noon and 3:00 pm,
so any last-minute decision concerning me would have to be made on the
spot. I walked up to the senior official who had called off the interrogations
of the children and handed him my British passport. He opened it, gave it a
glance and handed it back to me. I pushed open the glass doors, stepped onto
the tarmac—and swallowed hard.

The distance between the building and the plane was less than fifty
yards. I walked normally, but seemed to be floating on air in the stifling
heat, counting my steps and occasionally looked up at the azure sky. The
silence was deafening, nothing could have had a greater impact on me
than that short walk, that euphoric moment of doubt . . . and elation. The
plane's motors were turning. My part was nearly over, my role about to
end—a risky mission accomplished! I turned around, raising my hand in a
friendly greeting to those whose thoughts were with me and went on board.
Immediately, the doors closed, the noise of the engines increased and the
plane taxied toward its take-off position. A minute passed, then the engines
rose to a full throttle and the plane gathered speed and soared skywards.

I took a deep breath and then asked the steward if by chance he had
any champagne on board. "Yes Sir . . . it's already on ice for you." Clearly,
Michael Friedmann had guessed or knew all along, I thought. I was chatting
with the steward when he suddenly told me that sometimes the Moroccan
authorities obliged a plane, still in Moroccan airspace, to return even for
the smallest error found on one of the exit forms. He wasn't joking. I asked

him to keep the champagne on ice until we were over the Rock of Gibraltar, by which time it would be more chilled—and me a little less.

The flight was pleasant and the children were allowed to roam up and down the aisle. One young boy was so excited that I placed him next to the pilot where he calmed down. Twenty-five years later, he reminded me of this when we met at the Mimouna Event on May 1, 1986.[75] We landed at Bron airport, outside Lyon, a few hours later. Naphtali Bar-Giora was waiting to greet me, very enthusiastic, quite a different welcome than the meeting in Paris nearly three months earlier. The eighty-three children were put straight onto a special El Al plane for Israel. The blue Star of David shone brighter than ever on its silver frame. The next morning in Marseilles harbour, 147 children from the fourth convoy which had left Tangiers on Saturday disembarked, and were immediately re-embarked on another ship belonging to Israel's national carrier, the Zim lines, leaving for Israel—230 children in all, within twenty-four hours! Unfortunately, I only had one copy of the list of eighty-three children travelling by air and was reluctant to part with it on arrival, but there was no alternative—no faxes in those days. I insisted that I be sent a copy "for my records" but this never happened, as I had feared, so that the preliminary list I had prepared just before finalization and kept is not as exact as my final lists for the first four convoys.[76]

Bar-Giora and I continued on to Paris alone in our empty plane. There was a lot to discuss together. I soon learned when and why the final decision to bring me out had been taken. The "religious scandal" in Israel, resulting from the 9 July arrival of eighty-five children, had come as a bombshell. His assurance that he had managed to prevent two similar scatterbrained schemes, but that the third coup had been carried out without his knowledge or that of his supervisors in Jerusalem, barely calmed me. The risk that this uproar would eventually reach Moroccan ears, as well as last week's "Zionist" remarks made by the Jewish woman living above our office, had convinced him, when informed, that I could not remain any longer, even though daily departures were increasing by leaps and bounds. He had gone to Casablanca himself to verify the situation on the spot, viewing me from afar, so he informed me.

I reminded him that, aside from this act of betrayal, my mission could only have continued if my plan to bring a convoy of Muslim children for a fortnight had been accepted, thus allowing us to offer a similar free week or so to the children of the first convoy who were due back "after a month"— on July 26, latest August 1. This complicated "Muslim" plan had never been approved by him or anyone else; therefore, even without the scandalous act that appeared to have triggered my precipitate withdrawal, I could not have stayed any longer.

On another subject, he affirmed that when we first met in Geneva over six months ago, he knew he had found in me a rough diamond that merely needed polishing to prove its true worth. He added, as an afterthought, that we would certainly be invited officially to visit Israel. I remember replying: "There's no need to use public funds on us, but a letter of thanks would be appreciated by both of us—and perhaps also by our children." "Recognition" only came twenty-three years later—and not via him.

I hadn't been able to call Gisèle from Bron airport and only did so late that evening from Paris. She had been very anxious the whole day and had even called Mrs. Tordjman from whom she heard of my safe departure several hours earlier. Unfortunately, I could not join her immediately, for I was needed in Paris, Geneva and Morgins for debriefing, explanations and advice. We were only to be reunited at the end of that week of July.

Paris—Geneva—Morgins—London—Bournemouth

Georges was still on leave in Paris with his wife Ruth and their children and I was soon together with them. In my report, written in 1962, I penned my feelings for him and his team: "Having worked with him and his colleagues, I feel a bond between us, and when I said 'thank you' to him, to his boss in Casablanca and to those of our colleagues whom I had met, and heard the same words in reply, I realised that only those who share a difficult task thoroughly, and accomplish it, can appreciate one another truly." Then, and much later when my shorter personal narrative was published in Hebrew in 1986,[77] and today in 2011, I would put it differently, but I wouldn't change either my feelings or the message that I wished to express in my official

Report of 1961 which provided the essential facts and source documentation.

Georges was due to return to Casablanca in a few days and I described to him in detail the events of my last ten days in Casablanca since his departure. The next day I recounted for hours all that had happened during my 130 days séjour in Morocco—still so fresh in my memory—to my first Mossad "contact" in Paris, "Alex Korany," who had welcomed me then as a fledgling volunteer.

He and Naftali insisted that I write a documentary report, but it was many months before I found either the time—settling in Switzerland and starting to grapple with business responsibilities—or the inclination to comply with their request, and soon my wrath was such that it required Gisèle's constant prompting to galvanise me sufficiently to complete the task. It was fortunate she succeeded for otherwise no trace of Operation Mural would have remained—if one doesn't tell one's own true "saga," someone else will and that version will hardly resemble the events experienced directly.

In Geneva, two days later, I learned from Prof. Bloch and Miss Schirmann about the serious administrative problems that OSE had faced. I listened attentively, sympathised outwardly, but my mind was elsewhere—the Moroccan scene that I had left behind me seemed worlds away from these bureaucratic problems.

On the drive up to Morgins in the Canton of Valais, Arieh Reiffler was unable to understand the reasons for my remonstrations. For him the July 9 departure of eighty-five children for Israel had been an administrative master-stroke that had been accomplished without any serious repercussions. Why was I complaining? His face glowed with the self-important look of the official aspiring for more authority. Not content with one error, he now proposed—perhaps encouraged by others—another one. The "troublesome elements" were difficult for Youth Aliyah to absorb into "normal" groups; moreover, the two or three cripples, as well as a dumb sister and brother, only aggravated things for his organization. If I had complied with my instructions and organized a psychological screening on the spot, all these "problems" would not have arisen. He finally confided in me his brainstorm idea: some of these "unsuitable elements" could perhaps be sent back to Morocco on their respective collective passports, by ripping out most of the pages, leaving only those concerning the returning children. I could scarcely believe my ears! Now I understood their reiterated instructions only to accept individual passports, and why our on-the-spot decision to act pragmatically and use collective passports had first been refused.

I told him firmly that this would be an inhuman and totally irresponsible action and that I would denounce it wherever possible. I could conceive of no surer way of putting obstacles on the path of the whole mission, whose purpose was not solely to bring children to Israel, but to facilitate once again mass emigration—preferably to Israel—for those Jews who wished to leave Morocco.

A handful of Israelis were awaiting us at OSE's Home de la Forêt where most of the 230 children in the first and third convoys were housed (the others were in Mrs. Truffer's chalet which OSE had rented at Champéry, not far away). I was virtually ignored by these "experts" who spoke to one another in Hebrew. Then, as if suddenly reminded of my presence, the Israeli who seemed to be in charge approached me with Reiffler, thanked me perfunctorily and enquired, with a deadpan expression, whether I thought it would be possible to continue the holiday-camp system and why I had not organised at least one subsidized Muslim group to facilitate further departures of Jewish children. I was later told that my interlocutor was a high official from Jerusalem. I don't think he even bothered to introduce himself and, if he did, I couldn't remember his name when I wrote my report several months later which is perhaps fortunate. I was flabbergasted at the naivety of his remarks. He was totally out of touch and knew nothing about my repeated demands since April for just such a plan and its systematic refusal. I told him bluntly that it was a week too late to consider implementing what I had been recommending from the start. I don't think he appreciated my terse reply. As an independent person, unaccustomed to the rules of bureaucratic hierarchy, I have always had a habit of speaking my mind. I had heard enough foolhardy conceptions in the last few hours to loosen the tongue of a saint.

Reiffler seemed to be his main informant and the smooth process of merit-substitution had already begun and was gathering steam by a kind of natural osmosis difficult to define. The undoubted success of the Moroccan operation (for Youth Aliyah!) necessitated the apportionment of success from the top downwards. "Credit" in one form or another was up for grabs and there was no lack of candidates. When Aïda Schirmann accompanied the remainder of the children to Israel in August, she listened to many hot-air stories from several "sponsors" of the Moroccan operation. Such are the absurdities of bureaucracies and hierarchies in which a man must constantly justify himself in order to achieve promotion. Israel was (and remains) far from being an exception to this golden rule.

I had left Casablanca tired, but elated. I departed from Morgins exhausted in body and soul—and disillusioned from what I had heard, and from the ingratitude that I had experienced. It was only a foretaste of the silence over the next twenty-three years.

I remember making hurried arrangements for our autumn arrival in Geneva, going on to London, and then down to our family hotel in Bournemouth, the Palace Court Hotel, where Gisèle was awaiting me anxiously with Diana, who was plumper than ever. I recall that curious feeling as we walked along the sea promenade eastward to Sandbanks. My feet simply refused to go forward, the built in tension that had fortified me for the last weeks, without sleep, was no longer there to sustain a body that lacked rest, both physical and mental. I staggered back to the hotel on Gisèle's arm, slept through that day, and the next. The dream had ended.

Hardly more than two years earlier in Bournemouth, that same sea resort town that I knew since returning from America in 1945, I had asked Gisèle to be my wife. We had been excavating together on an archaeological dig near Salisbury and had gone down to the Palace Court Hotel in Bournemouth for two days. She was undecided, advised me to think it over carefully, and then went home to her parents in London. I crossed by ferry to the Isle of Wight, walking for hours on Tennyson Down, but the more I walked, the more I knew that we would "plight our troth" forever. One should never fly from one's destiny, but rather grasp it firmly. In the same way, our joint Moroccan decision, eighteen months later, could not have been otherwise, and Shakespeare's words which I wrote in my 1984 article were in my mind:

There is a tide in the affairs of men,

Which, taken at the flood, leads on to fortune;

Omitted, all the voyage of their life

Is bound in shallows and in miseries.

Julius Caesar: IV. iii. 218-21

My 1961 Report

The conclusion which follows is directly quoted from my detailed 1961 Report[78] which was also sent to Moshe Kol then Head of the Youth Aliyah on July 4, 1962.[79] Six months before I had sent him a three page letter informing him of my role in the mission to Morocco, of my bitterness to the way I was received in Morgins and Paris "by all but one of the Israeli representatives of those organizing the action" and of my regret for the lack of any written acknowledgement for what I had achieved.[80]

In April 1962, I handed over this report in Paris to Naphtali Bar-Giora (Mr. X in my Report) who forbade me to let anyone else see it, instructing me instead "to destroy all the spare copies in my possession" and to wait for further instructions regarding my spare copy. Instead, as mentioned in a letter dated April 10 1962 to Moshe Kol, I was instructed to send merely "a précis of the report to Jerusalem, giving simply the essential facts without details."[81] Two months later, David Umanski wrote me to convey Moshe Kol's request that I send him a copy of my report in a closed envelope marked: "Personal and Confidential" through Mr. Ben-Tzur, the Israeli ambassador to Switzerland.[82] It was only after I received the OK from my former contact in Paris, that I then sent Moshe Kol my 1961 Report together with other important documents.[83] In a letter dated August 1962, upon reception of my report, Moshe Kol expressed how "impressed by the degree of responsibility imposed" on me during the "rescue operation in the summer of 1961" and thanked me "on behalf of the whole Youth Aliyah family."[84] This was to be the first and last acknowledgment by an Israeli official of Operation Mural until 1984.

The Conclusion of the 1961 Report

"As to the possible repetition of such an action at another date in the same, or another—or something similar—I am doubtful. At the moment of course it is unnecessary in Morocco as both illegal and legal emigrations are still in full swing. Perhaps Algeria, one day?

Yet I can't help feeling that the Almighty himself was on our side from March to July 1961. We had a plausible plan, but we made too many unnecessary faults, which, coupled with the unfortunate circumstances that occurred, should have torpedoed everything. Yet, on the contrary, they did not, all problems ended in our favor, at the most unexpected moments, too! I cannot see such a concatenation of events arising again, unless the Almighty should once more enter the lists on the right side. Even then, without the connivance of the Moroccan authorities (or any other country's authorities, once they are against emigration, "officially") I do not think it is possible. Personally, I don't think the authorities were fully aware of what was happening. Some might have guessed (and been indifferent, or felt approval: some like Tajjedine were definitely antagonistic), but they could never be sure, and an international scandal would be the result of any hasty decision. Undoubtfully, there are liberal elements in the country (like the two adjoints of the Governor, D'Khissy and Hajjaj) who dislike carrying out illiberal policies. But it should not be forgotten that an enquiry was made (and just as quickly hushed up), for Mrs. Tordjman was called to the prefecture to give an explanation. They are not likely to be tricked again like this, UNLESS THEY WANT TO BE.

It is obvious that the organization—and achievement—of this whole action was due to the co-operation (often very close) of the three separate bodies involved, of which each played its own important part: The Jewish Agency, The Youth Aliyah, and the O.S.E. Suisse. It is important to stress this aspect with regard to this particular Moroccan action in view of some observation made by high-placed, yet ignorant, persons in Switzerland, who have tried, and continue to this day, to minimize the part played by O.S.E. Suisse, which in the known circumstances is quite ridiculous.[85]

For many years, the Youth Aliyah had been trying to launch such an action in Morocco. O.S.E. Suisse was clearly a suitable organization through which to work, and my chance arrival in Geneva completed the design. It only remained for Mr. X to prepare the whole scheme on a solid basis, which he quickly did.

To Prof. Bloch, the Director of O.S.E., goes the credit of having arranged with the authorities in Bern what was necessary from the Swiss side and having obtained their implicit consent, as well as the two ESSENTIAL letters of recommendation. It was he who recommended me to Mr. X when I started to work for the O.S.E., and in a sense I was lent by O.S.E. to the Jewish Agency and the Youth Aliyah for the mission in Morocco.

The Jewish Agency financed the operation with regard to the work in Casablanca, and my own expenses (in part). However, since we managed to save just about 3,000 dollars with the collective passports, the special price on the *S.S. Ionia*, and the nine free places on the first plane convoy (as recorded), the actual cost did not come to more than 300 dollars in all. Of course there were the normal cost of transporting the 530 children from Casablanca to Switzerland, which came to forty dollars a child, including everything. This is the equivalent of a normal third-class fare, single.[86]

This does not take into account the magnificent work of "Georges" and his group, which was really the nucleus of the whole action as I have tried to explain. Of course there were expenses involved here.

Excepting the last convoy from Tangier, O.S.E. was responsible for accompanying the children from Morocco and the conveying of them to Morgins and Champery. O.S.E.'s office in Geneva became the veritable centre of the operation. Prof. Bloch controlled the correspondence with Miss Schirmann and he sent the monitors.

The Youth Aliyah was responsible for the charges incurred for keeping the children in O.S.E.'s Homes in Morgins, as well as in Champery. This was honoured in great part, yet O.S.E. nonetheless registered a financial loss. The Youth Aliyah was responsible for transporting the children safely from Switzerland to Israel."[87]

After "Mural"

What was to become known within the Mossad as "Operation Mural" ("Mural" was the code name that members of the network used when referring to me) had succeeded beyond anyone's expectations. Soon afterwards, a new policy was initiated for a new situation that had developed as a result, firstly of King Hassan II's liberal policy that had begun in July, and secondly, of our success whereby, for the first time since Moroccan independence in 1956, Jewish children had been able to leave the country freely on collective passports, and the parents could then follow—an innovation in July–August 1961.

It was only much later that I grasped the key importance of Mural, particularly the system of collective passports, which Mr. Reinhard of the Swiss Red Cross had suggested to me as early as March after my arrival— and Muhammad D'Khrissy had approved at my first meeting with him on May 31. In the end, it was this system, used successfully in Operation Mural, that was chosen four months later by King Hassan II when he agreed to the mass departure of Moroccan Jews.[88]

By March 1962, almost all families of those who had left under OSSEAN's auspices had been able to join their children in Israel. This involved nearly 300 families, from 2,500 to 3,000 persons. More important was the fact that the Moroccan authorities preferred to ignore what had happened. True, an enquiry was started and Mrs. Tordjman was called to the préfecture for an explanation of her relationship with me, but the matter was quickly hushed up.

By November, the Moroccan government appeared to have accepted the innovative collective passport system as a regular travel facility for potential Jewish emigrants, tens of thousands of whom were thus able to leave Morocco for France, Canada, or elsewhere during the next three years—but not officially for Israel. Both Alex and Georges remained in Casablanca into 1962 and 1963 to organize these departures that involved other organizations. Clandestine operations were soon no longer necessary as the gates for the exodus were again opened wide.

This did not mean that there no incidents or arrests. On October 26, 1961 for example, *The Jerusalem Post*, quoting the *Maghreb Arabe Press*, announced the arrest of five Moroccan Jews seeking to emigrate to Israel and the hunt for two "Zionist Agents." The departures began on a big scale in November and *The Time York Times* announced on December 8, 1961 that 25,000 Moroccan Jews out of a population of 180,000 were expected to leave the country for France after an agreement had been reached with an American Jewish organization (probably HIAS). The *Jewish Chronicle* (December 15) referred to the "easing of restrictions" and the departure of 250 emigrants for Marseille by plane. After a suspension in January, *The New York Times* of February 8 and 10, 1962 again reported that "more than 1000 Jews had left Morocco in the last three weeks in ships bound for Marseilles" and that "the current departures of Jews had been 'duly authorized' by the Moroccan government."

This liberal policy nonetheless resulted in an inevitable increase in baksheesh payments by inexperienced operators. I learned of one particular case in February 1962 that raised my eyebrows. An orthodox group from Israel had sent out a representative to encourage parents to send their children to study in their religious schools (yeshivot) in Israel. The network had given it advice as to how it should act, but he had preferred bribery in order to speed up the collective passport procedure. The cost was sixty dollars (1,800 dollars today) per individual! The recipient of the bribes was . . . Tajjedine himself, who asked the willing briber whether he knew a certain Mr. Littman: "He certainly cheated us out of a lot of money!" Allegedly, the official baksheesh cost, per individual, in summer 1961 was 160 dollars per person (4,800 dollars today)! Tajjedine was later to be dismissed for corruption. A few months later, another incident was reported in the Italian weekly *Israel* of July 5, 1962. It concerned a passport scandal in Casablanca involving sixteen persons: six Jews and five officials of the passport department of Casablanca, one of whom was reported as being a member of the governor's cabinet, two others were in charge of the passport section and his assistant. All of them were arrested and accused of "corruption and illicit commerce in the obtaining of passport for Jews." The head of the organization was a certain Georges Harrar, an astrologer—fortunately no connection with "Georges." I never learned the names of the five officials arrested.

Notes

1   Fig. 91: Certificate of the "Hero Of Silence" Order with its translation in English.

2   See Part II: *Operation Mural: The Documentary.*

3   See Fig. 92: Verbatim transcript of Efraim Halevy's presentation as recorded on July 1, 2009 at the Israel Intelligence' Heritage & Commemoration Center in Glilot; and Fig. 93: Address by D.G. Littman at the Israel Intelligence Heritage and Commemoration Center in Glilot, July 1, 2009.

4   See below, Chapter 2: Geneva—Paris—Casablanca .

5   Raphael Mahler (eds.), *The Jews of Czestochava,* United Czestochower Relief Committee and Ladies Auxiliary, New York, 1947, p. LIV.

6   Alister Heath, "The rich have never been richer: their predecessors were small fry," *The Spectator,* July 13, 2006; cf. a similar article by Steve Doughty: "100 new millionaires created a day" in *The Daily Mail,* July 13, 2006.

7   As I later learned, in 1262 the Egyptian Mamluk Sultan Baibars had forbidden Jews and Christians to enter the ancestral tombs of Abraham, Isaac, Jacob and their wives. Six hundred years later in 1862 the first Christian, the Prince of Wales, was allowed to visit the sanctuary under armed Ottoman guards. After the British victory over the Turks in 1917, all Christians could enter the holy shrine, but Jews still had to wait until after the 1967 Six-Day War before they could visit or pray there. I was one of those who managed to visit the tombs twenty years earlier.

8   Fig. 1: Order of Mission from the fictive OSSEAN's Secretary-General, N. Lehmann (in fact Miss Aïda Schirmann).

9   Fig. 3: Letter from René Steiner, Secretary General of the Swiss Red Cross in Bern to A.E. Reinhard, chief delegate of the Red Cross Societies in Morocco, March 8, 1961.

10 Fig. 2: Letter of recommendation from M. Tromp, President for of the Commission for the Hospitalization of Sick Foreigners in Switzerland, March 2, 1961.

11 Fig. 7: Letter from Mr. Maeder of the Federal Police for Foreigners to Erwin Bernath, Swiss Ambassador in Rabat, March 21, 1961.

12 Fig. 5: Letter from D.G. Littman to N. Lehmann (OSSEAN), March 17, 1961; and Fig. 6: Letter from N. Lehmann to D.G. Littman, March 21 1961 .

13 Prior to the French occupation of Morocco in 1912, the condition of the Jews, as dhimmis, was very precarious. From 1970 I researched and published articles on this question in French, and in the London Wiener Library Bulletin (1975:28 n.s.35/36 and: 29 n.s.37/38); and "Mission to Morocco (1863-64)", in *The Century of Moses Montefiore* (OUP, 1985). See Paul B. Fenton & David G. Littman, *L'Exil au Maghreb. La condition juive sous l'Islam 1148-1912,* PUPS (Presses de l'université Paris-Sorbonne), Paris, 2010. Bat Ye'or (Gisèle Littman) has also written extensively on the subject of the dhimmis since 1971. (See her website: www.dhimmitude.org).

14 Fig. 4: Letter from the fictive Director of OSSEAN, Prof. Aberson (in reality Prof. Jacques Bloch) to D.G. Littman March 9, 1961.

15 Fig. 17: Letter from N. Lehmann to D.G. Littman, May 7, 1961.

16 Fig. 18: Letter from D.G. Littman to N. Lehmann, May 9, 1961.

17 Fig. 8: Letter from D.G. Littman to N. Lehmann, March 23, 1961.

18 Fig. 10: Example of medical certificate used by OSSEAN.

19 Fig. 8 and 9: Letters from D.G. Littman to N. Lehmann, March 23 & 25, 1961.

20 Fig. 12: Letter from D.G. Littman to N. Lehmann, April 8, 1961.

21 Fig. 11: Moroccan registration forms of David & Gisele Littman, March and April 1961.

22 Fig. 14: Prospectus in Arabic & French of OSSEAN's the "Home de la Forêt" in Switzerland.

23 Fig. 13: Letter from D.G Littman to OSSEAN, April 18 & 22, 1961; together with Fig. 15: visit card and Fig. 16: bill from OSSEAN's office in Casablanca.

24 Fig. 19 and 20: Letter from Prof. E. Aberson (Director of OSSEAN) to the Swiss Ambassador in Rabat, Mr. Bernath and to H.R.H. Princess Lalla Aïcha, May 9, 1961.

25 Thirty years later in a statement in March 1991 delivered to the UN Commission on Human Rights for the World Union for Progressive Judaism, I quoted this passage when speaking on Soviet *refuseniks*.

26 "'Operation Mural' Parents and Children: Separation" by Gisèle Littman (Bat Ye'or), in *Shorashim Bamizra'h* (Roots in the Orient), Vol. I. Editor: Itshak Avrahami, Edition Hakibbutz Hameuchad: Yad Tabenkin, 1986 , pp. 427–432 (First Compilation published by the Institute for Research on Zionism and pioneers from Oriental Countries).

27 Fig. 37: Letter from D.G. Littman to the Ministry of Foreign Affairs in Rabat, May 17, 1961.

28 Fig. 7: Letter from Mr. Maeder to the Swiss Ambassador in Rabat, March 21, 1961.

29 Fig. 21: Letter from D.G. Littman to Ambassador E. Bernarth, May 14, 1961.

30 Fig. 22: Answer from Federal Political Departement (EPD) from May 17 following Ambassador Bernath telegram dated May 15, and Fig. 24: Confidential letter from the Office of International Organizations at the Federal Political Department in Bern to the Swiss Ambassador in Rabat, May 18, 1961.

31 Fig. 21: Letter from D.G. Littman to Swiss Ambassador Bernath, May 14, 1961, and Fig. 23: Letter from Ambassador E. Bernath to the Federal Political Department in Bern (EPD), May 18, 1961.

32 Fig. 25: Confidential letter from J. Birchler, Swiss Consul in Casablanca to the Federal Police in Bern, May 23, 1961.

33 Fig. 41: Letter from Lehmann to D.G. Littman, June 16, 1961.

34 See Part II, *From the Presidential Residence to the Intelligence Center in Glilot (2008-2009).*

35 Fig. 24: Confidential letter from the Federal Political Department of Bern to Swiss Ambassador in Rabat, May 18, 1961.

36 Fig. 22: Answer from Bernath to the Department of Foreign Affairs at the Federal Political Department (EPD) May 15 and the answer from the EPD, May 17, 1961; Fig. 26: Confidential letter from Bernath to the Department for International Organizations of the Federal Political Department, Mai 25, 1961.

37 Fig. 28: Confidential letter from the Federal Political Department in Bern to the Swiss Embassy in Rabat, June 3, 1961.

38 Fig. 27: Letter from Mr. Ghomari from the Entr'Aide Nationale in Rabat to the Swiss Ambassador, June 3, 1961.

39 Fig. 29: Confidential letter from Bernath to the Federal Political Department, June 5, 1961.

40 Fig. 30: Telegram from the Federal Political Department to the Embassy in Rabat, June 9, 1961, and Fig. 31: Letter from Bernath in Rabat to Mr. Ghomari, Secretary-General of the Entr'Aide Nationale in Rabat, June 12, 1961.

41 Fig. 47: Letter from the Swiss Consul in Casablanca, Mr. J. Birchler to the Federal Police in Bern, June 26, 1961, and Fig. 53: Letter from the Swiss Consul in Casablanca, Mr. J. Birchler to the Federal Police in Bern, July 11, 1961, and Fig. 90: Speech by the Swiss Ambassador Walter Haffner at the private reception for Mr. & Mrs. Littman to commemorate Operation Mural at the Israeli President Residence, Jerusalem, June 1, 2008.

42 Fig. 37: Specimen of collective passports first used on June 26, 1961, for our first convoy.

43 Fig. 33: Letter from D.G. Littman to N. Lehmann June 1, 1961; Fig. 34: Letter from N. Lehmann to D.G. Littman, June 1, 1961; Fig. 35: Letter from D.G. Littman to N. Lehmann, June 5, 1961; Fig. 36: Letter from N. Lehmann to D.G. Littman, June 8, 1961.

44 This system of collective passports was preferred by the Moroccan authorities, it later became the linchpin for the simplest and most discreet method of Jewish immigration from Morocco to Israel: between 1962 and 1964 nearly 100,000 Jews arrived in Israel under the guise of Operation Yakhin with royal consent. The same system of collective passports was to be used elsewhere, especially in Ethiopia for Operation Solomon (1990). See Fig. 37: Specimen of collective passports, first used on June 26, 1961 for our first convoy.

45 Fig. 33: Letter from D.G. Littman to N. Lehmann June 1, 1961.

46 Fig. 38: Letter from D.G. Littman to N. Lehmann, June 9, 1961 and Fig. 40: Letter from D.G. Littman to Mr. Cheradi, Governor of Casablanca, June 11, 1961.

47 Fig. 39: Letter from D.G.Littman to N. Lehmann, June 10, 1961.

48 Fig. 40: Letter from D.G. Littman to Mr. Cheradi, director of the cabinet of Casablanca's governor, June 11, 1961.

49 Fig. 32: Letter from D.G. Littman to the Ministry of Foreign Affairs in Rabat, May 17, 1961.

50 Fig. 39: Letter from D.G. Littman to N. Lehmann, June 10, 1961.

51 Fig. 35: Letter from D.G. Littman to N. Lehmann, June 5, 1961.

52 Fig. 38: Letter from D.G. Littman to N. Lehmann, June 9, 1961 and Fig. 39: Letter of D.G. Littman to N. Lehmann, June 10, 1961.

53 Fig. 41: Letter from D.G. Littman to N. Lehmann, June 12, 1961.

54 Fig. 43: Telegram from D.G. Littman to N. Lehmann, June 16, 1961.

55 Fig. 44: Letter from D.G. Littman to N. Lehmann, June 18, 1961.

56 Fig. 45: Letter from D.G. Littman to N. Lehmann, June 19, 1961.

57 Fig. 47: Letter from the Swiss Consul in Casablanca, Mr. J. Birchler to the Federal Police in Bern, June 26, 1961.

58 Fig. 46: Letter from D.G. Littman to N. Lehmann, June 26, 1961.

59 Fig. 48: Letter from D.G. Littman to N. Lehmann, July 1, 1961.

60 Fig. 49 and 50: Letters from N. Lehmann to D.G. Littman, July 3, 1961.

61 Fig. 46 and 48: Letters from D.G. Littman to N. Lehmann, June 26 and July 1, 1961.

62 Fig. 48: Letter from D.G. Littman to N. Lehmann, July 1, 1961.

63 Fig. 51: Letter from D.G. Littman to N. Lehmann, July 4, 1961, and Fig. 52: Bill dated July 5, 1961 for the tickets of 85 children booked on the plane from Casablanca to Lyon on July 10, 1961.

64 Fig. 53: Letter from the Swiss Consul in Casablanca, Mr. J. Birchler to the Federal Police in Bern, July 11, 1961.

65 See chapter 4: "A traffic Accident" when George heard the news on the clandestine radio of Kol Israel Lagola; and chapter 5: "Farewell Casablanca" and "Paris—Geneva—Morgins—London—Bournemouth" the meetings with Naphtali Bar-Giora and Arieh Reiffler respectively; and in Part II: "Operation Mural hits the press" with the demand of Moshe Kol in 1984 to correct my critical reference to this specific decision in Samuel Segev's book. See also Fig. 71 and 74: Letters from D. Littman to Gershom Shoken, Editor-in-Chief of *Haaretz*, May 28, 1984 and Fig. 77: Letter to Naphtali Bar-Giora, December 31, 1985.

66 Fig. 52: Bill dated July 5, 1961 for the tickets of 85 children booked on the plane from Casablanca to Lyon on July 10, 1961.

67 Fig. 51: Letter from D.G. Littman to N. Lehmann, July 4, 1961.

68 Fig. 54: Letter from N. Lehmann to D.G. Littman, July 12, 1961.

69 Fig. 55 and 56: Telegrams from "Lehmann" to D.G. Littman, July 14-15, 1961.

70 See in Fig. 60 the P.S in my letter to Moshe Kol, Head of the Youth Aliyah in Jerusalem, January 24, 1962.

71 I learned later that Jacques's real name was Pinhas Katsir. In October 2006, 45 years later, I returned to Morocco with "Jacques" and "Georges" (Gad Shahar) to make a documentary movie on Operation Mural. See Part II, The return to Morocco 45 years later.

72 Fig. 58: Letter from N. Lehmann to Mr. de Blomac, August 15, 1961 and Fig. 59: Letter from D.G. Littman to Alex Korany, August 26, 1961, and Fig. 85: Letter from D.G. Littman to the editor of *The Jerusalem Post*, June 9, 1986.

73 Fig. 57: Telegram from N. Lehmann to D.G. Littman, 17 July 1961.

74 Fig. 58: Letter from N. Lehmann to Mr. de Blomac, August 15, 1961.

75 See Part II: "Operation Mural hits the press."

76 Appendix 1: Lists of the names and addresses of the 530 children who left Morocco during Operation Mural.

77 "Operation Mural: Mission to Morocco (March 16-July 24, 1961)" by David Littman, in *Shorashim Bamizra'h* (Roots in the Orient), Vol. I. Editor: Itshak Avrahami, Edition Hakibbutz Hameuchad: Yad Tabenkin, 1986, pp.365-425, (First Compilation published by the Institute for Research on Zionism and pioneers from Oriental Countries).

78 Report of the united action of the Jewish Agency, O.S.E. Suisse and the Youth Aliyah from March 16 until July 14, 1961 by their representative in Casablanca, David G. Littman. The 1961 Report and Mural's documents can be found at the New York Public Library in the Dorot Jewish Division (Archives of D.G. Littman and Bat Ye'or, boxes 55-56).

79 Fig. 63: Letter from D. Littman to Moshe Kol, Head of the Youth Aliyah Department, July 4, 1962.

80 Fig. 60: Letter from D. Littman to Moshe Kol, Head of the Youth Aliyah Department, January 24, 1962.

81 Fig. 61: Letter from D. Littman to Moshe Kol, Head of the Youth Aliyah Department, April 10, 1962.

82 Fig. 62: Letter from D. Umanski, Director General of the Youth Aliyah Department, to D. Littman, June 14, 1962.

83 Fig. 63: Letter from D. Littman to Moshe Kol, Head of the Youth Aliyah Department, July 4, 1962.

84 Fig. 64: Letter from Moshe Kol, Head of the Youth Aliyah Department, to D. Littman, August 12, 1962.

85 For his own personal reasons, the President of O.S.E. Suisse, Mr. M.J. Klopman, wishes to deny that O.S.E. Suisse occupied a principal place in the accomplishment of this action. This is perhaps because he was not aware of any of the facts—of necessity—until almost the end of the action. This curious idea could spread, and should be disproved.

86 The financial cost to the Jewish Agency with regard to our 130-day mission in Casablanca was minimal—between 3,000 dollars and 3,500 dollars (up to 100,000 dollars today). The use of no cost collective, instead of individual, passports, and extremely cheap rates on the *S.S. Ionia* and nine free places on the first TAI flight economized at least this amount. The cost to transport children by plane to Lyon and then Switzerland was under forty dollars a child, and the overall cost, including the ship passage

must have been roughly 20,000 dollars (about 600,000 dollars in 2011). At that time the actual "rate" of getting emigrants from Morocco to Gibraltar by clandestine boats cost twice the forty dollars figure, so I had been informed then.

87 See note 78, op. cit.

88 On November 27, 1961, General Muhammad Oufkir, then chief of security, signed the first collective passport for Jewish adults, heralding the start of the highly successful Operation Yakhin by which 100,000 Jews left Morocco from December 1961 to 1964. The importance of the collective passports was confirmed to me during conversations with Gad Shahar, Pinhas Katsir, Carmit Gattmon, Yehuda Domenitz and Shmulik Toledano in November 2003 (from the address in French by D.G. Littman at Beit Lavron in Ashdod, on January 13, 2004). (II Second Part).

Part II
From Oblivion to Recognition
1962–2009

CHAPTER 1

Following Two Decades of Silence

I began my personal narrative on Operation Mural with a brief preface relating to that moving event on July 1, 2009 when the deputy head of the Mossad awarded me their rare "Hero of Silence" Order—and to the unforgettable words of Alex Gattmon, the Mossad chief in Morocco, the night before I left Casablanca on July 24, 1961.

In this second part of the narrative, I shall endeavour to relate how this "story" finally became known from 1984, after twenty-three years of silence. Many unsung heroes deserve praise for their courageous actions. I had, what I call, providential luck on my side and am providing here some more details for the record.

The Unexpected Decease of the Mossad Chief in Morocco

Except for Moshe Kol's letter in August 1962, I had not received any official written thanks after the success of Operation Mural, despite Naphtali Bar-Giora's promise of an official invitation to Israel when we met at Lyon airport, and continued on to Paris on July 24, 1961.[1]

I was so disgusted by this utter silence that I twice refused Gisèle's request that we take a holiday in Israel—she had never been to Israel and was eager to visit the country for which she had risked her life. I changed my mind in 1964 and we made a long trip, touring the country and visiting my relatives and friends again after eight years. On this visit to Israel, we met former Mossad chief Alex Gattmon, his wife Carmit, and my Casablanca contacts, Gad Shahar ("Georges") and Pinhas Katsir ("Jacques"), as well as Shmuel Toledano, deputy to Mossad chief Isser Harel in Israel during Operation Mural—all of whom became close friends. From 1983 onwards, Toledano did everything he could for Operation Mural to be recognized in Israel officially.

In July 1981, Alexander Gattmon died of a heart attack while on a visit to Zurich with his wife Carmit and their two children. At his funeral, both Prime Minister Shimon Peres and Foreign Minister Yitzhak Shamir spoke highly of him, the latter referring to the "outstanding air force officer who lived by a principle that acts should speak and the mouth remains silent." His former boss in Tel Aviv, Shmuel Toledano—deputy to Mossad chief Isser Harel and later advisor to several prime ministers—referred to him as "a born leader." The obituary in *The Jerusalem Post* (August 6, 1981) spoke about his remarkable life from his birth in 1926 as Olek Guttman (in Bendin, Polish Silesia). Having joined the Polish underground at the age of fourteen, he survived torture and a hanging in Hungary, being saved by Soviet troops in Budapest (1944).

He reached Israel in 1948 and fought in the War of Independence, rising to become Lieutenant Colonel in the Israeli Air Force. During the summer of 1960, he resigned from the Israeli Air Force at the request of the Mossad, who then in turn prepared him for his new post in Morocco, where he arrived in late November 1960 with his wife, Carmit, to direct all clandestine activities, under the code-name "Armin." He and Carmit returned to Israel in mid-1963 after a very successful mission that included Operation Mural—and Operation Yakhin, for which he received a citation and a personal letter of congratulations from President Itzhak Ben-Zvi, as did his deputy Gad Shahar ("Camus"), my main "contact" in Casablanca, known to me only as "Georges." Alex Gattmon was to become a brilliant industrialist.

From January 1981—on the 23rd of the Hebrew month of *Tevet*—Prime Minister Menahem Begin's government decided on an annual "Day of

Remembrance" for the forty-four persons (twenty-three of which were children) who drowned near the port of Al Hoceima in northern Morocco, en route for Gibraltar on January 11, 1961 when their clandestine embarkation capsized (the *Piscès* or *Egoz*—"nut" in Hebrew). This date was also intended to honour those who had participated in the clandestine aliyah activities in North Africa, but no other details were provided then. From 1981, some articles began to appear in the European Jewish press.[2]

In a moving ceremony in December 1992, twenty-two bodies were re-buried on Mount Herzl in Jerusalem. On that occasion, Prime Minister Yitzhak Rabin warmly thanked Moroccan King Hassan II's gesture, and in his eulogy declared: "Here before us lay those who paid the price for the [Zionist] dream with their bodies and souls."[3]

Alex Gattmon's unexpected death in July 1981, and the brief obituary reference to his Moroccan mission, led to the Mossad's decision, with governmental approval, to authorise the publication of more details on all the clandestine aliyah activities in Morocco. A few months later, I received a letter, dated December 9, 1981, from Moshe Kol, former head of Youth Aliyah between the years 1948 to 1964, and later Minister of Tourism: "The purpose of my note is to ask you if I can mention your name in my book of memoirs as the man who did such an excellent job in 1961 by helping to rescue 500 children from Morocco. I want to tell the whole story of your courageous undertaking, but I don't know if you want your name to be mentioned after twenty years. If you agree, I will be happy."[4] I gave him my agreement on December 21, 1981,[5] suggesting that he obtain official agreement first. He replied briefly on December 30: "I needed your permission to mention your name and I am glad that you agreed."[6] Fortunately, I had prepared a detailed forty-five page report for Bar-Giora and the Mossad, a copy of which Mr. Kol had received from me in 1962—at his personal request—and after much hesitation by the Mossad.[7] Shmuel Toledano had received a presidential citation in 1962. Having become close friends with him and his wife after our first visit to Israel in 1964, he had promised to alert me if ever the "story" became public. On our visit to Jerusalem in 1983, he suddenly remembered and put me in touch with Shmuel Segev, a senior editor of a major Israeli newspaper, *Maariv*, who had been authorised to write a book on the Aliyah from Morocco since 1948—after Deputy Prime Minister David Levy, born in Morocco, had obtained the cabinet's approval. Fortunately, Mr. Kol was able to provide me the next day with a copy of my 1961 Report. When I later lunched with Segev, I gave it to him and he immediately expressed his astonishment on reading the precise details of the story, adding that no one had mentioned anything to him about this children's Aliyah, via Switzerland (Operation Mural)—with collective passports, soon to be used for Operation Yakhin (1962–1964). He then decided to add a chapter to his book referring to Operation Mural as "Miller" and "Milhar" at the Mossad's request. He also changed other names for security reasons, for instance Prof. Bloch became "Prof. Blumfield," and his organization OSE was renamed "Hilsfund"; Naphtali Bar-Giora, my Paris contact, became "Dan Ben Gar," and "Georges," my contact in Morocco, became "Gilbert." Over the years, these fictive names reappeared in the press and in books.[8]

CHAPTER 2

Operation Mural Hits the Press (1984)

On the book's publication, this whole chapter on Mural was reproduced in an entire page of the widely-read daily *Maariv* in its issue of April 20, 1984.[9] Soon after, I received a phone call from Mr. Kol informing me out of the blue: "You have become a hero in Israel!" He then asked me to send a correction on Segev's critical reference to a Youth Aliyah's decision that appeared in the article, copied from my report—the disastrous departure for Israel on July 9, 1961 of the eighty-five children from the first convoy. I informed him that this decision concerned our personal security in Morocco and had been fully described in my 1961 Report, which he had received from me; I could not contradict myself and describe differently now that grave event which was presently known to the public.[10] He was very disappointed with my reluctance to follow his wishes, and this incident tarnished our very friendly relations which had spanned over the previous twenty years.

Mr. Kol had been the only Israeli personality who had officially thanked both Gad Shahar and me on our 1964 visit, awarding both of us Youth Aliyah's 30th anniversary medal, just before he retired as its director. According to Gad, at the annual commemorative meetings honoring these clandestine events, Mr. Kol regularly mentioned us and Operation Mural, which had become for him a Youth Aliyah achievement.

As a result of Segev's book, at a special ceremony in the presidential residence on May 9, 1984, President Haim Herzog received about fifty of those persons who had worked in Morocco for Operation Yakhin in the early 1960s. During his presentation in Hebrew (which was translated for us), the President unexpectedly asked me to rise and be publically recognized for Operation Mural.

Moshe Kol wasn't present at the ceremony and I don't know what he wrote in his memoirs, but in an article which he published on May 16, 1984 in *Haaretz* titled "Thirty-five years of youth immigration from Morocco," he spoke highly of Operation Mural—calling it 'Milhar,' as required by the Mossad—in relation to Youth Aliyah's activities while referring to me vaguely, but without a name ("we chose a Jew with a British passport ... this Jew worked with Alex Gattmon"), and went on to explain his version of the July 10, 1961 "incident."[11] My detailed response of May 28, 1984 was refused for publication by the highly-respected editor, Gershom Shoken (on June 12, 1984), on account of it being "too long"; a shorter version that I sent six weeks later (on July 26, 1984), was also not published. Clearly, Moshe Kol's "version" was preferred—without any "reply."[12]

An English translation of Shmuel Segev's article, with fictive names, soon followed in two issues of *Newsview*, an Israeli Weekly, with an interview by journalist Simon Griver.[13]

Then followed a long version of my personal narrative, prepared in English in 1984, based on my 1961 Report. Gisèle had observed that the parents of the children had not been mentioned in any report and she provided a moving description in French on the parents—these two articles appeared in a Hebrew publication by the Institute Yad Tabenkin in 1986.[14]

In a letter dated December 31, 1985 to Naphtali Bar-Giora I relate to the various comments he had sent me concerning this text.[15]

On May 1, 1986, Gisèle and I were both nominated by Sam Ben Shitrit head of the *Beyahad* Movement, the ideological movement of Jews of North African Origin, to receive their special annual honor at the Mimouna Festival. Also present for that special event was our daughter Ariane, studying then at the Hebrew University, and our son Daniel, together with tens of thousands of people taking part in this colourful Mimouna Day, Moroccan Jewish national festivities held annually in the Sachar Park opposite the Knesset, closing the Passover' week. We received this special certificate of

David G. Littman speaking after receiving the Beyahad Award at the Mimouna Festival, Sacher Park, Jerusalem, May 1, 1986. On the podium: sitting next to Sam Ben Shitrit, second from the right, Vice-Premier and Foreign Minister Yitzhak Shamir, then Prime Minister President Shimon Peres, and Mayor of Jerusalem Teddy Kollek.

gratitude with warm words of appreciation from Prime Minister Shimon Peres after I had delivered a brief presentation in the presence of the Vice-Premier and Foreign Minister Yitzhak Shamir, the Mayor of Jerusalem Teddy Kollek and the Speaker of the Knesset Shlomo Hillel.[16]

A few days later at a very moving meeting in Tel Aviv—(after ads were placed in all newspapers) we met 120 of the 530 children (now married adults with their own children), who had arrived in Israel via Operation Mural.[17] All this was widely covered on Israeli radio, TV and in the press, with a comment by the Mossad head Meir Amit.[18] Following the articles by Abraham Rabinovitch in *The Jerusalem Post*, and by Michal Yudelman in the same newspaper, I wrote a letter to the editor of *The Jerusalem Post* where I stressed a few precisions concerning the Operation. Among them, I emphasized that it was OSE-Suisse who served as the Geneva cover for

David and Gisele Littman meeting with "children"

in Gan Oranim, Tel Aviv, May 14, 1986

Operation Mural and not the invented name "Hilsfund,"[19] in this same letter of June 9, 1986, I reiterated that no family documents or records of the
children were left in my Casablanca office but were all handed over the night
before my departure of July 24, 1961 with the last convoy. Unfortunately,
the person responsible for mailing the documents panicked at the thought
of being questioned at the post office, and threw them into a garbage bin.
This indeed had probably been the cause of much anguish for the families
who suddenly found themselves without these identity papers and were
obliged to explain their inexplicable loss to the Moroccan authorities, as
described by Prosper Alfasi in the article of M. Yudelman.[20]

A year later, on May 29, 1987, a long article by Michel-Meir Knafo, "Who
saved the Moroccan Jews?" appeared in *Haaretz* Magazine. From Rabat, at
age twenty-one, Knafo had been one of those guarding the groups leaving
clandestinely on boats like the *Egoz*, and had been arrested and tortured
in February 1961 after Operation Bazak. He interviewed many key players,
among them: Isser Harel, former head of the Mossad, Shlomo Havilio, head
of framework and of the Mossad in Paris in the fifties, Ephraim Ronel who
replaced Havilio in the sixties, and Shlomo-Zalman Shragai, then head of the
Jewish Agency's immigration department. Some key facts in Knafo's article
on Operation Mural were either inadequate or incorrect. For instance, he
states that it is time to tell the whole story of this clandestine aliyah from
Morocco (1961–64) by giving the factual details and the names of all those
involved. However, he then omits to mention Gad Shahar (code-name
"Camus"—known to me as "Georges"). This was rather strange since Gad
had received, together with Alex Gattmon, a personal letter from President
Itzhak Ben-Zvi, dated May 16, 1962, and delivered to him personally on
May 23, 1962 by Ronel himself—as well as a presidential citation on July 27,
1964 at the close of his long mission. Twenty years later in 1983, on Israel's
35th anniversary, Gad was one of the twelve chosen to carry a torch at the
"Year of Heroism" ceremony in Jerusalem, representing those who had
courageously worked in these clandestine operations for Aliyah from Arab
countries. In that same article, Ephraim Ronel named Naphtali Bar-Giora
as being the one who had had the idea of sending children on holiday in
Switzerland—and from there to Israel with their parents' permission. He

states that Bargiora "mobilised a Jew who was at the head of the holidays plan—it seems to me involved 140 children who reached Israel." Just as in Mr. Kol's *Haaretz* article from 1984, my name is not mentioned and the number of children is inaccurate: 140 instead of 530. These "facts" and "names" could easily have been checked.

On October 9, 1987, an illustrated page article by Simon Griver was published in London's newspaper, *The Jewish Chronicle,* on "Mission to Morocco," in which I put the record straight.[21] On the other side of *The Jewish Chronicle* page, there was another article, "Beyond the Barbed Wire: Forty years after the Exodus Saga." We were in good company.

CHAPTER 3

A Reputable Writer Publishes
a Distorted Story

The inaccuracies continued. One example is worth quoting at some length as it is a remarkable example of how "facts" can be twisted and related in an extraordinary manner. Tad Szulc, reporter and writer—an important Washington correspondent for *The New York Times* from 1953 to 1972, and even a Knight of the French Légion d'Honneur—published in 1991 (and in 1993 by Pan Books), *The Secret Alliance: The Extraordinary Story of the Rescue of the Jews Since World War II*. He described the details of Operation Mural on one page, for which his sole source appears to have been Naphtali Bar-Giora, who became overnight the chief organizer and hero, whereas there is no mention of me ("Mural") at all.

Szulc states, "Another venture of the Mossad was Operation Mural, which was cleverly designed to send Moroccan children on summer vacations to a full-fledged recreation camp in Switzerland. Naphtali "Nat" Bar-Giora, a German-born, Arabic-speaking specialist on legal and illegal immigration, who was "lent" by the Jewish Agency to the Mossad in 1959, came up with the idea of a Swiss vacation program which would be open to all children—with the understanding that Moslem children would return home and Jewish children would be sent on to Israel. He set up an office in Casablanca as part of Framework (Misgeret), and its Moroccan Jewish activists visited Jewish families, urging them to register their children for Swiss summer vacations. The parents of the Jewish children registered for the

Swiss camp "were perfectly aware that the children would not come back," said Bar-Giora, who operated in Morocco under the cover of a German businessman [. . .] All the children travelled on collective passports, which concealed the Jews among them, and over 800 Moroccan Jewish children made it safely to Israel during the two years of the Swiss operation [. . .]"

A few brief clarifications are needed to set this fictional record straight:

- Bar-Giora did not set up an office in Casablanca, I made the decision with Georges' agreement.
- Bar-Giora did not operate in Morocco under the cover of a German businessman.
- Bar-Giora might have come to Casablanca later, once or twice, to get an idea of what was going on.
- Bar-Giora refused "collective passports" until the very last moment despite my insistence.
- Bar-Giora was against my early idea to offer Swiss holidays for Muslim children.
- The number of children who reached Israel under the guise of holidays via Switzerland under Operation Mural was 530, not 800.
- There were five convoys (June 26–July 24, 1961), only three of which reached Switzerland. The mention "during the two years of the Swiss operation" is wrong.
- There is a general mix-up—either by Tad Szulc, or because of the "facts" he received from Bar-Giora regarding Operation Mural and Operation Yakhin—two totally separate operations.
- HIAS (Hebrew Sheltering and Immigrant Aid Society, the oldest Jewish American institution dealing with refugees established in 1890) was only involved in "Yakhin" with "Georges" and "Jacques," not with "Mural."

I have related this "version" at some length as an example of factual errors, published in a serious book—by a highly considered journalist and writer, probably relying solely on what Naphtali Bar-Giora had conveyed to him vaguely, and who suddenly became the key man in Operation Mural, like others before him.

Fortunately, when Sir Martin Gilbert—an old friend to whom I had shown the documentary film *Operation Mural* in his home in May 2007, which he liked—was preparing his last book, *In Ishmael's House: A History of the Jews in Muslim Lands* (2010), he consulted me and also Shmuel Segev[22] on Operation Mural. In his book, he devoted a brief accurate description with the full details and notes provided by me. In March 2009, a long article interview by Xavier Cornut was requested and published on five successful pages (March 23–26) by the Casablanca *Le Soir Echos*, revealing Operation Mural for the first time to a Moroccan public.[23]

CHAPTER 4

Operation Mural: The Documentary

Twenty years after Shmuel Segev's book and his full page *Maariv* article had led to two public recognitions of Operation Mural by President Chaim Herzog in 1984 and Prime Minister Shimon Peres at the Mimouna festival in 1986, another commerative event of Operation Mural took place in 2004: I was personally awarded by General Shaul Mofaz, then Minister of the Defense, a certificate of recognition for my role in Morocco and for the success of the activities of the Misgeret.[24]

This moving event, attended by the mayor of Ashdod and eminent personalities, was held at Beit Lavron, Ashdod on January 13, 2004, just prior to the commemoration service at the annual ceremony in front of the monument for the forty-four illegal Jewish emigrants who drowned in the 1961 *Egoz* (*Piscès*) tragedy. This was also the Day of Remembrance for the clandestine network of North Africa, held in Ibrahim Corchia Square, Ashdod and organized by Meir Knafo, the organization's president.[25]

It was after this event that I started thinking seriously about finding a professional film-maker who might be interested in making a documentary on Operation Mural. I raised the matter with Gad when visiting him at Kibbutz Regavim during our summer visit in 2006, and he had the genial idea of contacting an old kibbutz friend, Yehuda Kaveh, who had become a documentary filmmaker for Israel's Channel 1. He called me immediately and we mutually agreed on a scenario that he would prepare after I had provided him with all the necessary documentation. He came over to meet me at the home of our friends Prof. and Mrs. Raphi Israeli in their picturesque home at Ein Kerem near Jerusalem, and thanks to Raphi a contract was put together very quickly and signed. Never could I have imagined then that all would be fixed so quickly—I've never worked so hard and so fast on providing material—and that another contract would soon be signed with Ronit Dor, a top Israeli producer, and the two of them would then organize the project very quickly. In September, they came to Geneva for a several days of filming sessions with us; in October we were in Morocco for more filming; and in November other Israeli witnesses, who had not been able to join us in Casablanca, were interviewed.

David G. Littman receiving the Misgeret Award from
the Minister of Defense Shaul Mofaz, Ashdod, January 13, 2004

CHAPTER 5

The Return to Morocco
Forty-five Years Later (2006)

The return to Morocco after forty-five years was an adventure in itself. It had to be prepared very carefully by the film producer, Ronit Dor, as a tourist excursion with a "normal" Israeli group of tourists touring Morocco with Shimon Amir, our special guide. I met the group which of course included Gad Shahar ("Georges") and Pinhas Katsir ("Jacques") at Milan Airport and from there we continued, arriving in Casablanca airport which I had left in haste on July 24 1961 with our last convoy of eighty-three children. The return to Morocco with "Georges" and "Jacques," and this time with my daughter Ariane, was indeed a dramatic moment. I put aside any thoughts that we would be arrested after such a long period, but there remained the concern whether or not we could succeed in making a clandestine film with professional equipment, acting as a normal Israeli tourist group. In fact, Ariane and I were once followed by a policeman dressed in civilian clothes in the souk of Casablanca as the two of us were strolling, taking a short break from the group which was always flanked by two Moroccan armed guards. He stopped us and asked if she had official authorization to use her two professional cameras. Later in the afternoon, the police called our guide who arranged everything. I can't imagine what would have happened if we would have been asked to hand over the material we were filming without official authorization, telling the story of the clandestine Operation of 1961, and with three ex-Mossad agents travelling freely through the

The "tourists" in front of the Royal Palace in Casablanca during the making of the film *Operation Mural, Casablanca 1961*, October 2006: bottom first row, left to right: Director: Yehuda and Dalia Kaveh, Shimon Amir, Paul Fenton, second row: Gad Shahar, Ronit Dor, Ariane Littman, Orna Raz, top third row: Ram Li-Tal, Pinhas Katsir, David Littman, Nella Cassouto

streets of Morocco recalling past memories. The visits to the Don Camillo restaurant with "Georges," where we first met on March 26, 1961, was a moving moment, and the Sunday attendance in St. John's Anglican Church at Casablanca—filmed with the approval of the pastor—brought back vivid memories. The same emotion welled up in me with visits to our Casablanca office—105 rue Dumont d'Urville—and to the main post office where my wallet was stolen and handed back to me by the police in a providential moment on June 17, 1961. I strolled with Gad and Pinhas through the colourful Main Square of Casablanca, remembering the buses waiting to take the children on their journey to their Swiss holidays and walked along the Casablanca Corniche where I drove frequently in my green Renault-Dauphine to meet my contact "Georges" and where I had my extraordinary

David G. Littman and Pinhas Katsir
arriving in Casablanca, October 2006

David G. Littman with Gad, alias "Georges" and Pinhas, alias "Jacques" on the Place
Mohamed V in Casablanca during the filming of *Operation Mural*, October 2006

David G. Littman in the Main Square of Casablanca in 2006 showing a picture of parents and children at that same square in 1961

David G. Littman in front of the OSSEAN's office, rue Dumont d'Urville, Casablanca, 2006, with director Yehuda Kaveh and cinematographer Ram Li-Tal

Gad Shahar recalling his first meeting with David G. Littman
in the restaurant Don Camillo in Casablanca in 1961

meeting with Alex Gattmon on the eve of my departure with the last convoy of eighty-three children on July 24, 1961. On this travel through Morocco, from Casablanca to Tangiers, to Fez and through the Middle Atlas mountains down to Marrakesh, the question constantly arose in my mind: Would we succeed in producing a fine documentary film depicting that page in Israel's history and drink champagne on our departure as I had done on the plane that brought me safely back to Gisèle and Diana on July 24, 1961.

The documentary was surprisingly completed in a very short period. In May 2007, producer Ronit Dor organized a special premier of *Operation Mural: Casablanca 1961* in May 2007 at the Tel Aviv Cinematèque where over 350 persons participated, including all those involved in some way, old friends and relatives and about sixty ranking officers from the Israeli army invited by Major Yamin Kaanan—who himself appeared in the documentary with a vivid personal interview of his account of the clandestine aliyah in 1961, being a seven year old boy at the time. After the film was received with much applause, my wife and I were called to the podium where we received an unexpected standing ovation for several minutes. The film was much appreciated and its story too. This was the beginning of its success in several Jewish festivals in Israel and worldwide, and especially on Israel Broadcasting Authority's Channel 1, where it was first aired on December 19, 2007 and three times again, the last in summer 2010. It was also screened on French Canadian Television in March 2009.

Cover of the documentary: *Operation Mural, Casablanca 1961,*

directed by Yehuda Kaveh and produced by Ronit Dor, 2007

CHAPTER 6

From the Presidential Residence to the Intelligence Center in Glilot (2008-2009)

This public recognition of Operation Mural motivated Shmuel Toledano—without any prompting from me—to contact President Shimon Peres' secretary with the suggestion that the time had come for a presidential commemoration. Several months later the Mossad gave its OK and a special event took place at the presidential residence on June 1, 2008 in the presence of my spouse Gisele, our daughters and granddaughters, my friends Shmuel Toledano, Carmit Gattmon, Gad Shahar "Georges," Pinhas Katsir "Jacques," Miriam Korshia, Colonel Yamin Ka'anan (one of the "children") as well as the Swiss ambassador, Walter Haffner. I addressed in my speech the conciliatory role of Switzerland which the Ambassador acknowledged: "As an Ambassador of Switzerland I also pay tribute to those in the Swiss administration, who turned a blind eye, as Mr. Littman rightly put it, to Operation Mural, implicitly understanding at a certain moment, that the true goal of the operation was not a vacation in Switzerland but emigration to Israel. By issuing visas to some 500 children they contributed in their small way to the success of this wonderful operation . . ."[26] The whole event was filmed and photographed.[27] I was particularly moved by President Peres' words:

Well, it is a belated ceremony, but it doesn't lose its value, because what you did stands on its own legs and is not affected by time. I think that the saving of 530 children is, I imagine, the most moving experience a man can have. You say in Hebrew: 'The one who saves one life is like the one that saved the life of the whole world.' But when you save 530 children it's really unforgettable. I want to express, on behalf of our people, our nation, our recognition of your courage, your wisdom, of your determination under extremely difficult conditions at a time when our connections [in Morocco] were extremely weak. And I must say, whenever I read again the story, I am moved to see the ingenuity and the courage that you have shown, and the results. So, thanks to it we have 530 people, families, children alive and it's unique because in North Africa our connections were even weaker than in Europe, and the ground was less known. And, I think, if you wouldn't do it, it wouldn't be done. In order to do it, you were in touch with the Mossad and I wish to express the appreciation of the Mossad for all the performance, your activities, under cover, and successful result . . . It's for me a pleasure to have your families, the children, the grandchildren . . .[28]

David G. Littman listening to President Shimon Peres
at the Presidential Residence in Jerusalem, June 1, 2008

President Shimon Peres with David and Gisele Littman
together with Diana Littman and Elisabeth Wieder, June 1, 2008

President Shimon Peres with David G. Littman and his granddaughters,
Kalia-Gisèle, Tair-Délia and Daphnée-Cécile (from left to right), June 1, 2008

David G. Littman holding the "Hero of Silence" Order award,
to his left: Efraim Halevy, chairman of the MLM/IICC, Glilot, July 1, 2009

A year later, on July 1, 2009, The Israel Intelligence and Communications Center (MLM) awarded me the "Hero of Silence" Order, "an order of highest esteem and appreciation." Efraim Halevy, chairman of the MLM/ IICC acknowledged on this moving occasion the importance of Mural, a rescue operation, which "took place on the background of a crisis which had its origin in the entire operation of bringing the Jews out of Morocco."[29] While listening to Mr. Efraim Halevy speaking of "the solidarity of the people of Israel thoughout the world," I realized that by volunteering to bring Jewish children out from Morocco to Israel, via Switzerland, I had, together with my wife Gisèle and all the courageous people involved in Operation Mural, fullfilled the wish I committed to forty-eight years earlier: "to do something for The Jewish People, for Israel." It was an exhilarating moment which like our Casablanca mission will remain indelibly in our minds.[30]

Postscript

In spring 2011, the British Broadcasting Corporation (BBC) contacted me for a radio interview. Although serious health problems then occupied much of my mind and my time, I agreed to their unexpected proposal for a nine-minute "Witness" program on Operation Mural, which was then broadcast worldwide on July 22, 2011 and subsequent days during the next week—exactly fifty years after my hasty departure from Casablanca.

Ultimately, it was my daughter Ariane, in her mother's womb when we left Casablanca on July 24, 1961 and by my side in Morocco during the filming of *Operation Mural* (2006)—who, during a family visit in the summer of 2011, persuaded me that it was now the time to work seriously on my personal narrative. As she read through my 1961 Report and my correspondences with Mrs. Lehmann (Aïda Schirmann) of the OSSEAN's office in Geneva and others, she became even more involved in the story. Choosing a large quantity of original documents and photographs, she helped me greatly over the next months to put together this present book.

Notes

1   Fig. 64: Letter from Moshe Kol, Head of the Youth Aliyah Department, to D. Littman, August 12, 1962.

2   "Il y a 20 ans: la tragedie du Piscès" by Charlie Sutton, to which I replied, signing it "Mural," both published in *La Tribune Juive*, Paris, no. 654, Jan. 9–15, and no. 659, Feb. 13–19, 1981.

3   "Egoz victims laid to rest" by Bill Hutman, *Jerusalem Post International Edition* (weekly), December 26, 1992.

4   Fig. 65: Letter from Moshe Kol, Head of the Youth Aliyah Department, to D. Littman, December 9, 1981.

5   Fig. 66: Letter from D. Littman to Moshe Kol, Head of the Youth Aliyah Department, December 21, 1981.

6   Fig. 67: Letter from Moshe Kol, Head of the Youth Aliyah Department, to D. Littman, December 30, 1981.

7   Fig. 63: Letter from D. Littman to Moshe Kol, Head of the Youth Aliyah Department, July 4, 1962, Fig. 64: Letter from Moshe Kol, Head of the Youth Aliyah Department, to D. Littman, August 12, 1962 and Fig. 68: Letter from D. Littman to Moshe Kol, Head of the Youth Aliyah Department, January 18, 1982.

8   *Operation "Yakhin" The Secret Immigration of Moroccan Jews to Israel*, Ministry of Defence Publishing House, April 1984, Cf. pp. 216–233. Articles also appeared in *Libération*, April 17, 1984, and especially *Le Monde* (May 16, 1984).

9   Fig. 69: Article in Hebrew by Shmuel Segev published in *Maariv*, April 20, 1984.

10   Fig. 71: Letter from D. Littman to Gershom Shoken, Editor-in-Chief of *Haarez*, May 28, 1984.

11   Fig. 70: Article in Hebrew by Moshe Kol in *Haarez*, May 16, 1984.

12   Fig. 71: Letter from D. Littman to Gershom Shoken, Editor-in-Chief of *Haarez*, May 28, 1984; Fig. 72: Letter in Hebrew from Gershom Shoken, Editor-in-Chief of *Haarez*, to D. Littman, June 12, 1984; Fig. 73: Letter from D. Littman to Gershom Shoken, Editor-in-Chief of *Haarez*, July 26, 1984, and Fig. 74: Letter by D. Littman for publication in *Haarez*, July 26, 1984.

13   Fig. 75: "The Unlikely Secret Agents." Interview by Simon Griever in the first part of Shmuel Segev's article "Operation Yakhin" in *The Israel Weekly Newsview*, August 21, 1984, Vol. V, no. 33, pp. 12–18, and Fig. 76: Second part of the article "Operation Yakhin" by Shmuel Segev in *The Israel Weekly Newsview*, August 28, 1984, Vol. V, no. 34, pp. 18–21. In the English translation as in the Hebrew article, except for my name, all the names of the people involved in the mission were changed for security reasons, see note 95, op.cit.

14   "Operation Mural: Mission to Morocco (March 16–July 24, 1961)" by David Littman, pp. 365–425 and "Operation Mural, Parents and Children: the Separation" by Gisèle Littman (Bat Ye'or), pp. 427–432, in *Shorashim Bamizra'h* (Roots in the Orient), Vol. I. Editor: Itshak Avrahami, Edition Hakibbutz Hameuchad: Yad Tabenkin, 1986. (First Compilation published by the Institute for Research on Zionism and pioneers from Oriental Countries.)

15   Fig. 77: Letter from D. Littman to Naphtali Bar-Giora, December 31, 1985.

16   Fig. 78: Speech delivered by D. Littman at the Sacher Park on May 1, 1986; Fig. 79: Certificate of Gratitude (with French translation) awarded in 1986 by the Beyahad organization to David Littman and Gisèle Littman (Bat Ye'or).

17   Fig. 80: Speech in French by D. Littman to the "Children" and their families delivered in Tel Aviv on May 14, 1986, Tel Aviv.

18   Fig. 81: "A Thousand and One Nights" by Zvi Gilat, *Hadashot*, May 9, 1986, interviews in Hebrew with David and Gisèle Littman, Gad Shahar and David Bar Sheshat, pp.25–29; Fig. 82: Articles in Hebrew in *Maariv* and *Hadashot*, Mai 15, 1986.

19   The name "Hilsfund" first appears in the book of Shmuel Segev *Operation Yakhin* (1984) when for security reasons, the Mossad asked Seguev to use fictive names. Over the years these fictive names reappeared in the press, in articles and in books.

20   Fig. 83: "An Englishman to the Rescue," by Abraham Rabinovitch, *The Jerusalem Post*,

May 9, 1986 republished in *The Jerusalem Post. Int. Edition* as "The Mission," May 24, 1986, Fig. 84: "First reunion for children smuggled out of Morocco in 1961" by Michal Yudelman, May 9, 1986 and Fig. 85: Letter from D. Littman to the Editor of *The Jerusalem Post*, June 9, 1986.

21 Fig. 86: Simon Griver, "Mission to Morocco," *The Jewish Chronicle*, October 9, 1987. Unlike his previous interview in 1984, published in *The Israel Weekly* Newsview, this time Griver gives the real name of the Jewish organisation OSE and not the fictive one "Hilsfund" used by Segev in 1984 on the order of the Mossad and re-used in later publications including the book by Meir Knafo, *The Jewish Clandestine Activity in Morocco, The Misgeret and it's Secret Operations (1955–1964)* published in 2001.

22 Shmuel Segev in the chapter on Mural in his new book, *The Moroccan Connection, The secret ties between Israel and Morocco*, Matar Publishing House (2008), gives the genuine names of the people involved in Operation Mural but omits the July 9 departure of 85 children to Israel before the end of the Operation, an incident he had mentioned in his previous book *Operation Yakhin* (1984).

23 In the column of the Casablanca daily newspaper, I expressed my hope that this enduring relationship between Morocco and Israel serve as an example to other countries and an encouragement to negotiators, as well as a reminder to all that despite difficulties, reconciliation can be achieved. See "L'Agent Secret Humanitaire" by Xavier Cornut, *Le Soir-Échos*, March 23–26, 2009 and "The Moroccan Connection" in *The Jerusalem Post*, June 22, 2009.

24 Fig. 87: Certificate of recognition to David Gerald Littman signed by Meir Knafo, President of the Organization of the Clandestine Network of North Africa (*The Misgeret*).

25 During this event in the presence of family, dignitaries and friends, I described how I came to be involved in Operation Mural forty-three years earlier. One might ask, I said, how parents could accept to put as many as four of their children into the hands of an organization, supposedly non-Jewish, for "Swiss holidays," without being sure of seeing them again. And how can one explain that extraordinary love of Zion? A moving passage from Jeremiah [31:8-9] explains well that élan of the North African Jews, whose courage and dignity in the face of adversity had so inspired us (English translation of my address (in French) at Beit Lavron, January 13, 2004).

26 Fig. 89: Speech by D.G. Littman at the Presidential Residence, June 1, 2008: "At this truly memorable moment, I also wish to state—in the presence of the distinguished Swiss Ambassador Walter Haffner—that this Moroccan page of Israel's heroic history

occurred as a result of the diplomatic discretion of the Swiss authorities, who turned a blind eye to what might have become a potential exodus of Jewish children from Morocco to Israel via Switzerland, and implicitly accepted mass collective passport and Swiss visa facilities. This is now confirmed by the documents I received three months ago from the Federal Archives in Bern, thanks to the gracious initiative of the Tel Aviv Swiss Embassy. Fig. 90: Speech by the Swiss Ambassador Walter Haffner during the private reception for Mr. & Mrs. Littman to commemorate Operation Mural at the President Residence, June 1, 2008.

27 The whole event was graciously filmed by Rami Lital, cameraman of Israel Broadcasting Company Channel 1, who had filmed *Operation Mural: Casablanca 1961* (2006). A 14 minute DVD was later made by Ronit Dor, the producer and was put on a Swiss blog (drzz).

28 Fig. 88: Verbatim recording of President Shimon Peres during the private reception to commemorate Operation Mural at the Presidential Residence, June 1, 2008.

29 Fig. 91: Certificate of the "Hero of Silence" Order with its translation in English; Fig. 92: Verbatim transcript of Efraim Halevy presentation as recorded on July 1, 2009, at the Israel Intelligence' Heritage & Commemoration Center in Glilot.

30 Fig. 93: Address by D.G. Littman at the Israel Intelligence' Heritage & Commemoration Center in Glilot, July 1, 2009.

Part III

Parents and Children: The Separation[1]

Gisèle Littman

I remember those winter mornings, the mountains at dawn awash in warm pink light. Rocking my newborn daughter in my arms, glowing with happiness, I asked myself how I would express my gratitude for the gift of motherhood. December 1960: we were living in Lausanne. Only three years before, I had left my native Egypt in the mass exodus that uprooted the entire Jewish community. In London I experienced the hardships and anguish of a stateless, destitute refugee. And suddenly my life changed; my marriage and the birth of our first child filled me with bountiful joy. This gift of life created a moral obligation that I would have to fulfill. But how would I show my gratitude, and to whom? I sought and did not find an answer. But I sensed that I would be called to make an effort corresponding to the privileges bestowed on me. It was like an appointment with the future. I knew that the opportunity to pay my debt would arise sooner or later. Would I be up to the challenge? I waited, vigilant for the occasion. And every morning the deep pink light dawning on the horizon renewed my commitment, the oath carried by my newborn daughter.

One day early in February my husband announced: "I've been asked to go to Morocco to help with the secret emigration of Jewish children to Israel. It may be dangerous. But everything should work out all right." He explained the mission and we discussed it at length.

It was the first time I had ever heard about Moroccan Jews. And Israel?

I'd never been there. As a Jewish refugee from Egypt I could easily weigh the dangers involved in going back to an Arab country to take part in a secret Zionist operation. After living in Europe for three years I was just beginning to understand the meaning of "freedom." The non-existent personality imposed on me in Egypt, which was an essential survival mechanism of Jews in Arab countries, still stuck to my skin. But I knew that my mind was already made up. The decision had been forged, in spite of myself, in that dawn light that called to me and prepared me—a contented young mother—to go and face the risk of prison in an Arab country for the sake of a people and a country I didn't know. And I didn't even consider myself Jewish; I was a universalist.

Now I had to decide if I should take my daughter with me or leave her behind for several months. The thought of interrupting the powerful bond of love that had grown between us was too painful; I could not sacrifice my wonderful new happiness. My husband and I decided we would go together, all three of us, and that we would not ask for any financial compensation for our part in the mission.

We left Lausanne for London where I stayed with my daughter in my parents' house while my husband went first to Paris and then to Casablanca. We planned that I would join him a little later without our baby, so that we would have time to travel, make social contacts and get organized.

At the end of March, we settled in Casablanca where I assisted my husband in his work while at home gave a convincing image of a normal Christian couple, cheerful, sporty, and sociable. It was easy for me to go back to my familiar Egyptian habits. I could sense someone following me without turning around to look; I was constantly wary and alert; I could keep secrets, detect danger in the air, protect myself on all sides with the invisible armor developed by the survival instinct of Jews in Arab countries. I realized that my husband, who was born in London and lived in a democracy, could be careless and because of my experience as a Jew from an Arab country I could advice him.

At the start of the mission we spent a week touring the country, visiting institutions and meeting some leaders of various communities. They took us—at least officially—for a British Christian couple who had come to Morocco to organize children's vacation camps. Our conversations with Jews were neutral, apolitical but their attitude shocked me. Having lived three years in a European democracy my eyes were opened. In them I recognized the person I had been in Egypt: muzzled and deprived of my identity. They existed in an invisible prison that suppresses man's liberty and dignity, a prison made of evasive silence, eloquent omissions, stifled thoughts. Other encounters with Moroccan Jews confirmed my first impression. Whatever their superficial luxury or nonchalance, these Moroccan Jews survived on a tightrope of fear within a system of spiritual destruction. Of course I too lived in fear. It clung to me day and night, forcing me to control every word I uttered. But I knew that there were lands where people are free. In fact, that was the only difference between me and these bourgeois Moroccans: I too had been a Jew of Islam, but I was now a free woman. Knowing this made me more determined to pursue my mission to save those children.

My husband brought our five month-old daughter Diana from London in early May; she suffered terribly from the heat. I watched over her closely while I organized our social life and helped my husband with his correspondence, writing his letters in French or translating them from English. Three weeks after I had joined him in Morocco I discovered I was pregnant again. Whatever might threaten me now also threatened the child I was carrying. Anything that physically harmed me would also harm the new life growing inside of me. I was haunted by visions of danger for my child, chilling ordeals, interrogations, sadistic treatment common to prisons in Egypt, Iraq, Syria and all the other countries where Zionism is punishable by death. But what was the use of tormenting myself, I had made a binding oath and I would respect it to the very end.

I played a secondary role, assisting my husband. I made our cover convincing by acting in a normal carefree manner, spending mornings taking care of my daughter, and helping in the office during afternoons. My husband would give me his correspondence, we'd discuss different matters, and then I would translate the letters into French and go to the office to type them. It was only later in June that I saw them . . . the parents of the future "vacationers." At first I only saw the fathers. They started coming to the office, dressed in worn, patched, long *jellabas*, often black, with black caps and *babouches,* and registered their children for "holiday camp." For security reasons the "contact" had told them that my husband and I knew nothing of their ultimate destination. They were forbidden to mention it to us, and scrupulously respected the rule. I went to the office most afternoons to receive them. I knew they would come, I waited for them. They would walk in, silent and solemn, register their children, sign—sometimes with a thumbprint—pay for the "vacation in Switzerland," and then leave. We spoke no more than what was strictly necessary. I displayed the normal attitude of an employee doing an ordinary job, unconcerned by this "unexpected" flow of Moroccan Jews in our office.

It took me time to understand the quality of their gaze, the density of their silence, the solemnity that ennobled them despite their worn clothes. I would think of these fathers when I was giving my daughter her bottle, when I could feel the stirrings of the life within me; fathers who were willing, for the love of Israel and freedom, to separate from their children under dangerous conditions. How many family discussions, how much anguish, how many tears and sacrifices were contained in the mute appearance of the father on the threshold of the office? We exchanged just a few words, did not let our eyes meet. I did not want to see the apprehension that I was not allowed to calm, or encourage the questions on the tips of their tongues that I would harshly interrupt. But I will never forget the dense look in their eyes before they bent over the desk and committed themselves by a hesitant signature or thumbprint to allow one, two, three or four of their children to leave for Switzerland and from there to Israel, their hearts stung by the secret fear of an accident or a final separation. I remember the fear in the eyes of one father who timidly sought a reassuring smile on my face as he dared to whisper to me, "They are really going to Israel, aren't they?"

I scolded him harshly. The office was crowded with adults, strangers, talkative children and I had accumulated enough mistrust in Egypt for a thousand lives.

In the late night hours when I would be waiting for my husband in our Anfa studio apartment without a telephone, I would remember this father. My daughter was sleeping in her crib and another was taking shape within me. What would happen to my babies if the police arrested my husband and took me away with him? I was so worried about my children and I thought of those parents, those humble people who took on such dangers to fulfill the millennial dream of a return to Zion.

As the date for departures approached they came in greater numbers, hurried. After giving the French babysitter strict instructions for my daughter's bottles and meals and diapers and clothes, reminding her to carefully disinfect everything, I would go to the office. I would see them from a distance at the bottom of rue Dumont d'Urville still deserted in the intense midday heat. I could recognize them at a glance in their shapeless *jellabas*, in the slow heavy steps that led them to a goal they both feared and desired. Sometimes I found them already sitting silently and patiently on the doorstep. Some looked at me warily and others quizzically, searching my expressionless face for a glimmer of reassurance. Who was I behind my stern mask? What about the foreign organization that employed me, which was a total mystery to them; what would the organization do with their children? If there would be the slightest hitch where would these poor people go to find their children? Who could they ask when the danger was so great that it imposed silence and secrecy?

I unlocked the office door and opened it; they walked in from a long line, signed, paid, and then left. There was no communication between us. And yet I had come for them, for these Jews whose very existence was unknown to me just a few months ago. Their mute, humble moral force, clothed in worn garments, forced my admiration. Our common purpose, the rescue of children, created a silent secret fraternity with these strangers whose capacity for hope and courage was palpable. These fathers were giving their children, the most precious family possession, to Israel for a new life, new freedom. I never saw happiness or insouciance on their faces, but I discerned the solemn force, the anguished sadness of the tragic episodes of the Jewish condition. Theoretically, the operation would go off without a hitch, but parents and agents knew nothing about negotiations at the "summit"; all they knew was the concrete reality: they were involved in a secret illegal Zionist operation in an Arab country. For the parents to allow their children to leave and for the agents to work, they had to trust in the intelligence and ingenuity of the leadership . . . and hope the operation would succeed. The parents who came to sign up had deliberately chosen to reject doubt and opt for faith in the future.

But there was something more in the simple gesture of signing up. The children who were leaving would eventually be followed by the parents; an entire community would be uprooted, a departure with no return, abandoning ancient synagogues, venerated cemeteries, households bustling with memories of defunct generations. Their move would bring an end to two thousand years of history and open the way to a new life. I was observing them standing before me at the very moment when, silently, they tore themselves away from the past, feeling all the pain and anguish of a death so as to welcome the rebirth in Zion—so that the children would be liberated—so that the children would be purified of exile.

I had seen the fathers in the office; the children's departure showed me the mothers. With my husband and the escorts who had come from Switzerland, I waited for the "vacationers" near the buses that would take them to the port or the plane. The "contact" had warned us that members of the underground organization and plainclothes Moroccan policemen might be mingling with the crowd. The families arrived, fathers, mothers, holding the children by the hand. The worn clothing of the parents spoke eloquently of the sacrifices they had made to dress the children in their very best. They stood near the bus, silently kissed goodbye, no outbursts of emotion, no laughter. Then, without a word, the children boarded the buses and quietly took their seats.

The women were heavy from multiple pregnancies, they wore kerchiefs on their heads and nondescript cotton skirts. They looked straight ahead, dismayed, their eyelids reddened and swollen; but the tears did not flow. People walking by turned to look at us. You don't cry when your children are leaving "for a vacation in Switzerland" and their laughter will brighten the house again in just a few weeks. You cry if, taking a chance on freedom, you let the children go off to the unknown, having no idea of what they will find at the other end of the journey, no idea of who will take care of them or how. You cry when you yourself are the prisoner of a state; when you tremble at the thought that you might be unable to leave despite reassuring promises. You cry when you know that the children's bright laughter has deserted forever the home where you will be left behind.

I will never forget the expressions on their faces . . . the parents looking at the children, the children looking at the parents as the doors close,
the motor hums, and the bus pulls away. Hands wave, eyes meet. Silence.
Not a single tear. The bus disappears around the corner, the parents seem
petrified, as if they still don't believe the children are gone . . . and won't
be coming back. As if they dread going back to the empty house. No tears.
Groups break apart with plodding haste. They had arrived in big families,
they disperse in solitary couples walking away with shoulders bent, head
down, and sometimes a fleeting gesture of consolation from the father to
the mother. Going back to an emptied household they would live with a
mixture of anxiety and expectation for another liberating departure.

The children had kept the secret! Not a gesture, not a tear betrayed
them. Here and there a conspiratorial smile, a radiant expression effaced
the solemnity on childish faces, sole indication of the wonderful secret they
shared. They were leaving for Israel, the land of their dreams, the land they
loved. You could feel them balancing between laughter and tears, not daring to burst out in laughter not daring to cry, uplifted by radiant happiness
and heavy with the sorrow of secret adieux.

For the sake of those children I would sometimes go to the home of
Madame Tordjman on the eve of a departure. I would bring my baby, sleeping soundly in the straw basket that I'd fitted out with a ruffled cotton lining
and used to carry her around in Morocco. Mme. Tordjman would have all
the ingredients ready in advance. She told me, "I know those children; they
would die of hunger before they would eat anything that is not kosher. The
older ones will watch out for the younger ones." We would work together
until one or two in the morning, making kosher sandwiches for the children,
the very same children I threw out of my office when they made careless
compromising remarks while Muhammed, the young Moroccan assistant
employed part time by my husband, was within earshot.

Towards the end of our mission the pace of departures accelerated and
the groups were larger. I often had to stay in the office until daybreak to
finish the paperwork. Working with my husband and Muhammed I filled
out forms in French and prepared the collective passports forms. When my
husband had to go out unexpectedly or answer the phone I always stayed in

the same room as Muhammed and discreetly surveyed him, ready to take his attention in the case of a compromising incident. It happened more than once that a careless remark from the parents, the children, or a temporary escort would endanger our security and the success of the operation.

I left Morocco in haste with my daughter on July 22, 1961. My husband was en route for Tangiers with the fourth convoy of children and hoped to leave in two days with the last group of eighty-three "vacationing" children, bringing the total to 530. It was one thing to come into Morocco and another to leave after four months of collaboration with an underground Zionist emigration network. Would the airport police let me go? Mme. Tordjman took me to the airport. I remember how I chatted and laughed with her, pretending to be carefree as I waited for my flight, loaded down with a baby, a bathtub, bottles, diapers, bags and a fetus already wriggling in my womb. I made a long stopover in Paris where I saw "Georges," our first contact in Casablanca. It was strange to find each other again and suddenly be able to speak freely in public, without having to hide, without being on our guard. I had returned to freedom in Europe.

A few days later my husband joined me in the south of England, at the Palace Court Hotel in Bournemouth. We rested for a few weeks and then went back to register at the University of Geneva and resume our life as students. But I often thought about those young people I knew only by their faces and code names who were still working in Morocco. We came from different backgrounds, had different motivations, and we joined together—parents, volunteers, children—to give the best of ourselves for a purpose that went beyond our selfish personal needs: to bring out the children whose parents would follow them soon after. I did not know that the future reserved other commitments for me, because every day the light that dawns waits for you . . . It is there . . .

If I have the audacity to offer this testimony it is because I am convinced that my daughter played a decisive role in the mission we accomplished. If it had not been for her I would not have gone to Morocco and I would have tried to persuade my husband not to go. If we hadn't gone there together, all three of us, the operation would still have taken place but it would have been different, whether successful or not. Effaced in my insignificant role and, thanks to my daughter, endowed with a mother's heightened sensitivity, I could understand the dramatic situation of those parents in a way that may have escaped those who assumed the heaviest responsibilities and dangers in action. My daughter will never read these lines, will never know this story. Her mental handicap was not identified until a year after the mission. I didn't know it then . . . but she had assumed, from the day of her birth, the role given to the most humble among the humble who by their presence alone breathe into others the force to surpass themselves.

---

1   "Operation Mural Parents and Children: Separation" by Gisèle Littman (Bat Ye'or), in *Shorashim Bamizra'h* (*Roots in the Orient*), Vol. I. Editor: Itshak Avrahami, Edition Hakibbutz Hameuchad: Yad Tabenkin, 1986, pp. 427–432 (First Compilation published by the Institute for Research on Zionism and pioneers from Oriental Countries).

A Thousand and One Nights:
The Story of David Bar-Sheshat[1]

Zvi Gilat

In Ashdod lives David Bar-Sheshat, who left Morocco from Casablanca on July 10, 1961, clutching his two small brothers Nissim and Yitzhak by the hand. They were told they were going to Texas. He was eleven at the time.

Bar-Sheshat registers surprise. One has to be careful nowadays. He asks me if I have a press card. He has just come home from the night shift at the Acrilan plant. His eyes are red from lack of sleep but as he gets carried away with his story his eyes begin to shine.

"It all began with me. We moved to Casablanca about a year before the aliyah (immigration to Israel). We previously lived in Mogador. My father managed a sardine-canning factory. We had a magnificent home there, two stories and an Arab maid who slept in the kitchen. We were taken to school— a distance like from here to the 'A' neighborhood—on a cart by an Arab. He waited for us until lessons were over. We're nine brothers. I'm the middle one. Father was a hard man, irate, strict, always in control. Things began to deteriorate in Mogador, rumors about wanting to get rid of the Jews. Work slowed down in the sardine factory and we moved to Casablanca. Father became even more short-tempered. The one who now took charge at home was Mother, a very clever woman even though she still cannot read or write to this day. We never managed to fool her about our homework. I didn't like studies and had many fights with Arabs. Together with a friend I'd sneak into billiard dens. On one occasion Charlie, the big brother of a friend of mine, told me about Eretz Israel and asked me if I wanted to go there. 'It's always hot there,' he said, 'and they always wear shorts, and the people are good and pleasant, and nobody hits you.' I got really excited about those stories. He also took me to a club where they screened films on Israel and the kibbutz for me and for some kids I didn't know. They also referred to the Shoah. I gave Charlie my answer: 'Yes I do. Speak to my mother.'

"I gave him the address. He sent someone else, perhaps to prevent blowing his cover. Mother never said a word about it to me. In the meantime more and more people visited my mother and apparently someone else also spoke to my two brothers. The three of us slept in the same room but never exchanged words between us on the subject because we'd been sworn to secrecy. Finally, one day Mother closed the door of the room and told us she'd conversed with certain people and wanted to send us to Israel. 'There's a summer camp taking children to Texas,' she said. Both she and Father would join us later. We'd go on ahead by air and wait for them there, without breathing a word in the meantime to anyone. Not even to Father, because he was against it. We heard them later quarrelling. He: 'Why are you selling your heart for money?' He obviously didn't believe her and didn't believe in Texas. He thought it sounded not kosher. And she, appealing to his heart: 'Your father's there, your first-born son's gone already, and we too should be going. All's not well here. We'll arrive in Israel in three weeks' time, and then we'll have a home there.' Father wasn't convinced, but couldn't refuse her. I saw someone arrive at night and give her a gold bracelet. She wore it for a few days and later appeared with a wad of money, as though she'd sold it. Today I know it was all a put-on. In the meantime she quietly began to prepare things for us. She sewed blue-and-white pajamas and gave us money to buy shorts. We prepared suitcases, as if we were going to a summer camp.

"Then one day they told us we'd be leaving the following morning. Early at one o'clock Mother took us to another house to avoid the neighbors noticing. A taxi came at eight o'clock and took Mother and us to the airport. Father didn't come. He was annoyed. They dressed us in blue trousers, white shirts and peaked caps, like for a celebration. Mother told me, 'Look after your brothers and never separate from each other. Yitzhak has a sore ear and see he gets treated. And don't forget—you're going to Texas. You'll see cowboys and wild animals there. Wait for us, we'll join you in three weeks, and we'll all go together to Israel. But don't mention Israel.' Perhaps they promised she'd join us. Perhaps they just told her to say that.

"At the airport I was amazed. Dozens of taxis. I suddenly see kids from my school. Most of them I know. Are they all going to Texas? Yes, and they all have suitcases. Everything so well planned. And someone suddenly turns up and hands Mother passports, which she signs and gives them to someone in authority, and I hold on to my two brothers and say: 'Stay close by me.' We were a little sorry to be leaving home, but for us it was like going to a summer camp and enjoying ourselves, and the first time in a plane, too.

"In the plane, in the air, there was a brawny man who spoke to us in Hebrew, the kind we learned in Talmud Torah. He told us: 'We're flying to France and from there we change planes and fly to Texas. You'll all be tired so go to sleep. Don't worry. We'll look after you.' We landed in Lyons in the evening. Half asleep we were loaded onto busses that got going. We're not changing planes, but everyone's drowsy. Several young men and women in the bus calmed those who were frightened. So far it's just an outing, what's there to be frightened about?

"In the morning, we found ourselves surrounded by trees in a large wooden house. They told us the place was called Switzerland. What Texas? What Cowboys? They said there'd be a small delay and that our parents were informed. They gave us postcards to write to them and we got a reply in just two days. 'Don't worry,' wrote Father, 'we'll meet in Texas.' For some reason, he also added the address of Aharon, our eldest brother, in Lod. He wrote it in initials, and once again warned us not to get separated from each other. And I, all the time with my brothers, demanded to have Yitzhak's ear treated. A doctor saw him and gave him pills. We were served a super meal at lunchtime in a dining room, but some of the children were crying and screaming that they'd been cheated. As a result, we were all moved to a different house in the middle of a forest to prevent the other holidaymakers from hearing the noise going on. Pajamas were waiting for us on the beds at night, but we already had ours in our suitcases—the ones mother had sewn for us. We didn't want to wear strange pajamas. Perhaps we thought we shouldn't give up on anything lest the ones in charge should feel they could do whatever they wanted with us. They looked around for our suitcases all night long but couldn't find them. We finally agreed to wear their pajamas.

"This is how we spent the time there for twenty days. We played games. We went for walks in the forest. They showed us films on Israel —not on Texas. But Switzerland is also very beautiful. Until one day they assembled us and told us about a change, that we would fly straight to Israel. And wouldn't that be great with our future, our challenge, awaiting us there? They used nice comforting words and told us some parents were already there. They even gave their names. Many children were reassured. But there were some crazy boys who smashed windows, who shouted and cried, who wet their beds. They were isolated. And we are waiting. Up till then we hadn't opened our suitcases. Why open them? They only contain shorts and in Switzerland it's raining. We were given there all our clothing, beautiful new clothes.

"And one day they came in luxurious buses and took us to the airport. We were again warned to say we were going to Texas. And I and my brothers are holding hands and already know—so much for Texas. We're going to Israel."

Bar-Sheshat and his two brothers landed in Lod at the beginning of August. When he was asked where they would like to go, to a secular or to a religious youth village, David answered that he would not budge until his brother Aharon, a resident of Lod, came and decided for them. That's what his parents had ordered him to say. He was told they could not locate Aharon. He dug his heels in and insisted that he would not budge. The Aliyat Hanoar (Youth Aliyah) people tried once again to trace his brother and this time discovered that he was away doing reserve duty on Har Hatzofim (Mount Scopus). He could not get leave of absence before his thirty days were up. The young Bar-Sheshats then mentioned their grandfather, who also resided in Lod. The Jewish Agency people located him and promised the boys they would enable them to see him. David Bar-Sheshat gave in and agreed to go, with his brothers, to the Aliyat Hanoar village near Haifa.

"So much for Switzerland. So much for Texas," he says today with a smile. "It really was hot and so finally we did wear shorts; but in Haifa they gave us vegetables in battered tin bowls, the benches creaked, and the beds were not made of wood. There were no pine trees on the beach. It was no Switzerland. Many lads made a row and were obstructive. They demanded to see their parents. We remained quiet, and insisted only on one thing—we're going to Lod to see Grandfather tomorrow."

Next morning they were given railway tickets. A too-busy youth leader gave them hurried instructions how to get to the railway station in Tivon by bus. Hand-in-hand, the three Bar-Sheshat boys left the youth village taking with them their suitcases with the blue-and-white pajamas and determined not to come back.

They lost their way more than once before they got to Allenby Street in Tel Aviv. "And even though it was hot," relates David, "and we didn't have a penny, and we knew nobody, and we had been only one day in Israel, and my brother Yitzhak's ears hurt him, we nevertheless saw that what we'd been told about Israel was true. People are kind and you'll always come across someone willing to help. When a person spoke to us we simply said: 'Take us where we have to go. We don't know anyone here.' A restaurant owner in Allenby Street gave us a "transparent wurst" sandwich. You put the wurst on the bread—all its color disappears." They finally reached Lod and succeeded in locating their grandfather. He was living in a ruined Arab building, just like in Morocco. "Do you know Yosef Bar-Sheshat from Mogador?" asked the boys, holding their suitcases. "Yes," cried the old man who had never before set eyes on them, "has something bad happened to him?" "We're his children", they answered, kissing his hand. "We're your grandsons."

Father Was Mabsut (Happy)

A wonderful story. Three little Zionists who ran away from Aliyat Hanoar to a distant family, struggling with life's difficulties. With his weeping brothers shocked by the standard of life in Lod, David reminded them of the handsome buildings they had seen in Arlozorov Street near the railway station. "They'll put us up there one day," he told them. They later went to another Aliyat Hanoar village. They studied agriculture. They got to know Sabras (native born Israelis). They struck roots. They sometimes refused to go to Lod. After complaining bitterly about the food: "They put black beans on our plates and told us: 'Eat, its cholent.' You call that cholent? We remembered the pots cooking in the oven of the Arab in Mogador." After the cooks were replaced and Moroccans were brought in from Even Yehuda, they began to feel at ease. The village carpenter together with the young Moroccans organized a Kabbalat Shabat (bringing in the Sabbath ceremony), like the ones at home. Before that, the female youth instructor used to snuff out the candles immediately after they had been lit, in order to relight them the next Sabbath.

A year-and-a-half later, their parents arrived. They were dispatched to a tin-hut *ma'abara* (temporary camp) in Hatzerim. Their father, irate, blamed his children; they had cheated him. Never in his life had he endured such dreadful conditions. He refused to work and refused to speak. That was the only way left for him to protest. Their mother tried to mollify him, that selfsame mother who had sent her sons as *halutzim* (pioneers) before him. They are all in Ashdod now. Their father died eight months ago. He had rehabilitated himself and spent his last years managing a metal workshop in a plant in Ashdod. He had started as an unskilled worker but because he knew French he was the only one able to read the assembly instructions for the cutting edge machinery imported from Marseilles. His honor was restored. David is a shift foreman in the Acrilan plant; his brother Yitzhak is employed there as an electrician; Roni has a boutique in Dizengoff Center; Yolanda is married and resides in Ashdod; Aharon is in Ashdod; Albert is in Kiryat Malachi; Miriam is married and resides in Ashdod; Zion is in Ayanot. Nissim emigrated to France. He married a woman who does not want to live in Israel. "Patience," avers David Bar-Sheshat. "We'll bring them here, too. A sister of mine came on aliyah with her husband two years ago, using the same trick she learned from her mother. She sent her children to study in Israel. Her husband is still angry. He left a very good job. Never mind. He'll get over it. He'll get used to it. Just like what happened to Father. You should have seen the big fish he used to catch on Saturdays on the Ashdod sea shore. How *mabsut* he was."

---

1 Extract from the article "A Thousand and One Nights" by Zvi Gilat in *Hadashot*, May 9, 1986. (See Fig. 81).

The Old Man

Gisèle Littman

It was in the year 1986. Unexpectedly, David and I were the guests of honor at the Mimouna festival. Seated on the podium with the highest political leaders of Israel, or lost in the crowd, we discovered the multiple aspects of the Moroccan/Israeli community, with its joyful popular traditions and exuberance.

Of the Moroccan Jews we only knew the inquisitive faces of the children we anxiously rushed into the bus, surrounded by their silent and petrified parents. But this was in Morocco in 1961. Here in the Israel of 1986, the atmosphere was one of happiness and achievement. A liberation from the Galut (exile). Certainly, the Moroccan aliya felt discriminated and even rejected at times. But in Israel they could express their discontent and fight it.

I was eager to interview the parents. Many couldn't recapture nor express clearly the turmoil they had experienced in those times of confusion, pain and sorrow when they had to extract themselves out of centuries of history. Then came the years in the Ma'abarot (refugee absorption camps), with difficult climatic conditions of cold, mud and rain, unbearable heat and dehydration. They faced the challenges of learning a new language; and the training in new crafts; and the building of cities and towns in the middle of the desert; and the external combat against invading Arab armies, and internal Arab terrorism.

I was observing them, seated silently in front of me, astonished of being the subject of my interest. They never thought they were interesting people.

Strenuously they gathered their memories and spoke in the broken French they still remembered.

Among their stories I noted a particular moving one. The woman seemed to be in her sixties. I still remember her corpulent body and her absent and sad gaze while she was contemplating her past in Morocco. She recounted that after her mother had passed away, her elderly father moved into the house which she shared with her husband and numerous children. Being with his family and grandchildren nurtured the joy and happiness of his old age.

Every afternoon he would sit on a bench near the door. From there he would wait to see the children on the far away road returning home from school. His heart rejoiced while they were walking in the sun toward him.

And then one evening, while the children were sleeping, the family discussed the possibility of emigrating to Israel. Would they go? Would they stay? Jews in the surrounding villages were all leaving discreetly while around them, Muslim threatening hate was escalating. The couple decided to emigrate but the old father refused to leave Morocco. He would stay, her father declared. In the cemetery his loved ones asleep forever and all the others resting there for generations needed him. He wouldn't abandon them. This was the place where he would go and lie down, next to them.

His daughter insisted that he join them in Israel, but he remained firm in his decision. The thought of abandoning her old father, tortured her during her sleepless nights. But she knew that the children's interest required their departure toward a redemptive freedom, leaving the Galut. In vain she tried to convince her father and on the day of departure, leaving him, her home, her youth's memories, turning back toward him at the end of the road, she saw him for the last time, sitting alone on the bench.

For years, she told me, she would think of her father's loneliness in this empty house. Every afternoon she would imagine him going to sit on the bench from which he could see the road stretching far away inundated by the sun. He would wait and would wait there, but the road would remain forever empty and no children would run toward him. Until one day, he would go to lie down near his loved ones, among his own in the old cemetery he didn't want to forsake.

A Mother's Silent Distress

Interview with Rachel Sabbah

As we sit together in her living room in Jerusalem, Rachel Sabbah, an eighty-one year old widow, recalls the day the "Zionist girl who came to save the children" arrived at her apartment in Casablanca. "At first, I believed that Joseph was going on a vacation to Switzerland, later I understood that he was going to Israel."

Rachel only twenty-nine at the time, but already a mother of seven, was feeling very lonely after her parents and her siblings had left for Israel years before. "If Joseph left first, then my husband would accept to follow him," adding, "you see, Solomon did not want to leave Casablanca but I wanted very much to be close to my family."

Those thoughts did not alleviate her despair as her eldest son, Joseph aged twelve, was impatiently preparing for his trip. Her voice breaking, she recalls that fateful Saturday on July 22, 1961, when together with her husband Solomon, she accompanied Joseph to the Place des Nations Unies where all the children and the parents had gathered at dawn, waiting for the buses to pick them up.

"That Saturday was the annual fast of Tisha Be'av[1]," she remembers. And as she left the square distraught, having watched the buses driving away towards Tangiers: "I made the promise, although I was not religious, to never comb my hair on Saturdays nor to turn the lights on until I hug Joseph in my arms." And she adds: "I carry on this ritual to this day."

Solomon & Rachel Sabbah
with their three children,
Joseph, Alice and
Paulette, Casablanca, 1955

After the departure of her son, Rachel remembers that she was constantly crying; she felt ashamed to have parted from her son. She knew that he was not coming back from his Swiss holidays but she couldn't share her pain with anyone except for one neighbor, Juliette Perez who was a widow with seven children. "She sent Gaby (thirteen) and two daughters, Marcelle (eleven) and Hélène (nine)." Powerless to conceal her sadness: "I would tell my concerned neighbors that I missed my family."

Ten months after Joseph's departure, Rachel left Casablanca with Solomon, their seven children and a new baby. They went from Casablanca to Tangiers, then to Gibraltar, sailing to Spain and Italy till they reached the shores of Haifa. After their arrival in Israel, The Jewish Agency sent them to Zichron Ya'akov "because it was close to the youth village where Joseph was studying." Solomon found a job in Jerusalem and Rachel kept moving with her seven children to her parents and her brothers and sisters.

A year later she eventually left with her children for Jerusalem.

Rachel Sabbah never saw again her friend and neighbor Juliette Perez with whom she shared her pain after the departure of the children on that crucial Saturday in July 1961.

Today, when asked if she would ever send her twelve year old son, on his own, to a far-away country and without knowing if and when she would see him again, she categorically answers: "Never!"

Interview by Ariane Littman, conducted on September 10, 2013.

---

1 The fast of Tisha Be'av commemorates the destruction of the First and the Second Temple and the subsequent exile of the Jews from the Land of Israel.

Fragments of Memory

Yossi Shahar

Joseph Sabbah and his friend Gaby Perez lived on the same street and the same building at Djamaa Chleu no. 358, Casablanca.

The two boys, aged twelve and thirteen, parted from their parents on Saturday 22, July 1961. Together with 145 children from the fourth convoy, they sailed from Tangiers to Marseilles aboard the Djene.

Landing in Israel four days later, Joseph was then sent to high school at the youth village of Meir Shfeya in Zichron Ya'akov.

Ten years later, during his second year of study at the faculty of agriculture in Rehovot, he changed his family name, meaning "morning" in Arabic, to Shahar, meaning "dawn" in Hebrew. "All my siblings followed my example except for one who chose to be named Saddot, which means "fields" in Hebrew."

Yossi Shahar and his wife Jacqueline have been living in Maccabim for the past twenty-two years. They have four children and six grandchildren. Yossi travels the world in his capacity of head agronomist for the Israeli company Pelemix Ltd., a company that has worldwide activities in the production and marketing of fibers from the coconut tree.

Yossi Shahar recounts here the story of this departure from Casablanca to Israel, more than fifty years later.

"We had just reached the entrance to the house after a routine school day when my friend Gaby Perez and I were met by a young woman who asked us for directions to the Perez family.

"I accompanied him, apparently out of idle curiosity, as he took her up to his parents' home. It turned out that she had come expressly for the purpose of registering Gaby and his sister for a summer camp in Switzerland, i.e., aliyah to Israel. I don't remember the details of the conversation at the time but I do remember asking her there and then to register me as well.

"The woman, who years later I learned was only in her twenties, wanted first to meet my parents, who lived two stories below in the same building. I told her that since there was no way my father would willingly agree to register me she should register me first and try to get my parents' consent later.

"Another fragmented memory that comes back to me from the time of the preparations for the journey is going to a certain house in Casablanca for a medical examination. I think that we were accompanied there by that same woman.

"Getting my parents' approval about two weeks before the journey was very tough for all of us; there were scenes of crying particularly on the part of my mother, my father's defiantly stubborn refusal, and my desperate though hardly forceful efforts to explain how important it was for me to make aliyah to Israel. Many years later my mother reminded me that on that occasion I had said that the only way to convince my father to sell up his business and make aliyah to Israel (if and when they "opened the gates") was to send me ahead . . . Gaby's parents had already registered him for the journey.

"The stratagem succeeded but the atmosphere in my home was one of depression and sadness. Because I was their eldest son it was really very difficult for my parents to gauge the consequences of this step. One could easily understand their apprehension especially in view of the endless rumors coming from Israel that the "authorities" there were educating immigrant youngsters to rebel against their parents and their religion. At that stage I couldn't appreciate what was going on in my parents' mind. Only later did I hear from them about their fears that they might not see me again for years on end or perhaps even never. Israel for them was something incomprehensibly insubstantial and not only physically distant.

Piece of paper belonging to Yossi Shahar, then Joseph Sabbah, aged twelve. This paper was given to him by OSSEAN's delegate, D.G. Littman. This document states the date and the hour of Joseph Sabbah's arrival on Saturday July 22 at 6 a.m. at The United Nations Square next to the Main Central Post Office. Joseph Sabbah left on the fourth convoy from Tangiers to Marseilles on a ship from the Pacquet line.

"Despite my parents' financially comfortable situation they were given a sum of money in order to buy me a small suitcase, a pair of shoes, some clothing and a wash kit. This was a real intimation of a prospective long journey—up to that time I had never been separated from my parents for more than a few hours.

"Our ties to Israel had been on several levels. The subject had always been discussed and our father was well informed about events in Israel and regaled us children with stories about the country. I distinctly remember stories about Menachem Begin and the I.Z.L. (Etzel) as well as stories about the Kadesh and Sinai military campaigns.

"We were loosely connected to several relatives in Israel and I had been delegated to correspond with them in basic French. They sent us several postcards as well as photographs of uncles, aunts and cousins. Furthermore, one should not underestimate the importance of our relationship with them through prayer in the synagogue and study of Hebrew. My father read, wrote, and understood Hebrew and also spent some of his time engaged in what is called "practical Kabbalah" and writing amulets, so that Israel, Hebrew and Judaism were always an integral part of my life.

"My friend Gaby and I spent hours every day waiting tensely on the landing of our house for the expected letter inviting us to join the summer camp in Switzerland.

"Since we could not inform any outsiders about our secret operation even my best friend, Sami Moyal, had no inkling of the turmoil raging inside me despite the fact that we were meeting almost daily. As a result, when he came to visit me as usual in our home on the day after I had set out he was shocked to hear that I had "departed." It was only thirty one years later that after three months of intensive inquiry I traced his whereabouts in France. He told me that at first he had felt insulted by my reticence before beginning to understand and forgive. We have since renewed our friendship and see each other in France and in Israel, with each meeting full of joyful exchanges of memories. He and his family had remained for another twenty years in Casablanca before finally settling down in France. I have more than once thought that my course of life could have been similar to his and am so glad that it has turned out differently.

"On Saturday July 22, 1961, our group of boys and girls, accompanied by their parents, assembled as instructed early in the morning in The United Nations Square near the Main Central Post Office of Casablanca. We were met there by a tall man, who spoke to us for a long time in a deep voice. I don't remember a word of what he said but I clearly remember him standing beside a reception desk and talking passionately. For me, the aura was totally hallucinatory, with people crowding all around me and buses standing by, a jumble of scenes and sounds lodged in my memory.

"Farewell embraces, a tumult around the buses, tremendous excitement, clambering into our seats, and a long drive northwards to Tangiers. The drive was very long indeed. Part of the time we kept our spirits up by singing. Personally I was lost in deep thoughts which I could not control. I do not remember any fears or doubts but to a greater extent intangibles.

"We boarded a ship in the port of Tangiers and went down with our gear into the ship's hold, a large very crowded space lined with tiers of bunk beds. What I remember mostly of the voyage was the time we all spent on deck singing popular French songs as well as several vulgar youthful songs which were a revelation for me as I had never heard such things before. Apart from my friend Gaby I knew nobody else and was apparently one of the youngest kids in the group, and also a little shy. I remember the ambience during the trip to Marseilles as being spiritually a very stormy one for me. Everything was strange and new, rhythmic and riveting. I don't remember thinking about my parents or feeling homesick. Being part of a large noisy group allowed no time for ruminating about whatever could and would happen. We talked about Israel on the ship and exchanged information regarding relatives there. Several of the older youths who stood out among us during the voyage came with me to the Meir Shfeya Youth Village, but to my regret I have lost all contact with them.

"I can remember no details about my three-day stay in the camp in Marseilles. On July 26 we boarded a plane to Lod and there I clearly remember the brown building we entered and the first meal in Israel which was not to my taste. To this day, whenever I pass Ben Gurion Airport in Lod I try to identify this building, but to no avail.

"Our original large group was split in two. The group I was in was sent to the Meir Shfeya agricultural school and the other one to Ramat Hadassah. "Shock" is what I remember feeling when we reached the place called "Meir Shfeya Youth Village." To children who were born and lived in a bustling city and almost never set foot outside it, the village appeared tiny, miserable and poor. Gazing out of the windows of the bus upon arrival, the first scene that met our eyes was two young girls wearing shorts gathered with elastic at the waist and above the knees (which women customarily wore at the time for work in agriculture) with patches sewn onto the seat. The first task I was given was removing rubbish from the village on a mule-driven wooden cart. The boy I was teamed with on this task, Benjamin Moskowitz, a native of Safed, is a close friend of mine to this day and it is mainly thanks to him that I became successfully integrated in Israel. The food was different from what we had been used to, and some of the group began to complain about "conditions."

Yossi, aged twelve (on the right) with friends shortly after their arrival at the Meir Shfeya Youth Village in Israel, 1961

"Integrating the members of our group was difficult. A short while after our arrival in the village various rebellious outbursts erupted, resulting ultimately in the departure from Shfeya of most of the members of our group, with only about seven of us remaining.

"During my first year in Israel I managed to meet with relatives of both my father and my mother, most of whom I had previously not known. They were mostly Jerusalemites and I chose to stay with them whenever I was off duty every five weeks and on holidays.

"About one-and-a-half years after I arrived in Israel I received a letter from my parents, which came through undisclosed channels and in which they informed me of a new-born baby brother named Gaby. This is the only time I remember crying in the presence of my fellow "olim" and of Israelis."

Joseph Sabbah (third from the right) with friends
at the youth village Kfar Hanoar Meir Shfeya, winter 1962

The renewed meeting with my family:

"My dear friend Benjamin Moskowitz invited me to stay with him in Safed for a weekend. In that town, in the area known today as the artists quarter and which comprised at the time the ruins of abandoned Arab houses, lived another one of my mother's sisters of whom I had been unaware existed and never met before.

"During my visit to this aunt on the Sabbath eve Ben comes running up from his home and informs me that he has received a phone call from the village that my parents have arrived in Israel and have been sent to a house in Zichron Ya'akov by the Jewish Agency. It turns out that the first thing my father did when he arrived in Israel was to start looking for me. He managed to phone the village and was informed that I was in Safed.

להתראות
בארץ

Postcard from 1951 sent from Jerusalem to the family in Casablanca of a picture of Yossi's uncle Hanania (kneeling on the stairs) who emigrated to Israel and served in the Israeli army. Written in hand writing: "SEE YOU IN ISRAEL."

"I had no prior information about the arrival of my family in Israel. The contact with them had been almost nonexistent—as far as I can remember I had only received one letter from them all the while. At the same time I do not remember feeling any sorrow or yearning and perhaps life in the village had flowed so pleasantly that I was simply swept along with the flow.

"I returned to the village on Sunday morning, immediately discarded my equipment and set out on foot for Zichron Ya'akov to find my family. A glance at a map will show that I was either mad or extremely naïve. The only information I had was that they had been placed in the southern neighborhood. I didn't know where that place was. Its distance from the village was too great to cover on foot and I was totally unfamiliar with the roads. I finally managed, however, to get there and with the help of local folk I located the house.

"Knocking on the door I hear the yelling of children answering me from indoors. My siblings are on the other side of the door but it is locked and my parents are away.

"They had taken the new baby to the Kupat Holim health clinic. I scouted around the house until I found a small open toilet window, stacked a few wooden crates lying in the yard, and climbed up into the house to meet my siblings. When my parents finally arrived I was already feeling quite at home.

"The renewed meeting with my parents and siblings was very emotional. My father, who was an industrious and responsible person, began immediately to look for employment but because he had been a business man all his life it was very difficult for him to find suitable work.

"The proximity of Shfeya to Zichron Ya'akov made it much easier to renew contact between us and I took every opportunity to visit my family. My parents came to visit me in the village and were very upset to see the kind of life I was leading, which to them was so foreign. They went around in a state of shock at the sight of the simple poverty stricken village and I had to work hard to convince them that I really felt good there enjoying a full and interesting lifestyle. They were displeased that there was no religious ambience or study in the village but gradually became used to the fact that I was not living with them and that our meetings were few and far between.

"When after several months of fruitless hunting for work in Zichron

Ya'akov my father finally gave up, he moved the family to Jerusalem, where they became united to everyone's joy. This move, however, did not overcome the acclimatization difficulties that beset my parents. Like every average immigrant family mine also faced numerous obstacles, but my parents' desire to bring up their children in accordance with their simple Israeli and Zionist dream in which all their children had been brought up finally overcame all the difficulties. My father used to declare that it was better to eat bread and olives in Eretz Israel than to eat kingly delicacies in the Diaspora.

"I continued living in the village until my graduation from high school; six wonderful years of the most significant period in my life.

"In Israel two daughters were born to my parents, which endowed them with a family of ten children in all."

A Young Student in Geneva
with a Mission

Interview with Raphael Rebibo

In Morocco, Raphael Rebibo lived in the Mellah of Casablanca. He was one of the youth responsible of the 'Foyer Bialik,' the cultural center of DEJJ (Département d'Education de la Jeunesse Juive) for young Jewish adults from the Mellah, where he established an amateur theatre group which produced plays based on Biblical accounts. Rebibo left Casablanca to study at the Technicum of Geneva. In the summer of 1961, Prof. Bloch recruited him and asked him to escort the children from Lyon airport to the 'Home de la Forêt' in Morgins. In 1970 he finished the film school in Jerusalem and started a successful career, becoming a worldly acclaimed film director and producer both in Israel and in Switzerland, receiving many awards.

Rebibo recounts: "During the summer of 1961, Prof. Bloch from the OSE asked me to accompany Moroccan Jewish children, who had landed at Lyon airport in France, to their summer camp in Morgins, Switzerland. Consequently, without being aware of it, I became involved in a rescue operation of Jewish children called Operation Mural.

"After we boarded fancy buses in Lyon I had to make sure that there would be no problem crossing the border into Switzerland. These children had no individual passports, only a 'collective passport.'

"I was responsible for bringing them to the Home de la Forêt where Israeli officials responsible for the rest of the Operation awaited them. Once

Officials responsible for the Operation with the children at the Home de la Forêt, Morgins, 1961. From left to right: first row: Raphael Rebibo (kneeling); second row: Arieh Reiffler, Simcha Steuermann (housemother of the Home de la Forêt) and Aïda Schirmann, alias N. Lehmann, leaning against the parapet; third row behind Mrs. Steuermann: Mrs. Bloch, Prof. Bloch, Mrs. Reiffler and Meyer Steuermann (housefather).

arriving in Morgins, I stayed on, looking after them with other caretakers until they departed for Israel.

"At the time, I was a young student of nineteen in Geneva. I myself was a boy raised in the Mellah of Casablanca speaking fluently the language of these children. I took my mission very seriously, in fact almost as a divine mission that had to succeed at any price. This is what earned me, I believe, the friendship of David and Gisele Littman whom I both met on several occasions after the mission.

"Years went by and I became a filmmaker. This account with its numerous untold anecdotes remains vivid in my memory till this very day."

Interview by Ariane Littman, conducted in June 2014.

The Mossad Agents

Ariane Littman

Gad Shahar alias Georges Chemla, code name "Camus" while working as a Mossad agent in Morocco

"Camus"
Gad Shahar, alias Georges Chemla

Born in Tunis in 1923, Gad Shahar was active during the Second World War in clandestine Zionists activities. In 1945, he immigrated to Israel and was one of the founders, in 1949, of Kibbutz Regavim located in northern Israel. In 1960 Shahar joined the Mossad and left for Morocco as a salesman in import and export of agriculture equipment. Alias Georges Chemla, code-name "Camus." Shahar headed "Mak'hela" (Choir), the branch of the Misgeret involved with illegal immigration. During Operation Mural, he was known as "Georges," the contact between David G. Littman, the delegate of OSSEAN, and Alex Gattmon the head of the Misgeret in Morocco. After Operation Mural Shahar remained in Morocco, under a new identity, for another three years until the end of Operation Yakhin.

Gad Shahar alias Georges Chemla,
code name "Camus"

I met with Gad Shahar at his modest room in Kibbutz Regavim on September 2013. Aged ninety, he still has vivid memories of the secret vow he made when he left Tunisia in 1945. A young idealist involved in clandestine Zionist activities during the Second World War, he promised himself that if ever he was able to emigrate to Israel, he would pay his debt by coming back one day to North Africa and help Jews who wished to leave. In 1960 he gets the permission from the Kibbutz General Assembly. He successfully passes his exams and joins the ranks of the Mossad as head of the clandestine immigration section in Morocco. On December 11, 1960, he crosses the border into Morocco with a forged passport. "I'll never forget this date, as I was also born on December 11," he says to me.

Now a Belgium businessman, Shahar is in charge of the import and export of agricultural equipment, but at night he is "Camus" in charge of the clandestine departures of Jewish children. During the Christmas holidays, he organizes a holiday camp for children on the beach of the Gulf of Alhucemas on the Mediterranean coast, where children are smuggled out on boats. But one day, barely four weeks after his arrival in Morocco, the *Piscès* ("Egoz" in Hebrew)—an old RAF motor-boat carrying forty-two illegal Moroccan Jewish clandestine emigrants—sank shortly after it left the Moroccan shore near the Gulf of Alhucemas, on its way to Gibraltar, due to bad weather conditions. Among the victims were parents of the children that had left on Christmas, and twenty-four other children, an Israeli radio operator, Haim Sarfati, and a Spanish crew member. "I was one of the last persons to talk to them before their tragic disappearance," he emits pensively before pursuing, "after this disastrous event we needed to find other ways for Jews to leave Morocco."

Georges landing at the airport of Madrid on his way to discuss Operation Mural with Ephraim Ronel, head of the Misgeret at the headquarters in Paris. Taken by a photographer at the airport, Georges bought the picture and gave the other half to the Mossad, since he suspected being trailed by a Moroccan agent.

Following several meetings with his Mossad contacts in Madrid and Paris, Georges meets with Professor Bloch in Geneva where they discuss the possibility of children being sent to the Swiss Valais on a holiday. Heading "Mak'hela," one of the branches of the Misgeret in charge of clandestine immigration, Shahar receives his orders directly from his boss Alex Gattmon. Shahar, together with young Moroccan Zionists, is responsible for contacting the families in order to recruit Jewish children aged fourteen to seventeen, chosen among the poorest social strata living in the Mellah, and eager to leave Morocco out of a profound faith in the return to Zion and Jerusalem.

"It is important to understand," explains Gad Shahar, "that in Morocco the children were usually sent to work to help relieve the financial burden of these poor families. The organizers thought that if those children were sent to schools in Israel, they might stand a chance of avoiding this, even after the reunion with the parents." Shahar adds: "the motivation behind the parents' incredible decision to send their children on such a journey on their own, arose from the promise they received from the Misgeret that their names would be up-graded on the departure lists."

For Gad Shahar, Operation Mural was a completely different story, no longer a clandestine and risky mission at night on some shores along the coast, but instead the children were officially going on a vacation in Switzerland.

He recalls: "When I went to Don Camillio restaurant to meet my new contact for the first time, I was horrified. The man, I recognized by the carnation in his buttonhole and the newspaper in his hand, seemed too tall, too British and definitely too visible. At first, David was not aware of the Mossad connection. Very disciplined he meticulously executed the orders he received from me. I advised him to advertise OSSEAN's summer vacation in the newspapers and to travel throughout Morocco. He knew how to make social contacts with Moroccan dignitaries and with European upper-class society. Around the end of April, I revealed to him that he was actually working for an organization related to the "clandestine" immigration to Israel. And if at first he might have been astonished, he didn't show any reluctance, on the contrary. We organized our meetings by calls, each time from different public phone booths, working closely and on the same wavelength. "Mural" closely identified with our goals, often taking initiatives at odds with the orders from his contacts in Geneva.

"It was an ad hoc operation, an operation that would stop the very day the children would not return to Morocco at the end of their summer holidays. The system of collective passports promoted by "Mural," even though first used on a limited scale in the 1950s, was indeed a precedent that was later adopted during Operation Yakhin."

On July 14, 1961, "Georges" goes on a two week leave to Paris, three days before the departure of the third convoy. From an operational point of view, he does not feel anxious. "Mural was handling well the operation, helped by our undercover team while "Jacques" was nominated to replace me as the liaison between "Mural" and the boss, Alex Gattmon."

On July 22 at Orly airport, he meets Gisèle Littman returning with her daughter Diana from Casablanca and while she awaits her London connection at Orly airport, he reveals to her that his real name is not "Georges" but "Gad" and that he is an Israeli. She was flabbergasted.

His first "civil" meeting with "Mural" takes place at the end of July in a fancy restaurant on the Champs-Elysées. He laughs as he recalls: "I was shocked when David sent back two bottles of fine wine. But I was even more surprised when at the end of the meal the chamberlain said that it was an honor for him to serve such a wine connoisseur."

Soon after this last meeting, "Camus" is back in Morocco, where he is surprised to learn from Alex Gattmon of the secret talks with the King and of the end of all clandestine emigration. "Camus" goes back to Paris, gets a new identity and leaves for Morocco where he continued to be active for another three years until the very last day of Operation Yakhin.

"Mural" and "Georges" met every year in Israel at Kibbutz Regavim with their respective spouses, Gisèle and Ruth, the dedicated nurse of the Kibbutz. Both couples remained close friends, bound by their memories of the days of Operation Mural and by Ruth's admiration for Bat Ye'or's books.

Interview conducted in September 2013

"Armin" & "Arminette"
Alex Gattmon alias Georges Sellers
& Carmit Gattmon alias Christine Blake

Alex and Carmit Gattmon, both undercover Mossad agents, arrived in Casablanca in 1960 where Alex had been appointed head of the Misgeret ("Framework".) Working undercover, Alex, a wealthy British businessman named "Georges Sellers," was accompanied by his English mistress that went by the name of "Christine Blake."

Operation Mural was one of the numerous clandestine operations Gattmon supervised. Later, he was in charge of Operation Yakhin that brought approximately 100,000 Moroccan Jews to Israel during the years 1961–64.

In July 1981, Alex Gattmon, aged fifty-five, unexpectedly died of a heart attack while on a family vacation in Switzerland.

Alex and Carmit Gattmon in a café at the port of Mazagan,
south-east of Casablanca, after checking a possible port of evasion

I met Carmit Gattmon in Jaffa in November 2013, exactly sixty-six years after her arrival to Israel from Belgium. Facing the sea on a sunny day, she recalls with sparkling eyes, her encounter with Alex Gattmon, the handsome and tall man who would change her life forever. He was studying criminology at the University in Brussels when they first met in 1955 while she was graduating in Political Sciences.

Alex was an ex-Polish Jewish partisan who, in November 1944 aged eighteen, was saved by Soviet troops in Budapest barely two hours before being sentenced to death by the Gestapo. In 1948, he had emigrated to Israel, joining the Israeli Air Force and six years later had volunteered for the Mossad.

Carmit, a Roman Catholic born Christine Lenz in Hong Kong in 1935 to a German father and a Belgium mother, had spent the Second World War in Shanghai before returning to Brussels with her mother. She fell in love with Alex, a tall Israeli Air Force officer and in November 1957 she followed him to Israel. "I was touched by the kindness and the warmth of the people and fell in love at first sight with this country," she evokes pensively. She changes her name to Carmit and takes Hebrew lessons in an *ulpan* in Givatayim, meeting with a variety of people from all over the world: "I could not have it better!" She converts to Judaism in the religious quarter of Mea Shearim, one of the first places she had visited with Alex, and which deeply impressed her. "It was like going back in time," she remembers. They get married a month later and move to Tsahala, a fancy neighborhood, housing all the well known army officers of the time, including the famous Ariel Sharon whom they befriend.

"It was only three years after our wedding that Alex first revealed his secret 'missions' and his 'cover' as a student in criminology when we first met in Brussels." Alex then told her that he had been nominated for an important 'mission' in Morocco adding that she could stay in Paris. "I categorically refused," she says forcefully. Instead she starts her own undercover training. In November 1960, on their way to Casablanca the Gattmons make a stopover in Hamburg, where they met the owner of the German import-export firm Alex is to represent, and from there they flew to Paris, meeting Ephraim Ronel, the new commander of the Misgeret in North Africa.

Alex Gattmon in the apartment in the Liberté building in Casablanca
with the maid Hadouj, who was unaware that she was working for a Mossad agent

Alex Gatmon checking possible routes to take Jews out of Morocco,
near an unfinished bridge

Arriving in Casablanca, Alex and Carmit start their new social life, he as a successful British businessman going by the name of Georges Sellers and she as Christine Blake, his beautiful mistress and secretary.

Asking her why she joined Alex on the mission, she replies: "It's very simple, Alex told me that it was important to help Moroccan Jews and I didn't want to let him go on his own, so we left." To her family in Belgium she explains that she is going to Togo where Alex had been nominated ambassador. She writes letters to her mother, sent by diplomatic mail, full of details of her new life in Togo. "I had studied political sciences at university and I just invented myself a new life." Lost in her thought, she pauses for a moment and expresses regrets for not having told the truth to her mother before her death. "My mother would have probably loved to hear of my clandestine role as a Mossad agent."

In Casablanca, Carmit shares the social life of Alex as his mistress and secretary busying herself in the office they opened not far from a well-known hotel. They live in a nice building called 'Liberté' housing two other agents, among them Gad Shahar code-name 'Georges.' Her faithful maid, named Hadouj, is totally unaware of her real identity. Carmit code-name "Arminette" often accompanies Alex, code name "Morgan" or "Armin," on trips as they look for possible new ways of escape for clandestine emigration. "It was a schizophrenic life," she sights.

Emigration in these years was illegal and at night convoys of fifty to hundred Moroccans families would depart the shores of Morocco on small boats. Before each departure Carmit regularly called the Yacht Club to enquire about sea conditions. In January 1961, three months after Gattmon's arrival in Morocco, a small vessel sinks near Gibraltar, forty-three victims perish including many children. The *Egoz* tragedy brings the plight of Moroccan Jews on the front page of the international press. Alex, a black hood covering his head to protect his identity, would often attend these departures together with other local members of the Misgeret. Carmit adds: "Nonetheless, because of his deep voice, he was easily recognizable. But unlike me, he was never afraid. His detention by the Gestapo, he once told me, made him oblivious to fear." She remembers, a hint of excitement in her voice, how as Alex was holding a secret meeting with his undercover

Carmit Gattmon at Chaouen, Morocco

associates in his office, the military commandant of the airport, a relation they cultivated, unexpectedly rang the front bell. Christine (Carmit) did not lose her poise, smiled and invited him to step into her office which was crowded with files of a fictive correspondence lined on shelves. Meanwhile she rushed toward the back room to announce the arrival of this unexpected visitor allowing for the Mossad agents to swiftly leave through a separate entrance before Alex makes his way towards her office. "This connection," says Carmit, "proved to be valuable when a young agent, named Soli, in charge of the self-defense force of the Misgeret, had to be smuggled out of Casablanca. The quickest way was through the airport, so we accompanied him, making sure he did not open his mouth since he could barely speak English." Spotted by the commander, Alex, imperturbable, called him over, inventing a credible story to explain the reason of their presence with this young man. "The commander," she goes on, "escorted us to the tarmac." Recalling this dramatic moment, she adds: "I was extremely tense and only when the plane was out of my sight, could I breathe again."

Alex Gattmon was also in charge of Operation Mural, a clandestine operation that did not involve perilous offshore departures at night but that entailed dangers of its own. Contacts between David G. Littman, and Alex took place through the intermediary of Gad Shahar, alias "Georges." On Sunday, July 23, 1961, the night before the hasty departure of Littman, Gattmon met "Mural" in person in his green Renault Dauphine, driven at high speed along the coastal road by Mossad agent Pinhas Katsir alias "Jacques." That night, Alex warmly thanked Littman for the success of his mission, warning him that the staff at the airport had been changed but reassuring him that his network would get him out, maybe in the same way as Soli had been smuggled out.

Curious, I ask Carmit during our interview if she knew about this meeting. She is not sure, "for security reasons I was not aware of each meeting." But she recalls very clearly how fascinated Alex was by the personage of "Mural." He often wondered what he was doing in this "galleon." She remembers that Alex highly valued Littman's culture, his discipline and his candor that rendered him oblivious of real danger, so eager he was to succeed in his mission. Carmit adds: "As Israelis, we all had our interest in helping Jewish Moroccans families who wished to emigrate to Israel, but for him it was different. I believe that it was the gratuity of his act that made him a real hero."

David G. Littman would cherish this critical meeting the rest of his life, for at the time Alex Gattmon would be one of the rare Israeli officials to acknowledge and thank him for his role in Operation Mural.

While directing behind the scenes of Operation Mural and other clandestine departures, Alex Gattmon held at the same time secret talks with influential Moroccan Jews who had contacts with Moroccan officials and with King Hassan II. These negotiations eventually lead to Operation Yakhin in which Gattmon played a major role. First implemented in November 1961 and continuing until 1964, a total of one hundred thousand Jews were thus able to legally emigrate from Morocco in counterpart for very high financial compensations mainly financed by American Jewish fund-raising organizations channeled to the Jewish Agency in Israel. Alex Gattmon was personally involved in handing over to a Moroccan minister in Geneva a suitcase with five hundred thousand dollars in cash, as a down payment.

"We stayed in Casablanca for another three years. We returned to Israel only when everything was running smoothly and although it had been a fascinating adventure, I was glad to be back home. It was time for us to start our own family."

And as I listened to Carmit's concluding words, I feel tremendously privileged that she shared with me the memories of their courageous endeavor on behalf of the State of Israel.

Interview conducted on November 14, 2013

"Gino"
Pinhas Katsir alias "Jacques"

Katsir, code name "Gino," was born in Haifa in 1936 and headed in Morocco "Modi'in," the information and intelligence branch of the Misgeret during the years 1958–1962. He opened many offices of HIAS (Hebrew Immigrant Aid Society) in various cities during Operation Yakhin.

Pinhas Katsir was David G. Littman's contact during the last two critical weeks of Operation Mural after "Georges" left for Paris in mid-July 1960. He was driving the car during Littman's meeting—a day before his hasty departure—with the head of the Misgeret, Alex Gattmon who personally thanked him for the way in which he had handled the whole operation.

On a phone interview held on September 2013 "Jacques" stressed, that beside the actual success of the operation, David G. Littman's major contribution had been his insistence in using collective passports, a system which was used afterwards for Operation Yakhin.

One of "Jacques" numerous fictive student identity cards while studying for a PHD in Law at the Sorbonne from 1959–1963. He only attended to take his exams which he passed brilliantly.

Shmuel Toledano

Shmuel Toledano in the 1960s
while number two of Isser Harel

Born in 1921 in Tiberias, Shmuel Toledano is a former deputy head of the Mossad and a Knesset member. He was adviser on Arab affairs to three Israeli Prime Ministers: Golda Meir, Levy Eshkol and Yitzhak Rabin. Toledano shared together with Ephraim Ronel, based in Paris, the policymaking for Operation Yakhin.

During Operation Mural Toledano, operating from Tel Aviv, was number two to Isser Harel, Director of the Mossad during the years 1952–1963. He was one of the rare Israeli personalities to acknowledge the importance of Operation Mural and from 1983 onwards did everything so that it would be officially recognized.

During the course of an interview held at his home in Jerusalem on July 2013, Shmuel Toledano evoked memories of the moving ceremony at President Shimon Peres' residence in June 2008 in honor of David G. Littman as well as the "Hero of Silence" Order awarded Littman at the Israel Intelligence Heritage and Communications Centre in 2009—"an honor of the highest esteem," he emphasized. In the same interview he stated: "Operation Mural, which smuggled 530 Moroccan Jewish children to Israel, although smaller in size, was more complex than Operation Yakhin which brought 90,000 Moroccan Jews to Israel. It is my belief that the present book will not only be a document of historical importance in the history of the *Aliyah* (immigration) of Moroccan Jews to Israel, it will also bear out the heroic operation of one man to future generations."

Appendix I
Documents

ŒUVRE SUISSE DE SECOURS
AUX ENFANTS DE L'AFRIQUE DU NORD

Genève 1. Case postale 220

Genève, le 11 Mars 1961

ORDRE DE MISSION
====================================

Il est certifié par la présente que

Monsieur David LITTMAN, citoyen britannique,

est mandaté par notre Oeuvre d'organiser
en Algérie, Tunisie et au Maroc l'action au
profit d'enfants relevant d'un séjour de
repos ou d'une cure d'altitude en Suisse
selon le programme établi.

Toutes les organisations internationales
et nationales sont priées de bien vouloir faciliter la tâche de Monsieur Littman dans la mesure
de leurs compétences respectives .

OEUVRE SUISSE DE SECOURS AUX
ENFANTS DE L'AFRIQUE DU NORD

N. LEHMANN
Secrétaire Général

Fig. 1 Order of Mission signed by Miss N. Lehmann, March 11, 1961

Order of Mission signed by Miss N. Lehmann OSSEAN's secretary-general (in reality Miss Aïda Schirmann), certifying that Mr. David Littman, a British citizen was mandated by OSSEAN to bring children from Algeria, Tunisia and Morocco to Switzerland for a rest cure. She calls upon all national and international organizations to help him in his task.

KOMMISSION FÜR DIE UNTERBRINGUNG AUSLÄNDISCHER KRANKER IN DER SCHWEIZ
COMMISSION POUR L'HOSPITALISATION DE MALADES ÉTRANGERS EN SUISSE

Geschäftsstelle / Secrétariat:

~~14, Helvetiastrasse~~ Effingerstr. 6
Bern

Telephon (031) ~~215 02~~ 3 29 86
Postcheckkonto III 7622

Lettre de recommandation

La Commission pour l'hospitalisation de malades étrangers en Suisse confirme par les présentes que Monsieur David Littmann, citoyen britannique, exerce les fonctions de délégué de l'Oeuvre suisse de secours aux enfants nordafricains. Notre Commission connaît bien cette Oeuvre, qui s'occupe d'une action d'hospitalisation d'enfants marocains.

Nous prions instamment toutes les autorités et organisations privées qui prennent connaissance de la présente lettre de recommandation de soutenir de tout leur pouvoir l'activité de M. Littmann et, ce faisant, de la faciliter dans une large mesure. Cette activité, il l'exerce dans un esprit de solidarité et d'utilité publique; aussi mérite-t-il la collaboration compréhensive de tous les organismes et personnes intéressés.

Berne, le 2 mars 1961

Le président par intérim

Dr. iur. M. Tromp

Fig. 2 Letter of recommendation from Mr. Tromp, President of the Commission for hospitalizing foreigners in Switzerland, March 2, 1961

Mr. Tromp earnestly requests of authorities and private organizations to support by all means David Littman, delegate of OSSEAN in his efforts to bring Moroccan children for a rest-cure in Switzerland.

SCHWEIZERISCHES ROTES KREUZ

CROIX-ROUGE SUISSE · CROCE ROSSA SVIZZERA

BERN

Taubenstrasse 8
Telephon 2 14 74
Postcheckkonto III 877

> Délégué en chef au Maroc
> de la Ligue des Sociétés
> de la Croix-Rouge
> 584, Boulevard Mohamed Zerktouni
>
> C A S A B L A N C A .
> ------------------------ Maroc.

Ihre Zeichen Vos références		Unsere Zeichen Nos références	St/jk	Bern, den Berne, le	8 mars 1961.

Cher Monsieur,

Je me réfère à notre échange de correspondance au sujet du jeune garçon atteint d'hémophilie.

J'ai eu l'occasion de rencontrer entretemps Monsieur David Littman, collaborateur de l'Oeuvre de Secours aux Enfants en Afrique du Nord et au Maroc, qui prépare une action en faveur d'enfants répondant d'une cure en Suisse, au home "la Forêt" à Morgins.

Monsieur Littman, respectivement l'organisation qu'il représente, est à même, semble-t-il, de faciliter la venue de l'enfant en question, en liaison avec une organisation compétente en France.

Je vous prie de réserver bon accueil à M. Littman, qui se permettra de vous interpeller également au sujet de l'action qu'il entend réaliser.

Veuillez croire, cher Monsieur, à mes sentiments les meilleurs.

> CROIX ROUGE SUISSE
> Service du Secours aux Enfants:
>
> René Steiner

Fig. 3 Letter from R. Steiner, Secretary-General of the Swiss Red Cross (Children's section) to A. E. Reinhard, the chief delegate of the League of the Red Cross Societies in Morocco, March 8, 1961

This letter mentions the possible involvement of David Littman, the representative of OSSEAN (an organization he knows well), in facilitating the transfer with a competent organization in France for special medical care of a young Jewish Moroccan boy suffering from haemophilia.

ŒUVRE SUISSE DE SECOURS
AUX ENFANTS DE L'AFRIQUE DU NORD

Genève 1, Case postale 220

Genève, le 9 Mars 1961.

Mr.David LITTMAN,
3, Blakesley Avenue,
L o n d o n W.5.

Cher Monsieur Littman,

En nous référant aux conversations de ces derniers
jours concernant l'accueil d'enfants nordafricains dans des
institutions en Suisse, nous vous communiquons que le prix
forfaitaire de pension est fixé à Frs.10.- par jour et par
enfant.

Nous vous autorisons cependant, en cas d'enfants de
familles nécessiteuses, de réduire ce taux et d'appliquer
un prix de faveur qui correspond aux possibilités des
parents en question.

Veuillez croire, cher Monsieur Littman, à l'assurance
de nos sentiments les meilleurs.

ŒUVRE SUISSE DE SECOURS AUX
ENFANTS DE L'AFRIQUE DU NORD

p.

Fig. 4 Letter from the Director of OSSEAN, Prof. Aberson (in reality Prof. Jacques Bloch) to David Littman, March 9, 1961

"Professor Aberson" confirms that the inclusive payement is ten Swiss francs per day and per child, which can be reduced for poor families.

March 17th. 1961

The Secretary General
Oeuvre Suisse de Secours aux enfants
de l'Afrique du Nord,
Case Postale 220,
Genève, 1

Dear Madam,
   I arrived safely yesterday at midday and at the moment
am installed in the Hotel de Cernay, 8 Rue de Cernay. However this
is only temporary and the moment I have something more permanent I
shall inform you directly. Of course any urgent and important letter
can always be sent to the above address to be collected by me should
I have changed hotels in the meanwhile or taken an appartment.
   My Olivetti typewriter having been damaged by the airlines
on route I am using that of the hotel until mine can be prepaired, if
it is possible to repair it; perhaps I can get M. Reinhard's assistance
until then.
   Yesterday and this morning I had two most useful conversations
with M. Reinhard, le Délégué en chef au Maroc de la ligue des Sociétés
de la Croix-Rouge, and he will endeavour to give me every assistance
in our work for the aid of Moroccan children. On Monday he will take
me with him to Rabat where I shall meet an important personage in the
Moroccan department of health who can aid me and who can put me onto
the necessary authorities both here in Casablanca and in Rabat and
elsewhere. M. Reinhard is of the opinion that the demand will be large
for those having need of a rest or a cure in Switzerland and I would
strongly advise you to see what other Homes might be available should
this be the case and what sort of numbers we can cope with approximately.
   M. Reinhard has drawn my attention to the individual case
of a young Moroccan who is suffering from Haemophelia. I have examined
the correspondence and I feel that- although this case is not really
within our competence- we should try through our contacts with other
organizations to assist this boy. M. Reinhard has sent photocopies of
the relevant correspondence to M. René Steiner, the Secretary General
of the Red Cross in Berne, whom you know well, and he suggests that
we write to him for all these documents. I feel sure that something
can be done and I look forward to hearing from you on this matter. I
have informed M. Steiner that assuming we can find an appropriate
Home for this young boy and be able to cover the necessary expences
he could leave with the first group of Moroccan children leaving for
their rest-cure in Switzerland. He was most appreciative of my proposal.
When you have the correspondence you will note a letter of the 7th. July
1960 from the Association des Hémophiles in which they name the
Internat de LA QUEUE LES YVELINE (Seine et Oise) and the MONTAIN(Jura)
as possible schools where the boy can continue his studies without
coming to harm through an accident. Although the daily cost is 3000 Frer
francs, 80% of this is borne by the French Sécurité Sociale. If this is
indeed the case we must somehow see what can be done regarding the boy's
transport to France and the remaining 600 French francs per day and I
leave this in you own very capable hands. At Rabat I will see the father
   This morning I saw the Swiss Consul in Casablanca, but
unfortunately the letter from Mr. Maeder had not yet arrived(I trust

Fig. 5 Letter from D.G. Littman to N. Lehmann, OSSEAN's Secretary General, March 17, 1961

Littman announces his safe arrival in Casablanca except for the damage of his Olivetti

typewriter. He met twice with the chief delegate of the League of Red Cross Societies, Mr.

Reinhard who will endeavor to give him every assistance and would introduce him to a

high official at the Health Ministry in Rabat. Littman raises the possibility of assisting the

boy suffering from haemophilia and having him leave with the first convoy of Moroccan

children to Switzerland. He is still waiting for the letter from Mr. Maeder of the Federal Police

for Foreigners in Bern to the Swiss Ambassador and the Swiss Consul before he contacts

them. Expecting a large demand from families, Littman advices exploring vacancies in

other homes.

ŒUVRE SUISSE DE SECOURS

AUX ENFANTS DE L'AFRIQUE DU NORD

Genève 1, Case postale 220

Genève,le 2I marsI96I

Monsieur D. LITTMAN
Hôtel de Noailles
22 Bld II Janvier
C a s a b l a n c a.

Cher Monsieur Littman,

        Nous avons reçu avec grand intérêt votre let-
tre circonstanciée et vos 2 cartes,et avons pris connaissance avec
grand plaisir que vous avez déjà contacté M. Reinhard.Nous sommes
certains que ce dernier pourra vous faciliter dans une large mesure
vos démarches auprès des autorités.

        De notre côté,nous nous sommes mis en relation
immédiatement après réception de votre lettre,avec la Police Fédérale,mais nous avons appris que différentes préoccupations urgentes
en rapport avec la conférence d'Evian les ont empéché de faire partir la lettre à l'Ambassade et au Consulat Suisse.Ils nous ont promis pourtant que ces lettres partiraient au plus tard aujourd'hui,
Mardi,aux adresses de Rabat et de Casablanca.

        D'autre part,nous avons fait les démarches né-
cessaires pour mettre l'enfant souffrant d'hémophilie dans de meilleures conditions en France.Votre seule préoccupation devra donc
être de trouver les moyens de financer son voyage.

        Nous attendons avec intérêt le résultat des
premiers contacts avec le Ministère de la Santé.La maison en question pourra accueillir 30 enfants.Elle est située à Champéry/Vs,
et elle est très bien équipée.

        Je ne comprends pas tout à fait ce que vous
réclamez au sujet des formules.De toute façon si elles ne sont
pas bien faîtes,il sera baucoup plus simple de commander des formu-
les chez un imprimeur ou un bureau de Casablanca,que de les faire
venir de Suisse.

        Les formules de la Croix-Rouge vous seront en-
voyées dès que nous les recevrons.

        En attendant de vos nouvelles,veuillez agréer.
cher Monsieur Littman,l'assurance de nos meilleurs sentiments.

Oeuvre Suisse de Secours aux
Enfants de l'Afrique du Nord.
(O.S.S.E.A.N.)

N. Lehmann

Fig. 6 Letter from N. Lehmann to D. Littman, March 21, 1961

Mrs. Lehmann writes that the letters to the Swiss Consul and the Swiss Ambassador will be sent today by the Swiss authorities in Bern. OSSEAN has found a place in France for the child with haemophilia (which does not include the cost of the trip). She looks forward to the upcoming meeting with the official at the Health Ministry, and mentions the house Champery (in the Valais) that can take up to thirty children.

Berne, le 21 mars 1961

EIDGENÖSSISCHE FREMDENPOLIZEI
POLICE FÉDÉRALE DES ÉTRANGERS
POLIZIA FEDERALE DEGLI STRANIERI

Ambassade de Suisse
R a b a t

N° E 12/128 So/bu

Bitte in der Antwort angeben
A indiquer dans la réponse
Pregasi ripeterlo nella risposta

Ambassade de Suisse, Rabat
2 7 MARS 1961   00910
Réf.: G.65.40.

Monsieur l'Ambassadeur,

L'oeuvre suisse de secours aux enfants de l'Afrique du Nord a l'intention d'inviter en Suisse, dans les prochains mois, un certain nombre d'enfants marocains pour un séjour de convalescence et de repos de deux à trois mois dans le Home de la Forêt à Morgins (Valais). Ces enfants seront munis par les autorités compétentes marocaines de papiers nationaux réguliers assurant leur retour au Maroc. Les frais de cette action seront entièrement à la charge de l'oeuvre suisse de secours aux enfants de l'Afrique du Nord. L'oeuvre suisse de secours enverra au Maroc dans les prochains jours un délégué, M. David Littman, ressortissant anglais, qui devra aider les enfants et leurs familles à remplir les formalités nécessaires à l'obtention des passe-ports et des visas. M. Littman délivrera aux intéressés une déclaration prouvant qu'ils sont invités à Morgins par l'oeuvre de secours. Sur la base de cette déclaration et sur production de papiers nationaux réguliers vous pourrez octroyer sans autres formalités aux enfants marocains un visa d'entrée pour un séjour de 3 mois dans notre pays.
                    Nous adressons une copie de la présente lettre au Consulat de Suisse à Casablanca, pour son information.
                    Veuillez agréer, Monsieur l'Ambassadeur, l'assurance de notre considération distinguée.

POLICE FEDERALE DES ETRANGERS
LE DIRECTEUR:

Fig. 7 Letter from Mr. Maeder of the Federal Police for Foreigners to the Swiss Ambassador in Rabat, March 21, 1961 (File G.65.sd, Archives of the Historical Department, the Swiss Federal Department of Foreign Affairs in Bern)

Mr. Maeder writes in this letter to the Swiss ambassador (copy to the Swiss consul in Casablanca) that the "Oeuvre Suisse de Secours aux enfants de l'Afrique du Nord" (OSSEAN) will invite Moroccan children for a rest-cure in Morgins (Switzerland). All the costs are being covered by the association. Their delegate Mr. David Littman will be responsible for the necessary passports and visas formalities. On presentation of these legal papers, Mr. Maeder asks the Swiss authorities to provide the children invited by OSSEAN with a three months visa.

Hotel de Noailles,

Blvd. 11 Janvier, 22

Casablanca.   23rd. March 1961

Dear Madam,

       I do not even know if I am in actual correspondence with you for I have received no answer at all to my two letters and the postcards. This must have something to do with the irregularity of the postal deliveries here. I have been in Morocco exactly one week and thanks to th' ending of Ramadan at least two days(not counting the week-end) have been holidays; to-day His Majesty the king makes a triumphal entry into this city, so there is no postal delivery and to-morrow is announced as another day of rest in honour of this event. May I remind you to write " Air Mail "(and to put the additional stamps) on all letters as Morocco is outside of Europe and Air Mail is not automatic; sometimes " Express " would be most useful especially
(now.

       May I repeat that the letters from M. Maeder in Berne to the Ambassador and Consuls here in Morocco have not yet arrived. These letters are most important as you know and I hope you can deal with this matter promptly- it is best for all the Swiss Consuls to receive notification. Yesterday I was in Rabat again and was to have seen the Swiss Ambassador but firstly he had not received any letter at all from Berne regarding me, and secondly he was very busy owing to the fact that the next day he was leaving for a ten to fourteen days holiday in Switzerland. On my deciding to try to see him anyway just to introduce myself, as I had done with the consul in Casablanca, I was quite unable to get through to the Embassy thanks to the 'phone having gone out of order, and having already appointments with three important Moroccan officials I was forced to let the opportunity go. Perhaps it is not so unfortunate since M. Maeder might be able to contact His Excellency in Switzerland during his holiday and appraise him of the situation, or failing this M. Maeder's letter should have arrived before H.E.'s return: certainly the way things are arranging themselves at the moment I cannot see any necessity for Visas within the next two weeks, or even two months.

       I have made a number of useful contacts and seen a good many of the right authorities during my two days in Rabat, yesterday and Monday last. As instructed I have explained our programme as follows
1.) Convalescence, or rest for tired or exhausted children et cetera.
2.) A sort of " holiday camp "

       Regarding the first aspect I have had a meeting with Dr. Laraki of the Ministry of Health, who is I think the Secretary-General of the recently-formed Red Crescent. He made it quite clear that although he would be quite interested in sending children in the first category he would not make any contribution whatsoever (" pas un sou, M. Littman, pas un sou "),but if we were willing to pay for both the voyage and the complete cost of keeping the children he would willingly co-operate. Here the obstacle is unsupportable I fear.

       With respect to the " holiday camp " idea I had a more useful conversation with M. Mazzour the Director of ' La jeunesse et Sport 'in Rabat. I was once again accompanied by a M. Lazrak,who is the Director of the Red Crescent,and after half an hour's talk it was suggested that they ' might ' be able to bear the transport costs if something reasonable could be arranged with the air and sea companies concerned. M. Mazzour spoke about a group of thirty or forty for a period of about twenty-one days, starting in July only. Hardly more

than a 'symbolical' contribution can be expected for the cost of each

Fig. 8 Letter from D. G. Littman to N. Lehmann, March 23, 1961

Littman writes that he could not contact the Swiss Ambassador in Rabat since Mr. Maeder's letter has not reached the Embassy. He met with Dr. Laraki from the Minister of Health. The latter seems interested in sending Muslim children to Switzerland provided it is free of charges. Littman is conducting negotiations with Mr. Mazzour the Director of Youth and Sports about a possible Holiday Camp in the summer. The price of ten Swiss francs per child

child and if you were to ask me " how much " I couln't tell you. One thing
is certain, and that is that when I stated that perhaps 10 S.F. was too
much for those coming from necessitous families I was always informed
that all the children were in such a situation, other than those who
could afford to go to Switzerland privately. When I cut the figure in
half it didn't help too much and I would say quite frankly that in this
second category with regard to La Jeunesse et Sport I doubt very much
whether we would even get 4 or 3 S.F. per day per person, and this assumes
that they will in the end bear the transport costs. In the first category
(Dr. Laraky) you can expect absolutely nothing UNLESS somehow I can
get the a State department to make a contribution OR find co-operation
with Royal Air Maroc to fill-up empty seats, but neither of these possibilities looks too encouraging: I shall do my very best. But please let me
know what actual offer I can make to M. Mazzour for the cost of séjour
per child per day as without this information I can hardly continue on
these lines. I need hardly remind you of the importance of this matter
which is at the very base of all our plans of aid for North-African
children; everything is expected to be gratuitous and ten francs, however
reasonable for Europe, comes as a shock here. We must see whether we have
the resources to deal with such a problem. I have explained here that
no contribution(or a very small one) simply reduces the numbers we can
cope with; none the less I think you must be prepared to organize another
Home-properly equiped- in case of use: this is imperative, However I am
sorry to say that I do not see any real developement until the Summer
vacation in July(Jeunesse et Sport) unless we bear the entire cost and
transport a handful of children needing a convalescence (Dr. Laraky).
I think if you consider the whole problem from all sides you will also
come to the conclusion that it very much better to concentrate our
resources and energy on the Summer period, beginning towards the end of
June. The Easter vacation is only for two weeks and there is hardly time
to arrange anything in the time remaining; at the same time I doubt if
it is worth all the effort since the Summer is the normal period, and the
gap is really too long.
    I have spoken to the head of the French community and it is
possible that we might have a few children coming under their auspices.
Through the Red Crescent I was taken to see the Ladies looking after the
Jewish community's children in Rabat, and they also await something
positive from us on the financial side- again for the Summer.
    I had the good fortune to speak with M. Chaoui from the Consular
and Social division of the Ministry and he has assurred me that once a
definite plan has been drawn up and is meeting with success he the
necessary circular will be sent round to the appropriate authorities in
the various cities,relating to the issue of passports etc. which he says
is easily arranged and is merely a formality. I informed him that the
Swiss side was just as easily dealt with. On my taking my leave he told
me to see the respective airline and navigation companies, see what could
be arranged through our organization or the Swiss government (what about
Dr. Fischer in Berne, here is his chance to contribute in the actual
country of need) to alleviate the financial aspect and when everything
had been thoroughly prepared to call on him once again. He explained that
in the case where there were twenty children on one passport, and a few we
were due to stay in Switzerland a little longer than the rest, the Morocca
legation in Berne could always arrange matters, and that probably such a
passport is the best sort in such a case.
    I have been asked to see if there is a Swiss organization which
can help the Red Crescent in the case of a boy, Ahmed ? (I have forgotten
the full name), a boy of ten suffering from Myopathie Spardo Hypertroph-
iante- like Spastics - whose parents have no means whatsoever. What about
Dr. Fischer ? Any news regarding the Haemophilia case I wrote to you about'

seems too expensive writes Littman and one should opt for the summer vacations instead
of the Easter vacations. He has a positive meeting with Mr. Chaoui, Head of the Consular
and Social Department of the Foreign Ministry, who told Littman that collective passports
were preferable. In this letter Littman inquires about the boy with haemophilia and asks if
a Swiss organization could help the Red Crescent in the case of another sick boy.

Casablanca, 25th. March 196

Mlle. N. Lehmann,
O.S.S.E.A.N.
Genève. Suisse.

Dear Madam Lehmann,
                    I acknowledge receipt of your letters of the 21st.
and 22nd. March which arrived this morning. May I ask you to make sure
the envelope is properly sealed as one of the letters might well have
fallen out of its envelope and been lost en transit. I thank you for
all the information therein.

                    It is with great pleasure that I learn that the
letters from the Head of the Federal Police in Berne have been sent
to the Swiss Ambassador in Rabat and to the Consul in Casablanca. I
refer you back to the second paragraph of my letter of the 23rd instant
On Monday I must once more journey to Rabat and I shall enquire (in
the Ambassador's temporary absence) whether the letter was received,
and on Tuesday or Wednesday I shall do the same here in Casablanca.
Let me add that it would be most useful to have a governmental letter
of reference from Berne if that is at all possible. Of course the
Swiss government is cognizant of our work and is most appreciative of
our contacts and support for North African countries and I have
explained this to the authorities with whom I have spoken. In fact the
same authorities have suggested that perhaps the Swiss authorities or
for instance the " Swiss Aid for foreign countries " (Dr. Fischer)
might like to offer their help on the financial side- especially the
cost of travel- and I have been informed that a short while ago the
Belgian government received a group of children without any contribution
whatsoever from the Moroccan side. I have always replied to this with
the answer that for us to operate on such terms would completely alter
the purpose of our work by greatly reducing the number of children
which we thought would be in the hundreds. I refer you to the second
page of my letter of the 23rd. instant to which I await an urgent reply
I know you will do your utmost to obtain financial support from the
Swiss government or through Dr. Fischer in this important work which
would also be received here with much gratitude, but failing this any
appropriate letter from the same authorities as outlined above would be
most useful to my position here. Again I must know how much more of
the financial burden our Oeuvre can absorb first with regard to the
daily charge per child (and this must be made much more realistic for
the cost of living here, where organizations and not parents contribute
AND with regard to the travel expences, the details of which will be
set out below. In such a humane work we cannot afford to count the cost
and I feel sure their are many Swiss organizations of benevolence who
would contribute to such a worthy cause.

                    Your success in finding a suitable organization to
help the young boy suffering from haemophelia is most encouraging.
To-morrow evening on M. Reinhard's return from a tour of inspection in
the south I shall acquaint him with the news. I shall see what can be
done with regard to financing this boy's journey, but would point out
that it would be possible to get the boy from Casablanca to Marseille
for about 120 S.F.
                    which if it is not forthcoming here should be easy
to find on your side: I shall do my very best. I wonder if there is
any chance of coming to the aid of the Red Crescent in the case I
mentioned in my last letter? Perhaps you can make enquiries.

Fig. 9 Letter from D. Littman to N. Lehmann, March 25, 1961

Littman asks once more to reduce the costs as one should bare in mind the cost of
living in Morocco. Is there any chance of financial help from the Swiss authorities? He
writes, mentioning the importance of this humane work and the benevolence of Swiss

Concerning the Medical Questionnaires I have ordered 1000 copies
(more or less a minimum) which will be finished on Monday. As for the
prospectus of the Home de la Forêt it has seemed best to me to Arabize
it, and since the cost of re-printing the whole in Arabic, photograph
and all, would have been prohibitively costly (150 S.F. plus 60 S.F. just
for the translation), with the advice of a printer in Casablanca I have
decided to print simply on the obverse side the Arabic translation of
all that is printed above and below the photograph. Thus the 500 odd
copies I have with me will be so overprinted (I hope by to-morrow) to
enable me to take some with me when I go to Rabat on Monday at 7:00 a.m.
It would do no harm to put a packet or two more in the post as printed
matter just in case they should be needed, AND anything of a similar
nature on our other prospective Homes, if they are available, could prove
useful. I am not quite sure what I am to do with the Red Cross formulae
which you are sending me (I imagined I had all the Medical questionnaires
that were really necessary) but no doubt you will enlighten me. My thanks.

Concerning the cost of transporting children from Morocco to
Geneva I have much information and I trust you will bear with me. It
would appear that the airlines are not going to be too co-operative, and
neither Royal Air Maroc nor Air France has done more than offer the
normal 10% reduction for groups aller retour and then one must book well
in advance. Since the cost would work out at well over two times the
cheapest sea and land passage fares it can hardly be considered, even
though the latter journey would take 2 1/2 days by sea (from Casa)
and half a day by 'bus or train. The boat leaves in the evening and the
children would arrive at the Home three full days later in the evening.
I would mention but one advantage that Royal Air Maroc offers and that is
that children under 12 are carried at a cost reduced rate of 50% either
of the return fare or of the single as the case may be. In other words
for those few children we have under the age of twelve years we could
avail ourself of this offer which works at only a little more than the
boat and train(or 'bus) fare as you will see. However from the 26th.
June Caravelles will be introduced on the Geneva flight and the fares
will be augmented then about 3% or so. Of course I shall endeavour to
bring about a démarche with the airlines so that they will offer better
terms and perhaps Rabat will help, but I am sceptical. At any rate the
month of July and probably August is a difficult one anyhow. The Air
France flights to Lyon only operate their 50% reduction for children
under the age of 10 which is of no use; otherwise 10% for groups.

The Compagnie de Navigation Paquet offers a 20% reduction for
young people between the ages of 12 and 21 years, on the condition that
they travel aller et retour: this is to Marseilles. The group must compose
at least ten persons. If the group is as much as 50 in number an educator
is taken free of charge in the same class on the same boat.
There are two boats which are equipped to take both young boys
and young girls in 4th. class dormitories and here the round trip to
Marseille and back with the 20% reduction is 244 Dirhams(here more or
less equal to the French franc) per child. A single journey without
reduction is 150 dirhams— you can see the difference. There is another
boat a little older than these two which works out at 223 1/2 223 1/2 Drhs.
in comparison with the single fare of 137 Drhs. However on this boat
there are no facilities to accomodate BOTH girls and boys in dormitories.
In this case only boys can be taken 4th. class. However this might have
its uses and I therefore mention it. There are about three or four
sailings each week and the boat stops in Tangier early the next morning
from where the cost is 36 Dirhams less on a return fare.

organizations to worthy causes. He will inform M. Reinhard that a suitable organization was
found for the young boy with haemophilia and will inquire about the new case put forth
by the Red Crescent. Medical certificates were ordered as well as the translation in Arabic

The French Railways give a reduction of 50% for children between 10 and 21 years old if they comprise a group of at least ten, and for each ten the person in charge is also granted a 50% reduction. It is possible that this reduction might operate as far as Aigle, but it is absolutely certain that it does so as far as Geneva. Once again of course this applies for aller et retour. The return fare therefore works out at about 41 Dirhams per child, which is about 35 S.Fs. at the exchange here. Probably you will argue that it is best to hire a coach ('bus that is) since even if this should cost as much as 1000 S.Fs. it would only be necessary to have 25 children in it for it to be worth while and then it is more convenient; on the other hand if a group of thirty, forty, or even seventy(?) to come the same 'bus would be sufficient to take all the children. What a pity we have not a 'bus of our own; in a situation like this it would almost pay to buy one and re-sell it later. This I leave, dear Madam, to your wisdom.

You will have calculated that all in all the cheapest means of transported the children to and from Switzerland is between about 265 and 285 Dirhams, that is to say the top price is about 240 or better 250 Swiss francs at the exchange rate here in Morocco. On Monday I shall inform the various authorities of this curious bit of research and will see what sort of offer they will make towards defraying the cost. It would also be interesting to know whether or not we are able to make any contribution in this field as well should I find myself up against a brick wall, and I trust you will not fail to inform me of the prix de séjour(revised) for each child on the lines advised upon here and in my previous letters. This information I must also pass on as quickly as possible.

There seems no alternative but that I must remove myself to Rabat to set up a permanent office there— " everyone"concurs. I have asked to rent a room in the Red Crescent building and I shall know on Monday with r not they are willing. They have been most co-operative ever since M.Reinhard introduced me five days ago. I shall endeavour to find a flat there as well,although at first I shall move into the " Nouvelle Hotel." It would be wisest if you continued to address your letters to me here at the Hotel de Noailles until that time when I can give you exactly my new address.

of the OSSEAN's prospectus on the 'Home de la Forêt' in Morgins. In this letter he provides details on all possible means of transportation by land, air and sea.

ŒUVRE SUISSE DE SECOURS AUX ENFANTS DES PAYS DE L'AFRIQUE DU NORD

QUESTIONNAIRE MEDICAL CONCERNANT L'ENFANT
(à remplir par le médecin demandant le placement)

Nom : _____ Prénoms_____ Né le_____

Lieu de naissance : _____ Nationalité : _____

Domicile habituel : (adresse complète) _____

Profession du père : _____

Antécédents et état de santé familiaux : _____

_____

_____

Antécédents personnels ; (état à la naissance, maladies antérieures etc)_____

_____

_____

Vaccinations faites :   Antivariolique : _____ Antidiphtérique ;_____

(dates)   Antitétanique : _____ Antityphoïdique : _____

B.C.G. : _____ Autres : _____

Cuti-réaction : _____ Résultat : _____

Radioscopie (graphie) pulmonaire : _____

_____

Autres examens : (dates résultats) _____

_____

_____

Etat actuel : Général:_____

psychique:_____

Sommeil : _____ Appétit :_____

Travail scolaire : _____ Enurésis :_____

Traitements effectués:_____

Indications du séjour à la montagne :_____

Points à surveiller, régime:_____

Traitements proposés:_____

Durée nécessaire du séjour :_____

Observations:_____

Date _____ Nom et adresse_____

Fig. 10 Example of medical certificate used by OSSEAN

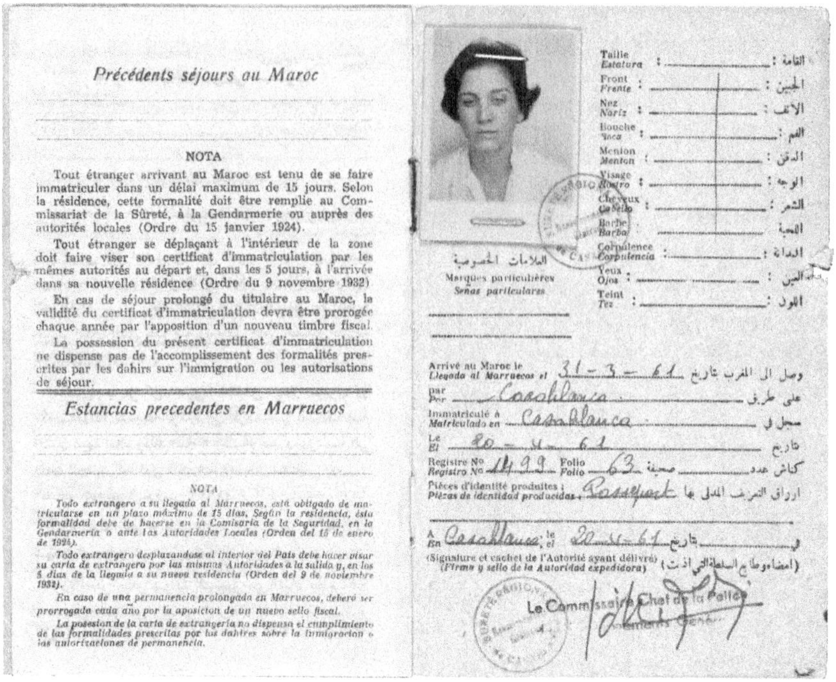

Précédents séjours au Maroc

NOTA

Tout étranger arrivant au Maroc est tenu de se faire immatriculer dans un délai maximum de 15 jours. Selon la résidence, cette formalité doit être remplie au Commissariat de la Sûreté, à la Gendarmerie ou auprès des autorités locales (Ordre du 15 janvier 1924).

Tout étranger se déplaçant à l'intérieur de la zone doit faire viser son certificat d'immatriculation par les mêmes autorités au départ et, dans les 5 jours, à l'arrivée dans sa nouvelle résidence (Ordre du 9 novembre 1932).

En cas de séjour prolongé du titulaire au Maroc, la validité du certificat d'immatriculation devra être prorogée chaque année par l'apposition d'un nouveau timbre fiscal.

La possession du présent certificat d'immatriculation ne dispense pas de l'accomplissement des formalités prescrites par les dahirs sur l'immigration ou les autorisations de séjour.

Estancias precedentes en Marruecos

NOTA

Todo extrangero a su llegada al Marruecos, está obligado de matricularse en un plazo máximo de 15 dias. Según la residencia, ésta formalidad debe de hacerse en la Comisaria de la Seguridad, en la Gendarmería o ante las Autoridades Locales (Orden del 15 de enero de 1924).

Todo extrangero desplazandose al interior del Pais debe hacer visar su carta de extrangero por las mismas Autoridades a la salida y, en los 5 dias de la llegada a su nuevo residencia (Orden del 9 de noviembre 1932).

En caso de una permanencia prolongada en Marruecos, deberá ser prorrogada cada año por la aposicion de un nuevo sello fiscal.

La posesion de la carta de extrangería no dispensa el cumplimiento de las formalidades prescritas por los dahires sobre la inmigracion o las autorizaciones de permanencia.

Taille / *Estatura* : القامة
Front / *Frente* : الجبين
Nez / *Nariz* : الأنف
Bouche / *Boca* : الفم
Menton / *Menton* : الذقن
Visage / *Rostro* : الوجه
Cheveux / *Cabello* : الشعر
Barbe / *Barba* : اللحية
Corpulence / *Corpulencia* : البدانة
Yeux / *Ojos* : العين
Teint / *Tez* : اللون

العلامات الخصوصية
Marques particulières
Señas particulares

Arrivé au Maroc le / *Llegada al Marruecos el* 31-3-61 وصل الى المغرب بتاريخ
par / *Por* Casablanca على طريق
Immatriculé à / *Matriculado en* Casablanca مسجل في
Le / *El* 20-4-61 بتاريخ
Registre No / *Registro No* 1499 Folio / *Folio* 63 صحيفة كناش عدد
Pièces d'identité produites : / *Piêzas de identidad producidas* : Passeport اوراق التعريف المدلى بها

A / *En* Casablanca, le / *el* 20-4-61 بتاريخ
(Signature et cachet de l'Autorité ayant délivré) / *(Firma y sello de la Autoridad expedidora)* (امضاء وطابع السلطة التي اذنت)

Le Commissaire Chef de la Police

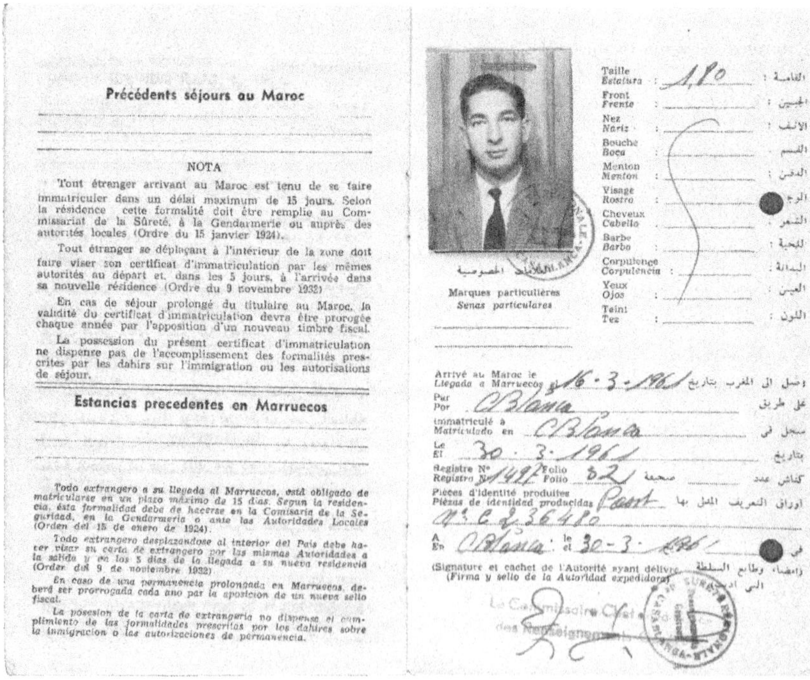

Précédents séjours au Maroc

NOTA

Tout étranger arrivant au Maroc est tenu de se faire immatriculer dans un délai maximum de 15 jours. Selon la résidence cette formalité doit être remplie au Commissariat de la Sûreté, à la Gendarmerie ou auprès des autorités locales (Ordre du 15 janvier 1924).

Tout étranger se déplaçant à l'intérieur de la zone doit faire viser son certificat d'immatriculation par les mêmes autorités au départ et, dans les 5 jours, à l'arrivée dans sa nouvelle résidence (Ordre du 9 novembre 1932).

En cas de séjour prolongé du titulaire au Maroc, la validité du certificat d'immatriculation devra être prorogée chaque année par l'apposition d'un nouveau timbre fiscal.

La possession du présent certificat d'immatriculation ne dispense pas de l'accomplissement des formalités prescrites par les dahirs sur l'immigration ou les autorisations de séjour.

Estancias precedentes en Marruecos

Todo extrangero a su llegada al Marruecos, está obligado de matricularse en un plazo máximo de 15 dias. Segun la residencia, ésta formalidad debe de hacerse en la Comisaria de la Seguridad, en la Gendarmeria o ante las Autoridades Locales (Orden del 15 de enero de 1924).

Todo extrangero desplazandose al interior del Pais debe hacer visar su carta de extrangero por las mismas Autoridades a la salida y en los 5 dias de la llegada a su nueva residencia (Orden del 9 de noviembre 1932).

En caso de una permanencia prolongada en Marruecos, deberá ser prorrogada cada ano par la aposicion de un nuevo sello fiscal.

La posesion de la carta de extrangeria no dispensa el cumplimiento de las formalidades prescritas por los dahires sobre la inmigracion o las autorizaciones de permanencia.

Taille / *Estatura* : 1,80 القامة
Front / *Frente* : الجبين
Nez / *Nariz* : الأنف
Bouche / *Boca* : الفم
Menton / *Menton* : الذقن
Visage / *Rostro* : الوجه
Cheveux / *Cabello* : الشعر
Barbe / *Barbo* : اللحية
Corpulence / *Corpulencia* : البدانة
Yeux / *Ojos* : العين
Teint / *Tez* : اللون

العلامات الخصوصية
Marques particulières
Senas particulares

Arrivé au Maroc le / *Llegada a Marruecos el* 16-3-1961 وصل الى المغرب بتاريخ
Par / *Por* C/Blanca على طريق
Immatriculé à / *Matriculado en* C/Blanca مسجل في
Le / *El* 30-3-1961 بتاريخ
Registre No / *Registro No* 1497 Folio 82 صحيفة كناش عدد
Pièces d'identité produites / *Piézas de identidad producidas* Passt N° C 236480 اوراق التعريف المدلى بها
A / *En* C/Blanca le / *el* 30-3-1961 في
(Signature et cachet de l'Autorité ayant délivré) / *(Firma y sello de la Autoridad expedidora)* (امضاء وطابع السلطة التي اذنت)

Le Commissaire Chef des Renseignements

Fig. 11 Moroccan registration forms of David & Gisele Littman, March and April 1961

8 April 1961

Mlle N. Lehmann,
O.S.S.E.A.N.
Genève, Suisse

Dear Madam Lehmann,
I am sorry that there has been a gap of two weeks
between this letter and my last one and I thank you for yours of the
27th. March. I wonder if you have had any good fortune in your approach
to the "Swiss government authorities"?

Unfortunately I have not been too well since the 27th.
and after my wife's auspicious arrival on the 31st. the cold I was
enduring was complicated by a severe nose bleed which had to be cauter-
izised,with the result that I was completely indisposed and in bed
throughout the Easter period. Happily this is all over now and I can
report a certain amount of success for the initial phase of our
programme.

Early to-morrow my wife and I are leaving on a little
trip to Ksar el Souk via Fes. The Secretary-General of the Entre'Aide,
of whose work you are well aware, has given me a very kind letter of
introduction to visit their establishments in various parts of the
country, and on our return I shall endeavour to obtain be presented to
Her Majesty, Lalla Aicha, the sister of the king,whose reputation is
world-wide and who is the Président of the Entre'Aide. On this same voyage
we shall visit one or two hospitals, and the Minister of Health, himself
was good enough to give me a letter for this purpose. This will enable
me not only to see the fine work that is being done in these two fields,
but also to correlate this with our programme of helping children to come
for a cure, repos, or convalescence in Switzerland. At the same time we
shall visit a few Red Cross centres where M. Reinhard will show us what
is being done to help the Algerian refugees et cetera. If we can spare
a moment to see Fez and the other cities en route as well as to ride a
camel in the desert we shall do so, but I am dubious about the possibility

The Swiss Consul has received the letter from
M. Maeder and has promised to facilitate this side of my work and has
left orders that in his absence there should be no delay. The British
Consul is a charming personality and with his help I shall begin (my
wife and I, rather) to meet the largish British community; he,himself,
is an early morning Tennis player. I am happy to say that there is a
Church of England church here, so our spiritual needs will not be
neglected. He is anxious to introduce me to persons engaged in similar
sort of work to ours.

Would you please tell me to which Home the boy
with Haemophilia will be sent, and all related information on this
subject since M. Reinhard would like to approach the boy's father and
cannot do so without explaining the entire matter to him? This is most
important and your immediate co-operation would be much appreciated
If you have the "cliché" of the photograph of the
Morgins Home,please send it immediately as I shall be inserted an
announcement in two newspapers in about two weeks and without it I must
pay a further 23 to 30 Dirhams.

In about two weeks I must go to London (my expense)
of course) via Gibralter, which is much cheaper, to bring out our baby
daughter. This operation will take two days.

With great good fortune I have been able to rent a
office from the 15th. April, monthly at 250 Drhs. The address is: 105,
Rue Dumont d'Urville, Casablanca (under the name of the Oeuvre).

Fig. 12 Letter from D.G. Littman to N. Lehmann, April 8, 1961

During his one-week tour in southern Morocco, Littman plans to visit establishments of the
Entr'Aide Nationale and hospitals as well as Red Cross centers to see if there are children
in need of a cure in Switzerland. He received letters of recommendations from both the
Entr'Aide Nationale and the Health Ministry. Upon his return he hopes to meet with Her
Majesty, Princess Lalla Aïcha, the sister of the king and the President of the Entr'Aide. He
finally meet with the Swiss consul who promised to facilitate the visa procedure and has
made contact with the British Consul. He will open an office of OSSEAN at Rue Dumont
D'Urville in Casablanca.

105, Rue Dumont D'Urville, Casablanca. Tel: 265.53

The Secretary-General,
O.S.S.E.A.N.
Case Postale, 220
Genève, 1.

Dear Madam,

We returned from our week's tour on the 16th. April and I was pleased to receive your letter awaiting me at the Hotel Anfa. The tour itself was most interesting and gave us an insight into the good work being done here in so many fields.

The Oeuvre is now installed in offices at the above address and I have given you also the telephone number (subject to confirmation which should be functioning in a few days. I have taken these offices until the end of April, and thereafter on a monthly basis, notice being given either on the 15th. or the 30th. of any month for ending the letting

I asked, in my last letter of the 8th. April, for the cliché of the Morgins Home photograph. This has not yet arrived, nor do you refer to the matter in your letter of the 13th. April. I have decided to let the newspaper re-make a cliché from the prospectus photograph, especially as one of the journalists whom I met promised to write an introductory article with the photograph without cost, and I shall follow this up by inserting small announcements every week. This kindness on the part of this journalist will save the Oeuvre about 200 S.F. and it is an example of the co-operation one finds here in Marocco towards our work. At the same time I am endeavouring to obtain the assistance of another newspaper (there are two main ones), and also to have something printed in an Arab language newspaper. But all this takes time(it has taken me three days simply to contact one journalist), yet in the end it will help considerably to publicize our action in favour of Maroccan children and will enable both the private person as well as the institutions to come into contact with us, which is of the utmost importance as you well know. The introductory article which I mentioned above should be published this week or early next week and I shall send you a copy.

With reference to the financial aspect and your contacts with our delegate in Berne, I must re-iterate once again that our price is not feasible in any sense when compared with the cost of living here. It is quite clear that our programme can only interest those financially easy and I shall endeavour to get in contact with the appropriate schools through the Minister of Education. Of course this will still serve the purpose of establishing an entretien between Marocco and Switzerland, but the poor will not be able to afford it and the various institutions have not as yet shown any interest to co-operate financially. Only this morning the Entre'Aide Scolaire - a Jewish organization - represented by its President, made it quite clear that they(like the Entre'Aide National and the Jeunesse at des Sport etc.) had no funds available for such "luxuries"; they more or less hinted that we were wasting our time, although they agreed that individual cases might present themselves, and in fact the secretary suggested that he might wish to send his own son , and I left a prospectus. Our good intentions have so far not yielded their fruit but perhaps this will change soon. You are sure the price cannot be in any way reduced ?- and how much for the " special cases " ? Unless a group is sent with its teacher (an orphanage for example) it is difficu to envisage anything developing before the summer holidays the end of Jun On this point I am sure, and it is understandable.

Fig. 13 Letter from D.G. Littman to OSSEAN, April 18 and 22, 1961

Littman encloses in this letter the leaflet of OSSEAN translated into Arabic which will be published in a French and an Arabic newspaper. This should allow private people and institutions to contact him, but it is impossible to expect people to pay ten Swiss francs per child,

With regard to the boy suffering from Haemophilia I cannot co-relate
your letters of the 21st. March and the 13th. April. In the former you
state that the boy will be taken care of and put in the "meilleurs
conditions",and in the latter you refer to the necessity of finding the
means to " placer l'enfant." M. Reinhard is slightly perplexed, but
will endeavour to discover the details about the boy's cousin (of which
he was ignorant) so that the father will know to what sort of establishment his unfortunate child is going. On the other hand it would be as
well for you to give me all the details as to where the boy will be sent
et cetera,when you have them, as M. Reinhard has already once asked me
and as yet I have not received a reply, which complicates matters.

2/4/61
    I delayed this letter in order to be able to send you the
newspaper clipping, but due to the furore caused by the Algerian news
the article on the Oeuvre will not appear until ~~until~~ Monday.

    May I ask you to endeavour to find suitable Homes during the
Summer months (especially the months of July and August) in the
eventuality that they will be required. I am aware that the Home at
Champéry/Vs is available until the 25th. June and naturally enough
I shall do my very best to arrange something before this expiry date,
but you must understand that it is not easy to send suitable children
during the school term- unless, as I stated above, a professor or
teacher goes with an entire class, probably an orphanage. Of course
during July and August it will be difficult to find accommodation at
Morgins itself and I must leave you to decide upon the double issues
involved here. It would seem that we should endeavour to have available
a smallish Home (like that of Champéry) able to take about 30 children
and another rather larger to take the place of Morgins should the latter
be full. For the moment all arrangements must be tentative until such
time as I can arrange something sure, and now that most of the necessary
contacts have been made or will be made within the next week or so the
going should be easier,- but such operations take time! I know all too
well that it ~~decided~~ is difficultfor you, yet that is the situation.
    I have ~~decided~~ it is wiser for me to travel to London to collect
our baby,via Paris,instead of via Gibralter. This journey will most
probably take place the week after next during the early days of May.
Since I have decided to take this route I shall stop off to see a cousin
I have not seen for many years and if there is any little commission
I can do on behalf of yourself, Madam, or of the Oeuvre I will be only
to happy to comply. My departure dates are changeable and you could
telegraph me:"ANFOTEL Casablanca." Naturally I will telephone you from
Paris,where the cost is not so great, to convey my personal good wishes.
    I hereby enclose a detailed list of all the moneys I have laid
out with most of the bills that go with it. This is a tedious business
and you might let me know if I should continue in the same manner my
reports in this respect or in a different way. Please bank the total in
the Account specially opened for the purpose and have them send me a
full Statement as soon as possible. I would like to start drawing from
this account.

    I remain , dear Madam, your humble and obedient servant.

        (D.G. Littman)

P.S. Enclosed a specimen of one of my new cartes de visites, and a copy
of the prospectus in French and Arabic. I wonder if you put any more
in the post to me here. If not I shall probably print a combined French/
Arabic one if I feel it is necessary. At least I shall have the photograph
put on the bac

0222
1:)
reo.

he writes, after meetings with Muslim and Jewish institutions. He inquires about the boy
with haemophilia and asks that two homes be found for the period of July–August. Littman
is about to fly to London via Paris to 'collect' his baby daughter, Diana.

المؤسسة الخيرية السويسرية لاعانة اطفال شمال افريقيا

دار الغابة

بمورجن (فالى) البالغ علوها عن سطح البحر 1400 متـرا
مفتوحـة للرواد خـلال السنـة كلهـا

Fig. 14 Prospectus in Arabic & French of OSSEAN's the "Home de la Forêt" in Switzerland
This leaflet advertises OSSEAN's "Home de la Forêt" situated in the mountainous village of Morgins in the Swiss Valais, a place particularly suited for convalescence. There, children benefit from suitable lodging, medical care and many sport activities. The leaflet originally in French was translated into Arabic and appeared in a French and Arab language newspaper.

ان الغرض الاساسي والهدف المنشود للمؤسسة السويسرية لاعانة اطفال شمال افريقيا هو العناية بصحة الاطفال الذين يقيمون بالمناطق التي كانت مسرحا للاحداث الاخيرة المفجعة ، ولنفس هذا الهدف لقيت هذه المؤسسة تشجيعا واعانة تامة من طرف المنشئات السويسرية الاخرى التي وضعت رهن اشارتها دار الغابة بمورجن وبضم منازل اخرى في نفس الناحية حيث يمكن للاطفال ان يقضوا عطلة ممتعة ومقاما طيبا في هواء نقي وبعيد عن البحر .

ان دار الغابة الواقعة على علو 1400 متر من سطح البحر وفوق نجد تحيط به غابات الصنوبر وعلى حدود ، الفالي ، ومقاطعة ، السافوا ، العليا تشرف عليها سلسلة جبال ، الالب ، الممتدة من وادي ، الرون ، الى الجبال التي تقع تحت اقدام ، الرأس الابيض ، وتمتاز ناحية مورجن بطقس جميل يساعد الخصوص على الاستحمام من العناء الفكري وضيق النفس ونقص التغذية ومن فقر الدم والضعف الناشئين عن الامراض المعدية واجراء العمليات الجراحية .

لقد نظمت دار الغابة بعناية رجال اختصاصيين ، وتوجد بها 40 حجرة منها حجرة ذات فراشين واخرى ذات ثلاثة افرشة كما توجد بها فصول دراسية وقاعات للالعاب ومعامل ومصحة ورشاشات وحمامات ، وقد اتخذت جميع الاجراءات والوسائل حتى يستفيد الاطفال اقصى ما يمكن من اقامتهم بالجبل ومدة الاقامة العادية شهر واحد . وبما أن دار الغابة تملك مدرسة منظمة من طرف ولاية (فالي) فيمكن الاطفال ان اقتضى الحال ان يطيلوا اقامتهم اكثر من شهر دون ان يضيعوا دراستهم .

وتعطى اهمية كبرى في الدار الى الرياضة البدنية والعاب الهواء الطلق فالتلال السهلة التسلق والمزالق وركوبات الاطفال تتيح امكانيات كثيرة وفرصا سعيدة للقيام بجولات مختلفة ورياضات متنوعة سواء في فصل الصيف او خلال فصل الشتاء .

وتقبل الدار من الاطفال من تتراوح اعمارهم بين 12 الى 16 سنة .

وتتوجه طلبات القبول مصحوبة بشهادة طبية الى العنوان التالي :

المؤسسة الخيرية السويسرية لاعانة اطفال شمال افريقيا
105 زنقة ديمون دورفيل الدار البيضاء : تلفون : 265.53
يقبل التسجيل ابتداء من 8 ماي 1961 و في ايام الاثنين و الثلاثاء، و الاربعاء في كل اسبوع ساعات التسجيل 9 الى 12 و من 3 الى 6 مساءً
105, Rue Dumont d'Urville · Casablanca · Tél. 265-53

ŒUVRE SUISSE DE SECOURS AUX ENFANTS DES PAYS DE L'AFRIQUE DU NORD

HOME DE LA FORÊT

**MORGINS (Valais) Altitude 1400 mètres
Ouvert toute l'année**

Doc. 8

L'Œuvre Suisse de Secours aux Enfants de l'Afrique du Nord s'occupe en premier lieu de la santé des enfants résidant dans les zones éprouvées par les derniers événements. Dans ce but, elle s'est assurée la collaboration d'œuvres suisses qui ont pu mettre à sa disposition le Home de la Forêt à Morgins, ainsi que quelques autres maisons de la région, permettant à ses protégés de faire d'excellentes cures d'altitude et de plein air.

Le Home de la Forêt situé à 1400 mètres d'altitude, sur un plateau entouré de vastes forêts de pins, à la frontière du Valais et de la Haute-Savoie, est protégé par la chaîne des Alpes Valaisannes qui s'étend de la Vallée du Rhône jusqu'aux contreforts du Mont-Blanc. La station de Morgins jouit d'un climat particulièrement favorable pour le traitement du surmenage, de l'asthme, de la sous-alimentation, de l'anémie et de l'asthénie à la suite de maladies contagieuses ou d'interventions chirurgicales.

La maison a été aménagée sous la surveillance de spécialistes. Elle possède 40 chambres à deux et trois lits, des salles de classe, salles de jeux, ateliers, infirmerie, douches et salles de bains. Toutes les dispositions ont été prises pour assurer aux enfants la possibilité de profiter dans la plus large mesure de leur séjour à la montagne. Le séjour normal s'étend sur un mois, mais comme la maison possède une école primaire organisée par l'Etat du Valais, les enfants qui nécessitent un séjour plus prolongé peuvent parfaire leur santé sans perdre une année scolaire.

Beaucoup d'attention est donnée à l'éducation physique, ainsi qu'aux jeux en plein air. Les collines faciles à escalader, la patinoire, les ski-lifts, télésièges et monte-pentes offrent d'excellentes possibilités pour les excursions et le sport tant en été que pendant les mois d'hiver.

Le Home admet des enfants de 12 à 16 ans.

Les demandes d'admission accompagnées d'un certificat médical sont à adresser à :

*Œuvre Suisse de Secours aux Enfants de l'Afrique du Nord
Genève 1 Dépôt, Case postale 220*

D. G. LITTMAN
DÉLÉGUÉ
DE L'ŒUVRE SUISSE DE SECOURS AUX ENFANTS
DES PAYS DE L'AFRIQUE DU NORD

DOMICILE :
HOTEL ANFA
TÉL. : 502-22
CASABLANCA

BUREAUX :
105, RUE DUMONT D'URVILLE
TÉL. : 265.53
CASABLANCA

Fig. 15 Visit card of D.G. Littman, delegate of OSSEAN

L	125 00
~~Concierge~~	7 50 taxe édilité
~~Eclairage~~	
~~Timbre~~	
~~Eau~~	
TOTAL	132 50

QUITTANCE DE LOYER

N° 15

Reçu de M onsieur Littman
la somme de Cent trente deux Dirhams cinquante frs
pour le montant d'une période de loyer des locaux qu'il occupe dans la maison située 105 Rue Dumont d'Urville
le dite période commençant le 15 Avril et finissant le 30 Avril 1961 sous toutes réserves de droit : DONT QUITTANCE

NOTA. — Un locataire ne peut déménager :
1° Qu'il n'ait justifié au propriétaire par une quittance du Receveur qu'il a acquitté toutes ses contributions personnelle et mobilière de l'année courante.
2° Qu'il n'ait donné ou reçu congé par écrit, dans les délais prescrits.
3° Qu'il n'ait fait faire toutes les réparations locatives à sa charge suivant l'usage ou d'après l'état des lieux s'il en existe un.
Il ne pourra sous louer, en tout ou en partie, les locaux cédés sans le consentement du propriétaire.

DUPLICATA

Loyer	265
Concierge	
Eclairage	
Timbre	
Eau	
TOTAL	265

QUITTANCE DE LOYER

N° 33

Reçu de M onsieur Littman
la somme de deux cent soixante cinq Dirhams
pour le montant d'un mois de loyer des locaux qu'il occupe dans la maison située 105 Rue Dumont d'Urville
le dit mois commençant le 1er juillet et finissant le 31 juillet 1961 sous toutes réserves de droit : DONT QUITTANCE

NOTA. — Un locataire ne peut déménager :
1° Qu'il n'ait justifié au propriétaire par une quittance du Receveur qu'il a acquitté toutes ses contributions personnelle et mobilière de l'année courante.
2° Qu'il n'ait donné ou reçu congé par écrit, dans les délais prescrits.
3° Qu'il n'ait fait faire toutes les réparations locatives à sa charge suivant l'usage ou d'après l'état des lieux s'il en existe un.
Il ne pourra sous louer, en tout ou en partie, les locaux cédés sans le consentement du propriétaire.

Fig. 16 Bill from OSSEAN's office at Rue Dumont D'Urville in Casablanca

ŒUVRE SUISSE DE SECOURS
AUX ENFANTS DE L'AFRIQUE DU NORD

Genève 1, Case postale 220

Genève, le 7 Mai 1961

Mr.D.G.LITTMAN,
Oeuvre Suisse de Secours
aux Enfants de l'Afrique du Nord,
105, rue Dumont d'Urville ,
C a s a b l a n c a .

Cher Monsieur,

En rapport avec nos divers échanges de dorrespondance,
nous nous empressons de vous communiquer ce qui suit:

1. Prix de pension et réductions:

Après consultation avec nos amis de Berne, il a été décidé
qu'une réduction du prix journalier en dessous des Frs.13.-
exigé par Madame TRUFFER, directrice de l'Hôtel du Parc à
Champéry ne peut être consentie, tant que l'action n'ait pris
une plus grande envergure.

Il faut donc d'abord organiser un transport de
100 à 200 enfants au taux complet. Seulement au moment où ce
chiffre sera atteint et où on verra que l'action se développe
avec l'effectif prévu, nos amis de Berne seront d'accord
de changer leur attitude et de consentir des réductions pour
un certain pourcentage de cas.

Il faut donc absolument que vous tendrez compte
de ces instructions et que vous preniez vos engagements en
suivant ces directives.

2. L'Hôtel du Parc à Champéry dans lequel nous proposons de
réaliser la colonie marocaine dispose de 105 places, mais
entre le 25 Juillet et le 7 Août, il doit héberger 70 anglais.
Donc, du 20 Juin au 24 Juillet, on pourra héberger un effectif
de 100 enfants et à partir du 8 Août de nouveau le même nombre,
tandisque entre le 25.7. au 7.8., on ne pourra pas avoir plus
de 30 lits, pour notre groupe.

3. Cadres: Comme il est difficile de trouver sur place du personnel
qualifié, parlant le français et l'arabe, notre organisation est prête à accepter l'encadrement du groupe envoyé par
vous, et ces éducateurs seraient hébergés gratuitement. On doit
compter un éducateur (ou éducatrice) sur 12 à 15 enfants.
Il serait nécessaire qu'il y ait au moins une personne du sexe
féminin parmi les éducateurs, car pour les fillettes, il sera
nécessaire d'avoir une femme. La meilleure solution serait
qu'un couple marié prenne la direction du groupe. Le Salaire de
ces éducateurs ne peut pas être pris à notre charge.

Nous attendons de vos nouvelles avec grand intérêt
et vous prions d'agréer, Cher Monsieur, nos meilleures salutations

O.S.S.E.A.N.

Fig. 17 Letter from N. Lehmann to D.G. Littman, May 7, 1961

In this letter N. Lehmann writes that after consulting with "their friends in Bern" (Naphtali Bar-

Giora of the Jewish Agency and Arieh Reiffler from the Youth Aliyah in Marseilles) it has been

decided that the rate will be thirteen Swiss francs per child, unless there are a hundred to

two hundred children registered. She also mentions that between July 27 and August 7, there

will be a group of British tourists in Champery and therefore only a small amount of beds

will be available. She informs Littman that their office can't provide for the monitors' salary.

105, Rue Dumont d'Urville. Casablanca/Maroc.

May 9th. 1961

Mlle. N. Lehmann,
Oeuvre Suisse de Secours
aux Enfants de l'Afrique
du Nord. Case Postale, 220.
Genève, 1, Suisse.

Dear Madam,
  Your Express letter of the 7th; May arrived this morning,
for which I thank you.

1.) Prix de pension et réductions:
  I have taken note of your remarks on this subject and would refer
your attention to my last letter to you from London where I discussed
this at great length in my poor English. I cannot possibly be more
clear than this; let it be translated into Swiss German for the
benefit of the Berne office who must approve all financial matters.
It is just no good at all informing me at this late stage that the
new Home(or hotel) at Champéry/Vs. is Frs.13 per day etcetera,
after I have been negotiating on a top price of 10 Frs. with possible
reductions for necessitous children. I have had a few demands from
wealthier persons and these might pay Frs.13- if I accept their
children- but to expect me to go back to the Ministère de l'Education
Nationale and the Secrétaire-Général and raise the prices is wishful
thinking. Berne must be made to understand that (a.) the cost of
living here is very much lower than in any part of Europe,(b.) it is
most unusual for parents, institutions, or governmental bodies to
send children to Europe for convalescence or holidays when they can
find accomodation here in Marocco for a nominal cost, (c.) our
Oeuvre is attempting to make it possible for these children to benefit
from a stay in Switzerland et cetera, and therefore we must accept a
much greater financial burden than we do for European children. Our
good-will shall have its human rewards and Berne can rejoice with
you, Madam, and all our colleagues when our economic advisers there
see the happy faces of these Maroccan children on the arrival in
Switzerland and their return home. The conditions laid down in my
letter of the 6th. May will apply.
  If there should be a definite disapproval of my actions from
a distance of 2000 kilometres and an attempt made to tie my hands in
advance, I would ask you, dear Madam, to arrange for my replacement
by a more able colleague. I would remind you that from the beginning
I insisted on the months of July and August, and that Homes should
be " more or less in readiness "- however difficult it might be. To
present me at this late stage with a hotel at Frs. 13 is not my
affair. I shall do my best to resolve this minor financial problem,
but I must concentrate on completing my task for the benefit of these
children and in this respect once again I refer you and our Berne
colleagues to the calculations in my previous letter. I understand
the sine quâ non (translate!) and expect co-operation not obstruction

2.) L'Hôtel du Parc à Champéry: Do I understand that we must take all
  the available beds for the whole summer period not occupied by the
English group, or can we restrict our obligations. I very much doubt
if you will have the numbers and groups you require for this Home as
early as the 20th. June. YOU HAVE NOT REFERRED TO THE SMALLER HOMES
which you mentioned to me on my recent visit to Geneva and I would
be most grateful if you could give me all the details IMMEDIATELY
for otherwise I cannot work properly. These Homes are on a 10 Frs.

Fig. 18 Letter from D.G. Littman to N. Lehmann, May 9, 1961

In this letter, Littman sarcastically replies to Lehmann that thirteen Swiss francs. per child

is totally unrealistic in view of the local cost of living and in view of the fact that it is very

unusual of parents or institutions to send children to Europe for convalescence. He expects

co-operation and not obstruction and should this be disapproved by their contacts in Bern

basis so you stated. It is important that the Valaisian countryside
is scourred for suitable Homes so that WHEN you know the numbers I
have on this side you can arrange everything accordingly.

I trust that you have already posted the four letters requested
and the copies to me. This is most important.

On Thursday, the 11th. I am going to Rabat for a meeting with
M. Omar Senoussi, representing the Minister of Education. Unfortunately
M. Ahmad Ghoumari will not be in Rabat until Friday morning and I hope
that something solid will result from my conversations on these two
days, assuming M. Ghoumari is actually in his office on Friday morning.
On the same Thursday I have a meeting at the 'Division Consulaire et
Sociale' of the Ministère des Affaires Etrangers. M. Chaoui, the head
of this department dealing with passport formalities, is on pilgrimage
to Mecca, and I can only hope that his temporary retirement will
facilitate my job. On the telephone yesterday there was a suggestion
that each child's parents apply for an individual passport if that is
what is desired, but to me on Wedne Thursday we shall discuss the
whole question of collective and/or individual passports, and I trust
this small issue will be resolved satisfactorily.

When I speak to M. Choumari I shall attempt to outline the
reductions we spoke of on my last visit. Of course I am awaiting
your letter on this point confirming these instructions, and I shall
say the same to M. Ghoumari, but it is necessary that I make some
gesture immediately and thus receive a more or less categorical reply.
As agreed upon the reductions will be on a proportional basis. I
suggest the following:- Assume for convenience total of 100 children.
5% of children coming from Entr'Aide Nationale: at 5 Frs. (750)
10% of   "   "   "   "   "   "   "   : at 6 Frs. (1200)
25% of   "   "   "   "   "   "   "   : at 7 Frs. (1875)
65% of   "   "   "   "   "   "   "   : at 10 Frs. Original cos
The figures in red are the amounts in Swiss francs that these
further reductions will cost the Oeuvre, assuming they are applied to
100 children for a period of one month. The Total figure is 3825 Frs. f
To send such a number of children the Entr'Aide Nationale would have
to provide more than seven times this amount and at the same time
provide the transport as arranged. The Ministry of Education, who has
agreed to pay the full 10 Frs. " if the Entr'Aide arranges the transpor
will not be offered the same reductions- I will know more about his
requirements on Thursday, but a figure of from thirty to fifty childrer
was mentioned on my last visit.
This additional cost is not great and should be accepted to allow
the sails to open to their fullest extent. I realize that if we have
to turn to the hotel at Champéry/Vs. at 13 frs.,then for 100 children
during one month we must add a further 9000 Frs.,yet I cannot be
expected to raise the 'prix de séjour' and therefore I cannot consider
this late developement as my responsibility. Even adding these two
figures together the figure is not so large that the Oeuvre cannot
support it,viewed from the results, of good-will which should follow
to produce these results. Let us put the horse before the cart!; be
assured that the horse will not part without the cart.
3.)Cadres:
This will be taken into consideration,but can only apply to group:
sent by those who can provide an éducateur. I will keep you informed.
I await your Express letter with all the information you omitted
in your last, plus the copies of the letters you sent to Rabat, and
the letters referring to reductions and the kitchen. On Thursday I shal
hhave to act without the former.

(Bar-Giora and Reiffler) he asked to be replaced by a more able colleague. He mentions his upcoming meetings with a high official at the Minister of Education, Mr. Omar Senoussi and with an official replacing Mr. Chaoui currently on pilgrimage to Mecca. In these meetings he plans to discuss possible reductions for Muslim children of the Entr'Aide and the collective or individual passports.

ŒUVRE SUISSE DE SECOURS
AUX ENFANTS DE L'AFRIQUE DU NORD

Genève 1, Case postale 220

Ambassade de Suisse, Rabat
16 MAI 1961
B4 $6.65.40$

01545

Genève, le 9 Mai 1961

Monsieur Erwin BERNATH
Ambassadeur de la Suisse
Case Postale 169
R a b a t .

Monsieur l'Ambassadeur,

Vous avez certainement été informé par la Police Fédérale
des Etrangers que notre Oeuvre a entrepris, par son délégué,
Mr. D.G.LITTMAN, une action ayant pour but d'accueillir des
enfants marocains dans des homes en Suisse pour y passer leurs
vacances d'été.

On a suggéré à notre délégué, des instances gouvernementales
qu'une intervention de notre part auprès de Son Altesse Royale,
la Princesse Lalla Aïcha pourrait simplifier les démarches
pour l'obtention de facilités de transport et de documents de
voyage. C'est pourquoi nous prenons la liberté de vous demander
de bien vouloir transmettre la lettre ci-jointe à Son Altesse
Royale, et nous vous remercions très sincèrement de votre
sollicitude.

En réitérant nos remerciements, nous vous prions d'agréer,
Monsieur l'Ambassadeur, l'assurance de notre haute considération.

OEUVRE SUISSE DE SECOURS AUX ENFANTS
DE L'AFRIQUE DU NORD

Le Président

Prof.E.ABERSON

**Fig. 19 Letter from Prof. E. Aberson, President of OSSEAN to the Swiss Ambassador
E. Bernath, May 9, 1961 (File G.65.40.sd)**

Prof. E. Aberson (OSSEAN) mentions Mr. Maeder's letter related to OSSEAN's action in
bringing Moroccan children to Switzerland during the summer vacation. Prof. Aberson
would like to forward through the Swiss Embassy, a letter to her Excellency Princess Lalla
Aïcha. Governmental authorities told him that the Princess could help in facilitating the
transportation and the necessary documents for the children's journey.

ŒUVRE SUISSE DE SECOURS
AUX ENFANTS DE L'AFRIQUE DU NORD

Genève, Case postale 220

à Son Altesse Royale,
La Princesse Lalla
A g d a l - Rabat

Votre Altesse Royale,

Connaissant l'intérêt que Votre Altesse a
manifesté à maintes reprises pour le travail social que nous faisons,
nous prenons la liberté de vous exposer en quelques mots le but
de notre Œuvre au profit des enfants nord-africains.

Suivant la tradition suisse qui tend à faire bénéficier
du climat et des conditions favorables les enfants des pays
plus divers, nous avons entrepris, avec l'appui moral des autori-
rités de notre pays, de efforts pour mettre à la disposition des
enfants du Maroc des homes situés dans les Alpes Valaisannes, où
des groupes de jeunes marocains seraient accueillis pendant les
mois d'été pour y passer leurs vacances. Préférence devrait être
donnée, à des enfants ayant besoin d'une cure d'altitude, et nous
avons essayé de leur offrir les conditions les plus favorables.

Nous serions infiniment reconnaissants à Votre Altesse
Royale de bien vouloir accorder une audience à notre délégué,
Mr.D.G.LITTMAN, qui, au cours de son séjour au Maroc, ces derniers
temps, a eu l'occasion de prendre contact avec les autorités compétentes du pays, entre autres avec Mr. Ghoumari, Secrétaire Général
de l'Entr'Aide Nationale. Ceci permettrait à notre délégué de vous
exposer les problèmes de l'action entreprise.

En vous remerciant très sincèrement de toute aide
que vous voudrez bien accorder à notre délégué afin de lui permettre
de mener à bien cette action qui est dans l'intérêt de la santé et
du développement des enfants marocains, nous vous prions d'agréer,
Votre Altesse Royale, les sentiments respectueux de notre haute
considération.

ŒUVRE SUISSE DE SECOURS AUX ENFANTS
DE L'AFRIQUE DU NORD
Le Président

Prof.E.ABERSON

Fig. 20 Letter from Prof. E. Aberson, President of OSSEAN, to H.R.H. Princess Lalla Aïcha, May 9, 1961 (File G.65.40.sd)

Prof. E. Aberson (secretary-general of OSSEAN) explains to the Princess the aim of OSSEAN in bringing Moroccan children to spend their summer vacation in the Swiss Alps, preferably children in need of a cure. He asks the Princess to agree to meet with their delegate, D.G. Littman who has already had an interview with Mr. Ghoumari, the Secretary-General of the 'Entr'Aide Nationale.'

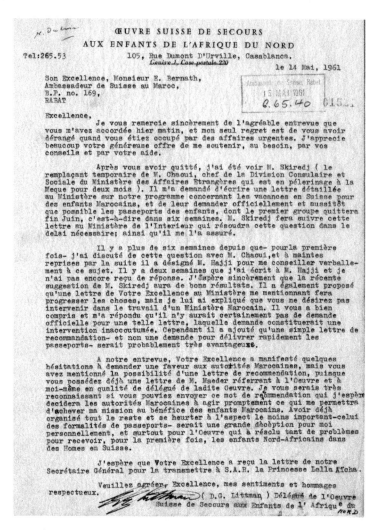

Fig. 21 Letter from D.G. Littman to the Swiss Ambassador in Rabat, Mr. E. Bernarth, May 14, 1961 (File G.65.40.sd)

Littman thanks the Ambassador for receiving him, and informs him of his meeting with Mr. Skiredj replacing Mr. Chaoui at the Consular and Social Division of the Foreign Ministry. Mr. Skiredj asks for a detailed letter on the summer holiday camp together with an official demand for passports to be forwarded to the Ministry of Interior. Mr. Skiredj believes that a letter from the Swiss Ambassador mentioning Mr. Littman would help speed up the passports formalities for the first convoy leaving in six weeks. A letter of recommendation, writes Littman, not a letter asking for a favour from the Moroccan authorities would be very helpful. Littman ends this letter hoping His Excellency received Prof. E. Aberson's letter to be forwarded to Princess Lalla Aïcha.

G.65.40 15 MAI 1961

"P"

EPD No.19 "ch"

Fremdenpolizei ermächtigt mich mit Brief vom 21. März Visas
für marokkanische Kinder, die sich zu einem Erholungsaufenthalt
nach "Morgins" auf Einladung und auf Kosten des schweiz. Kinder-
hilfswerkes für nordafrikanische Kinder stop Littman, Delegierter
                                       individuelle
des Werkes teilt mit mit erstens dass er zahlreiche/Anfragen,
durch Erziehungsministerium und "Entr'aide nationale" erhalten hat
zweitens dass Transportspesen vollständig zu Lasten der Teilnehmer
fallen und Aufenthaltskosten teilweise stop Littman, der gewisse
Organisationsschwierigkeiten hat verlangt Unterstützung durch Botschaft
um ihn bei der Prinzessin, die Hilfswerk leitet, und beim Aussenmini'
sterium etc. einzuführen (zu empfehlen) Kabelt ob einverstanden.

AMBASUISSE

Fig. 22 Telegram from the Swiss Ambassador E. Bernath to the Department of Foreign Affairs at the Federal Political Department (EPD), May 15, 1961 and the answer from the EPD, May 17, 1961 (File G.65.40.sd)

In this telegram in German to the Department of Foreign affairs, the Ambassador writes that following the March 21 letter from Mr. Maeder, (Federal Police for Foreigners) he will issue visas to the children invited by OSSEAN for a recreational stay in Morgins. Mr. Littman told him that he received requests from both the Ministry of Health and the Entr'Aide Nationale. The participants will fully cover transportation and partially the accommodation expenses. The Ambassador mentions that D.G. Littman asks for a recommendation from the Embassy and would like to be introduced to Princess Lalla Aïcha (President of the Entr'Aide Nationale) and to the Minister of Foreign Affairs. The Ambassador waits for instruction from the Political Department regarding this matter.

Réf.: 6.65.40

"p"

Telegramm No. 19 "ch" des EPD

Im Einverständnis mit FREPOL bitten wir Sie Ihre Intervention
auf Ausstellung Visas im Rahmen ihres Briefes vom 21. März zu
beschränken und sich von anderen Demarchen fernzuhalten stop.

Politique

The EPD (Federal Political Department) in Bern asks the Ambassador to restrict his intervention to issuing visas for the children as mentioned in Mr. Maeder's letter but nothing beyond this.

01117

18 mai 1961

G.65.40 - DU/ap

A la Division des affaires politiques
du Département politique fédéral

B e r n e

Oeuvre suisse de secours
aux enfants de l'Afrique du Nord

Monsieur le Ministre,

Je vous remercie de votre communication rapide du
17 mai 1961 concernant la demande d'intervention présentée
par M. Littman, délégué de l'Oeuvre citée en marge.

Selon vos directives, je m'abstiens de recommander
M. Littman auprès des autorités marocaines et me bornerai à
délivrer en temps voulu des visas d'entrée aux enfants marocains détenteurs d'un passeport national valable et en possession d'une invitation délivrée par M. Littman, conformément à la lettre du 21 mars 1961 de la Police fédérale des
étrangers.

A toutes fins utiles, je vous remets, pour votre information, la photocopie d'une lettre du 9 mai 1961 adressée
à SAR la Princesse Lalla Aïcha, Présidente de l'Entraide Nationale à Rabat, que M. E. Aberson, Président de l'Oeuvre
suisse intéressée, voulait acheminer par l'entremise de l'Ambassade. Je remettrai cette lettre à M. Littman lui-même à
l'occasion de sa prochaine visite à l'Ambassade. Je vous saurais gré de bien vouloir en informer M. Aberson si vous le jugez utile.

Ne connaissant pas l'Oeuvre suisse de secours aux enfants de l'Afrique du Nord et étant quelque peu étonné par sa
façon de procéder, je vous serais obligé, vu que cette Oeuvre
semble appelée à exercer son activité dans les pays de l'Afrique du Nord, de bien vouloir me donner toute information utile
la concernant.

Je vous en remercie d'ores et déjà et vous prie d'a-
gréer, Monsieur le Ministre, l'assurance de ma considération
distinguée.

L'Ambassadeur de Suisse :

Annexes : photocopies de 2 lettres
du 9 mai 1961

Fig. 23 Letter from Ambassador E. Bernath to the Political Affairs Division of the Federal Political Department (EPD) in Bern, May 18, 1961 (File G.65.40.sd)

In this letter to the Minister heading the Division of Political Affairs, the Ambassador refers to the telegram from the 17th asking him to refrain from giving a letter of recommendation to Mr. Littman but allowing him to issue visas to children invited by OSSEAN with valid passports. He sends the Minister copies of the letters from Prof. E. Aberson and writes that he will hand back to Mr. Littman the letter addressed to Princess Lalla Aïcha. The Ambassador is unaware of this specific organization and is somehow astonished by its rather improper way of proceeding. He requires information on OSSEAN from the Federal Political Department.

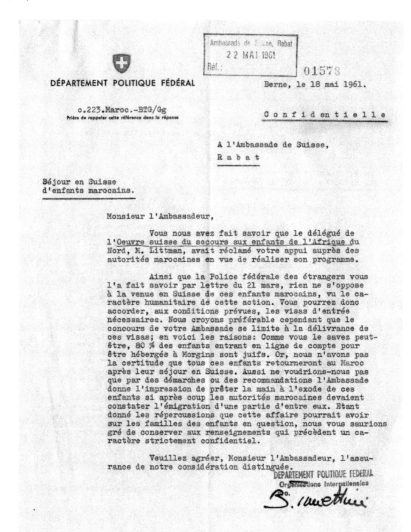

Fig. 24 Confidential letter from the Federal Political Department (International Organizations) in Bern to the Swiss Ambassador in Rabat, May 18, 1961 (File G.65.40.sd)
Although nothing opposes the emission of visas to Moroccan children coming on a humanitarian mission to Switzerland, it is preferable, that the Embassy limits itself to granting visas for the following reasons: firstly, eighty percent of the children coming to Morgins are Jewish and secondly some might not return to Morocco after their vacation. Should the Moroccan authorities were to notice the emigration of some of these children, the Swiss Embassy should not be seen as having helped this 'exodus.' The Minister asks for his information to remain confidential so that it doesn't have repercussions on the families of the children.

COPIE *confidentiel*

Copie à l'Ambassade de Suisse pour
son information. *Mich*

CONSULAT DE SUISSE
CASABLANCA

CASABLANCA, le 23 mai 1961
81, Boulevard de Paris
Téléphones 601 11 – 601 12
Boîte Postale 5

...ade de ...se, Rabat
25 MAI 1961
Réf.: **6.65.40**

01623

Réf.:   X.4.1.61 – JB/hl

ad: B 12/128 Bo/bu

Police Fédérale des Etrangers

B e r n e

Monsieur le Directeur,

Vous avez bien voulu m'adresser, pour mon information, une copie de votre lettre du 21 mars 1961
à l'Ambassade de Suisse à Rabat, au sujet de l'Oeuvre
suisse de Secours aux enfants des pays de l'Afrique du
Nord.

A trois reprises, j'ai eu la visite de son
délégué, M. David Littmann, que j'ai mis en rapport,
entre autres, avec le Docteur Eric WITZ, médecin de confiance du Consulat, au sujet de la visite sanitaire à
laquelle sont astreints les enfants se rendant en Suisse
sur invitation de l'Oeuvre en question.

A ce propos, j'ai reçu du Dr Witz une communication ayant la teneur suivante :

" Monsieur D.G. Littmann, délégué de l'Oeuvre suisse
de secours aux enfants des pays de l'Afrique du Nord,
est venu me trouver en ma qualité de médecin de confiance du Consulat.
          Il m'a présenté le questionnaire médical qu'il
avait l'intention de faire remplir par le ou les médecins chargés d'examiner ses jeunes protégés.
          J'ai attiré son attention sur les faits suivants :
ce questionnaire, certainement valable pour la Suisse,
a été conçu avec une méconnaissance totale de l'esprit
des gens de ce pays. Il présente, par ailleurs, des
lacunes à mon avis très importantes, à savoir par
exemple : – absence de sérologie syphilitique,
                  – absence d'un examen du cuir chevelu.
En effet, la syphilis et les teignes (favus et
teigne tondante trichophytique) règnent ici avec un
caractère endémique. J'espère que ce délégué tiendra
compte de mon avis et exigera ces deux examens."

Je tenais à vous faire part de ce qui précède,
en vous laissant le soin d'intervenir auprès de la Direction de l'oeuvre en question, dans le sens de la suggestion
faite par le médecin de confiance du Consulat.

...

**Fig. 25 Confidential letter from the Swiss Consul in Casablanca, Mr. J. Birchler, to the
Federal Police in Bern, May 23, 1961 (File G.65.40.sd)**

The Consul acknowledges the letter by the Federal Police of March 21 and writes that Mr.
David Littman visited him three times. He put him in contact with Dr. Eric Witz. the trusted
doctor of the Consulate regarding the obligatory examination for the children sent by his

- 2 -

Par ailleurs, plusieurs personnes m'ont demandé de les renseigner sur cette oeuvre et son délégué, qui est sujet britannique.

A titre confidentiel, j'ajoute que mes interlocu- teurs semblaient s'étonner quelque peu qu'une oeuvre de secours suisse soit représentée en Afrique du Nord par un délégué étranger.

Vous m'obligeriez vivement en me faisant parvenir quelques renseignements sur cette oeuvre charitable.

Veuillez agréer, Monsieur le Directeur, l'assu- rance de ma considération distinguée.

Le Consul de Suisse

J. Birchler

organization. Witz had emitted reservations on the medical certificates Littman brought him since syphilis and lice exams do not figure on those certificates. The Consul conveys to the Ambassador Witz's observations hoping that the Director of OSSEAN will consider them. The Consul concludes his letter by mentioning that several people have inquired about OSSEAN and its British delegate, and were astonished that a Swiss organization acting in North Africa should be represented by a foreign delegate. He asks for more information regarding this charity.

25. Mai 1961

G.65.40. - EB/be
ad: o.223.Maroc.-BTG/Og

<u>Vertraulich</u>

An die
Abteilung für Internationale Organisa-
tionen des Eidgenössischen Politischen
Departements

<u>Bern</u>

Herr Minister,

       Ich danke Ihnen für Ihr Schreiben vom 18. Mai, mit
dem Sie sich zu meiner Anfrage betreffend das "Oeuvre suisse de
secours aux enfants de l'Afrique du Nord" und seinen Delegierten
in Marokko, dem britischen Staatsangehörigen Herrn Littman,
Russern. Herr Littman, der für die genannte Organisation den
Aufenthalt marokkanischer Kinder in der Schweiz organisieren soll,
hatte sich bekanntlich mit der Bitte an mich gewandt, ihm in ver-
schiedener Weise dabei behilflich zu sein. Ihr Schreiben hat sich
übrigens mit meinem Brief vom gleichen Datum gekreuzt, den ich
jedoch an die Abteilung für Politische Angelegenheiten richtete.

       Die Auskünfte, die Sie mir inzwischen erteilten,
haben mich, offen gestanden, beunruhigt, denn es war mir nicht be-
kannt, dass ein grosser Prozentsatz der für den Aufenthalt in der
Schweiz in Frage kommenden Kinder der jüdischen Gemeinde angehören.
Wenn es zutrifft, dass 80 % der Kinder Juden sind und diese zum
Teil nicht mehr nach Marokko zurückkehren, so haben wir ohne Zweifel grösste Schwierigkeiten zu befürchten. Und zwar müssen wir
damit rechnen, auch wenn die Botschaft sich jetzt aller Interven-
tionen enthält, denn erstens bezeichnet sich die Organisation als
"Schweizerisches Hilfswerk" und zweitens lässt sein Delegierter die
hiesigen Behörden nicht im Zweifel darüber, dass das Hilfswerk zum
mindesten die moralische Unterstützung unserer Behörden geniesst.
Professor Aberson schreibt in seinem Brief an die Prinzessin Lalla
Aïcha, von dem ich Ihnen eine Photokopie sandte: "Suivant la
tradition suisse... nous avons entrepris, avec l'appel moral des
autorités de notre pays, de efforts...".

       Ich bitte Sie, die Angelegenheit unter diesem Ge-
sichtspunkt nochmals zu prüfen und mir nach Fühlungnahme mit der

- 2 -

**Fig. 26 Confidential Letter from the Ambassador E. Bernath to the the Federal Political
Department in Bern, May 25, 1961**

The Ambassador writes that following the information disclosed in the last letter, he is

frankly worried. If it is correct that eighty percent of the children are Jewish and that some

of them will not return to Morocco, he expects problems, even if the Embassy abstains from

all interventions. First, he writes, because this organization (OSSEAN) calls itself a 'Swiss aid

- 2 -

Abteilung für Politische Angelegenheiten Ihre Stellungnahme
bekanntzugeben.

Ich versichere Sie, Herr Minister, meiner
vorzüglichen Hochachtung.

Der Schweizerische Botschafter

sig! E. Bernath

Kopie geht zur Kenntnisnahme an
die Abteilung für Politische
Angelegenheiten des EPD.

organization' and secondly because their delegates do not leave the local authorities any doubt about the moral support they receive from the Swiss authorities, as mentioned in the letter to Princess Lalla Aïcha by Prof. Aberson. The whole issue should be reconsidered after contacting the Political Department (EPD).

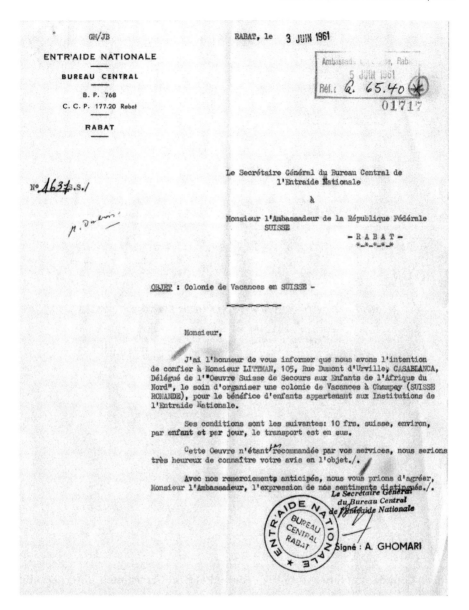

Fig. 27 Letter from Mr. Ghomari from the Entr'Aide Nationale in Rabat to the Swiss Ambassador, June 3, 1961 (File G.65.40.sd)

Mr. Ghomari writes to the Swiss Ambassador in Rabat informing him that the Entr'Aide Nationale is sending children with Mr. Littman for a the summer holiday in Champery and asking his advice since the Organization (OSSEAN) is not recommended by the Embassy.

DÉPARTEMENT POLITIQUE FÉDÉRAL

Berne, le 3 juin 1961

o.223.Maroc.-BTG/mg
Prière de rappeler cette référence dans la réponse

Confidentielle

ad G.65.40.-DU/ap
.-EB/be

A l'Ambassade de Suisse

R a b a t

Oeuvre suisse de secours aux
enfants de l'Afrique du Nord.

Monsieur l'Ambassadeur,

Nous avons bien reçu vos lettres des 18 et 25 mai
dernier concernant l'Oeuvre suisse de secours aux enfants
de l'Afrique du Nord et avons pris connaissance de leur
contenu avec intérêt.

Tout en comprenant vos préoccupations, nous
pensons qu'il n'y a pas aujourd'hui d'autre solution pour
votre Ambassade que de délivrer les visas qui vous seront
régulièrement demandés, conformément aux instructions de la
Police fédérale des étrangers, et de limiter votre concours
à l'octroi de ces autorisations d'entrée en Suisse, à
l'exclusion de toute autre démarche. En revanche, nous
croyons que vous ne devriez pas prendre l'initiative de
donner à qui que ce soit des renseignements sur l'Oeuvre
suisse de secours aux enfants de l'Afrique du Nord, mais
que si l'on devait vous interroger à ce sujet, vous pourriez
vous borner à répondre qu'il s'agit d'une organisation
privée, à laquelle les autorités suisses n'ont aucune part.

Nous serions heureux que vous nous teniez au
courant, le cas échéant, des développements ultérieurs de
cette affaire.

Veuillez agréer, Monsieur l'Ambassadeur, l'assurance de notre considération distinguée.

DEPARTEMENT POLITIQUE FEDERAL
Organisations Internationales

Fig. 28 Confidential letter from the Federal Political Department (International Organizations) in Bern to the Swiss Embassy in Rabat, June 3, 1961 (File G.65.40.sd)

The Minister writes in this confidential letter to Ambassador E. Bernath that he took notice of the concerns he expressed in his letters of May 18 and May 25 but that there is currently no other solution than issuing visas for the children. Following the instructions of the Federal Police for Foreigners, he should just deliver the authorisation to enter Switzerland on the display of identity cards. He tells the Ambassador, if asked about OSSEAN, not to divulge any information and mention that it is a private organization and that the Swiss authorities are not involved.

par avion

5 juin 1961

G.65.40.sd - DU/ap

ad o.223.Maroc.-BTG/Gg

CONFIDENTIEL - Urgent

A la Division
des organisations internationales
du Département politique fédéral

Berne

Monsieur le Ministre,

Me référant à ma communication confidentielle du 25
mai 1961 concernant "l'Oeuvre suisse de secours aux enfants
de l'Afrique du Nord", je porte à votre connaissance que, par
lettre du 3 juin 1961, le Secrétaire général du Bureau central
de l'Entr'aide nationale à Rabat me demande ce qui suit :

"J'ai l'honneur de vous informer que nous avons l'intention de confier à Monsieur LITTMAN, 105, Rue Dumont
d'Urville, Casablanca, Délégué de l' "Oeuvre Suisse de
Secours aux Enfants de l'Afrique du Nord", le soin d'organiser une colonie de vacances à Champey (Suisse Romande), pour le bénéfice d'enfants appartenant aux Institutions de l'Entr'aide Nationale.

Ses conditions sont les suivantes : 10 frs. suisses, en-
viron, par enfant et par jour, le transport est en sus.

Cette Oeuvre n'étant pas recommandée par vos services,
nous serions très heureux de connaître votre avis en
l'objet."

Cette demande est plutôt embarrassante. N'étant pas
en mesure de recommander cette institution (cf. votre lettre
du 18 mai dernier), je crains qu'en éludant la question les
autorités marocaines se ravisent et ne donnent plus suite à
la proposition d'hébergement d'enfants en Suisse.

Je vous saurais gré de bien vouloir me faire connaître au plus tôt votre point de vue en l'espèce et vous en remercie d'avance.

Veuillez agréer, Monsieur le Ministre, l'assurance de
ma considération distinguée.

L'Ambassadeur de Suisse :

Fig. 29 Confidential letter from the Swiss Ambassador Mr. E. Bernath to the Federal Political Department in Bern, June 5, 1961 (File G.65.40.sd)

In this express and confidential letter, the Ambassador refers the Minister to his letter dated May 25 and to the letter received on June 3 from Mr. Ghomari regarding the Entr'Aide Nationale sending (Moslem) children on holidays in Switzerland with Mr. Littman, delegate of OSSEAN. It is quite embarrassing, he writes, referring to Mr. Ghomari's request for advice, since he cannot recommend this organization. He fears that in the future the Moroccan authorities might not allow children to come to Switzerland anymore.

Fig. 30 Telegram from the Federal Political Department in Bern to the Swiss Embassy in Rabat, June 9, 1961 (File G.65.40.sd)

In this telegram Bern asks the Ambassador to follow the instructions in the letter dated June 3 and to mention that OSSEAN is a private organization unrelated to the Swiss authorities.

Double au Consulat de Suisse, à Casablanca

01323

12 juin 1961

G.65.40 - DU/ap

ad no 1637 S.S./

Au Secrétariat Général
du Bureau Central
de l'Entraide Nationale

B.P. 768

R a b a t

Monsieur le Secrétaire Général,

Me référant à votre lettre du 3 juin 1961 concernant l' "Oeuvre Suisse de Secours aux Enfants de
l'Afrique du Nord", j'ai l'honneur de porter à votre
connaissance qu'il s'agit, en l'occurrence, d'une organisation privée, à laquelle les autorités suisses
n'ont aucune part.

Veuillez agréer, Monsieur le Secrétaire Général, l'assurance de ma considération distinguée.

L'Ambassadeur de Suisse :

Copie à la Division des organisations internationales du DPF,
à Berne, en me référant à sa lettre du 3.6.61 (ad o.223.Maroc
-BTG/mg)

Fig. 31 Letter from the Swiss Ambassador in Rabat to Mr. Ghomari, Secretary General of the Entr'Aide Nationale in Rabat, June 12, 1961 (File G.65.40.sd)

In his answer to the letter of Mr. Ghomari (June 3) the Ambassador writes that the Organization (OSSEAN) is a private organization unrelated to the Swiss authorities. A copy is sent to the Federal Political Department (EPD) in Bern.

ŒUVRE SUISSE DE SECOURS
AUX ENFANTS DE L'AFRIQUE DU NORD

Tel: 265.53   105, Rue Dumont D'Urville, Casablanca.
Genève 1, Case postale 220
le 17 Mai, 1961

Ministère des Affaires Etrangères
RABAT.

Monsieur,

Suivant le conseil de M. Skiredj, directeur par intérim
de la Division Consulaire et Sociale du Ministère des Affaires
Etrangères, nous vous adressons cette brève explication des buts
de notre Oeuvre et nous ajoutons ci-inclus la liste des références
et recommandations demandées. M. Skiredj nous a expliqué que cette
lettre sera envoyée au Ministère de l'Interieur qui se mettra/avec en rapport
nous et nous permettra de terminer les formalités de passeports
avant le départ du premier groupe des petits Marocains la fin Juin.

Il existe en Suisse de nombreuses Oeuvres qui s'appliquent
à renforcer les liens entre la jeunesse de pays divers et celle de
la Suisse; et ces Oeuvres, afin d'aider les plus nécessiteux,
abaissent leur prix de séjour- et ceci nous concerne particulièrement-
pour permettre aux parents, ou à des institutions gouvernementales
ou privées, d'envoyer ces enfants pour une convalescence nécessaire
ou simplement en vacances dans les montagnes de Suisse. Dans cette
intention l'Oeuvre Suisse de Secours aux Enfants de l'Afrique du Nord
a fixé un prix de séjour spécial pour le Maroc et s'efforce de
recevoir pour la première fois un contingent d'enfants Marocains
envoyés par l'Entr'Aide National, probablement par le Ministère de
l'Education, et par les particuliers Marocains qui inscrivaient
leurs enfants au bureau de l'Oeuvre à Casablanca. Les autres Oeuvres
humanitaires Suisse appuient moralement notre Oeuvre et les autorités
Suisse nous connaissent. Pour une plus ample information je vous
adresse ci-inclus un prospectus en Arabe et en Français. J'ai laissé
plusieurs prospectus à M. Senoussi du Ministère de l'Education National
et à M. Ghomari, Secrétaire Général de l'Entr'Aide Nationale.

Je vous cite les references suivantes:
S.E. l'Ambassadeur de Suisse au Maroc, Monsieur E. Bernath.
M. le Consul de Suisse à Casablanca, Monsieur M. Birchler.

Ils possèdent une lettre officielle de Berne les priant de me
donner toute l'assistance nécessaire pour conclure les formalités de
visas pour les enfants Marocains (ces visas seront valables pour un
maximum de trois mois).

Fig. 32 Letter from D.G. Littman to the Ministry of Foreign Affairs in Rabat, May 17, 1961

Littman shown this letter whenever questioned by government officials. Addressed to the
Ministry of Foreign Affairs (on the advice of Mr. Skiredj) it presents the goals of OSSEAN, a
charity organization, interested in enhancing the ties between youth from all over the world.

ŒUVRE SUISSE DE SECOURS
AUX ENFANTS DE L'AFRIQUE DU NORD

105, Rue~~Gen~~ ~~outas~~ ~~Journalize~~, Casablanca.

M. René Steiner. Secrétaire Général de la Croix Rouge Suisse,
Services de Secours aux Enfants; Taubenstrasse, 8 , BERNE.
M. Steiner a écrit une lettre à M. A.E. Reinhard, Délégué
en chef au Maroc de la Ligue des Sociétés de la Croix Rouge,
me recommandant à lui. Il connait bien les activités humain-
itaires de notre Oeuvre.
Dr. M. Tromp. Président de la Commission pour l'Hospitalisation
de Malades Etrangers en Suisse; Effengerstrasse, 6 , BERN.
J'ajoute une photo-copie d'une lettre de recommandation du Dr. Tromp.
Dr. Fischer. Secrétaire Général de " L'Aide Suisse aux Pays Etrangers.
Dr. Fischer est maintenant en Tunisie, mais avant mon départ
pour le Maroc, j'ai eu le plaisir de le voir en compagnie du Professeur
Aberson notre Président. Dr. Fischer a précisé qu'il serait
très heureux, sur une demande, d'envoyer une lettre de recomm-
endation pour l'Oeuvre et son délégué au Maroc.
Le Président de l'Oeuvre a écrit une lettre à S.A.R.
la Princesse Lalla Aicha et une lettre a été envoyée à M. Nacer el
Fassi, chef de l'Enseignement Secondaire, Ministère de l'Education.
. . . .
Depuis mon arrivée au Maroc, fin Mars, je suis en
rapport avec M. Cha oui, chef de la Division Consulaire et Sociale,
pour organiser au mieux les formalités de voyage pour les enfants
Marocains. M. Chaoui a proposé d'envoyer une circulaire aux Gouverneurs
des villes desquelles les enfants viendront, spécialement Casabla nca.
Je n'ai pas encore reçu de communication officielle dirigeant mon
action. Ce silence est peut-être due à l'absence de M. Chaoui qui
est en pélérinage à la Meque.
J'apprécierai beaucoup votre avis, Monsieur, à ce
sujet. Nous pouvons utiliser des passeports collectifs (l'Entr'Aide
préfère cela) ou des passeports individuels quand ce sera nécessaire.
On m'a suggéré qu'une"feuille de route collective" serait plus facile.
Si les autoités Marocaines préfèrent cette dernière solution,
j'essayerai d'organiser les convois en conséquence. Comme il n'y a que
six semaines ou moins avant le départ du premier groupe d'enfants,
puis-je demander votre assistance pour me permettre de terminer ces
formalités à temps. Je préparerai les premières listes d'enfants de
Casablanca, et je vous serai reconnaissant si vous pouviez aviser
le Gouverneur de la ville aussitôt que possible.

OSSEAN which offers a special vacation rate for Moroccan children hopes to receive for the
first time a contingent of children from the Entr'Aide Nationale and the Ministry of Education
but also from individual families. Littman gives the names of his references in Switzerland
and writes that the Swiss Embassy and the Consul received an official authorization from

/3.)

ŒUVRE SUISSE DE SECOURS
AUX ENFANTS DE L'AFRIQUE DU NORD

Genève 1, Case postale 220

En m'adressant à vous, Monsieur, je me permet en qualité de délégué de l'Oeuvre Suisse de Secours aux Enfants de l'Afrique du Nord de vous exprimer les espoirs du e notre Président, notre Secrétaire Général à Genève, et les miens que ces débuts ouvrent le chemin à une plus ample co-operation pour rapprocher la jeunesse Marocaine et celle d'autres pays dans le site superbe des Alpes Valaisiennes.

Veuilles agréer, Monsieur, mes sentiments distingués.

(D.G. Littman)

Délégué au Maroc de l'Oeuvre Suisse de Secours aux Enfants de l'Afrique du Nord.

Bern to issue visas. He mentions the letters written to Princess Lalla Aïcha and to the Ministry of Education and his metting with Mr. Chaoui from the Foreign Ministry regarding a possible collective travel paper or collective passports. He adds to this letter the Arabic and in French prospectus of OSSEAN.

ŒUVRE SUISSE DE SECOURS
AUX ENFANTS DE L'AFRIQUE DU NORD

105, Rue, Dumont D'Urville, Casablanca, Maroc.
Genève 1, Case postale 220

June 1st. 1961

La Secrétaire Général,
L'Oeuvre Suisse de Secours
aux Enfants de l'Afrique du Nord.
Case Postale, 220,
Genève, 1

Dear Madam,
      I enclose a letter sent last night to M. Phazi of the
Entr'Aide Nationale. I shall only telegraph you Friday night if there
is really anything important to communicate.

      Our efforts are now yielding their fruit. Since my last
letter to you I have been receiving many parents who have arrived
with all the documents required and the Questionnaire Medical filled
in adequately by a doctor. Within a very few days(perhaps this
Saturday, or Monday the 5th. June) I shall be able to hand to M.Hajja
all the demandes,fully completed and signed by the Chef de chaque
Arrondisement,for the first collective passport, containing about
eighty names. The other lists will follow very shortly after when I am
able to complete the preliminary work as I have almost done for the
first list, with the help of course of all the parents concerned.
      Yesterday afternoon I was called to the Le Service de la
Préfecture du Gouverneur de Casablanca to speak with M. Dkhissy.
It appears that he had heard about us through M. Ghomari, and of course
I immediately showed him the letter I had written to the Ministère des
Affaires Etrangères. He is a most pleasant personality and was very
impressed with our efforts to bring Maroccan children to Switzerland.
He likes Switzerland very much and considered that our special
reductions for Marocco, and especially for l'Entr'Aide National were
praiseworthy. He thought that we should have contacted the Maroccan
legation in Berne and offered to show them one or two of the Homes
in which we propose to house those Maroccan children. I explained
that this was not done, because being a private organization we
hesitated to interfere in such a way. However I stated that we would
be only toohappy to make contact with the legation and take one of its
members on a tour of the Homes which will be used to house Maroccan
children. I suggest that a telephone call (or a letter) be made to
the Legation, M. Dkhissy's suggestion mentioned, and if they are willi
to send someone perhaps Professor Aberson, our President, or another
distinguished Lady or Gentleman from our committee could arrange to
a visit to Champéry(giving Mme. Truffer prior notice) or any other
Home which will be used by those children from Marocco. I realize that
the two large Homes at Morgins are undergoing repairs at the moment,
and anyway these are all reserved for children from Europe, but perhap
the third Home at Morgins, or those in the vicinity, are presentable.
I leave this matter to your wisdom, Madam, and I am sure it will
receive your immediate and considered attention. On behalf of the
Oeuvre I informed M. Dkhissy that we would be delighted and honoured
if he, himself, would visit us in Switzerland either this year(when
the children from the Entr'Aide are with us in August) or next. We
doubted if he could manage it this year, but he thanked me for the
offer.
      He is a close friend of M. Hajjaj (who is helping me with
the passport formalities), chef de division, Place Mirabeau, and has
promised to get in touch with him, so that the quickest possible
attention is given to the Oeuvre in this field. He spoke most strongly
in support of collective passports, and I acquiesced. Apart from being

---

Fig. 33 Letter from D.G. Littman to N. Lehmann, June 1, 1961

Littman informs Lehmann that parents started coming to the office with the required documents. He hopes to meet on June 5 Muhammad Hajjaj (head of the administrational division of the prefecture of the governor) regarding the collective passports. Mr. Muhammad D'khissy, an important Moroccan official at the prefecture of the Governor in

very much cheaper- in fact there is no charge- he feels that
children should not have individual passports to go where they please;
the Jeunesse et Sport always organises their travel with collective
passports and he feels that we should do the same. I agreed heartily
and added that we felt ourselves responsible for these children and
would take charge of them on the journey to Switzerland, their stay
there, and their safe return to their own country, Morocco. I explained
how we proposed to arrange the transport and asked him whether he
thought it was possible for all the ~~facilities~~ formalities to be
terminated to enable the first groups to leave by June 26th. when ~~the~~ a
Greek ship would be leaving for Marseille, offering extremely reduced
rates (actually, less than 100 Dirhams to Marseille; the return fare
by Paquet costing about 125 Dirhams). Yes, he knew about this ship,
the"Ionia"! His own opinion was that the formalities should not take
more than two weeks(I am completing the bulk of them, myself, as
mentioned in my last letter and here) and that we could safely buy
the tickets for the children to leave on the 25th. June. We then stated
that he would have a word with M. Hajjaj to facilitate this.

This ship the "Ionia" has 86 places, as dormitory accomodation,
and I have for the moment booked them all. At the same time there are
about from 60 to 70 places in Tourist Class "B" with food. The company
is willing to give food for those children travelling by Dormitory
class at an extra cost. I have asked confirmation from Greece on the
final reduced cost if the Oeuvre takes all ~~that~~ the remaining places
in ~~the Sen~~ Tourist "B"(about three-quarters of those available) and
all the dormitory places. At the moment the cost per child would work
out(with a 20% reduction) at from 93 to 96 Dirhams to Marseille. When
this figure is added to the return fare by Paquet, it is clear that
it is less than the return fare by Paquet.The advice is to take this
opportunity, and I have done so. There rests only the difficulty that
might arise if I purchased all the tickets very shortly and the formalities were not completed in time for the children to leave. The Agents,
S.I.R.T.A.M., cannot hold the tickets too long, and it has been with
considerable difficulty that they have agreed to wait one week. If there
is a demand during that time for large numbers of tickets they will
notify me immediately and I will have the choice to take or reject the
reserved places. Myself, I think that the Dormitory accomodation will
remain available for the week at least, but the Tourist "B" places, six
in each cabin,could well diminish: here is the dilemma!

Mme. Nordjman is a Swissess from Bâle and asked many questions
about our Oeuvre. She will be in Geneva in about one week's time and
I suggested, herself, that she contact Swissair to see what sort of
arrangement they could make for the return of the children as well as
the transport at the ~~se~~ same time of those from the Entr'Aide in August.
I emphasized that we would use either a chartered aircraft or the
Paquet line. At the same time she wishes to arrange the Marseille/Geneva
part of the journey either by train or by 'bus. Pleaselet me know how
you propose arranging this aspect, whether you prefer the train or the
'bus, and whether payment should be made here in both cases, or what?

To-day I opened an account in the Banque Franco-Suisse pour le
Maroc in the name of the Oeuvre. They are affiliated to the Société
de Banque Suisse, and the Sous-Directeur, M. Willy Hufschmid, with whom
I spoke(~~has~~ another Swiss from Bâle) is most genial and will arrange
all the transfers necessary. Strangely enough he knows M. Chenevière,
from ~~my~~ the S.B.S. in Lausanne where I bank. It seems best to arrange
the transference of money from Casablanca to the S.B.S. in Geneva. If
you have any suggestions on this, please let me know.

So that this reaches you by Saturday, Let me close now with
cordial greetings from my wife and myself, dear Madam.

Casablanca, was very positive regarding sending Moroccan children to Switzerland, even
proposing a Moroccan delegate in Bern visit the homes in Morgins. He prefers collective
passports for "children should not have individual passports to go where they please,"
Littman agrees. Mr. D'Khissy tells Littman that there should be no formalities delay regarding
the first convoy of eighty children to board the Greek ship *S.S. Ionia* on June 26. The rest
of the letter deals with transportation logistics and the opening of a bank account for
OSSEAN in Casablanca.

ŒUVRE SUISSE DE SECOURS
AUX ENFANTS DE L'AFRIQUE DU NORD

Genève 1, Case postale 220

GENÈVE, le 1 Juin 1961

Monsieur D.G. LITTMAN
Oeuvre Suisse de Secours aux Enfants
d'Afrique du Nord,
105, Rue Dumont d'Urville,
C a s a b l a n c a .

Cher Monsieur,

1. Entr'Aide Nationale: Il n'est absolument pas clair combien d'enfants
   l'Entraide va finalement nous envoyer. La seule
   chose que nous avons compris de vos longues explications, c'est que
   la date du 10 août (Mme Truffer insiste que ce soit le 10.8.) conviendra
   mieux que de placer un groupe déjà au cours du mois de juillet.

   Mais, nous vous prions de bien retenir qu'il nous faut absolument avoir
   une confirmation par écrit de la part de l'Entr'Aide Nationale, car
   sans cette confirmation, nous ne pouvons exiger de Mme Truffer de nous
   GARDER LES PLACES, et de notre part, nous ne pouvons donner aucune
   garantie que ces places doivent rester à notre disposition.

2. Passeports: Vous devriez comprendre vous-même combien il est important
   que des enfants venant de si loin, soient en possession des
   passeports individuels. Il est toujours difficile de recevoir les
   certificats nécessaires pour sortir des enfants malades qui doivent
   prolonger leur séjour, du passeport collectif, et nous aimerions
   éviter ces désagréments.

3. Quant aux questionnaires médicaux, nous sommes d'accord à ce que ceux-
   ci soient remplis par les médecins des familles.

4. Moniteurs: Nous demandons que le groupe de Champéry soit encadré par
   des moniteurs du pays, qui resteront avec les enfants
   pendant tout leur séjour et qui les raccompagneront à la maison à
   la fin de leur séjour.

5. Transport: Un détour par Bâle est exclu: Ceci est beaucoup trop
   compliqué, vu que la maison se trouve en Suisse Romande,
   et que l'Aeroport de Genève est beaucoup plus proche de Champéry.

6. Programme: Le programme sera celui de toutes les colonies de vacances:
   jeux en plein-air, excursions, baignades (Il y a une piscine
   à Champéry); C'est d'ailleurs l'affaire des moniteurs d'établir les
   détails du programme.

7. Prosper Bitton: Nous faisons des démarches pour trouver une participation
   financière, car un prix journalier de 35 francs suisses
   est en-dessus des possibilités des Oeuvres privées. Il faut trouver
   plusieurs participants. C'est cela l'unique raison qui nous empêche de
   donner encore notre accord au transfert du garçon.

8. Piera: Votre Piera s'ennuie énormément car, comme elle dit, il n'y
   à Morgins pas assez d'hommes pour la distraire- donc elle

Fig. 34 Letter from N. Lehmann to D.G. Littman, June 1, 1961

This letter is critical of the length of Littman's detailed letters. It is divided in several points, among them Mrs. Lehmann asks to have a written confirmation from the Entr'Aide Nationale so that places can be booked at the homes and she adds her preference for individual

ŒUVRE SUISSE ·DE SECOURS
AUX ENFANTS DE L'AFRIQUE DU NORD

Genève 1, Case postale 220

– 2 –

Un déplacement à Bruxelles nous semble vraiment peu indiqué,
si l'on tien compte des difficultés d'adaptation de cette personne.

9.   Appartement : Nous avons reçu des plans et descriptions d'un
        immeuble locatif qui est en construction. Nous
     vous envoyons ce matériel par lettre imprimée, et vous pourrez
     choisir en toute tranquilité l'appartement qui convient à
     à vous, à Baby et à votre femme.

Avec nos meilleures salutations

N. Lehmann

passports to collective ones in case a sick child needs to extend his stay. She mentions Pierra, the Littman's maid that was sent to the Morgins' home while the Littmans were in Morocco.

ŒUVRE SUISSE DE SECOURS
AUX ENFANTS DE L'AFRIQUE DU NORD

105, Rue ~~Deseat Dessewille 20~~asablanca June 5th. 1961

Madam N. Lehmann,
Oeuvre Suisse de Secours aux Enfants
de l'Afrique du Nord.
Case Postale, 220,
Geneve, 1
Suisse.

~~Dhlue~~ Dear Madam,

I thank you for your letter of the 1st. June, and
will try to answer briefly.

Entr'Aide: No more long explications !; just simple facts.
On the 3rd. June- when I telephoned him- M. Rhazi asked for a further
week in order to receive the long-awaited answers from the various
branches in Marocco. He again said "thirty to forty"- for the month
of August. You have my letter to him of the 31st. May; I repeated
that we no longer held ourselves responsible for reserving the places.
Please do not ask me for any more confirmation which I am unable to
give you; like your délégué here you must wait,without being responsible should there be no places available thanks to THEIR delay.

Passports: I shall endeavour to explain your anxiety to the
authorities here- and it is one shared by the Swiss Consulate- and
see whether individual passports cannot be obtained. I must, in all
fairness, point out that the procedure for individual passports is
very much more cumbersome than for collective passports, and the
authorities(as I mentioned) are not now prepared for this. My
orders were to ask for collective passports ! It is so ! Yet I shall
try. However when you consider that so far,of all those more or less
inscribed on the lists, only 50 have so far been able to bring me:
1) an Acte de Naissance,ou Livret d'Etat Civil
2.) Carte d'identité(scholaire ou autre)
you will understand that this formality concerning the collective
passport, although seemingly so easy, is not so, for reasons I cannot
understand. In order to have individual passports a Certificate de
résidence is necessary, which itself takes time to obtain. M. Hajjaj
was kind enough to set aside this document for collective passports;
now you ask me to insist on individual passports(thus, the certificate
de résidence), at a moment when only 50 children have managed to
bring me the above two documents, the most easy of all. With these
two documents, it should take less than one week to have the collective
passports. I prefer to send in the first list for the first passport
when at least eighty children(of those inscribed) are fully
documented. This I really expected to have been completed by Saturday,
3rd. June, as explained before, but it would appear that this will
not be the case until at least the 7th., if not later. You will
understand that this is entirely outside of my hands; I can but wait.
At the least one must prove the child's identity, and I am astonished
that the parents had not thought of this before !

Questionnaires Médicaux: These have been satisfactorily filled in ,
usually with another written note that the child suffers from
no contagious disease. I will begin forwarding them to you
the moment all the other formalities are complete, for
the passports and visas.

Fig. 35 Letter from D.G. Littman to N. Lehmann, June 5, 1961

Answering to Mrs. Lehmann, Littman writes that since he has not yet received any
confirmation from the Entr'Aide Nationale, OSSEAN can't be held responsible should there
be no places available. He doubts that individual passports can be obtained since they need
a more cumbersome procedure which the authorities are not prepared for. Even collective
passports are not a simple matter, as children have no legal identity documents proving

ŒUVRE SUISSE DE SECOURS
AUX ENFANTS DE L'AFRIQUE DU NORD

Genève 1, Case postale 220

Moniteurs: I refer you back to my letter of the 29th. May. This
matter is not an easy one. Be so kind as to let me know how I can
possibly " encadre " those children whose parents have come to me
individually. I understand your good reasons but the problem needs
more ample consideration and discussion from all sides, and you will
be hearing more of this in the very near future.

Air Transport: We both agree that Genève is closer to Champéry than Bâle.
But this is not the issue, which is whether T.A.I will receive
permission to fly to Genève or not. If they don't, they can only
go to Mulhousen, near to Bâle. For the moment we can leave the
questions of air transport until we have definite information.

Sea Transport: The position in regard to the S.S. Ionia, sailing from
Casablanca to Marseille, probably on the 26th. June is most favourable. It now appears that there are 213 places for couchettes
accomodation in dormitories of the taking about 20 children each.
The main office in the Piraeus has offered these places to us at
90 Dirhams with food, this being a group reduction. In addition
there are in fact 90 places remaining in Tourist B at approximately
95 Dirhams with food, this being a group reduction.
          I have confirmed with S.I.R.T.A.M., the Agents here,
that we will be taking the 90 places in Tourist B, and in two or
three days I shall leave a deposit of about 15%. At the same time
they will endeavour to guard all the dormitory accomodation until
that moment when I am able to inform them that I the formalities
for all the children are complete. Unfortunately this result is
highly unlikely; if it has taken so long just to obtain the
documents for fifty children, how long indeed will it take for
those other hundreds inscribed to bring to me what I need to
arrange the passport formalities,for which one must allow a minimum
(it shouldn't be more) of one week. The boat sails in three weeks
time: I shall be happy if at least there are 90 on board. This is
a very great pity, for to have send the great bulk of the children
on one ship at such a reasonable cost would be most covenient in
all respects from the administrative side.
          At the same time I have tentative reservations until
the 10th. June (perhaps I can prolong them), for 70 boys on the
30th. June; 50 boys and fifty 50 girls on the 2nd. July. This is
with the Compagnie Paquet, who can also offer a large number of
places on the 9th. July(200 I think), 70 on the 15th. and as many
as required on the 16th July. You will see that accomodation is
not lacking even if we are unable to arrange matters so that the
greater portion of the children leave for their holidays on the 26th
June.

Haemophilia case: I understood the cost to be 3000 frs. fr. ancien,
per day, of which the French government paid 600. Do I understand
then, that after almost three months I must tell M. Reinhard that
the boy cannot leave with the first party, since the funds to suppor
him in the appropriate Home are not forthcoming ? Indeed a pity.

Piera: A rare phenomenon of contradictions! Try and make her go out
for her day off (almost impossible to do).Does she work at all ?
If not, please mention Brussels to her and contact my sister-in-law
at the same time: I don't know what else to say on this.
Apartment: Letter with information impatiently awaited by couple
with one beautiful baby and another seemingly and inexcusably "on
the way, who expect to return to Genève in September and have nowhere to go. Please enclose small map of Genèva to see position.
... ... collaborators and cordial

their identity; only fifty children were "fully documented." Concerning the sea transport,
Littman mentions that he tentatively booked ninety places with the travel agency S.I.R.T.A.M.
on the Greek ship *S.S Ionia* sailing from Casablanca to Marseille on June 26. He informs
Lehmann about medical questioner, monitors, air and sea transportation. He understands
that the boy with haemophilia will not leave with the first group of children due to a lack
of funds to support him in the appropriate home.

ŒUVRE SUISSE DE SECOURS
AUX ENFANTS DE L'AFRIQUE DU NORD

Genève 1, Case postale 220

Genève, le 8.6.1961

Monsieur D.G. L I T T M A N
Oeuvre Suisse de Secours aux
Enfants de l'Afrique du Nord
105, rue Dumont d'Urville
C a s a b l a n c a .

Cher Monsieur,
                              1 et 5
            Merci de vos lettres du 1er juin qui montrent que les choses
commencent à prendre une forme concrète ce qui facilite grandement
les démarches à entreprendre de notre côté. Si nous continuons à vous
harceler pour plus de précisions, veuillez nous comprendre: Ce n'est
que le désir de faire un travail rationnel, car nous ne disposons
que d'un temps très limité .

1. Nombre des groupes: Afin de prendre les dispositions nécessaires,
            il nous faudra savoir au plus vite combien
d'enfants sont prévus pour Champéry et combien pour Morgins. Les
directions des deux homes doivent faire les préparatifs par
chambres: Pour cela, il faut connaître le nombre de participants
et aussi - pour chaque groupe - le nombre des garçon et celui des
filles.
- Ceci est également important pour mettre à la disposition des
groupes les Cars nécessaires à transporter les enfants, soit
du port, soit de l'Aéroport, à leur lieu de séjour en Suisse.

2. Passeports: Nous comprenons vos difficultés. D'autre part, nous
            sommes convaincus que vous comprenez également notre
raisonnement, résultat d'une longue expérience avec les transports
de groupes. Il serait peut-être possible de trouver une solution de
compromis: C'est de faire - non pas un seul passeport collectif,
mais de faire des passeports collectifs par groupes: C'est à
dire: Un pour le groupe Champéry, un pour le groupe Morgins.

3. Convoyeur: Nos amis de Berne ne trouvent pas bien que vous quittiez
            Casablanca pour accompagner le premier convoi en Suisse.
Ils pensent qu'il faudra vous envoyer quelqu'un pour mener ce convoi
et que vous, entretemps restiez afin de ne pas interrompre votre
travail en faveur du deuxième convoi.

4. Moyens de locomotion: La solution "bateaux" nous semble excellente
            vu la grande différence de prix. Si cette
solution sera choisie, on pourra venir en Car jusqu'au port de
Marseille et mener directement les groupes à leur destination.
Si, par contre, on choisira tout de même le transport aérien
via Mulhouse, il faudra diriger les cars là-bas.

5. Séjour groupe Champéry: Madame Truffer est très heureuse de la
            nouvelle que le premier convoi va
arriver vers la fin du mois. Pendant qu'elle ne savait que du
groupe venant en Août, la chose ne l'intéressait que peu, depuis
la confirmation pour fin juin, elle est prête à toutes les
sacrifices. Ainsi, elle propose - et nous sommes d'accord avec
elle - que vous ameniez en Juin autant d'enfants que possible qui

Fig. 36 Letter from N. Lehmann to D.G. Littman, June 8, 1961

N. Lehmann is glad to see that things are progressing. She inquires on the exact number of children (boys and girls) for the two homes. She understands the difficulties involved with individual passports but asks that collective passports be made for each group and recommends the boat as a possible mean of transportation.

ŒUVRE SUISSE DE SECOURS
AUX ENFANTS DE L'AFRIQUE DU NORD

Genève 1, Case postale 220

— 2.

sont destinés pour un séjour de deux mois. Ces enfants resteront alors à Champéry pendant le mois de Juillet jusqu'à l'arrivée des anglais, et pendant le séjour des anglais, Mme Truffer les amènerait en excursion à Randa ou dans un autre Chalêt, et ils retourneront au 10 aout à nouveau à Champéry.

Surement vous aurez des intéressés pour un séjour de deux mois suivis. Mais pour ces cas-là, le passeport collectif doit être à part. Vous voyez déjà par cet exemple, combien les passeports individuels facilitent les choses, quand les durées de séjour sont différentes.

S'il y a , parmi les enfants de parents aisés, des cas où les parents peuvent payer plus que 10.—, tant mieux, car de notre côté, nous devrons donner 13.—

6. Moniteurs: Vous ne croyez pas que parmi les jeunes instituteurs, il y en aurait qui seraient tout heureux de pouvoir faire des vacances bon-marchées, en Suisse? La question est très importante; surtout à cause de la langue — on ne trouvera certainement pas des éducateurs appropriés en Suisse.

Nous vous envoyons, aujourdhui les plans promis concernant les appartements. Excusez le retard. Il n'était vraiment pas voulu, mais j'ai dû garder le lit pendant une semaine à cause d'une très mauvaise angine, ce qui a retardé tout le travail, — à un moment peu opportun, j'en conviens.

En attendant de vos nouvelles, et en vous remerciant de tout ce que vous avez déjà fait pour faire aboutir notre action, nous vous présentons, à vous, votre femme, bébé présent et bébé futur nos meilleures salutations.

O.S.S.E.A.N.

N. Lehman

يخصص للتعريف بحائزي الجواز الجماعي
RESERVE A L IDENTIFICATION DES TITULAIRES

Nom de Famille : _____ : الاسم الباطلي
Prénoms : _____ : الاسم الخاص
Nationalité : _____ : الجنسية
Date de naissance : _____ : تاريخ الازدياد
Lieu de naissance : _____ : مكان الازدياد

Profession : _____ : المهنة
Adresse : _____ : عنوان السكني
Référence de la carte d'identité : _____ : الاحالة الى ورقة التعريف
Produite : ___ n° _____ : التخصيصة البدلى بها وعدد ها
Date : _____ : تاريخيا
Délivré à : _____ : سلمة ب

(N.B. sur chaque feuillet ne doivent figurer que deux personnes)_____

تنبيه : لا يمكن ادراج اكثر من شخصين اثنين في كل ورقة

يخصص للتعريف بحائزي الجواز الجماعي
RESERVE A L IDENTIFICATION DES TITULAIRES

Nom de Famille _____ : الاسم الحائلي
Prénoms) _____ : الاسم الخاص
Nationalité : _____ : الجنسية
Date de naissance : _____ : تاريخ الازدياد
Lieu de naissance : _____ : مكان الازدياد
_____ : الجنسية
Profession : _____ : المهنة
Adresse : _____ : عنوان السكني
Référence de la carte d'identité _____ : الاحالة الى ورقة التعريف
Produite : ___ N° _____ : التخصيصة البدلى بها وعدد ها
Date : _____ : تاريخيا
Délivré à : _____ : سلمة ب

(N.B. sur chaque feuillet ne doivent figurer que deux personnes) _____

تنبيه : لا يمكن ادراج اكثر من شخصين اثنين في كل ورقة

Fig. 37 Specimen of collective passports first used on June 26, 1961

ŒUVRE SUISSE DE SECOURS

AUX ENFANTS DE L'AFRIQUE DU NORD

105, Rue Dumont d'Urville, Casablanca, Maroc.

Genève 1, Case postale 220

le 9 Juin, 1961

Madam N. Lehmann,
Oeuvre Suisse de Secours aux Enfants
de l'Afrique du Nord.
Case Postale, 220
Genève, 1
Suisse.

Chère Madame,

J'ai reçu votre lettre du 8 Juin dont les encouragements
et l'enthousiasme m'ont d'autant plus peiné que j'ai assisté hier à
une scène pour le moins décevante. Voici brièvement le bilan de nos
efforts:

Après avoir correctement rempli les fiches de 103 enfants pour une
demande de passeports, je les portais à la Préfecture chez M. Hajjas.
Celui-ci en ma présence téléphona à M. Allaoui Tajjedine (le khalifat
du premier arrondissement) et lui dit d'expédier rapidement les formalitées. J'allais alors chez M. Tajjedine qui me reçu avec beaucoup
de courtoisie et était disposé à tout terminer en une demi-journée.
Il prit une fiche, puis une deuxième et une troisième, après en avoir
examiné cinq, il les jeta toutes avec un geste d'humeur sur le bureau
et s'ecria avec violence: "Non, xkxxmaxxgxxxkkxxxtxgxx je ne donnerai pas
les passeports!" Devant mon étonnement, il continua: "C'est une émmigration, c'est un éxode!" Je répliquais surpris: "Que voulez-vous dire? Ces
enfants vont en Suisse pour des vacances!" Il me répondit: "Ils sont
tous israélites." J'étais éberlué: "Comment le savez-vous? demandais-
je. Pour ma part je n'ai vu que des noms et des enfants marocains."
M. Tajjedine m'apprit que tous les noms étaient de familles juives
marocaines. "C'est une affaire politique poursuivit-il, je ne puis
donner de passeports, c'est une trop grande responsabilité. Vous n'auriez pas dû vous compromettre dans cette affaire, Monsieur! "
Jugez mon étonnement. Les propos sybillins de M. Tajjedine rendaient
la situation extrèmement obscure. Je lui expliquais que mon travail
consistait justement à créer une colonie de vacances marocaine en
Suisse et que je m'efforçais de travailler avec les particuliers
aussi bien qu'avec le gouvernement. Je lui citais les 40 enfants que
l'Entr'Aide Nat. avait promis d'envoyer. Ferait-il aussi de pareilles
objections à ce départ? Bref M. Tajjedine téléphona devant moi à M.
Hajjas pour lui demander conseil. J'ignore le sens de cette conversation, mais je crûs comprendre que M. Hajjas était clairement d'une
opinion différente. M. Tajjedine me demanda de lui laisser toutes les

Fig. 38 Letter from D.G. Littman to N. Lehmann, June 9, 1961

D.G. Littman recounts in detail the 'incident' taking place on June 8, when Si Alaoui Tajjedine,
Khalifa of the 1st district of Casablanca, refused to sign the passports. The latter accused
Littman of being involved in "an exodus" saying that all the registered children were

ŒUVRE SUISSE DE SECOURS
AUX ENFANTS DE L'AFRIQUE DU NORD

~~Genève 1, Case postale 220~~

fiches de son arrondissement aux fins d'une enqu^ete.Je quittais le
Khalifat de très mauvaise humeur.

Ainsi tout notre travail est suspendu,et j'en ignore le dénouement
au moment où les départs sur les bateaux sont bien organisés, les
listes d'enfants prêtes,et quand j'avais l'assurance que par faveur
spéciale on terminerait en un jour toutes les formalitées de passeport. Je suis sûr que votre étonnement égale le mien. J'organise des
colonies de vacances en Suisse pour les enfants marocains, au nom
d'une Oeuvre appuyée par le gouvernement Suisse, et voilà que les
autorités marocaines y voient une éspèce d'action politique, une sor-
te d'éxode, d'immigration incômpréhensible pour des buts inconnus,
sous prétexte qu'il se trouve des enfants israélites dans les groupes,
malgré que je leur ai assuré que ces jeunes enfants n'ont de visas
valable que pour la Suisse,pour un maximum de 3 mois,et qu'ils séjour-
neront sous la surveillance de moniteurs qualifiés en Suisse.

Je vous tiendrai au courant des développements ultérieures
et en attendant, veuillez agréer mes salutations distinguées.

(D.G. LITTMAN)

Jewish. Utterly surprised by this accusation, Littman answers him that he is not expected
to distinguish the religion of a Moroccan child by its name. He asks Tajjedine to call Mr. Hajjaj
who will confirm that he is in contact with the Entr'Aide Nationale. Baffled by Tajjedine's
accusations, Littman concludes that surely Mrs. Lehmann must also find such accusations
extremely strange adding that for the time being everything is on hold.

ŒUVRE SUISSE DE SECOURS

AUX ENFANTS DE L'AFRIQUE DU NORD
105, Rue Dumont d'Urville, Casablanca. Maroc.

Genève 1, Case postale 220   10 June 1961

Madam N. Lehmann,
Oeuvre Suisse de Secours aux Enfants
de l'Afrique du Nord.

Dear Madam,
          This letter comes so quickly after its predecessor because
during that time there has been considerable activity by your délégué
and it seemed wisest for me to report immediately the most recent
developements; and in fact I have kept back my letter of astonisment
and indignation- here enclosed- so that you will receive it and this one
together on Monday and will more easily understand the unusual situation.
Meeting with M. Hajjaj:
          At 18;00 h. on Thursday evening I left Si Alaoui Tajjeddine
after our most extraordinary meeting. It was too late to return to
M. Hajjaj, but the following morning(yesterday) I was able to fix
a meeting for 18:30h. the same day. Unfortunately,after having waited
until 19:45, M.Hajjaj- engaged in an important conference- passed out
a message that he would see me this morning, the 10th. As usual he was
most courteous and showed his astonishment at the reception given me
by M. Taggeddine; so shocked was he that he asked for a letter from
me describing the scene,to be addressed to the Prefecture of the
Governor, asking for the Governor's intervention. He confirmed the
fact that all the children are Jewish and when I asked how he could
explain this curious fact, since we had made so much propaganda,he
explained that it was not so customaty for Moslem children to be sent
abroad in colonies de vacances. When I asked him what I should do,
especially as the tickets had been paid for in part due to his assurance
and that of M. Dkhissy,and that never before had the Oeuvre encountered
a similar situation, he first asked for me to write the letter to the
Prefecture du Governor and added that he felt sure that everything
would be arranged before the departure of the boat on June 26th. He is
a most sympathetic man and it was a real pleasure to speak with him
after the most unfortunate experience I had with the Khalifa of the
I Arrondisement.

Meeting with Si Berrode Abdellaoui; Khalifa du II Arrondisement.

          Morning 10/6/61 waited more than an hour in the ante-room with
scores of other persons, I was finally able to speak to the Khalifa.
I explained to him my conversations with the Khalifa of the I Arrondisement and M. Hajjaj. It was most regrettable that the demand for the
colonie de vacances had come from only one section of the population,
I explained, but this was not the Oeuvre's fault. He received me with
all courtesy and immediately detailed someone to begin the work of
sorting out the documents I had brought with me concerning the children
to see that they were accurately disposed on the demandes de passeport
forms. This quickly done and on Tuesday I have been instructed to
call in order to collect the demands- already stamped in my presence-
and take them to M. Hajjaj for the collective passports to be made out.
In the meantime the necessary enquiry will be carried out amongst the
families wishing to send their children to Switzerland in the colonie
de vacances; in the II Arrondisement in effect their are sixteen
families and 35 children at the moment.

Meeting(the second) with Si Alaoui Tajjeddine; Khalifa du I Arrondise-
          With all speed your délégué hastened to see once more the
a

Fig. 39 Letter from D.G. Littman to N. Lehmann, June 10, 1961

This letter, enclosing the previous one written a day before, relates the various meetings

Littman had with Moroccan officials after the incident with the Khalifa of the 1st district

of Casablanca. Mr. Hajjaj, shocked by the incident, advised Littman to write a letter to the

Mr. Cheradi, director of the governor's cabinet. The meeting with Si Berrode Abdellaoui,

Khalifa of the 2nd district, writes Littman did not elicit any angry reactions or accusations.

ŒUVRE SUISSE DE SECOURS
AUX ENFANTS DE L'AFRIQUE DU NORD

Genève 1, Case postale 220

the Khalifa of the I Arrodisement. This time I was received without
insults or hasty words. I was told that the enquiry had been carried
out and that the forms had been filled in correctly. The number of
children was 59 and that the dossier had been sent to M. Hajjaj at
the Prefecture. The Khalifa stated that he was not against the idea
of the colonie de vacances, but that he had noted in his report that
the parents of the children were mainly poor and wondered how they
could afford the luxury of such a trip(it is possible of course, and
I suggested this to him) that a charitable Oeuvre or their own economie
have permitted this happy occasion to materialize). He had made
certain reservations in his report, to the effect that:-

1;) The children should all travel on one passport.
2.) The Oeuvre should take full responsibility in the case where any
   • of the parents defaulted in paying the fees demanded, or in case
     of illness(I told him that they were all insured).
3.) The Oeuvre would be fully responsible for the transport to Geneva
     and the Home,and the return to Marocco after the month's holiday.
4;) The parents of the children are all poor.
He made some other minor points which I cannot recollect at
the moment, which expressed his doubts on the whole subject, but at
least he was not aggressively rude as he was on Thursday. He has this
idée fixe and it is difficult to explain to him the disinterestedness
of the Oeuvre's efforts. I left with him a letter written to the
Ministry of Foreign Affairs on May 17th., a copy of which I forwarded
to you a week ago or more.
      My impression being somewhat altered after this second meeting,
I am a little uncertain whether or not to write the letter to the
Governor (mentioning M. Tajjeddine' attitude at our first meeting),
but as M. Hajjaj advised me to do so I shall probably comply. I trust
their will be no scandal, which would be deplorable; yet M.Hajjaj
felt that such a letter was necessary in the circumstances, especially
considering what had been said,so wrongly, by M. Tajjedine. I shall
send you a copy of this letter.

———————————————

      There is just about two weeks before the departure of the
SS. Ionia. I am endeavouring to arrange that the greater part of those
inscribed will be able to leave on that date, but you see my difficulties. I can hardly ask the religion of the parents who come to inscribe
their children, but the curious fact is that all appear to be Jewish.
What does Professor Aberson think ? Can we possibly limit the number
of one religious denomination; I hardly think so, but on the other
hand it is inexplicable why there is no demand from individuals
profe ssing the Moslem religion. A most delicate question this, and
one hesitates to embarras the authorities on this score. I really
am in adilemma; the Khalifa of the I Arrondisement expained in his
harangue that one could see from the names that all were Jewish: woe
is me who see simply:Ifrah, Knafou, and Malka ! In our second year in
Marocco we must do our utmost to attract the Moslem youth so that
such absurd aspersions cannot be levied against the Oeuvreand its reput-
                                                              (ation.
      A further letter will follow dealing with yours of the
8th. June- for which I thank you- but in the meanwhile understand well
that this first group of about 100 children must be well-housed at
Champéry (is it not ?) and that you will have to provide one or two
persons to accompany them from Casablanca. We must set our usual high
standard so that a visiting Maroccan delegation will be in no doubts
about the good conditions and high standards provided by the Oeuvre
for all those children who come under its care.
            Cordial greetings to

The second meeting with Si Alaoui Tajjedine was more diplomatic but the Khalifa said that

he wrote his reservations in a report to his superiors. In the last part of his letter Littman

wonders about "the curious fact that all appear to be Jewish" saying that "it is inexplicable

why there is no demand from individuals professing the Moslem religion," and that "in our

second year in Morocco we must do our utmost to attract the Moslem youth so that such

absurd aspersions cannot be levied against the Oeuvre and its reputation."

COPIE POUR M. ~~HAJJAJ~~ GENEVE

ŒUVRE SUISSE DE SECOURS

AUX ENFANTS DE L'AFRIQUE DU NORD
105, Rue Dumont D'Urville, Casablanca, M
~~Genève 1, Case postale 220~~

le 11 Juin, 1961

M. Cheradi,
Directeur du Cabinet du Gouverneur,
Casablanca.

Monsieur,

Je vous adresse cette lettre sur la suggestion de M. Hajjaj, chef de Division de la Préfecture centrale. Veuillez croire que je regrette sincèrement qu'une telle lettre soit nécessaire.

Depuis mon arrivée au Maroc il y a trois mois, je me suis toujours éfforcé d'établir des contacts avec les autorités et les organisations intéressés à Rabat pour que notre Oeuvre puisse être efficace auprès des enfants marocains. Mes rapports à mi-Mars avec le Ministère de la Santé Publique (Dr. Laraqui) et avec La Jeunesse et Sport (M. Mezzour et M. Drissi-Kacemi) furent infructeux par la difficulté de trouver des contributions financières pour les enfants qu'ils enverraient en Suisse pour une convalescence ou des vacances. L'Entr'Aide Nationale et le Ministère de l'Education Nationale furent plus intéressés par nos offres, et l'Oeuvre proposa pour les enfants de l'Entr'Aide un tarif spécial. M. Ghomari, le Secrétaire Général, après avoir proposé d'envoyer 100 enfants réduisit dernièrement ce chiffre à 40; j'attends la liste finale des noms des enfants partant. M. Senoussi, du Ministère de l'Education Nationale, informé par M. Nacer El Fassi, chef de l'Enseignement Secondaire Musulman, me fit savoir que le Ministère payerait le prix de séjour pour environs 30 enfants si l'Entr'Aide se chargeait de son côté du coût des transports. Quand M. Ghomari décidait que l'Entr'Aide payerait les transports de ses pupilles seulement, ~~le~~ M. Senoussi m'informa que malheureusement il ne disposait pas de fonds pour payer le transport aussi. Cependant le Ministère était satisfait que l'Entr'Aide enverrait un groupe choisi probablement parmi les enfants des martyrs de l'indépendance.

J'ai été toujours été en contact avec M. Chaoui, chef de Division Consulaires et Sociales du Ministère des Affaires Etrangères, et le 17 Mai j'adressai une lettre au Ministère leur exposant nos buts, avec des références et récommandations, et leur demandant de me facilit er ma tâche. J'ai laissé une copie de cette lettre avec M. Hajjaj, M. Alaoui Tajjeddine, et je crois avec M. Dkhissy quand je lui ai parlé de notre programme à la Préfecture du Gouverneur il y a dix jours.

Fig. 40 Letter from D.G. Littman to Mr. Cheradi, Director of the cabinet Casablanca's Governor, June 11, 1961

In his three-page letter in French addressed to Mr. Cheradi, on the advise of Mr. Hajjaj, Littman summarizes his activities in Morocco on behalf of OSSEAN. He refers to his letter to the Foreign Ministry (May 17) and to the various meetings he held with Moroccan officials, stressing Entr'Aide Nationale's interest in sending children from "The Sons of the Martyrs of

ŒUVRE SUISSE DE SECOURS
AUX ENFANTS DE L'AFRIQUE DU NORD
Tel: 265-53   105, Rue Dumont D'Urville, Casablanca.
~~Genève I, Case postale 220~~

(2.)

Mon travail consistait justement à créer une colonie de vacances
en Suisse pour les enfants marocains, et je m'éfforçais de travailler
avec les particuliers aussi bien qu'avec les institutions plus ou moins
gouvernmentales. Depuis six semaines des particuliers sont venus au
bureau de l'Oeuvre, pour inscrire leurs enfants. J'étais toujours
en contact avec M. Hajjaj qui était aussi courtois que encourageant.
Il m'a autorisé à terminer les demandes de passeports des enfants inscrits
pour les colonies de vacances. Je devais prendre ces fiches, déjà
signées par ~~les~~ un des parents, aux Khalifats respectifs qui les signer-
aient et les retourneraient à M. Hajjaj pour faire les passeports collectifs

Jeudi, 8 Juin, j'allais voir Si Alaoui Tajjeddine, Khalifat du
1er Arrondisement. Il me reçut très aimablement et m'assura qu'il
n'aiderait à terminer rapidement les formalités. Il prit une fiche, puis
une deuxième et une troisième; après en avoir examiné cinq il les jeta
toutes avec un geste d'humeur sur le bureau et s'écria avec violence:
" Non ! je ne donnera pas ma signature." Devant mon étonnement il
continua:" c'est une émmigration, c'est un éxode !c'est une affaire
politique !; vous n'auriez pas dû vous compromettre dans cette affaire
M. Littman." J'étais éberlué. Ces propos sybillins de M. Alaoui rendait
la situation extrèmement obscure.Il semble que la colère que M. Alaoui
montra devant ses subordonnés et qu'il dirigea en partie contre moi
était provoquée par le fait que les cinq fiches portaient des noms
israèlites- incident que je n'aurais certes pas remarqué. (Par la
suite M. Hajjaj m'a appris, à ma grande surprise, que tous les noms
de la première liste était de familles juives.) J'expliquais à M.Alaoui
que j'avais été en contact avec de nombreuses organisations et autorités
marocaines et que l'Entr'Aide National enverrait des enfants, mais il
me répondit que tous ces discours n'étaient " que des mots,"et qu'il
n'agirait pas jusqu'à réception d'un document écrit officiellement.
Il accepta, cependant, le dossier après avoir parlé au téléphone avec
M. Hajjaj, mais me prévint qu'il ferait une "grande enquête." Jamais
je ne me serais attendu à de telles remarques qui sont en contradiction
totale avec les travaux de notre Oeuvre en Europe et au Maroc.
Si Berrode Abdellaoui, le Khalifat du II Arrondisement, était
par contraste très aimable et m'a promis les fiches pour mardi.
Cependant je dois dire que à ma deuxième entrevue hier,
M. Alaoui a été plus poli et m'a expliqué qu'il avait déjà envoyé le
dossier à M. Hajjaj. Mais il fit allusion à ses premières remarques.

the Resistance Organization" to Switzerland. He gives a detailed description of the incident
with Si Alaoui Tajjedine and requests the intervention of the Governor. Although an article
on the Oeuvre's summer camp was publicized in local newspapers, Littman acknowledges
that to his amazement all the children are Jewish. He stresses that it is not in the habit
of the Oeuvre to ask the religion of the children but that he would be glad to organize a

ŒUVRE SUISSE DE SECOURS
(3.)   AUX ENFANTS DE L'AFRIQUE DU NORD

~~Genève 1, Case postale 220~~

Puis-je vous demander, Monsieur, d'intervenir auprès du
Gouverneur de la ville de Casablanca ? Avec les encouragements de
M. Dkhissy et M. Hajjaj j'ai commencé le payement des billets de ~~x~~
transport pour ces enfants marocains. Le départ du bateau est fixé le
26 Juin, et je dois encore obtenir les visas suisses et les passeports.

Il semble maintenant que tous les particuliers de Casablanca
qui ont inscrit leurs enfants à mon bureau sont Israélites, fait
surprenant car la Vigie a publié un important article sur notre Oeuvre
(le 25 Avril) et d'autres annonces ultérieurement. La nationalité
de tous les enfants ~~enfants~~ inscrits, sans exception, est Marocaine,
et vous comprendrez facilement que notre Oeuvre ne peut demander la
religion de chaque enfant. Cependant je puis assurer Son Excellence,
le Gouverneur, que je serai très heureux d'essayer d'organiser- même
à cette date si retardée- un convoi d'enfants de Casablanca, exclusive-
ment Musulmans, pour des vacances en Suisse au tarif normal, si les
parents viennent ~~de~~ les inscire.

Il serait vraiment dommâge que les efforts de l'Oeuvre Suisse
pour renforcer les liens entre les jeunesse de divers pays échouent
au Maroc à cause de cet incident. J'ose éspérer que ceci s'arrangera
et que l'année prochaine nous intéresseront toutes les classes de la
population,de la ville de Casablanca.

En m'excusant d'avoir retenu votre attention si longtemps,
et en espérant que vous vous intéressez à cette affaire que je vous
ai amplement exposée sur la demande de M. Hajjaj, veuillez agréer,
Monsieur, ma consideration respectueuse.

                        D.G. Littman

                        Délégué au Maroc de l'Oeuvre
                        Suisse de Secours aux Enfants
                        de l'Afrique du Nord.

convoy of exclusively Moslem children. He ends this letter by emphasizing that it would
be deplorable should the Oeuvre fail to bring youths of different countries together due
to this unfortunate incident.

105, Rue Dumont d'Urville, Casablanca, MAROC.

12 June

~~14~~th. ~~May~~ 1961

11

Madam N. Lehmann,
Oeuvre Suisse de Secours aux Enfants
de l'Afrique du Nord.
Case Postale, 220,
Genève, 1. SUISSE

Dear Madam,

Enclosed you will find the letter I addressed to M. Cheradi and which I handed to him personally two hours ago at the Préfecture; at his request I have also left a copy with M. Hajjaj.

It appears that M. Alaoui is well-known for similar outbursts and both M. Cheradi- with whom I spoke this morning- and M. Hajjaj touched their foreheads as if to suggest that he was not quite normal. At the same time I understand that he is merely the Khalifat par interim of the I Arrondisement and is not liked.

M. Cheradi confirmed what M. Hajjaj had said on Saturday, that on no account was I to close my bureau and that there was no question of my asking the religion of the parents who come to inscribe their children for the colonies de vacances in Switzerland. As soon as the Governor returned he would bring the matter to his attention, and in the meantime he would have a word with M. Hajjaj so that all the formalities would be terminated before the departure of the S.S. Ionia on June 26th. He stated that I had done well to make my report.

S.S. Ionia, sailing either 25th. or the 26th. June(the latter date prob-
(able

We are now able to have at least 92 places in Tourist B, and there is a possibility that a further 6 will become available shortly. There are twelve cabins for six persons each, and two cabins for ten. The Dormitory accomodation still remains vacant and if I can complete the necessary formalities for the other children already inscribed it might be possible to take some of the 213 places available. The cost in Tourist B is approximately 99 Dirhams to Marseille, and the Dormitory class works out at 90 Dirhams a child.

Convoyeurs: I had no intention of accompanying any of the convoys by boat- thus committing myself to the sea's ravages- and since,it would appear that there will be no aeroplane convoys, the question does not arise. BUT this is a very important question, especially as the first large convoy will leave in exactly two weeks with the S.S. Ionia, and it is absolutely essential that the necessary persons be sent from Switzerland to take the children in hand. Remember there could well be from 100 to 200 children in this covoy and there must be ample personnel to keep them in hand not only from Marseille (are the 'busses certain ?), but on the two and one-half days' journey from Casablanca on board ship. For each 50 children, the company offers accomodation free for one accompagnateurs, and since they are being reasonable it is clear that they would probably offer a place free even for a good proportion of fifty. Thus there is no cost from Casablanca for from two to four accompagnateurs (if so many are needed) assuming that the number of children is from one to two hundred. It is hardly reasonable to expect more than that number.

Fig. 41 Letter from D.G. Littman to N. Lehmann, June 12, 1961

Littman writes to Lehmann that other Moroccan officials told him that Tajjedine was "not quite normal." On no account, he was told, should OSSEAN's office be closed nor should the religion of the parents be inquired. Littman reminds Lehmann to send the adults accompanying the children sailing aboard the *S.S. Ionia* on June 26, the children (sixty boys and fifty girls) are not to stay for more than one month. He tells Lehmann that the

2.)

12th.June 1961

All the booking arrangements for the return journey are being
arranged satisfactorily after a successful meeting this afternoon.
There is still the suggestion that my letters are incomprehensible;
well then " if the eyes of the blind"cannot be opened with words let
them be opened with acts. Geneva must be beautiful at this time of year;
one sees the lake, the mountains, and one is tempted to dream a little.
I hope you are taking care of my plateau I left with you, although
sometimes I tremble when I think how easily it might have broken in the
transport. Do be careful in the future and don't let anyone touch it; in
fact no-one at all ! It is extremely fragile,much more than you would im-
(agine.

Séjour groupe Champéry: No-one is coming for two months; all those
children coming on the S.S. Ionia will be staying for one month, as the
parents cannot afford more than that. If one adds the time needed for
travelling to and from Switzerland they will be away a little over five
weeks. I insist that you take the necessary measures to,see that the
promised accomodation is of the highest standard for these children who
will be our guests for the greater part of July. I assume that you will
be making use of both Morgins and Champéry during this period when such
an arrangement is feasible. Of the first 110 names on the first list,
sixty are boys and fifty are girls.

Entr'Aide National: I have received absolutely no reply of any sort
from M. Rhazi. I would suggest that the Oeuvre offer a special"prix de
séjour" of about 5 frs. or less for fifty children from the Entr'Aide.
This good-will would be much appreciated and contribute to a more
general result of our efforts. But you will soon be hearing of this idea
again; for the moment bear it in mind.

Questionnaires Medicaux: I shall begin sending you these concerning the
first 110 children, which I have stamped and signed with my approval.
The others will follow in due course. There is only one case which I
hesitated to approve, but in the end I consented since there is no
infectious disease involved. All the others are 100% fit!

I haven't the strength to go on, even though there are points
to discuss. Keep me well informed by Express Air Mail, don't ask the
impossible, and if my grammar and prolixity still causes concern may it
also cause reflection. You will receive much more information very
shortly from this side.

May I remind you, Madam, that the information forwarded me
concerning an appartment hardly relates to your letter of the 23rd. May
when one is supposed to be ready at " the end of the year."

Kindest regards from both my wife and myself to you, Madam,
and all our collaborators. We were very sad to hear of your illness
and trust that all is now well.

Yours very sincerely,

(D.G. Littman)
Délégué au Maroc de l'O.S.S.E.
A.N.

P.S. I trust that Professor Aberson arranged all facilities
with the Federal authorities in Berne. This is important as I
understand that M. Birschler, the Swiss Consulate in Casablanca
was awaiting a reply.

Entr'Aide Nationale has not yet replied and suggests that the rate be reduced to five Swiss

francs per child. As to the critics regarding the length of his letters he ironically writes: "and

if my grammar and prolixity still cause concern may it also cause reflection." He scoffs at

those who quietly sitting in Geneva far from the realities that he has to overcome, request

impossible and quick results.

ŒUVRE SUISSE DE SECOURS
AUX ENFANTS DE L'AFRIQUE DU NORD

Genève 1. Case postale 220

Mr.D.G.LITTMAN,
Oeuvre Suisse de Secours aux
Enfants de l'Afrique du Nord
105, rue Dumont d'Urville
C a s a b l a n c a.

16/6/61

Cher Monsieur,

Hier, nous vous avons telegraphié que nous avons
prévu trois convoyeurs pour prendre en main le transport qui
devra quitter Casablanca. Ces trois personnes arriveront séparé-
ment: comme première, Mlle Schirmann qui devra venir Mercredi/Jeudi
pour vous aider avec les dernières mises-au point de choses
administratives; le Dr.Dreyfuss est prévu pour Vendredi-soir
et notre moniteur Michel viendra Samedi. Les trois accompagneront
les enfants par bateau.

Nous espérons recevoir aujourd'hui votre télégramme
concernant la délivrance des passeports et le nombre d'enfants.

Certainement, nous allons utiliser Champéry également
pour le premier groupe. Tout est prévu de ce côté. Nous sommes actu-
ellement encore à la recherche de personnel éducatif qualifié,supplé-
mentaire , mais ce problème sera réglé ces prochains jours.

En ce qui concerne le Consulat suisse, Mr-Birschler
est en possession de toutes les instructions nécessaires. Nous
nous sommes assurés à Berne. Ces instructions correspondent exacte-
ment à ce qu'on vous a communiqué lors de votre discussion à Berne,
et sont - en bref -les suivantes: Dès que vous présentez les documents
nécessaires, exigés par le autorités suisses, vous aurez les visas.
Mais il est absolument exclu que le consulat puisse vous être utile
dans l'accomplissement de vos démarches pour avoir les documents.
Tel n'est pas le rôle d'un consulat, et il est extrêmement important
que vous compreniez cela, et que vous agissiez strictement selon ces
directives, afin de ne pas vous créer encore des complications à
la dernière minute.Nous, les suisses, sommes assez formalistes, et
la fantaisie n'est pas notre fort.
Nous faisons partir cette lettre d'urgence.
Dès que nous serons en possession de votre télégramme, nous
vous communiquerons les détails concernant l'arrivée des accompagnateurs. Il faudra leur réserver des chambres, si possible dans votre
Hôtel, où à proximité.

Espérant que tous les préparatifs seront terminés
à temps.

Bien à vous

O.S.S.E.A.N.

p. *Lehmann*

Fig. 42 Letter from Lehmann to D.G. Littman, June 16, 1961

In this letter Lehmann writes that three chaperons, Miss Aïda Schirmann (the fictive N.
Lehmann), Dr. Dreyfus and Michel Steurermann. will accompany the children on the 26. She
writes that once all the documents requested are ready the Consul, Mr. Birschler, will provide
the visas but that Littman should not ask the Consulate to help obtain the documents. That
is not the role of a Consulate adding that "we Swiss are quite formalists and fantasy is not
our strong point."

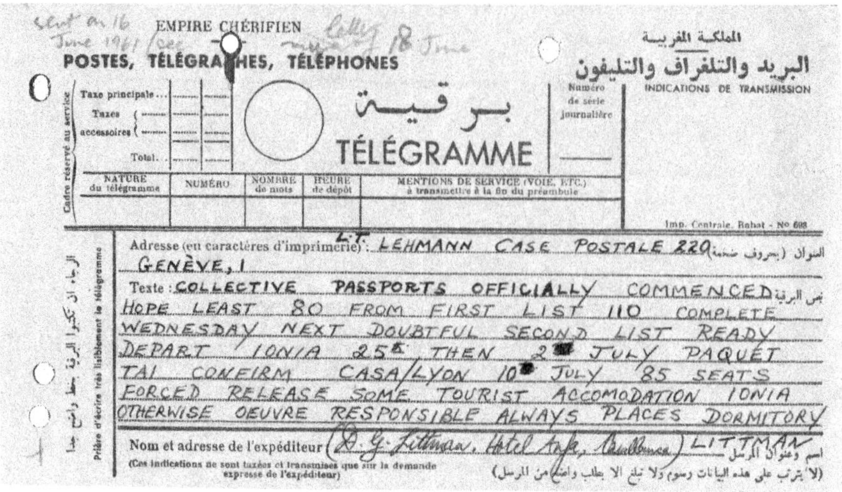

sent on 16 June 1961 (see ... 18 June

EMPIRE CHÉRIFIEN

POSTES, TÉLÉGRAPHES, TÉLÉPHONES

المملكة المغربية

البريد والتلغراف والتليفون

Taxe principale

Taxes accessoires

Total.

برقية

TÉLÉGRAMME

Numéro de série journalière

INDICATIONS DE TRANSMISSION

Cadre réservé au service

NATURE du télégramme	NUMÉRO	NOMBRE de mots	HEURE de dépôt	MENTIONS DE SERVICE (VOIE, ETC.) à transmettre à la fin du préambule

Imp. Centrale, Rabat - No 698

Adresse (en caractères d'imprimerie) : L.T. LEHMANN CASE POSTALE 220 GENÈVE, 1 العنوان (بحروف ضخمة)

Texte : COLLECTIVE PASSPORTS OFFICIALLY COMMENCED HOPE LEAST 80 FROM FIRST LIST 110 COMPLETE WEDNESDAY NEXT DOUBTFUL SECOND LIST READY DEPART IONIA 25th THEN 2nd JULY PAQUET TAI CONFIRM CASA/LYON 10th JULY 85 SEATS FORCED RELEASE SOME TOURIST ACCOMODATION IONIA OTHERWISE OEUVRE RESPONSIBLE ALWAYS PLACES DORMITORY نص البرقية

Prière d'écrire très lisiblement le télégramme

الرجاء ان تكتبوا البرقية بخط واضح جدا

Nom et adresse de l'expéditeur (D. G. Littman, Hotel Anfa, Casablanca) LITTMAN اسم وعنوان المرسل

(Ces indications ne sont taxées et transmises que sur la demande expresse de l'expéditeur)

(لا يترتب على هذه البيانات رسوم ولا تبلغ الا بطلب واضح من المرسل)

Fig. 43 Telegram from D.G. Littman to Lehmann, June 16, 1961

Telegram from Littman announcing that the collective passports actually began. Hoping that at least eighty children from the first list of one hundred and ten will sail on the *S.S. Ionia* (June 25) and later on the ship *Paquet* (July 2) and the TAI flight from Casablanca to Lyon (July 10).

Anfa Hotel
Tel:502.22
Chambre 62/3
Tel: 265.53 (bureau)105 Rue Dumont D'Urville, Casablanca, Maroc.

Madam N. Lehmann,
O.S.S.E.A.N.
Case Postale, 220,   midi, le 18 Juin,1961
Genève, 1. SUISSE.

Dear Madam,
          I thank you for your telegramme, and your letter which
reached me yesterday. I trust you received my telegramme sent off the
night of the 16th.June. Let me here give you the latest position.

Number of children likely to leave for Switzerland on board S.S.Ionia:

1.) Curiously enough the chief difficulties now emanate from the
    Khalifat of the II Arrondisement, who has refused his signature
    for approximately 12 children from the first list (which totalled
    110, of which 59 live in the II Arrondisement). No reasons are
    offered, but it would appear that he refuses to sign for those who
    are actually working and not at school: most astonishing ! At the
    same time the necessary enquiries have not continued, and at least
    6 children from the first list have therefore not been accepted
    due to this fact. What will happen to the second list I wonder ?

2.) The Khalifat of the I Arrondisement on the other hand simply gave
    his unfavourable opinion-after our most unfortunate meeting- and
    passed the passport forms on to M. Hajjaj to do as he pleased. Here
    the number was 59. The collective passports were begun with these
    names. It is possible that the same procedure will be adopted with
    the second list vis à vis the I Arrondisement,but one can't be sure.

3.) To make matters worse, some parents were foolish enough to give me
    school identity cards, sometimes without the signature of the
    Director, at others without the official stamp. This was the case
    with thirty children; it was only on the 17th.(yesterday) that
    M. Hajjaj gave the order to write in the names, even when the
    school identity card is incompletely signed, and this work on the
    passports will begin to-morrow: I have promised M. Hajjaj that I
    will have the cards correctly signed and stamped by Wednesday, the
    21st.June. If they are not sent back to me by then the whole
    arrangement will grind to a halt, thanks to the incredible lack of
    foresight of the parents concerned; they are responsible ! The
    Swiss Consulate MUST have the passports on FRIDAY, the 23rdin order
    to make out the collective visas, and he prefers Thursday. I have
    enclosed a copy of the Swiss demands; only the last paragraph
    perplexes me a little. THE S.S. IONIA will now arrive on the 24th.
    of June, and will leave on the 25th. June(not the 26th. as supposed
    The Agents will try to insure that the departure is in the evening.

4.) From the first list of 110 children, 7 failed to bring the proper
    legal document or prove their identity, or gave a wrong address by
    accident; at least 12 would seem to have been refused by the Khalifa
    of the II Arrondisement, and about 7 are still awaiting the enquiry.
By the parents! Assuming that I will have all the school identity cards returned to
    me on Monday or Tuesday, about 85 (eighty-five) children should
    be able to leave on the S.S. Ionia, the 25th. June.

5.) I have just this moment prepared the second list of children.

Fig. 44 Letter from D.G. Littman to Lehmann, June 18, 1961

Some problems arose, writes Littman, when the Khalifa of the II district refused to sign for

a number of children on the first list. Also some school-identity cards lack official stamps

and this has delayed to the very last day the visas from the Swiss consulate. The number of

children to leave on the *S.S. Ionia* is not final, between seventy to a hundred writes Littman.

/ 2.)

midi, le 18 Juin

This includes ALL those who have brought me the required documents by yesterday (Saturday) evening. Surprisingly enough the total is only 49 (forty-seven), and of these 6 are inadequately documented, and I still await school or other identity cards for 8,— but these should arrive. It is just possible that some from the second list will be approved and will be able to leave also on the 25th., but this I cannot say, and can only know on Tuesday at the earliest.

Under such circumstances—not of my making !— it is impossible to give you anything like an accurate figure for those sailing on the S.S. Ionia. The figure could drop as low as seventy (70), and lower if I have not received the identity cards; on the other hand it could reach 100 (one hundred), though I doubt it.

So far, adding the two lists together, there is a total of 159 children, 13 of whom are badly documented, and 12 (so far) seemingly refused. 124 is the remainder ! When one considers how many parents came to see me, wishing to send their children for a holiday in Switzeralnd, it is quite extraordinary that only this number remains at this late date,—sure! The S.S. Ionia offers the cheapest accomodation, but I doubt if we will fill one-third of the accomodation we could have. In fact I am forced to let some of the Tourist accomodation go (as mentioned in my telegramme), or otherwise we shall be responsible for paying for empty bearths. However, as the dormitory remains empty, with normal accomodation for 86, and additional accomodation for a further 110, there is no danger of losing what in the end we will require On this point I seek your advice, which is probably on the way already.

For those who cannot leave on the 25th. there is the possibility of the 2nd. July by Paquet (if I can hold the places, in such an uncertain situation), or T.A.I. who have offered a 'plane from Casa to Lyon on the 10th. July with 85 places. The cost should be less than the 220 Dirhams per child offered for the Casa/Genève journey, but I have not yet received the official figure. An Agent here for Travel feels sure that if we cannot fill the aeroplane, she will be able to use the remaining places for her clients. Again your advice! Of course there is more boat accomodation from the 16th.July onwards.

Let me say how happy I am that Mlle. Shirmann will soon be arriving; has she by chance another portable typewriter; the English one I left with you in Geneva, unfortunately, is not functioning well, so it is no use bringing that. My wife and I cannot operate the same machine. This is not so serious however. The important point is that Mlle.Shirmann not only arrives as quickly as possible, but stays on a little while. Should more parents come forward with the appropriate documents in the next two weeks I cannot cope with this as well as pushing the formalities which entails hour-long waits before one is able to speak with the person desired. Dr. Dreyfuss and Michel(a warm welcome awaits them) should be able to enough to accompany the children, and only two places are given free for 100 a group of 100 children.
DO NOT FORGET THAT THE S.S.IONIA SAILS ON THE SUNDAY THE 25th. JUNE and not the 26th. Mlle.Shirmann should not come later than Wednesday, as there will be a lot to do here on Thursday and Friday, made worse because Saturday is a national holiday. Advance also the arrival dates of Dr. Dreyfuss and Michel. I shall telegraph to-morrow or probably Tuesday night (by ordinary rate, not night) in the hope that you will receive it before 10:00 or 11:00 p.M. the same day. I shall endeavour to give you an exact figure of those leaving, assuming I am actually in a position to do so. My most cord

Transportation logistics are as following: by boats on the *S.S. Ionia* (June 25th) and the *Paquet* (July 2nd), and by air with TAI airlines (July 10th). He asks Miss Schirmann to bring him another portable typewriter and to stay for a while to help should more children be registered.

⟋ 105, Rue Dumont D'Urville, Casablanca, Maroc.
————————————————
                                    June 19th. 1961
                              11:15 a.m.
Mme. .N. Lehmann
O.S.S.E.A.N.
Case Postale 220,
Genève, 1

Dear Madam,

   I have just this moment come back from the Préfecture.
Three of their men are mobilized to complete the work of issuing
the passports (collective- about three or four). It appears that in
the end only 4 (four) from the II Arrondisement have been refused.
I was told that 91 names were being inscribed on the passports, BUT
if the School Identity cards are not brought for these children
before Wednesday, their names will simply be BARRED from the list.
The parents must be mad ! To arrive at this stage just before the
departure and then to lack about 30 school identity cards properly
signed is idiotic. Of course the remaining 50 or 60 whose identity
cards are properly filled in, stamped and signed will be able to
leave, and there are a further two (2) who already had individual
passports for travel to Spain, which will now be made valid for Switzerland as well. Thus you see the total could reach to NINETY-THREE 93
(NINETY-THREE) if I receive the identity cards, and it is just possible
that some from the second list will be able to leave also on the 25th.

   I can give you no more information at the moment, but
I feel that this is enough. As I said before:"at least 80" all being
well, and possibly up to 100. I am hammering away on all sides, but
there are too many nails.

   Mlle. Shirmann must come on Wednesday-not later, and stay
here, if possible, a few days after the departure of the Ionia, the
25th. The earlier the better for Dr. Dreyfuss and Michel.

   T.A.I. have just telephoned to confirm the Casa/Lyon
trajet for 10th. July at 18,450 (eighteen thousand, four-hundred
and fifty dirhams), which works out at about 217 Dirhams a child.
This is not too bad, if compared with the Paquet fare to Marseille
and the bus to Genève. Perhaps if thirty places or so are taken by
the Agents interested, they can pay a little more and the children
a little less. I am awaiting advice on this.

   Let me close with my most cordial greetings for all
our colleagues, three of whom I am looking forward to seeing here
shortly. Please do not fail me on your side.
                              Yours Sincerely,

Fig. 45 Letter from D.G. Littman to N. Lehmann, June 19, 1961

This letter confirms the one from June 18. Collective passports are being issued at the
prefecture but Littman is upset that school-identity cards are not properly signed. Children
from the second list might be leaving as well he adds.

105 Rue Dumont D'Urville, Casablanca, MAROC
————————————
4:30 p.m. 26 th June 1961

Madam Lehmann,
O.S.S.E.A.N.
Case Postale, 220
Genève, 1. SUISSE

Dear Madam,

The S.S. Ionia steamed out from the "Gare Delande" at about 12:30 P.M. this afternoon. She carries 127 children of Maroccan Nationality who will be taking their month's holiday in Switzerland with the full collaboration and help of the Oeuvre, a good beginning I trust to the Oeuvre's efforts in North Africa. The ship is due in at Marseille between 10.00 a.m; and 11.00 a.m. on Thursday the 29th. June and the autobuses should be at the dockside as early as possible. At the latest count there were 66 boys and 61 girls. Unfortunately, ELBAZ, Amram and SASPORTAS, Charles Simon and Moïse did not arrive at the convocation. The first was not well; in the case of the other two it appears that the parents preferred that SASPORTAS, Charles stayed to take an examination in ironing clothes. It was only with much persuasion, just before the departure of the boat, that I made it quite clear to the parents that they would have to bear all the costs involved. It was then decided that SASPORTAS, Moïse would take his holiday without his brother Charles who will remain for the examination in ironing. I shall refuse to take this child on any future convoy and will insist that the parents bear the full cost of their last-minute decision, which did not create a favourable impression at the port. It is possible that the parents will wish that Moïse return home before the official depature from Marseille on 1 August, but unless special papers can be procured from the maroccan legation in Berne this is impossible, as he is on one of four collective passports. These passports are valid until the 15th.August and if I recollect the Swiss visas are valid until the 5th. August. I have already reserved 100 places on a ship from the Company Paquet for the 1st. August and I hope to take a further 27 for the same date I trust this meets with your approval.

At 1:00 p.m. I sent off a telegramme announcing the departure.

Let me express my thanks to Mlle., your free-lance Shirmann monitrise, Dr. Dreyfus, and M. Steuermann, who organized the departure of the children so efficiently. Without them it would have been quite impossible to arrange matters and I am afraid they didn't have very much time to rest, especially Mlle Shirmann, who helped me enormously.

Whether or not the second convoy can leave on the 10th. July by aeroplane depends on many factors, but it is equally clear that at least two persons will be needed on this occassion to organiz the departure, although it is just feasible that one will suffice. I shall keep you fully informed, yet now I can tell you that full confirmation is unlikely until the very last days. In the end there might not be any alternative than that the children leave once again by boat, on or after the 16th. July.

I am sure everything will be done to take good care of the children in Switzerland during the full month and that Messrs. Leoni and Berger will strain the Oeuvre's resources to provide many short but satisfying excursions in the mountains during this time. Here I leave the sound reason and imagination of Professor Collisen to exert its influence over the exuberance of our two dear collegues kindest greetings from my wiffe and myself to you all.

Fig. 46 Letter from D.G. Littman to N. Lehmann, June 26, 1961

D.G. Littman writes to N. Lehmann (alias Aïda Schirmann) that the *S.S. Ionia* steamed out carrying on board 127 children, sixty-six boys and sixty-one girls. He was upset he recounts, that some children did not show up at the convocation. He thanks Miss Schirmann, Dr. Dreyfus and Mr. Steuermann for their help, jokingly concluding his letter regarding Leoni and Berger (The Israelis Bar-Giora and Reiffler) providing the children with satisfying excursions in the mountains during the holidays.

COPIE Copie à l'Ambassade de Suisse à Rabat pour son information.

01914

| Ambassade de Suisse, Rabat |
| 2 3 JUIN 1961 |
| Réf.: G.65.40 |

26 juin 1961

X.4.1.61 - GI/hl

ad: E 12/128 So/Bu

Police Fédérale des Etrangers

B e r n e

Messieurs,

Vous avez bien voulu m'adresser copie de votre lettre du 21 mars 1961 à l'Ambassade de Suisse à Rabat, par laquelle vous l'informiez de l'intention de l'Oeuvre suisse de secours aux enfants d'Afrique du Nord d'inviter en Suisse de jeunes Marocains.

Le 23 de ce mois, j'ai délivré aux 127 enfants figurant sur la liste ci-jointe, un visa d'entrée en Suisse valable jusqu'au 10 août prochain. Ils sont tous de nationalité marocaine, et inscrits dans quatre passeports collectifs. Pour les enfants Lisa et David OHANA, titulaires de passeports marocains valables, les visas y ont été apposés.

Par ailleurs, je vous informe que M. Littmann, délégué au Maroc de l'Oeuvre précitée, m'a remis une attestation déclarant que ces enfants se rendront à Morgins et à Champéry/VS, et seront à la charge de cette institution.

Les enfants seront accompagnés par Mlle Aïda Schirmann, née le 14.10.1914, de nationalité suisse.

Le séjour en Suisse est prévu du 29 juin au 1er août 1961.

Veuillez agréer, Messieurs, l'assurance de ma considération distinguée.

Le Consul de Suisse

J. Birchler

Annexes
2 listes

Fig. 47 Letter from the Swiss Consul in Casablanca, Mr. J. Birchler to the Federal Police des Etrangers in Bern, June 26, 1961 (copy to the Swiss Ambassador in Rabat)

In this letter the Consul informs the Federal Police in Bern that he has issued visas of entry valid until August 10 for the 127 children on the list. All the children are Moroccan, he writes, and are inscribed in four collective passports, except for two children, Lisa and David Ohana who are in possession of Moroccan passports. The delegate Mr. Littman, has acknowledged that the children are going to Morgins and Champery under the responsibility of the Oeuvre. The children will be escorted by a Swiss citizen, Miss Aïda Schirmann, born on the October 14, 1914. The children will remain in Switzerland from June 29 until August 1, 1961.

105, Rue Dumont D'Urville, Casablanca, MAROC

Madam Lehmann,
Oeuvre Suisse de Secours   1 Juillet 1961
aux Enfants de l'Afrique du Nord.
Casa Postale, 220,
Genève, 1

Dear Madam,
            I would have appreciated a telegramme to say that the
children arrived safely in Switzerland last night! Many parents have
been telephoning and calling at the office for news. I have given them
the Case Postale address to which they may write to their children.

            I have confirmed with TAI for the 10th. July from Casa to
Lyon, since I am fully confident that I can fill the eighty five (85)
places. At last the parents have understood what documents are required
and the flood is difficult to control. When I say that I hope to send
the second convoy with 85 children on the 10th. July, I must warn you
that a third convoy is also in preparation. One must push the authoritie
somewhat, but now they are used to my hustling ways we understand one
another better and the formalities take less time. However I doubt if
I can go on sleeping four hours a night for another month, and the
work involved is taking its toll.

            It is indeed a pity that the majority of the population,
the Moslems, have not been attracted sufficiently to send their children
to Switzerland for the holidays. I am trying every way to rectify this
situation, and will keep you well informed. Professor Aberson, himself,
I understand has shown considerable concern at our receiving children
from the minority (the Jews) of the population only. M. D'khissy
however has assured me that we should not let this bother us; it seems
that they are better organized than the Moslems(so he told me, when
we dined with he and Mme. D'khissy last night) but he thought that
what counted was that they were Marocains and our work is appeciated.
M. D'khissy is most helpful and never fails to aid me in pushing in
the right direction when it is necessary, and only yesterday he
telephoned to the Khalifat of the II Arrondisement to ask him to speed
up his "enquêtes"; the Khalifat of the I Arrondisement is now most
courteous and returns the passport demands within two days. Our
unfortunate first meeting is all but forgotten.

            It is my opinion that I could arrange the departure of the
children by aeroplane on the 10th. July without anyone coming from
Geneva, since TAI will provide hostesses for the flight. Of course
it is essential that the moniteurs and the buses are prepared to receive
the children at LYON (not Geneva) when the 'plane arrives. This
economy should please Herr Berger no end ! Do let me know IMMEDIATELY
what you feel about this suggestion; perhaps you prefer to send Mlle.
Shirmann. Of course if the third convoy is a large one and a ship is
used, then colleagues will be needed.

            Homes must be found to house all these children should your
booking from Europe and Marocco outnumber the space already availaable.
This is Professor Aberson's forte and we look to him to provide the
very best accomodation for these Maroccan children; and to Herren Berger
and Leoni to arrange those short but satisfying excursions into the
mountains. I have given some suggestions to Mlle. Shirmann when she was
here and she, Doctor Dreyfus, and Michel were in full agreement!

Fig. 48 Letter from D.G. Littman to OSSEAN, July 1, 1961

In his letter to Schirmann, Littman asks about the children who arrived in Morgins on June

29. He confirmed a plane to Lyon on July 10 with eighty-five children and a third convoy is

in preparation. He regrets that no Moslem parents are sending their children to Switzerland,

Mr. D'khissy, he writes, believes that it is because Jews are better organized than Moslems; to

him the important thing is that they are Moroccans children. Littman ends this letter wishing

"Herren Berger and Leoni" will organize short but satisfying excursions into the mountains.

ŒUVRE SUISSE DE SECOURS
AUX ENFANTS DE L'AFRIQUE DU NORD

Genève 1, Case postale 220

3 Juillet 1961

Mr.D.G. LITTMAN
Oeuvre Suisse de Secours
aux Enfants de l'Afrique
du Nord,
105, rue Dumont- d'Urville
C a s a b l a n c a .

Cher Monsieur,

Excusez le retard apporté à notre correspondance.
Comme vous pouvez bien vous imaginer, nous avons été pleinement
occupés par l'accueil de votre premier groupe, et nous réjouissons
de pouvoir vous donner quelques bonnes nouvelles:

En premier lieu, nous tenons à vous remercier de la
bonne préparation administrative de ce transport qui s'est
déroulé sans aucune difficulté aux multiples contrôles de police
et de douane. Même les tapis que vous avez eu l'amabilité de nous
envoyer comme cadeaux pour notre maison d'enfants, ont pu entrer
en Suisse sans charges supplémentaires.

Donc, les enfants sont arrivés en trois cars, JEUDI,
entre 3 et 5 heures du matin. Tout le monde était bien fatigué,
et les bons lits et l'entourage sympathique de la maison de
Morgins et de Champéry ont vite fait de restorer les voyageurs,
qui sont émerveillés des beautés de la montagne.

Par contre, nous avons à vous signaler une chose
très regrettable: Le choix des enfants n'a pas été fait avec assez
de perspicacité. Il y a , parmi le groupe, des éléments indésirables
qui n'ont aucune notion de discipline et qui se conduisent d'une
façon impossible. Pour vous donner un exemple: Nous avons dû
payer pour 350 dirhams de dégâts sur le bateau (matelas brulés,
draps déchirés, serrures arrachés etc., etc.) Et vous pouvez
facilement comprendre que s'il y a une dizaine de grands garçons
de ce calibre dans un groupe, ils arrivent facilement à désorganiser
le travail des moniteurs. Nous sommes donc en face de graves problèmes, et tout ce que nous pouvons vous dire pour le moment, c'est de
vous demander de procéder à un contrôle plus sévère concernant le
caractère de l'enfant. Il ne suffit pas de faire un contrôle médical
il faudrait un contrôle psychologique sérieux concernant l'état
mental et moral de l'enfant. Autrement, on mettra en danger toute
la continuation de notre action. Excusez-nous de devoir vous
adresser cette remarque, mais croyez-nous qu'elle est de la plus
grande importance. Nos amis de Berne qui sont venus accueillir les
enfants, approuvent notre point de vue et ont insisté à ce qu'on
vous signale ces faits.

Fig. 49 Letter from N. Lehmann to D.G. Littman, July 3, 1961

In this letter Lehmann announces the arrival of 127 children to Morgins and Champery. All
went smoothly with the customs she writes, thanking Littman for the good administrative
preparation. The major problem, she says, concerns the choice of children. This was not
carried with enough perspicacity. A fine had to be paid for the damages (burned mattresses,

ŒUVRE SUISSE DE SECOURS
AUX ENFANTS DE L'AFRIQUE DU NORD

Genève 1, Case postale 220

- 2 -

Mrs. Aberson vous remercie beaucoup de votre lettre,
qui lui a fait grand plaisir. Elle a beaucoup admiré les tapis
à la maison des ALOUETTES et aimerait en avoir un pour elle,
si ceci est possible. Mais je vous écrirai encore à ce sujet.

Comment vont les préparatifs pour le deuxième convoi:
Ecrivez-nous dès que vous aurez quelques précisions sur le nombre
approximatif des différents groupes, et surtout quelles sont les
prévisions pour Champéry. Madame Truffer doit être fixée là-dessus.

Veuillez dire au bureau de voyage que nos convoyeurs
et notre organisation les/ remercie de tout coeur de l'effort
qu'ils ont fourni, et que Mlle Schirmann a transmis les salutations à leurs parents en Suisse.

Recevez, cher Monsieur, l'assurance de nos sentiments
les meilleurs et nos hommages pour Mme

torn up sheets and broken locks) caused on the *S.S. Ionia* by "undesirable elements." It is not enough to make medical control but serious psychological examinations should be undertaken to evaluate the mental and moral condition of the child, our friends in Bern (Bar-Giora and Reiffler), she writes, insist on this point.

ŒUVRE SUISSE DE SECOURS
AUX ENFANTS DE L'AFRIQUE DU NORD

Genève 1, Case postale 220

3.7.1961

Mr.D.G.LITTMAN
OEUVRE SUISSE DE SECOURS AUX
ENFANTS DE L'AFRIQUE DU NORD
105, rue Dumont-d'Urville
C a s a b l a n c a.

Cher Monsieur,

A peine notre lettre partie, nous avons reçu vos nouvelles selon lesquelles vos inscriptions marchent maintenant à un rythme accéléré et que vous prévoyez un nouveau trasport pour le 10 Juillet. Nous vous félicitons de ce bon résultat.

Toutefois, les choses ne marchent pas si bien de notre côté, et nous devons vous demander de ne pas encore confirmer définitivement vos réservations pour l'avion de TAI, car les places pour ce groupe doivent être trouvées, et cela pose quelques problèmes. Veuillez donc attendre notre confirmation télégraphique. Les choses vont se décider en deux, trois jours.

Une autre question: Il faudra barrer de votre liste tous les adolescents au dessus de 15 ans, car les grands du premier convoi sont effectivement les pires éléments, et il faudra éviter à tout prix l'envoi de garçons et de filles de ce genre qui ne sont plus de l'age d'une colonie d'enfants. Le danger d'incendie à cause des fumeurs obstinés, les fréquentation entre filles et garçons, etc.etc. dépassent les limites d'une maison d'enfants.

Il nous est pénible de freiner votre bel entrain, mais vous comprendrez facilement nos difficultés.

Bien à vous

N. Lehman

Lehman

Fig. 50 Letter from N. Lehmann to D.G. Littman, July 3, 1961

In reply to Littman's letter of July 1, Lehmann asks him not to confirm for the flight on the 10th because of a lack of places for this new group. There are "problems," and it is necessary, she writes, "to bar from the list all the adolescents above the age of fifteen," explaining that it is difficult to manage the mixture of girls and boys of this age group.

105, Rue Dumon D'Urville, Casablanca, MAROC

Madam Lehmann,
Oeuvre Suisse de Secours aux Enfants
de l'Afrique du Nord.   11:30
Case Postale, 220.   11:30 a.m 4/7/61
Genève, 1

Dear Madam,
                    I have just this moment sent off a rather long telegramme
which in the circumstances was necessary.
                    The first part states that I have signed the contract with
TAI on the Oeuvre's behalf for the de-commercialization of one of their
aeroplanes, which will be put completely at our disposal to transport
84 children and one monitor from Casablanca to Lyon on MONDAY, the 10th.
July. The 'plane is due to leave Casa at 13:30 hours and should arrive
at Lyon aeroport at 18:00 hours French time, after a flight of 3 1/2 hours
We shall probably arrange that instead of the children eating on the
'plane at 14:00 hours, they will be given sandwich baskets just before
the arrival at Lyon, thus allowing the autobuses to make the four hours
or more drive direct to Morgins and Champéry without stopping to eat(at
least) on the way. We shall ask the parents to make sure that the
children eat lunch before they assemble for the buses to take them to
the aeroport on this side. I hope you are in agreement with all this.
                    It was necessary to sign the contract and start paying the
money(finally reduced to 18,400.00 Dirhams., or 216.5 Dirhams per child.)
or otherwise the TAI would have been forced to sell more seats; as it is
I have obliged them to empty the 'plane of 15 passengers and leave it
entirely at our disposal. The passport situation is developing nicely
and by to-morrow the collective passports should be ready to receive the
signature of M. Hajjaj. Unfortunately, I have been able to prepare a list
of about 95 to 100 names, already accepted by the Khalifa, but the 'plane
can only take 84 children, plus the moniteur- a total of 85.
                    However those who cannot go on this convoy will be able to
head the third convoy. There must be at least 60 children awaiting the
necessary "enquete" and the Khalifat's signature in the II Arrondisement
before they will be in a position to be presented for the collective
passports, but I do not doubt that within ten days at the most(Inshallah)
they also will be ready to leave. Transport is a great difficulty now,
since space is not easily available from the Paquet Company for 4th.class
(dormitory) during this period. TAI, once more, are coming to the rescue
and have offered a 'plane for the 24th. July. In my turn I informed them
that I preferred the 20th.July, but my situation is extremely delicate.
All depends upon whether the formalities are finished in time ! I should
have just enough names to fill another 'plane; I trust that your Homes
are being prepared to receive these youngsters.

MOST IMPORTANT: TAI- after much parrying- have AGREED to give ONE free
ticket to our chef du Transport to allow him or her to travel from
Paris to Casablanca. This I telegraphed. This offer is for the 6th. or
the 8th. July from LE BOURGET on TA 51 at 08:30 hours. Whoever is travelling must be certain to collect the ticket at LE BOURGET from UAT where
it will be kept at the counter , registered for the flight TA 51, in
the Oeuvre's name; the person travelling can then give his or her proper
name to be put on the ticket. I would advise that if you have not already
done so, you cable me immediately here in Casablanca giving me the name
of the person coming as chef du Transport and the date (6th. or 8th.July)
which has been chosen; I will then inform the Director of TAI and all
will be in order.

          Let me know

(Second Letter afternoon 4/7/61 ....)

Fig. 51 Letter from D.G. Littman to N. Lehmann, July 4, 1961

At 11:30 a.m. Littman writes that he just cabled Geneva that the contract with TAI on the

Oeuvre's behalf was signed. The plane from Casablanca to Lyon has been de-commercialized

in order to carry eighty-five children and one monitor on Monday the 10th. The passports

situation is developing nicely and tomorrow Mr. Hajjaj will sign them. A third convoy is under

Let me know immediately whether the group of thirty or forty about which I spoke with Mlle. Shirmann can come in the last two weeks of July as well as the first two weeks of August(arrival date, I mean). They will stay for approximately twenty days although one month is possible. Treat this request with the utmost urgency and let the moniteur who comes know all the details in this respect, without fail. This matter does not concern Herr Berger at all, as I have already explained to Mlle.Shirmann.

Again I advice that UBS forms be sent with the Chef du Transport, but since this is a question which touches Herr Berger to the quick, and his liveliness on this topic leaves aside all reason, I will not repeat the request. My opinion, past, present, and future, will remain always the same with regard to such short-sightedness. At the moment it is my own resources alone which allowed me to sign the contract and pay the deposit, which is such a ridiculous situation that I stand aghast!

My kindest regards to all in Geneva, also to Herr Leoni; I shall reserve any greetings I might have for Herr Berger when I have the occasion to see him next. On second thoughts, Cordial greetings to him also- it is my birthday to-day and I am in excellent spirits! My wife sends her best regards.

Yours sincerely,

(D.G. Littman)

Délégué au Maroc

P.S. I trust that the carpets arrived safely in Geneva without mishap. There will be a few other personal things arriving on the 10th. July, with the children's luggage and I look to you, Madam, to take care of this personal affair for me.

preparation, he writes, but transportation is a problem as it isn't easy to find available places in 4th class on the boat *Paquet*. He inquires once more about a matter previously discussed with Miss Schirmann (which doesn't concern Herr Berger) regarding the possible arrival of a group of thirty to forty (Moslem) children covered by OSSEAN's generosity. Littman asks to receive the forms from the UBS bank since as of now he has been paying the deposit for the de-commercialization of the plane from his own resources.

AGENCE MAROCAINE DE TRANSPORTS

Agent Général pour
l'Afrique du Nord de la

Agent Général pour le Maroc
de la "PAN AMERICAN"

Cⁱᵉ de TRANSPORTS AÉRIENS INTERCONTINENTAUX

SOCIÉTÉ ANONYME AU CAPITAL DE 10,000 DIRHAMS
SIÈGE SOCIAL. IMMEUBLE DU GRAND HOTEL DE TOURISME
27, Avenue de l'Armée Royale
Casablanca

Ad. Télég.: Cotransavia-Casablanca
Tél. : 660-01 / 02 / 03
C. C. P. Rabat 637-46

R. C. Casa 20.923
C. A. S. 18.015

Casablanca, le 5 Juillet 1961

FACTURE Nᵒ 4963/BP
AVOIR Nᵒ

Monsieur D.C. LITTMAN
Délégué de l'Oeuvre Suisse de secours aux
Enfants des Pays de l' Afrique du Nord
105, rue Dumont d'Urville
CASABLANCA

| 85 | billets de passage d'enfants
Trajet CASABLANCA/LYON ....
Décommercialisation de la TI52 du 10.7.61 | 18.400,00 |

ARRETE LA PRESENTE FACTURE A LA SOMME DE : DIX HUIT
MILLE QUATRE CENTS DIRHAMS./.

Fig. 52 Bill, July 5, 1961

Bill for the plane tickets of eighty-five children from Casablanca to Lyon on July 10, 1961.

Double, pour son information, à l'Ambassade de Suisse à Rabat.

COPIE   G.65.40   juillet 1961.

X.4.1.61 - GI/yb.

ad: E.12/128 - So/bu.

Police fédérale des étrangers

B e r n e

Messieurs,

Faisant suite à ma lettre du 26 juin dernier, j'ai l'honneur de vous informer que, le 8 de ce mois, j'ai visé trois passeports collectifs dans lesquels étaient inscrits les 93 enfants de nationalité marocaine, figurant sur la liste ci-jointe, invités en Suisse par l'Oeuvre suisse de secours aux enfants d'Afrique du Nord.

M. Littman, délégué au Maroc de l'oeuvre précitée, m'a remis une nouvelle attestation déclarant que ces enfants se rendront à Morgins et à Champéry/VS et seront à la charge de cette institution.

Notre compatriote, Mlle Aïda Schirmann, est à nouveau responsable du convoi.

Le séjour en Suisse de ce groupe est prévu du 8 juillet au 10 août 1961.

Par ailleurs, vous constaterez que le nom du petit Amram ELBAZ, 1951, figure également sur la présente nomenclature bien qu'il ait déjà été mentionné sur la liste antérieure. Ceci est dû au fait que l'enfant, par suite de maladie, n'a pas pu prendre part au premier convoi.

Veuillez agréer, Messieurs, l'assurance de ma considération distinguée.

Le Consul de Suisse:

J. Birchler.

1 annexe.

Fig. 53 Letter from the Swiss Consul in Casablanca, Mr. J. Birchler to the Federal Police in Bern, July 11, 1961 (File G.65.40.sd)

In this letter the Consul informs the Federal Police in Bern that on July 8 he issued visas for the three collective passports on which ninety-three Moroccan children invited to Switzerland by the Oeuvre Suisse de Secours aux Enfants d'Afrique du Nord (OSSEAN) where listed. The delegate Mr. Littman testified that they were going to Morgins and Champery under the responsibility of the Oeuvre. Miss Aïda Schirmann, is again responsible for this convoy. The children will remain in Switzerland from July 8 until August 10 1961. The Consul specifies the name of the little boy Amram Elbaz, 1951, listed on the first convoy but who due to illness will be travelling on this convoy.

ŒUVRE SUISSE DE SECOURS
AUX ENFANTS DE L'AFRIQUE DU NORD

Genève 1, Case postale 220

12.7.1961

Mr. D.G.LITTMAN
Oeuvre Suisse de Secours aux
Enfants de l'Afrique du Nord
105, rue Dumont d'Urville
C a s a b l a n c a .

Cher Monsieur,

Contrairement à nos habitudes, cette lettre sera longue, car il y a beaucoup à vous communiquer:

1. En premier lieu, Prof. et Mrs.Aberson vous remercient très sincèrement de vos gentils cadeaux. Ils ont beaucoup apprécié la poupée marocaine et le magnifique cuir travaillé.

2. En deuxième lieu, je vous communique que les tapis (2) et la caisse (1) sont arrivés sans histoires et se trouvent aux ALOUETTES, avec les premiers envois.

3. Les enfants sont bien arrivés, et les difficultés du transport ont été beaucoup moins graves qu'avec le transport en bateau. C'est pourquoi nous vous prions de continuer les transports par avion et ne plus organiser des convois par bateaux - même que cela coutera plus cher. Nos amis de Berne sont tout à fait formels à ce sujet. xxxxxxxxxxxxxx

4. Vous avez dit à notre convoyeuse, que vous prévoyez les prochains convois entre le 22 et le 25 Juillet. Encore une fois, veuillez partager les groupes jusqu'au nombres de 100 (maximum) et ne pas envoyer des grands convois ensemble - autrement, nous serons dans l'impossibilité à loger tout le monde.

5. En ce qui concerne le groupe spécial, veuillez nous communiquer au plus vite pour quel date vous prévoyez l'envoyer. Comme Mlle Schirmann vous a dit, nous comptons louer encore un Chalêt, mais nous devons être fixé sur la date d'arrivée.

6. Votre deuxième convoi comprenait des éléments beaucoup plus disciplinés que le premier. De ce point de vue, nous sommes très contents. Mais nous répétons notre demande de limiter l'âge d'admission à 15 ans et d'exclure des cas d'invalidité ou de maladies. Vous comprenez que ceci complique l'organisation du programme de vacances, surtout avec le nombre d'enfants,actuellement dans nos maisons.

7. L'argent que la convoyeuse a pu prendre (payement pour la pension des enfants) n'a pas pu être changé encore, mais ceci se fera dans quelques jours. Veuillez le dire aux personnes intéressées.--

8. Nous avons commandé le lait Guigoz qui sera envoyé directement à Londres.
Quant à votre Piera, elle a déclaré vouloir venir à Londres seulement le 25 Juillet. Elle s'en ira demain à Lausanne où elle veut se reposer une dizaine de jours. Veuillez nous envoyer le billet ou nous écrire, si nous devrions le faire. (On a oublié de le donner à Mlle Schirmann)

Fig. 54 Letter from N. Lehmann to D.G. Littman, July 12, 1961

In this letter Lehmann writes that the children (from the second convoy) arrived safely specifying that "our friends from Bern" have asked Littman to organize in the future for children to travel by plane and not by boat even if it is more expensive. She asks for the dates of the arrival of the special group (of Muslim children) adding that, as Miss Schirmann

ŒUVRE SUISSE DE SECOURS
AUX ENFANTS DE L'AFRIQUE DU NORD

Genève 1, Case postale 220

- 2 -

9. Nous espérons que vous avez fait le nécessaire pour rembourser Mme
   Aberson pour l'avance qu'elle a fait.

10. Mlle Schirmann a été enchantée de l'excursion que vous avez faite
    avec elle à Rabat et vous remercie encore de votre gentillesse.
    Elle vous transmet que malgré le manque d'organisation que vous lui
    reprochez, elle a pu tenir le coup et en même temps finir toutes les
    fiches de police française qu'elle a remplies dans l'avion.
    Est-ce qu'il ne serait pas possible de trouver une ligne de Transports
    Aeriens qui viendra directement à Genève-Cointrin ? Nous nous excusons
    de la question naïve, mais ceci serait naturellement encore plus
    facile pour les convois. Les longues voyages en car fatiguent beuacoup
    les enfants.

       C'est tout ce que nous avons à vous dire pour le moment, sauf
    encore une réponse à vos questions:

    Les enfants ont tous écrit aux parents; L'envoi de lettres a été
    contrôlé, et les enfants qui n'avaient pas fait leur courrier ont
    été rappelé à le faire de sorte qu'à l'heure actuelle, tous les parents
    devraient être en possession dee messages de leurs gosses.

                    Avec nos meilleures salutations

                         OEUVRE SUISSE DE SECOURS
                         AUX ENFANTS DE l'AFRIQUE DU NORD

                              N. LEHMANN

(alias Lehmann) told him, they will hire a chalet for them. The second convoy was more disciplined then the first one, she writes, asking once more that the age be limited to fifteen years old and that invalid or sick children be excluded (because it complicates the holiday program). Lehmann also enquires if there is a direct line to Geneva. She ends this letter by mentioning that all the children wrote to their parents. Gisele Littman's request of sending to London the powder milk of baby Diana, has been done.

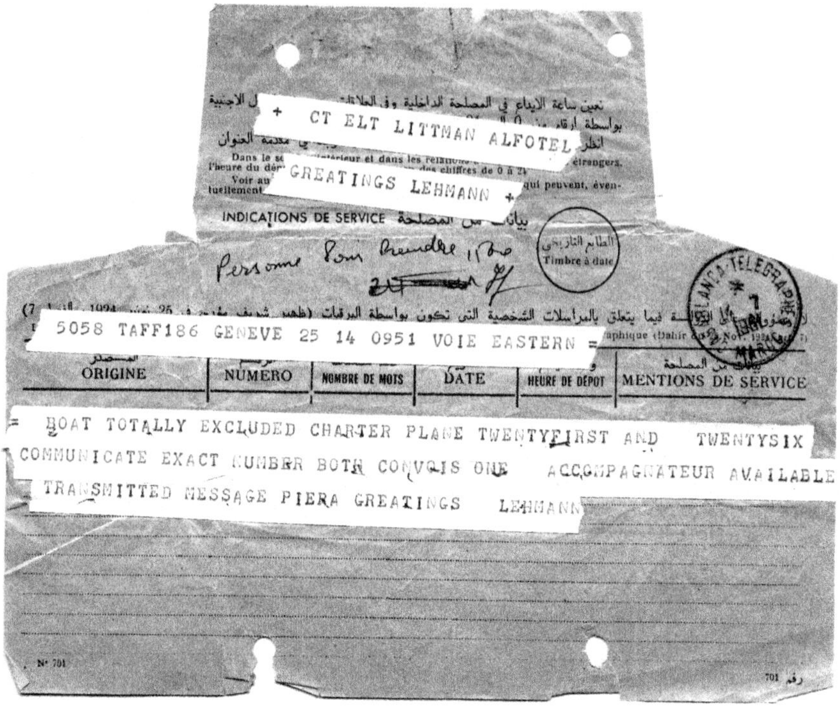
+ CT ELT LITTMAN ALFOTEL
GREATINGS LEHMANN +

INDICATIONS DE SERVICE بيانات من المصلحة

5058 TAFF186 GENEVE 25 14 0951 VOIE EASTERN =

ORIGINE	NUMERO	NOMBRE DE MOTS	DATE	HEURE DE DÉPOT	MENTIONS DE SERVICE

= BOAT TOTALLY EXCLUDED CHARTER PLANE TWENTYFIRST AND TWENTYSIX
COMMUNICATE EXACT NUMBER BOTH CONVOIS ONE ACCOMPAGNATEUR AVAILABLE
TRANSMITTED MESSAGE PIERA GREATINGS LEHMANN

Fig. 55 Telegram from Lehmann to D.G. Littman, July 14, 1961

Telegram from Lehmann peremptory asking that children not be sent by boat but by charter plane.

Fig. 56 Telegram from Lehmann to D.G. Littman, July 15, 1961

Telegram from Lehmann asking the date of the next convoy and the number of boys and girls on each convoy to land preferably in Geneva. She asks about the "special group" (Muslim children from the Entr'Aide Nationale).

Fig. 57 Telegram from N. Lehmann to D.G. Littman, July 17, 1961

Important prearranged cable from Geneva explaining among other things the difficulties in finding accompaniers for the last convoys. This cable was the official alibi for D.G. Littman to leave Casablanca with the children boarding the plane on July 24.

Genève, le 15 Août 1961

Monsieur H.de BLOMAC
F.E.A.U.-Maroc
Immeuble Liberté
Place Lemaigre Dubreuil
C a s a b l a n c a

– Bureaux 105 rue Dumont d'Urville –

Cher Monsieur,

    Nous vous remercions de votre lettre du
4 août 1961 et vous envoyons sous ce pli les copies de nos
lettres adressées à la S.M.D. et aux P.T.T., contenant –
en dehors de la prière de résiliation – des détails sur les
sommes déjà versées et les dépots en notre faveur. Nous
présumons que les notes de ces deux compagnies ne vont pas
dépasser 100 à 135 dirhams, et il restera donc un solde en
notre faveur de 100 dirh. env.

    En ce qui concerne la réclamation que nous
nous avez adressée, nous vous informons que Monsieur Littman
a remis les documents appartenant aux parents des enfants dont
il s'est occupé, à un messager qui, entretemps, a dû les délivrer
au domicile de ces familles. Dans les bureaux, aucun document
personnel n'est resté. Monsieur Littman a d'ailleurs laissé
la clef à la concierge qui était chargée de nettoyer ces locaux,
et vous pouvez récuperer la clef chez elle. Le contrôle des
locaux vous montrera qu'il y a uniquement du matériel de propa-
gande qui pourra être récupéré par le nouveau délégué qui sera
envoyé au Maroc, mais qui n'a pas encore été nommé.
    Espérant que ces explications suffiront à éclair-
cir la situation, nous vous prions d'agréer, Cher Monsieur,
l'assurance de nos sentiments très distingués.

OEUVRE SUISSE DE SECOURS AUX
ENFANTS DE l'AFRIQUE DU NORD

N.Lehmann

Fig. 58 Letter from N. Lehmann to Mr. de Blomac, August 15, 1961

Letter from N. Lehmann to Mr. de Blomac, from the estate agency F.E.A.U. – Maroc. In this letter she encloses copies of the bills and the initial deposits left with the telephone and electricity companies. She writes that Mr. Littman gave a messenger all the family documents and the parents should by now have received them. No personnel documents were left in the office except propaganda material to be picked up by the next delegate still to be nominated.

(I was trying to underline the tel.no.)

August 26th,1961

Dear Alex.,

I am a terrible sort of fellow. This delay grieves me quite as much as it does you, I can assure you.

You can have no idea of the mess in which I found my personal affairs on my arrival here. We have to leave for Geneva on about the 15th.September and I doubt very much if I will be finished. I am in London during the week-days and by the sea for the week-ends. By trying to relax for the first few days instead of writing the report and sending you the accounts, I was asking for trouble, and now a month has passed and I feel quite ashamed. Mind you, I was very tired on arrival, and then my personal and family obligations complicated the matter. I trust no-one is very angry with me and that all the "squeezing"you did in Paris has served its purpose. I do, nonetheless, sincerely apologise.

I am most disturbed that a letter which I sent to you, Express, on the 11th. August has just been returned to me. Surely it was correctly addressed I Although I knew your actual address, I see from your card that there is a postal box address, would you be kind enough to drop me a note informing me that this time you received my letter with all the various enclosures I will not send the Report to you until I know that the postal box address is the correct one, and as it is I am not happy about sending anything. I have enclosed the envelope of the letter posted on the 11 August.

From Geneva, I understand that the boy, Charles Bonscussan, has been sent an air ticket from Paris to Casablanca and a conciliatory letter. This is the wisest course- as there are no places on the boat- even if it be a little more costly. Unless he has left already for Casablanca, his address is c/o Mme. Levy, 14 Rue Marie Stuart,Paris 2e.

From the letters which I herewith enclose (re-directed to me from Geneva) you will see that the parents are still desperately trying to find their livrets de famille. I have not answered the letters myself, but I must point out that this situation should never have been allowed to develope to such an embarrassing state. Before his departure "George" had advised me to hand over all the "livrets de famille" to him or one of his colleagues for distribution. This I did, it was really impossible to do otherwise at the last moment-every minute was precious- and there just was not time to post such a quantity of documents, nor would it have been wise to do so from the security point of view. Let me say that I appreciate the difficulty involved in returning these documents, but the scandal that could arise if they are not returned also to be considered. At the same time the parents are in great need.

Fig. 59 Letter of D.G. Littman to Alex Korany, the Mossad's No. 2 for security in Paris, August 26, 1961

Littman writes to Korany that he hasn't started writing his "Report" yet and that he will not send it before he knows Korany's correct postal box address. He writes about "the parents still desperately trying to find their livrets de famille," an incident that "should never have been allowed to develop to such an embarrassing state." As advised by Georges who left for

of their livrets de familles, without which they have no legal identity,
nor can they collect social aid, et cetera. Please do see whether this
matter cannot be satisfactorily sorted out soon.

Dear Alex., let me once more thank you for your kindness
towards my wife during her stopover in Paris, and to me during my two visi
This was very much appreciated. Should you be in contact with our
dear friends "over there", please convey to them our sincerest thanks
coupled with the fullest gratitude for all they did, for without their
activity and sterling advice nothing could have been accomplished.
We both, my wife and I, hold "George"(Gad, actually) in fondest
affection and would be grateful to hear good news of the success of his
work and his continued safety. For " Jacques " also we have kind thoughts,
and I personally was most grateful to their chief for seeing me himself
before my departure. Such an action is understood and appreciated.
We pray that all are in the best of health and spirits, that their
brave work flourishes, and that they will soon be safely back home when
the work is done.
I am driving back to Geneva on about the 15th of September and
could conceivably pass through Paris if there was any need of me(in case
you wish to 'squeeze' any more information out of the orange). I await
news to this effect at the Palace Cout Hotel, Bournemouth.

Best Wishes then to you from my wife and myself (the baby is
fine), and I look forward to hearing from you soon.

Regards to Naphtalie.

Yours very sincerely,

(David Littman)

P.S.   Do let me know when Gad is likely to be back in Paris,
and assure me at the same time that he and his colleagues
are well in every respect.

Paris, he gave the family documents to a colleague of Jacques. Although he understands
the difficulties involved in returning the documents "they are crucial to the families without
which they have no legal identity." He asks Korany to "see whether this matter cannot be
satisfactorily sorted out soon." He ends his letter by warmly praising the work of Georges and
Jacques and thanking "their chief" (Alex Gattmon) for seeing him in person while praying
for their safe return back home once the work is done.

O.S.E. SUISSE
11, rue du Mont-Blanc
GENÈVE

Genève, le 24th. January 196 2

Téléphone 32 33 01

Compte de chèques postaux I. 9688

Mr. Moshe Kol,
16, Arzelaroff Street,
Jerusalem.
ISRAEL.

Dear Mr. Kol,
My wife joins me in thanking you sincerely for
your gift of Herzl's " Altneuland " and for your kind inscription
within. The novel- and its unique presentation- is most interesting
and a pleasure to read. Prof. Bloch has recently informed me that
you have been suffering from ill health of late and it was therefore good news to learn of your full recovery. My wife and I
extend to you and yours, good wishes for the year,- and good health.

What follows in this letter should perhaps be written
to another, but as I am ignorant of any other name and yet wish
its contents to reach the higher echelons, rather than be confined
to the waste-paper basket of the lower echelons, I have addressed
it to you, who occupy such an honoured position as Head of Youth
Aliyah. ....

After my return from Casablanca exactly six months
this day, I was asked to write a report of the action undertaken
there (through the collaboration of the Jewish Agency and the
Youth Aliyah) which resulted in the exodus of 530 Jewish children.
In Paris I immediately explained, in considerable detail, all the
more important facts and gave verbal portraits of those persons
with whom I had come into contact, so that this varied information
might be utilized quickly and profitably- as I understand has been
the case during the past six months. My full-length written report,
on the other hand, was to be of a " historical " nature (so I was
told),-for the records.

More than four months in Morocco had somewhat
confused my personal affairs and at first I did not find very
much time for my " historical " task. With the passing of the
weeks I began to doubt the real necessity of the request, for not
only had I been somewhat brusquely received in Morgins and Paris,
by all but one of the Israeli representatives of those organising
the action, but no written acknowledgement of any description
whatsoever had yet arrived either for my wife or for myself.
Of course, on my arrival from Morocco in Europe, the passive
dirigents of the action coming from Marseilles and Paris repeated
statements (of one kind and another (e.g. that the very State of
Israel was grateful to me for what I had done, etc., etc.). I had
replied that a simple letter of acknowledgement of such feelings
would be sufficient to please both my wife and myself immensely.
This letter never arrived and it took my friends of the Jewish
Agency in Paris more than two months to give their instructions
for their officials in Geneva to pay to me the money long since
expanded by me in the work necessary for the exodus of the children.
My surprise changed to bitterness and I took no more interest in
the " historical " report. The months continued to pass justifying
my feelings,- still nothing ! Sir Winston Churchill had said once
during the war that " all Greeks were heros "; even if this statement
should be truthfully and uncritically applied to " all Israelis "
this surely should not hinder some appreciation being proffered
to an outsider who had played, with his wife, a central and crucial
part in such an action, some of the accruing advantages of which,

Fig. 60 Letter from D. Littman to Moshe Kol, Head of the Youth Aliyah in Jerusalem, January 24, 1962

Littman thanks Moshe Kol, head of Youth Aliyah, for the book he sent him. He informs him of the crucial role he played in the action resulting in the Exodus of 530 Jewish children from Morocco to Israel via Switzerland thanks among other things to the "innovative collective

(page 2.)   Mr. Moshe Kol, 16 Arzoloroff Street, Jerusalem. ISRAEL

O.S.E. SUISSE

11, rue du Mont-Blanc
GENÈVE

Genève, le 24th. January 1962

Téléphone 92 33 01

Compte de chèques postaux I. 9588

(such as the continued use of collective passports) were still
being reaped in Morocco itself. We were not just " accompagnateurs "
of the children at the last minute from Morocco to Switzerland, or
Marseilles; nor had I sat watching from afar in Paris or Marseilles
giving general and often contradictory advice: in fact without a
moment's hesitation I had accepted to leave Switzerland immediately
for Morocco to undertake an unexpected mission entrusted to me,
and had even taken out my wife and five-month old baby daughter.
There we stayed from March until July until I could sufficiently
develope a plan to bluff the children out of the country under the
very noses of the authorities. The directors of the action (both
those in Israel and in Europe) never expected- nor could they have
reasonably done so- such a success; yet all was forgotten in an
instant, almost as quickly, as the saying goes,-" as it takes to
say Jack Robinson."

Although we had not received any news from Israel
until your thoughtful gift a few weeks ago, my work in Casablanca
brought us into contact with Jewish men and women (many being
Israelis) for whom we hold the highest admiration and the warmest
feelings. Our danger, in a soi-disant " official " capacity, was
as nothing to theirs, working they do, underground. Never shall I
forget the sincerity of their chief who, wishing to express his
appreciation and not considering the telephone to be sufficiently
communicative, decided to see me the very night before my departure
(after my wife and child had left) in order simply to express
his gratitude to me for having obtained the collective passports
(an innovation !) for those 530 children which his colleagues
had selected and documented, with so much difficulty, during the
previous six weeks. He put himself in physical danger just to shake
my hand and thank me, and to assure me of the preparations made
for my safety should the Moroccan authorities attempt to hinder my
departure for any reason. Such an immediate and typical action is
indeed sincere and I have treasured the memory of it as well as
that of my co-workers in Casablanca ever since.

I recognize, dear Mr. Kol, that you, yourself, are
an important man, who has been busy not so long ago with elections
and other pressing matters, and your health has not been well.
I have only drawn your attention to this unfortunate affair (and
with much hesitation and considerable misgivings, believe me !)
as it would appear that those of your colleagues responsible- and
the same applies to those working for the Jewish Agency- have
failed even after six months to give proper notice to their
superiors of the actualities and the chief personalities concerned
in the long-since-forgotten action last summer, which resulted in
the Youth Aliyah and the State of Israel receiving a further 530
children (not to mention their large families soon to follow them
by other ways); children both good and difficult,-yet Jewish children.
I say this for I am sure that it is only recently that you have
even become aware of our name, or of our existance, for it is clear
that you, as well as your equal in the Jewish Agency, would never HAVE
consider it burdensome to fulfil the formality of writing a letter
of acknowledgement to those who surely merited that. I feel it is
important that you are made aware of such lapses which can cause
unnecessary misunderstanding and astonishment to the innocent party.

At any rate I shall hasten to finish off my rather long-
winded report of an old " action " so that the " historical " record
is preserved if it is truly wanted. Please accept cordial greetings

passports." He expresses his astonishment and disappointment that six months have passed
without any written acknowledgment for a mission he had undertaken together with his
wife and a five-month old baby daughter. While critical of the Israeli higher echelon he
praises the courage of those Jewish men and women (many being Israelis) who worked
underground adding that he will never forget the "sincerity" of their chief (Alex Gattmon)

(page 3.)   Mr. Moshe Kol, 16 Arzoloroff Street, Jerusalem. ISRAEL

O.S.E. SUISSE

11, rue du Mont-Blanc
GENÈVE
—

Genève, le   24th. January 196 2

Téléphone 32 33 01

Compte de chèques postaux L 9686

addressed to you such a letter, which is forced from me almost
in despite of myself.

         With all respect, dear Mr. Kol, I remain,

                                    Yours truly,

                            David Littman

P.S. I must draw your attention to an error, this time on our side.
    I understand that Prof. Bloch accidentally omitted to put the
    name of M. Bruno Kern on the list of those who had contributed
to the success of the action as accompagnateurs. M. Kern, a German-
    speaking Swiss, working in a governmental position in Geneva,
    (address: 22, Baulacre, Genève.) is not Jewish, and although
    at first ignorant of our real objects in Morocco, he ~~inevitably~~ now
    realized them. On being approached by Dr. Dreyfus, a friend, and
one of the accompagnateurs of the first convoy, he agreed to go to
    Morocco and took a week of his holiday time to help us. I can
    testify to the devoted service of M. Kern, who possesses only
    one hand, for if it had not been for this non-Jew I cannot
    conceive the possiblity of the 4th. covoy (which left from
    Tangier) having left at all, he being the only one willing to
    work into the earliest hours of the morning of the departure
    of the boat, with my wife and I, on the necessary port formalities
    for 147 children. I am told that without him on the three-day
    boat journey, there would have been turmoil. Unlike others he saw
    almost nothing in Morocco from a tourist's viewpoint. Irony of
    ironies, this worthy man received no thanks until his wife, I
    understand, came to the offices of O.S.E. last Autumn to ask for
    an explanation, after which a letter was sent on our behalf,
    thanking him. When I remember M. Kern's goodness and tact I am
    ashamed to know that he, too, has not been remembered, and perhaps
    this error can still be rectified by some few words from you, to him.

who put himself in danger to thank him in person. He ends with the report he will "hasten

to finish so that 'historical' record is preserved if it is truly wanted."

In a P.S. he heartily speaks about Bruno Kern, a non-Jew, who volunteered to accompany the

fourth convoy sailing from Tangier to Marseilles on July 22 and was accidentally omitted by

Prof. Bloch from the list of those who had contributed to the success of the action.

10th. April   62

The Director of the Youth Aliyah,
P.O.B. 92
JERUSALEM
ISRAEL

Dear Mr. Kol,

Although I have not received a reply to my registered
Express letter to you of the 26th. January, it was a pleasure to
have a few words with your Vice Director, Mr. Umanski, when he
passed through Geneva last week-end. It was also kind of you to
remember Mr. Bruno Kern, for whom you sent an inscribed volume.
Actually he has already been posted for one year to Libya by the
I.L.O.; having spoken to him on two occasions before his departure,
he expressed his willingness to aid in whatever way he could in the
future. I have relaid this information, and his present address, to
those who might be interested in the course of a recent visit to Paris.
When I next write to him, I shall inform him that your handsome gift
has arrived; I am sure he will be pleased.

Whilst I was in Paris last March I handed over to a certa
gentleman there my 37-page report on the action. After he had read it
himself and passed it onto his immediate superior, he forbade me to let
anyone else see it and ordered me to destroy all the spare copies in
my possession. I was instructed not to send a copy to Marseille. It
would appear that the details- and especially the proper names- mentioned by me in the report could still compromise persons and events.
It is difficult for me to disobey this order, especially as I was
instructed to send merely a précis of the report to Jerusalem, giving
simply the essential facts- without details. I have explained the
situation to Mr. Umanski, before his departure for Paris, and he said
he would see the gentleman concerned, read the report in his possession, and that I would then receive further instructions whether or not
I was to send the spare copy I have, which has not yet been destroyed.
Before sending you a précis (for the records) it is perhaps wisest to
await the result of Mr. Umanski's approach

Fig. 61 Letter from D. Littman to Moshe Kol, Head of the Youth Aliyah Department,
April 10, 1962

Littman thanks Moshe Kol for sending a present to Mr. Bruno Kern currently posted in
Libya and mentions that he met with his Vice Director, Mr. Umanski. He mentioned to him
his detailed 'Report on the action' handed in March to a 'certain gentleman' in Paris. This

page (2)   Mr. M. Kol, Jerusalem

10th. April 1962

During his visit here Mr. Umanski took all details about
ALBERT ABENAIN, including a copy in German of the latest, medical- "intellectual
examination". We all hope that finally Youth Aliyah will see its way
to helping this Jewish youth, in the same way as it helps thousands
of others, no better, nor worse, in general, then Albert. If nothing
is done for him to go to Israel soon, there to be integrated into a 2
communal life, he will probably have to return to an orphanage at
Strassbourg. The boy is hardly yet 13 years old, and it is still
possible to give him a future,- and his thoughts turn always to Israel.
No doubt, Professor Bloch, will reiterate on this question during his
three-weeks' stay in Israel, and can provide you with all the
additional information; you will excuse me joining my voice to his.
It is some three years since O.S.E. Suisse first took up the case
of Albert with the Youth Aliyah, which was strongly pressed (by us) last
Summer during the Moroccan action, when it would have been so easy
to have joined him to one of the many convoys leaving for Israel via
Switzerland. Can nothing be done for this unfortunate boy, who is
no more backward than 25% of the Moroccan children you are receiving
regularly, and probably as intelligent as the great majority?

Trusting that your health has fully recovered, I remain,
dear Mr. Kol,

Yours truly,

D.G.Littman)

"gentleman" (Naphtali Bar-Giora) forbade him to let anyone else read it, asking him instead
to destroy all the spare copies in his possession. Umanski promised to read the report and
send further instructions whether or not to send the spare copy to Marseilles or Jerusalem.
Littman ends this letter by making an appeal through the Youth Aliyah for a thirteen years
old Jewish orphan boy, Albert Abenain.

YOUTH ALIYAH

THE JEWISH AGENCY • הסוכנות היהודית לארץ·ישראל • המחלקה לעלית ילדים ונוער •

Cable Address: JEVAGENCY • TELEPHONE 24231, 26473, 26479 • JERUSALEM, P.O.B. 92

558/62   June 14th, 1962.

Mr. D. G. Littman
O. S. E. Suisse
11, rue du Mont Blanc
Geneva.

Dear Mr. Littman,

        Mr. Kol, Head of this Department, has received
your letter and I am sure that he will communicate with you directly as soon as his rather busy schedule will allow him to do
so.

        In the meantime I was asked by Mr. Kol to con-
vey to you his request that you forward to him copy of the report on your activities. In order to ensure full confidentiali-
ty, Mr. Kol suggests that the report should be sent to him in a
closed envelope marked ' Personal and Confidential " through Mr.
Bentsur, Israeli Ambassador to Switzerland.

        He will be grateful to you for your kind co-ope
ration in this matter.

                       Yours sincerely,

                       David Umanski
                       Director General,
               Youth Aliyah Department

cc: Mr. Moshe Kol

ZW/dmb.

Fig. 62 Letter from David Umanski, Director General of the Youth Aliyah Department, to D. Littman, June 14, 1962

In this short letter to Littman, David Umanski writes that Mr. Moshe Kol, Head of the Department, will soon be in touch. Meanwhile he asks Littman to send through the Israeli Ambassador to Switzerland, Mr. Ben-Tzur, a copy of the Report in a closed envelop marked "Personal and Confidential."

chemin des palettes, 13
Grand Lancy/ GENEVA
SWITZERLAND

4th. July 1962

Mr. Moshe Kol,
16, Arzoloroff Street,
JERUSALEM

Dear Mr. Kol,

I have received a letter from Mr. David Umanski, the Director-General of the Youth Aliyah Department, in which he has informed me of your request for a copy of my report on certain activities in Morocco last summer. More recently - following on this request - I have obtained permission from my former contact in Paris to send you the report as requested. In the file containing the report you will also find the following additional information:-

1.) Photocopies of the two original Swiss letters of introduction and recommendation mentioned in the text.

2.) Copies of two letters written in French to important Moroccan officials and referred to in the reports as "Letter I" and "Letter II" respectively.

3.) Four additional pages of Addenda which I have recently written rather hurriedly to complement the report and to emphasize and heighten certain aspects of the Action.

Both in the report and in the Addenda there are rather too many corrections I admit, but without the help of a typist either for the first draft or for the final copy the fuzziness in my head of so much typing was bound to result in mistakes both in grammar, syntax, and also in omissions; and of course I could not use a typist for such a work, just as I could not use one in Morocco. I would like to have re-typed the whole thing, with the addenda fitted into the context, but I really couldn't spare either the time, the energy. I trust it is at least readable and comprehensible. Certainly it is somewhat "dated", now in the summer of 1962, at a time when Israel is receiving more than 10,000 emigrants a month!

As suggested by you I am sending all the data and this letter in a closed envelope marked 'Personal and Confidential' to Mr. Bentsur, Israeli Ambassador to Switzerland, for forwarding to you. I will pleased to learn that it has reached you intact.

Yours truly,
(David Littman)

cc: Mr. David Umanski

Fig. 63 Letter from D. Littman to Moshe Kol, Head of the Youth Aliyah Department, July 4, 1962

Letter to Mr. Kol informing him that he received the permission from his former contact in Paris (Naphtali Bar-Giora) to send him his report. He has added to "The Report" additional photocopies of the two Swiss letters of recommendations, letters to important Moroccan officials and four pages of Addenda emphasizing certain aspects of the action. All this will be sent through the Israeli Ambassador, Mr. Ben-Tzur.

YOUTH ALIYAH

THE JEWISH AGENCY • המחלקה לעלית ילדים ונוער • הסוכנות היהודית לארץ־ישראל

Cable Address: JEVAGENCY • TELEPHONE 24231, 26473, 26479 • JERUSALEM, P.O.B. 92

MK:lk   August 12, 1962

Mr. David Littman
Chemin des Palettes, 13
Grand Lancy   Geneva

Dear Mr. Littman,

I received your interesting and comprehensive report, together
with your letter of June 4, 1962, through our Ambassador in
Switzerland, Mr. Ben-Tzur.   I was very much impressed by the
degree of responsibility imposed on you during the period of
the rescue operation in the summer of 1961.

Now, one year later, we can state that the large majority of
the children have settled down nicely in the various absorption
places of Youth Aliyah, and are quite content with their lot:
their well-being is certainly due to you in no small measure.
With Youth Aliyah they have every prospect of developing cul-
turally and socially which they would never have achieved otherwise, and you have every reason to be gratified with the carrying out of your responsible mission.

I again thank you on behalf of Youth Aliyah and in my own name,
and would also ask you to convey my warmest greetings and thanks
to Professor Bloch and to all those who were associated with
this mission.   You can serve as a model in the performance of
this rescue operation, whilst Prof. Bloch put his life and soul
into the task.   I can only repeat our deepest appreciation on
behalf of the whole Youth Aliyah family.

With kindest regards,

                                              Yours sincerely,

                                              M. Kol

                                              Moshe Kol.

cc: Mr. David Umanski

Fig. 64 Letter from Moshe Kol, Head of the Youth Aliyah Department, to D. Littman, August 12, 1962

In this letter, Mr. Kol's acknowledges receipt of The Report received through the Ambassador, Mr. Ben-Tzur, writes how impressed he was by the degree of responsibility imposed on Littman during "the rescue operation in the summer 1961." After a year, most of the children have settled down nicely he writes, ending the letter with warm greetings and thanks on behalf of the Youth Aliyah family to Littman, Prof. Bloch and to all the others associated with the mission.

MOSHE KOL
10, Jabotinsky St., Jerusalem

משה קול
ירושלים, רח' דבוט:נסקי 10

December 9, 1981

Mr. David Littman
░░░░░░░░░░░░
Switzerland

Dear Mr. Littman:

    I have not heard from you for a long time. I hope that you and your family are well. Have you visited Jerusalem? How could it have happened that I was not contacted, if you were here?

    The purpose of my note is to ask you if I can mention your name in my book of memoirs, which I am now writing, as the man who did such an excellent job in 1961 by helping to rescue 500 children from Morocco. I want to tell the whole story of your courageous undertaking, but I don't know if you want your name to be mentioned after twenty years. If you will agree, I will be very happy.

    With best wishes and a Happy New Year to you and your family.

       Yours,

       Moshe Kol

:em

Fig. 65 Letter from Moshe Kol to D. Littman, December 9, 1981

Mr. Kol asks for permission to mention the name Littman, "as the man who did such an excellent job in helping rescuing 500 children from Morocco" in 1961, in the memoirs he is currently writing.

Mr. Moshe KOL
10 Jabotinsky

JERUSALEM / Israel   21 December 1981

Dear Mr. Kol,

Thank you for your letter of 9 December.

You are quite right, we owe you both an apology. We were in Israel in
October and spent a marvellous 12 days with two of our children at Neviot.
- the *last*, probably ! We were then much taken, in Jerusalem, organizing
our daughter's entry and installation into the Hebrew University. Ariane
Yaël (born in January 1962) is getting along fine there and intends to
complete her *aliya* at the end of her studies.

She was in fact conceived in Casablanca, which brings me back to the
subject of your letter.

Concerning our Moroccan mission, you are probably aware that this whole
"Story" has always been considered by the powers that be, too delicate
for publication. The first newspaper references were only made early this
year on the 20th anniversary of the tragedy of the Pisces and again on
the death of Alex Gattmon last July (see Jerusalem Post 6 Aug. 1981) and
in the Hebrew press), a great man, my ex-boss in Casa and a dear friend.

It was most thoughtful of you to remember our Mission to Morocco which,
against all the odds, permitted 532 Jewish children to leave Morocco
between 26 June- 24 July 1981 for Israel and was instrumental in finally
persuading the Moroccan authorities to allow open Jewish emigration once
again to Israel, thus resulting in about 100,000 immigrants arriving
there between 1962-65.

In fact the whole operation was known "known..d circles" by the code
name of *Mural*, which was in fact the name by which I was designated throughout these 130 Moroccan days of my life (16 March- 24 July 1961). My
wife joined me on 31 March and was indispensable, inter alia, as my se-
creatry and in the first week of May - during a brief trip to Geneva to
report on progress - I brought over to Casablanca our 5½ month old daughter Diana. (It was discovered two years later that she was mentally
handicapped). We thus *innocently* provided ourselves (and the "Mission")
with a perfect cover.

This is a very long story and curiously enough I still possess my 20 year
old, 60 page, detailed, report (plus some relevant documents) which I had
thought, one day, of developing into an historical document, as otherwise nothing will be remembered of this event.

Actually, you were the only Israeli personality who officially thanked us
in 1964 for what we did in 1961 at great personal risk. You awarded us
then a Youth Aliyah medal. Other than this, we never received even a few
official words of thanks for our work and success.

./.

Fig. 66 Letter from D. Littman to Moshe Kol, December 21, 1981

In his reply on December 21 to Mr. Kol D. Littman adds some details about the "Story," too

delicate for publication until 1981. He thanks Mr. Kol for remembering his role in the mission,

which received, in the Mossad circles, the code name Mural (a name designating Littman

during his 130 Moroccan days of his life). Littman refers to the indispensable role of his wife

-2-

I have no objection to my name (and that of my wife½) being mentioned
by you in your book of memoirs, but may I suggest, humbly, that as far
as on-the-spot details of our mission (and the whole operation) are concerned, you allow me to make suggestions and offer advise, once you hav
approximatively prepared your text related to this period. You might
also wish to enquire beforehand whether it is now permitted by the offi
cial censor to refer (or give details) of these events.

We will be in Israel in 1982, I'm sure, but as Ariane will be home for
2 weeks in February, we probably won't be in Jerusalem for at least six
months. Do not hesitate to correspond with me on the above subject, if
you feel so inclined.

With every good wish to you and Mrs. Kol from both my wife and myself
and a healthy and happy 1982 to you and yours.

The times are fraught with danger for Israel and the world, unfortunately !

Sincerely,

David Littman

P.S. Enclosed my wife's latest article. Her book "Le Dhimmi" is being
translated into Hebrew for a 1983 publication.

and their baby daughter, Diana, and to his 60 page detailed Report. He reminds Moshe Kol
that he was the only Israeli personality to officially thanked them and adds that he has no
objection that their names be mentioned in his book of memoirs.

MOSHE KOL
10, Jabotinsky St., Jerusalem 92142
Tel. 669788

משה קול
ירושלים, רח׳ ז׳בוטינסקי 10

December 30, 1981

Mr. David Littman

(Vaud) Suisse
Switzerland

Dear Mr. Littman:

Thank you very much for your letter of December 21, 1981.

I have your report and I do not need more information for everything is included. I needed your permission to mention your name and I am glad that you agreed.

I hope that next time when you are in Israel you will visit us. Please tell your daughter that she can call on me and we will be pleased to invite her to our home.

With best wishes to you and your wife, and with the hope that 1982 will be a better year than 1981 for the world, Israel and the Jewish people.

Yours,

Moshe Kol

:em

מרכז תרבות העמים לנוער
ת. ד. 8009 – ירושלים
INTERNATIONAL CULTURAL
CENTER FOR YOUTH
P. O. B. 8009 — Jerusalem – Israel

Moshe Kol

Fig. 67 Letter from Moshe Kol to D. Littman, December 30, 1981

Mr. Kol answers D. Littman that he has The Report and needs no more information and that he is glad to have his permission to mention his name.

Mr. Moshe KOL
10 Jabotinsky
JERUSALEM 92142
Israel   18 January 1982

Dear Mr. Kol,

Thank you for your letter of 30 December.

On receiving it, I went down to my archives and recovered my old "
Morocco" file. There I found, inter alia, my letter to you of 4 July 1962
in which I mentioned that I had finally been authorised to send you my
37 page report via the Israeli Ambassador in Bern. I also sent you four
pages of "addenda", as well as other relevant correspondence.

It is indeed strange that I forgot that I had dispatched all this to you
twenty years ago. I also found your personal letter of appreciation to me
of 12 August 1962. Of course, I have other "documentations" of this Mission, and have a very clear memory on many details not mentioned in my
report, which I will eventually put on record. For your purposes, however, you are probably right in considering that you do not need more
information than you already have on this "Mission to Morocco".

When will your book be published ? - in a Hebrew or an English edition,
or both ? We would be honoured to receive a copy of the English edition.

Kind regards.

                                                Yours,

                                                David Littman

Fig. 68 Letter from D. Littman to Moshe Kol, January 18, 1982

In his answer to M. Kol, D. Littman writes that after looking into his archives, he found a
letter dated July 4 1962 regarding the 1961 report sent via the Israeli Ambassador in Bern
together with the personal letter of appreciation dated August 12 1962.

Fig. 69 Article in Hebrew by Shmuel Segev in *Maariv*, 20 April 1984

Article by Shmuel Segev in the Hebrew newspaper, *Maariv* on Operation Mural. Shmuel Segev, after receiving the 1961 report in 1983 and unaware before that of Operation Mural, decided to add a chapter about it in his new book *Operation "Yakhin" The Secret Immigration of Moroccan Jews to Israel.* In the book as in the article, except for Littman, all other names were censored for security reasons at the demand of the Mossad. "Operation Mural" became "Operation Milhar" or "Miller," Prof. Bloch was called Prof. Blumfield, his organization O.S.E was renamed "Hilsfund," Naphtali Bar-Giora from the Youth Aliyah was called "Dan Ben Gar" and "Georges" became "Gilbert." In this detailed article, Segev mentions the unfortunate departure on July 9 of eighty-five children for Israel, a decision that endangered the lives of the persons still involved in the Operation.

35 שנה לעליית הנוער ממרוקו

מאת משה קול

MISSION PERMANENTE D'ISRAEL
9, chemin Bonvent
CH-1216 Genève / Cointrin
Tél. 98 05 00

20/5/84

Dear David

"Haaretz" article of 16th May 1984
by Moshe Kol describes his - yours
activities to save Jewish children
from Morocco in the 1950s.
although not being mentioned by your
name your performance is highly
appreciated in his article.

Sincerely yours
David Daniel

Fig. 70 Article in Hebrew by Moshe Kol in *Haaretz*, May 16, 1984

The article by Moshe Kol "Thirty-five years of youth immigration from Morocco" appearing a month after Shmuel Segev's article in *Maariv*, Kol recounts his involvement in the Aliyah of children from Morocco in the 50s and 60s. Writing on the operation that brought 530 Morrocan children to Israel, he mentions a "Jew with a British passport" enrolled thanks to the help of Professor Bloch, who, provided with letters of recommendation from the Swiss authorities, acted under the orders Alex Gattmon, a Mossad agent in Morocco. A possible group of Muslim children coming to Switzerland had been dismissed, he writes, because it was too compromising but on the whole The "Jew," accompanied by his wife and baby daughter, was very successful in his mission. The Operation had to end after religious groups in Israel held demonstrations asking for the children to be integrated into religious frameworks. The man and his family, writes Kol, had to leave Morocco in haste.

TELEPHONE

(VAUD) SUISSE

Mr. Gershom SHOKEN
The Editor-in-Chief
HAARETZ
Zalmar Shoken, 21
(POB 233)

TEL AVIV / Israel   28 May 1984

Sir,
          Moroccan Aliya : Operation "Milhar" (1961)

In his recent article, published in your columns ("35 years of youth
immigration from Morocco", Haaretz, 16 May), Mr. Moshe Kol refers to me
several times rather mysteriously - i.e. "a Jew possessing a British
passport," this Jew", "the man"". I would be obliged if you would kindly
publish these clarifications concerning Operation "Milhar."

(1) On 9 December 1981, Mr. Kol wrote to ask me whether he could mention
    my name in his book of memoirs "as the man who did such an excellent
    job in 1961 by helping to rescue 500 children from Morocco. I want
    to tell the whole story of your courageous undertaking, but I don't
    know if you want your name to be mentioned after twenty years. If
    you will agree, I will be very happy."

    In my reply (21 Dec. 1981) I authorised him to mention both my name
    and that of my wife who collaborated with me in Casablanca in the
    1961 operation. We were therefore somewhat surprised to discover that
    only our names were suppressed in his 16 May article.

(2) My 40-page detailed report (with addenda and documents attached) was
    sent to my Paris contact "Ben-Gar" in January 1962. At that time,
    Mr. Kol insisted on receiving a copy, which I was authorised to send
    him six months later, via the Israeli Embassy in Bern. He acknowled-
    ged its reception in a letter to me dated 12 August 1962, in which
    he sent his "deepest appreciation on behalf of the whole Youth
    Aliyah family",one year after completion of our successful mission.

    This official report is the main source for Operation "Milhar" (my
    code-name in Casablanca), which covered the period 16 March-24 July
    1961. Its success enabled 530 Moroccan Jewish children,between the
    ages of 8 and 17, to reach Israel's shores "legally", via Switzer-
    land, at a time when very few passport facilities were available to
    the Jews of Morocco, and immigration to Israel was illegal.

(3) In order to write his book (Operation "Yakhin : The secret immigra-
    tion of Moroccan Jews to Israel, Misgav Habitakhon, 1984), Mr. Shmuel
    Segev was officially authorized to consult secret government archives.
    He also interviewed many of those who worked in Morocco at various
    periods, including my wife and myself in November 1982. On that occa-
    sion, he received from me a photocopy of my 1961 report, which I was
    able to obtain in Jerusalem from Mr. Kol himself. I later sent to
    Mr. Segev other documents and photographs.

    The chapter which he devoted to Operation "Milhar" (largely reproduced
    in Maariv, 20 April 1984 ; an English version of which will appear
    shortly in Newsview) is basically an accurate description of those
    130 days. Confirmation is easily available from others - particularly
    from "Alex" Gatmon's widow, Carmit, who was her husband's close

Fig. 71 Letter from D. Littman to Gershom Shoken, Editor-in-Chief of *Haaretz*, May 28, 1984

This letter entitled: Moroccan Aliya: Operation Milhar (1961) refers to Moshe Kol's article of

May 16. In his detailed 7-points letter, Littman puts forwards clarifications about Operation

Milhar which he hopes will be "acceptable" in the columns of *Haaretz*. Astonished to have

become an anonymous "Jew with a British passport," Littman recalls that Mr. Kol asked for

his permission in 1981 to name him in his Memoirs. Littman writes to Shoken that a month

-2-

(from)
collaborator in Morocco, as well as) "Gilbert", my main contact in
Casablanca, a founder member of Kibbutz Regavim.

Having given Mr. Kol permission in 1981 to use our names in his
memoirs, there seemed no valid reason to refuse the same permission
to Mr. Segev in 1982. As this authorisation concerned a personal
testimony from a non-Israeli citizen, this might account for the
fact that, surprisingly, our names are the *only* ones which were not
censored for "security" reasons in Mr. Segev's book.

Mr. Kol informed me by 'phone a month ago that he was not happy about
this, nor the fact that Youth Aliyah was criticized for some of its
initiatives in this chapter. I told him then that all of these criticisms were already made in my *1961* report and I advised him to read
it again carefully. No further information has ever reached me during
the past 23 years to invalidate the criticisms I felt obliged to
make in my 1961 report. Quite the contrary.

(4) In his article, Mr. Kol explains how Operation "Milhar" (which he
does not name) suddenly came to an end because of a scandal which
occurred in July 1961, when a group of religious extremists tried
to force all the newly-arrived children into orthodox-administered
institutions. He omitted to mention that this situation *only* arose
as a result of a decision (in contradiction with a firm promise given
three weeks earlier to "Gilbert" - then in Europe) to bring the first
85 Moroccan "holiday camp" children to Israel from Switzerland on 9
July 1961. This unpardonable act - for which Youth Aliyah was either
solely or jointly responsible - only came to the ears of "Gilbert"
by pure chance whilst he was capting Kol Yisrael at night on the
Moroccan coast. *This* scandalous decision seriously endangered the
safety of my wife (then pregnant), our eight-month-old daughter and
myself - and effectively spelled the end of Operation "Milhar". That
we were not arrested or imprisoned, as a result of this precipitatous
departure,was providential.

(5) With regard to Mr. Kol's vague statement in his article concerning
a "Muslim convoy", I recommended regularly in my letters from March
1961 onwards that at least one group of Muslim children be brought to
Switzerland at reduced rates (for reasons amply developed in my
report and by Mr. Segev in his chapter), but this initiative was
never *seriously* considered by those sending me instructions from
Israel and/or Europe. This lack of imagination was, in itself, sufficient to end Operation "Milhar" - within one month of the departure
of our first convoy of 127 Jewish children on 26 June 1961.

It was only on 26 July that the crucial importance of my idea in
organizing a Muslim convoy was appreciated by a "high official" from
Jerusalem, whom I met in the Swiss mountain resort of Morgins (from
whence the remaining 350 children were being prepared for their
journey to Israel), but by then it was far too late to implement it.

(6) My wife and I learned much from our youthful experiences as rather
naïve "agents" at a crucial period of the Moroccan aliyah. The Israelis with whom we collaborated directly agreed with us then that
the "man on the spot" can more easily *feel* the reality of the situation than those giving instructions at a distance of 1000 to 3000
kilometres. Two final examples are noteworthy :

./.

earlier, after Shmuel Segev's article in *Maariv*, Mr. Kol seemed unhappy with the criticisms

levelled by the latter against the Youth Aliyah in *Maariv*. He called Littman asking him to

change the record regarding the eighty-five children sent to Israel on July 9 in the midst of

the Operation. Littman refused, judging this unfortunate decision "unpardonable." He also

refers to some of the points described by Mr. Kol, pointing out that the option of a "Muslim

-3-

a) All instructions received concerning a "selection" on any basis whatsoever (i.e. psychological tests, etc.) were ignored by "Alex", "Gilbert" and myself. We had to get as many young children as we could out of Morocco by the new-found "legal" manner, so that they would not have to join their courageous parents on clandestine ships at night from deserted beaches - a hazardous undertaking before the period of liberalization began a few months later.

b) The decision to request "collective" and not "individual" passports is the crucial example. The idea had been suggested to me quite innocently by a senior Swiss Red Cross official in Casablanca. It was the most practical method for processing hundreds of passport demands in a short time (I was churning out 50 every 48 hours in the last days). The instructions I received were on no account to accept collective passports (for a number of reasons). Again, we decided on the spot to ignore these instructions and get on with the job for which we were taking such risks, and when I was told to strike out children over the age of fifteen, or cancel a plane - because the flow of children to Switzerland was too great - I refused and was fully backed by "Alex" and "Gilbert".

Paradoxically, the mass emigration of 100,000 Jews during the subsequent period of liberalization (1962-1964) was effected principally through this very method of "collective" passports which had been categorically refused from afar, but had succeeded beyond all hopes in Operation "Milhar". This means was to become an acceptable system of emigration for the Moroccan authorities.

(7) Youth Aliyah has carried out a splendid job over a period of fifty years and all its collaborators deserve and have received public recognition for their devotion to its multifarous achievements. It is certainly not my intention to criticize such a hallowed institution, nor Mr. Moshe Kol, its distinguished head at a crucial period of its activity (1948-1966).

On the other hand, now that the events concerning the Moroccan aliyot have been released from "secrecy" by the Israeli government, the public is entitled to know the truth about all the various episodes preserved either in government archives, or by eye-witness participants still alive. To this effect, my wife and I have prepared a more complete report, based on the original documents still in our possession, which will be published by an Israeli institute.

It was indeed a moving moment, when so many of those who had worked in Morocco met after so many years at Bet Hanassi on 9 May last, welcomed by President Chaïm Herzog on the occasion of the appearance of Shmuel Segev's Operation "Yakhin", which recounts an unknown chapter of Israel's modern history. There, we found Carmit, "Gilbert", "Ben-Gar" and so many others. Mr. Kol had been invited, but was unable to attend because of another appointment. His article was published in Haaretz a week later.

I apologise for the length of this letter - necessitating translation into Hebrew - but having remained silent for so long, I sincerely hope that these clarifications and comments will be acceptable in the columns of your estimable newspaper.

Yours faithfully,

David Littman

convoy," was never seriously considered by his contacts in Switzerland. The man on the spot' is a better judge than someone sitting in an office thousands of kilometres away, writes Littman, while referring to his decisions regarding the "collective passports" and the demand of "selection," which were contradictory to the instructions he received from Geneva, yet fully endorsed by the Misgeret (Framework) in Morocco.

עתון יומי/המו"ל   הוצאת עתון "הארץ" בע"מ/תל-אביב, רחוב זלמן שוקן 21, בית "הארץ"   הארץ
טלפון 82 42 61   תבת דאר 233   למברקים: הארץ תל-אביב

בתשובה נא להזכיר מס' ....

12 ביוני 1984

לכבוד
מר דוד ליטמן
גלנד, שוייץ

מר ליטמן הנכבד,

קיבלתי את מכתבך מן ה-28 במאי.

אני יכול להבין שהדברים שאתה מעלה במכתבך בקשר לעליית ילדים ממרוקו
לפני למעלה מעשרים שנה מאד קרובים ללבך, מאחר שמילאת תפקיד בולט
בפרשה זאת. אך לצערי אינני רואה אפשרות לפרסם מכתב ב"הארץ"
שנכנס לפרטי פרטים כאלה. ישנן מגבלות למה שאפשר לפרסם בעתון
יומי שאינם יכול להתעלם מהן.

רצוף לזה אני מחזיר לך את מכתבך.

בכבוד רב,

גרשום שוקן

Fig. 72 Letter in Hebrew from Gershom Shoken, Editor-in-Chief of *Haaretz*, to D. Littman, June 12, 1984

In this short letter, Mr. Shoken acknowledges receipt of the letter from May 28. Shoken writes that although he understands the importance of this affair for D. Littman who played an essential role in it, unfortunately he cannot publish such a detailed letter in *Haaretz*. There are limits, he writes, about what can be published in a daily newspaper. The letter was returned to Littman.

TÉLÉPHONE

(VAUD) SUISSE

Mr. Gershom SHOKEN
The Editor-in-Chief
HAARETZ
Zalmar Shoken, 21
(POB 233)

TEL AVIV / Israel   26 July 1984

Dear Mr. Shoken,

I received your letter of 12 June and decided to reply after the elections, knowing that you would have little time before then to consider
events which occurred "more than twenty years ago".

Indeed, it would have been difficult for Haaretz to have printed *all* of
my detailed 28 May letter, but I was surprised that you decided that *none*
of it was publishable. Editors are well qualified for pin-pointing the
essential paragraph from lengthy letters.

Thus, for the readers of your newspaper, an unfortunate falsification
by omission - already made in 1961, and now perpetuated by Mr. Kol in
his 16 May 1984 article - has been allowed to stand unchallenged. I
regret it !

Just as Israel has its "Peace Now" movement, there is no reason why voices should not be raised for a "Truth Now" campaign regarding past events
which are a recognized part of the country's "Aliyah history."

What I find particularly galling is that, over the past thirty years,
some "Zionist agents" - as a result of official acts of unpardonable
incompetence - were either executed, imprisoned or barely escaped.
Usually these "errors" were (and probably still are) immediately covered
up by the establishment on the grounds of "security", whereas, more often than not, personal prestige is involved.

Had I just emerged from a Moroccan prison, I suppose that my *mise au
point* would still have been refused for one reason or another.

Let me try once again ! Enclosed a very brief letter. As I am a British
citizen living in Switzerland, is it really "too late" for you to accept
its publication even three months after the article to which I am refe-
ring? Your positive reaction would confirm that the colums of Haaretz
are open to those who merely wish to put the historical record right.
Those able and willing to contradict me need only do so publicly.

                                        Yours sincerely,

                                        David Littman

P.S. I have just completed a meticulously detailed 100 page report on my
1961 Mission which will be published by a Kibbutz institute. I have used
there the same historical methods of research as I did in my recent 70
page article on the visit of Sir Moses Montefiore to Morocco (1863-64)
for the forthcoming publication of the Centenary volume (Oxford University Press).

Enc.

Fig. 73 Letter of D. Littman to Gershom Shoken, Editor-in-Chief of *Haaretz*, July 26, 1984

D. Littman is surprised that Mr. Shoken won't publish any of his clarifications. This means,
writes Littman, that this "unfortunate falsification by omission" already made in 1961
and perpetuated again by Mr. Kol in 1984 will stand unchallenged. Probably, he writes,
this explains how such acts of incompetence leading to the execution or imprisonment
of "Zionist agents" were covered up in the past by the establishment on the ground of
"security." He sends back a concise letter in the hope that its publication will "prove that the
columns of *Haaretz* are open to those who wish to put the historical record right.'"

TÉLÉPHONE

(VAUD) SUISSE

Mr. Gershom SHOKEN
The Editor-in-Chief
HAARETZ
Zalmar Shoken, 21
(POB 233)
TEL AVIV / Israel   26 July 1984

Sir,

Moroccan Aliya : Operation "Milhar" (1961)

In his article "35 years of Youth Aliyah from Morocco" (Haaretz, 16 May)
Mr. Kol explains how Operation "Milhar" (which he does not name) suddenly came to an end because of a scandal which occurred in July 1961, when
a group of religious extremists tried to force all the newly-arrived
children into orthodox-administered institutions. He omitted to mention
that this situation *only* arose as a result of a decision (in contradiction with a firm promise given three weeks earlier)to bring the first
85 Moroccan "holiday camp" children to Israel from Switzerland on 9 July
1961. *This* scandalous decision seriously endangered the safety of my
wife (then pregnant), our eight-month-old daughter and myself - and
effectively spelled the end of Operation "Milhar". That we were not arrested or imprisoned, as a result of this precipitatous departure, was providential.

Operation "Milhar" is referred to in detail by Samuel Segev on pages
216-233 of his Operation "Yakhin" : The secret immigration of Moroccan
Jews to Israel (Misgav Habitahon, 1984), reproduced in Maariv (2oth
April), and shortly to appear in Newsview.

Both Mr. Segev and Mr. Kol received a copy of my 1961 "Confidential
Report" and both requested (and received) authorisation to refer to me
by name. Mr. Segev did so, but Mr. Kol still prefers the mysterious
appelation : "a Jew possessing a British passport," or "the Jew ".So
be it !

                                        Yours sincerely,

                                        David Gerald Littman

P.S. If you accept this letter for publication, but still find it "too
     long", the last paragraph could be eliminated.
     I would appreciate it if you could kindly reply to me briefly in
     English.

Fig. 74 Letter by D. Littman for publication in *Haaretz*, July 26, 1984

In his shorter letter for publication Littman only relates to the "scandalous" decision to "bring
the first eighty-five Moroccan 'holiday camp' children to Israel from Switzerland on July 9
1961." He also mentions Shmuel Segev's book and article in *Maariv* and his 1961 "Confidential
Report" sent both to Mr. Kol and Mr. Segev with an authorization to refer to him by name.

The unlikely secret agents

David and Gisele Littman played a key role in the smuggling of Jewish children out of Morocco.
Their efforts have now been publicly acknowledged by President Chaim Herzog.
They were interviewed by Newsview's Simon Griver

David Littman never realized that he and his wife Gisele were working for the Mossad back in 1961, when they succeeded in getting over 500 Jewish children out of Morocco. The fact is he did not even know that an Israeli secret service called the Mossad existed.

"It sounds naive," observes Littman, a recent visitor to Israel, "and naive I certainly was. Of course I knew we were engaged in undercover work for what I understood was the Jewish Agency, but I did not appreciate the dangers involved. I knew the assignment was covert, but until we were in the thick of things, it never occurred to me that the price of failure could be torture and worse. I had heard vaguely of an Israeli security organization called Shin Bet, but the name Mossad meant nothing to me."

Recalls Littman: "It was all a far cry from my English upbringing at an Anglican public school in Dorset. There, from 1950 to 1951, I was captain of the cricket, tennis and boxing teams in a world where nothing untoward ever happened. On accepting the task in Morocco, I ingenuously assumed that my British citizenship would protect me if I were caught. My wife Gisele, who had arrived in London as a refugee from Egypt, had led a less sheltered life and she perceived the risks, but she did not tell me of her fears."

Twenty-three years later, sitting in the sedate surroundings of Belgium House at the Givat Ram campus of Jerusalem's Hebrew University, David and Gisele Littman seem an unlikely couple of undercover agents. The outgoing David contradicts the tight-lipped image of the secret service operator, and his sunglasses do not screen the casual observer that here is a man of international intrigue. Gisele, though, cuts a more authentic figure. Petite and pretty, she has a poker face and chooses her words carefully.

"It is difficult to believe that we were the same persons in those days," remarks David. "The truth of the matter was that I thrived on the sense of adventure. It is difficult to describe the thrill of being the man on the spot, the person out there on his own making spur-of-the-moment decisions. Fortunately, my job was made easier because I was a man of independent means, so when the Jewish Agency told me not to buy a car because the budget was not available, I was able to ignore them and purchase a second-hand car with my own money."

Born in England 50 years ago, David Littman was the sixth of seven children. His father, Joseph Aaron Littman, was a successful real estate agent. After earning a degree in history at Trinity College, Dublin, he enrolled in a postgraduate program at the London Institute of Archaeology, where he met Gisele in November 1958. She and her family had been forced to leave Cairo in the wake of the 1956 Sinai Campaign. David and Gisele were married in 1959 and then moved to Lausanne, Switzerland.

With time on his hands (Littman had inherited a fortune following his father's death in 1953), and a drive "to do something significant" for his people, Littman began knocking on the doors of all the international Jewish organizations in Geneva, volunteering for a job. The response, however, was not very enthusiastic. No one took him very seriously — some were even suspicious — until his last call, at a Jewish children's organization called Hilsfund. It housed needy Jewish children in Switzerland during school vacations and had saved thousands of youngsters during World War Two.

The day before Littman's visit, Hils-

fund's elderly director, Professor Jacques Bloch, had an unexpected visitor from the Jewish Agency in Paris, Dan Ben-Gar, who needed a young man to undertake a delicate mission in Morocco.

Littman fitted the bill. Gisele could accompany him as collaborator and secretary. "I need not have gone and no doubt David could have done the job without me," she claims, adding: "But I myself had been a refugee relying on help when my family arrived in London. Now that I was in more fortunate circumstances — with a beautiful baby daughter — I felt a burning need to repay a debt."

Arriving in Casablanca in March 1961, Littman posed as an Englishman working for a Swiss children's organization interested in bringing Moroccan children to Switzerland for vacations.

For David, his role was natural. Yet it was decided that he should be known by his middle name, Gerald, because David was a typically Jewish first name in Morocco. Gisele called her husband Gerald even in the privacy of their hotel room. However, the name change, the couple recalls, led to one of their most embarrassing incidents — occurring near the end of their mission — which almost blew Littman's cover. What had happened was that Johnny, one of their contacts, had arrived outside Littman's office one night, calling out from the street, "David." Johnny, it seems, was unaware that a Moroccan clerk was working late, completing collective passport forms for a group of children due to leave in a few days. Littman, in a state of shock, went outside to talk to Johnny. They had a brief, tense conversation. Upon returning to the office he casually remarked to Gisele that, like King Edward VIII, his first name was also David. It was strange, he said, that old school friends from England still remembered him as David, rather than Gerald, his preferred name. The clerk, who had been surprised and had sus-

Fig. 75 "The Unlikely Secret Agents" interview by Simon Griever in the first part of Shmuel Segev's article "Operation Yakhin" in *The Israel Weekly Newsview*, August 21, 1984, Vol. V, No. 33, pp. 12–18

Interviews of D.G. Littman and Gisèle Littman by Simon Griever on their role in Operation Mural published in the first part of an article by Shmuel Segev "Operation Yakhin" and published in *The Israel Weekly Newsview*, August 21, 1984, Vol. V, No. 33, pp. 12-18.

piciously gone over to the window, continued his work, seemingly convinced. Still, it had been a moment of great stress.

Littman had another close shave when his wallet was pickpocketed at the main post office a week before the first convoy's departure. Hidden was a list of the names – all clearly Jewish – addresses and ages of the 127 children ready to leave the country. Though the passport authorities also knew the children leaving were all Jewish – and grudgingly accepted the fact because they believed, due to falsified "official" information, that Muslim children would be sent later – a list brought to the attention of the police would certainly have had unforseeable repercussions.

Littman took a gamble and decided to report the stolen wallet. His anxiety became acute when Gisele received a message at the hotel the next day summoning him to the police station – no reason given. Arriving an hour later, Littman wondered if the game was up. Led into a room where five wallets had been placed on a table, he was asked by a policeman whether one of them was his. Littman then wondered whether this was a trap. Yet he felt he had no other choice but to identify his wallet. Asked to check the contents to see if anything was missing, he felt his heart pounding and a pain in the pit of his stomach, due to an ulcer condition. At that point, the policeman was distracted by a visitor for a brief instant, allowing Littman to check that the list and all his money were still in the wallet. Studying the policeman's seemingly benevolent face, Littman felt sure that the list had not been discovered. The only thing missing was a picture of Gisele in a bikini. Asked by the policeman if anything was missing, Littman blandly replied, "Nothing," profusely thanked him and made a donation to the police fund.

While David arranged passport formalities, Gisele worked in the office interviewing parents sent by Mossad agents. Recalls Gisele: "The parents knew their children would not be coming back to Morocco, though nothing was said. They had limitless trust. Their selfless desire to do what was best for their children changed my view of people. I had come from a bourgeois Cairo family. At first I was surprised to see these shabby, poor Jews, some of whom were illiterate. I had been taught that nobility of soul is attained through education, culture and enlightenment."

Gisele, who, despite a potentially dangerous assignment in Morocco, had refused to be separated from her own child and was pregnant with a second, fully appreciated the parents' pain in parting with their children.

Gisele says she was able to cope with the tension of their covert existence because of the experience she had living "on her guard" during her last years in Egypt. "But I should stress," she says, "that the atmosphere in Morocco could not be compared with that which prevailed for the Jews in Nasser's Egypt during the fifties." She adds, "Our greatest regret after our mission ended was that we had been able to forge friendly relations with a few Moroccans and yet we were compelled to deceive them."

In the event, the Littmans, with the help of the Mossad, succeeded in legally sending out 530 children in three chartered planes and two ships. Gisele left Casablanca on July 22; David was to follow two days later, accompanying the final flight of 83 children.

Recalls Littman: "On the last evening, as the Swiss consular official stamped in the last three-month visas, it was evident that he realized what was happening. But he had no reason to react. So long as the Moroccans had issued collective passports, the final destination of the children was not their business. Perhaps in Bern it was remembered that during Hitler's time less than 30,000 Jews had found a temporary refuge in Switzerland, and never more than 8,000 foreign Jews resided there at any given moment out of a total of 100,000 refugees.

But there was a last hitch. The head of Mossad operations in Morocco asked to meet Littman the night before his departure – an unusual move. After taking seemingly endless precautions, he found himself in the back of a car seated next to a robust, imposing man. "Alex" simply said he wanted to thank Littman personally. He then warned him to be on his guard at the airport the next day because the entire staff had been changed. This might have been due to suspicions aroused by the departure of 93 Jewish children on July 10, and another 80 nine days later. If Littman was prevented from boarding the chartered plane on some pretext, advised Alex, he was not to panic or argue. He should just return to his hotel and go to a designated café the next day. Arrangements would be made for his immediate departure from Morocco, Alex assured him.

In the end, David was allowed to leave. Though many of the smaller children were questioned about their destination, they behaved magnificently, he recalls. All went smoothly at the airport on July 24. After take-off, David ordered champagne. The stewardess remarked that a special bottle had already been prepared. As an afterthought, she added that sometimes planes had been ordered to go back because of last-minute security checks by the Moroccan authorities. David then told her to keep the champagne on ice until the plane was out of Moroccan airspace, preferably over the Rock of Gibraltar. Eventually, the bottle was opened.

Apparently deciding to ignore what had happened, the Moroccan government later adopted a policy of liberalization regarding Jewish emigration. Within six months all the families had been reunited, a total of some 3,000 people. In fact, the "collective passport" system initiated by Littman (with the approval of Alex and Gilbert and disapproval of his contacts in Jerusalem, Paris and Marseille, who instructed him to seek individual passports only) had an unforeseen outcome. The Mossad, from 1962 to 1964, found ways to continue the system and managed to get over 100,000 Jews out of Morocco legally – with the tacit approval of the government of King Hassan II. Most eventually reached Israel.

In 1966, David Littman volunteered to help bring out the remaining 7,000 Jews trapped in Libya. But there were still no concrete plans by the time the Six Day War broke out in June 1967. Scores of Jews were killed in Tripoli, and those who were spared were only allowed to leave via the International Red Cross and other organizations.

For the past 15 years, the Littmans, still living near Geneva, have devoted their time to writing and research. Both have published articles and books on the subject of minorities in Islamic countries. They have a son and two daughters, one of whom is currently studying at the Hebrew University. During their visit here, the Littmans, as well as others involved in bringing Moroccan Jews to Israel, were received by President Chaim Herzog and publicly thanked for their efforts. On that occasion, the Littmans were reunited with Ben-Gar, with Gilbert and his wife and with Alex's widow, Carmit, who had worked with her husband in Morocco. The latter three had received official citations from President Ben Zvi in 1963. Now, the Littmans feel, a historical injustice has finally been righted by Israel's recognition of two unlikely but very successful secret agents.

Simon Griver

Operation Yakhin

by Shmuel Segev

Newsview presents the second and final extract from a new book, Operation Yakhin *(Ministry of Defense Publishing House, Tel Aviv, 1984), which tells of the clandestine efforts by the Israeli authorities to arrange the aliyah of the Jewish population of Morocco.*
In last week's extract we began the story — which has waited 20 years to be told — of Operation Miller, in which a young Englishman, David Littman, and his Egyptian-born wife, Gisele, organized the smuggling to Israel of 530 Jewish Moroccan children.

$\mathbf{B}$y the beginning of June, Littman had a list of 103 Jewish children. Due to the sluggish pace of negotiations with the Moroccan authorities, not one Muslim child had been included. The first group was scheduled to depart on June 26, 1961. Switzerland, obviously, did not favor one religion or community over another, so it would be quite inexplicable if the whole holiday-camp program were postponed for lack of Muslim participation.

Reassured by Haj's attitude, Littman went on June 8 to see the *khalifa* (inspector of police) in Casablanca's First District. This area included the Mellah, where 60 percent of the Jewish children on the list lived. The khalifa glanced at the names. As soon as he realized they were all Jewish, he flung the document to the floor in disgust. "No," he declared, "I will not sign this! It signifies pure and simple emigration. It is a political problem and has nothing to do with health. I'm surprised, Mr. Littman, that you got mixed up in this. I shall not sign these forms unless I receive written instructions to do so from my superiors."

Littman immediately informed Haj of this setback. He expressed the fear that an international incident might develop if Morocco were seen discriminating against sick children on religious grounds. It was a violation of human rights and clearly contradicted Morocco's many public pronouncements on her citizens' freedom of movement and the availability of a passport to any Jew who wanted to leave the country. Haj undertook to deal with the problem urgently.

The network had further resources. Gilbert promptly arranged a meeting between Littman and a leader of the Jewish community, who promised to approach the governor of Casablanca and demand the dismissal of the khalifa. Gilbert also contacted one of Haj's Muslim friends, who lost no time calling Haj to express his alarm at what had occurred. Littman met D'Khissy and explained that the Swiss were not in the habit of interrogating people about their religion, and if this affair got out, Morocco's good name would suffer. Furthermore, if it were not settled quickly, he would recommend that Hilsfund close its Casablanca office and cease activities in Morocco. D'Khissy urged Littman not to close the office or despair. He promised to deal with the matter and added that it wasn't Littman's fault if the children were all Jewish; the main thing was they were all Moroccan.

On the morning of June 10, Littman was back at the khalifa's office. He found him more courteous this time, but still reserved. He even warned that he intended launching a major investigation into Littman's activities in Morocco. He pointed out that whereas his district had once contained over 80,000 Jews, there were now barely 40,000 left. The Jews were leaving illegally, smuggled out of the country without passports, lured by Zionist propaganda. Many of the emigrés "subsequently regretted their action." Littman avoided any direct discussion; he merely indicated that if Zionist propaganda were enjoying any success, it must be because Morocco refused to grant passports to Jews. If these restrictions were lifted, they might not want to leave.

But this meeting proved as fruitless as the previous one. The khalifa still refused to sign the forms, without which the governor's office was powerless to issue a collective passport. Haj suggested that Littman write to the governor. On June 11 he did so, describing all his efforts to send a group of Muslim children for a vacation in Switzerland and mentioning the various meetings at government ministries and the list of sons of Moroccan "Martyrs of the Resistance". The Jewish children had all been registered in response to an article in the press about Hilsfund.

Fig. 76 Second part of Shmuel Segev's article on "Operation Yakhin" published in *The Israel Weekly Newsview* August 28, 1984, Vol. V, No. 34, pp. 18–21

The article describes in details Operation Mural, named Milhar or Miller as required by the Mossad and as it appeared in his book: *Mivtsa Yakhin / Operation "Yakhin." The Secret Immigration of Moroccan Jews to Israel*, Ministry of Defence Publishing House, April 1984.

Clément? Mural

Mr. Naftali BARGIORA
Bamberger Lane
Old City

<u>JERUSALEM</u> / Israel   31 December 1985

Dear Naftali,

Gisèleand I were happy to find you and Yaffa at home and were pleased
to get to know better Pinhas and Miriam.

You, yourself, seem to be very active in research and churning out books,
which is as good a way of "retiring" as any other. Congratulations !

It was only <u>after</u> I had spontaneously offered to let you read through
our texts that I realized the problems involved. Clearly, you would not
find all/of it to your taste.

Concerning your "comments" and "corrections", I did not see the editor
before we left and was preparing to send everything to him by express
post, when Dr. Paul Fenton visited us unexpectedly. He was able to read
your remarks in Hebrew and this has allowed me to instruct the editor.

p. 208 I remember hearing : "three or four" (shlichim). I have corrected
it to "more than one". The source is <u>you</u> (and perhaps Moshe Kol?. The
story of the doctor who brought out *only* his own baby after several weeks
or months is authentic.

p. 214 Re : arrests, etc. I did not refer <u>specifically</u> to "Operation
Mural"; my word in English was : "brutalised". My source is Gad and I
have asked that <u>he</u> decide what is inaccurate in my statement. I admit to
one mistake. He told me 20 years ago that two persons had been arrested
before my arrival, water was pumped into them during interrogation to
make them talk, and that <u>one</u> of the two died <u>later</u> in Paris as a result
of this <u>torture</u>.In my text, by an inadvertence, I incorrectly referred
to <u>two</u> deaths: "(Several 'agents' had been — and were to be — apprehended by the authorities before, during, and after our mission. Many of
them were brutalised and two died from the effects of torture}".

p. 224 I have nothing more to add to my comments on Mr. Reiffler.

p. 225/238 You admit in your letter that your superiors took the fatal
decision (9 July 1961). I covered this probability in my text, although
I endeavoured to exclude your possible responsibility in this decision.
I <u>still</u> disagree with your estimation re: the necessity of taking such
an "operation decision, while admittedly imposing an additional risk..."
Had I been gaoled for several weeks, months, years or decades, the subject would be less recondite today. It <u>was</u> a "betrayal" (whether you
appreciate the term or not). However, in order not to vex you (the "libel"
threat does not impress me — it is not the first time that I have heard
such *echos*), and particularly because Dr. Fenton informed me that the
word for "betrayal" in Hebrew is the same as "treason", I have modified

Fig. 77 Letter from D. Littman to Naphtali Bar-Giora, December 31, 1985

In this letter Littman refers to Bar-Giora's comments on his article soon to be published in

Hebrew in *Shorashim Bamizra'h (Roots in the Orient)*, Vol. I, Editor: Itshak Avrahami, Edition

Hakibbutz Hameuchad: Yad Tabenkin, 1986. One of the comments relates to the incident

of July 9 1961 which Littman calls a "betrayal."

-2-

this word. As only one word could be used — these are the last proofs — my choice was limited, but it should quieten the "somebody" you refer to in your letter.

Neither Mrs. Tordjman, nor any member of her family lives in Morocco and when we met at the Presidential reception in May 1984, she had no objection to being mentioned.

Thanks for the spelling and other mistakes. In view of Fenton's help and my long express letter to the editor, there is no need for you to meet with him, especially as I have sent him all the pages with your comments, as well as my remarks. He will decide (after discussions with Gad) what should be modified and what can still be changed ! X

A Healthy and Happy New Year to all from us here.

Address by David G. Littman

Prime Minister Shimon Peres, Vice-Premier and Foreign Minister Yitzhak Shamir, Members of the Government, Speaker of the Knesset Shlomo Hillel, Commander-in-Chief of the Army Moses ha-Levy, Mayor of Jerusalem Teddy Kollek, Chairman of 'Beyahad' Sam Ben Shetrit, distinguished guests, citizens of Jerusalem, people of Israel.

My wife and I are profoundly moved and greatly honoured to receive this testimonial from Prime Minister Shimon Peres on behalf of the organisation Beyahad, the sponsors of the Mimouna Festival. Our heartfelt thanks go out to you all.

It is written in Isaiah chapter six, verse eight: *"Also, I heard the voice of the Lord, saying: Whom shall I send, and who will go for us? Then said I, here am I; send me."*

Twenty-five years ago, my wife and I were receptive to that call, each in a very specific manner, and we were able together — behayad — to accomplish our mission with the collaboration of Alex Gattmon, chief of Mossad operations, of Gad Shahar (my "contact" in Casablanca) and their devoted network (misqueret). By this method, 530 Moroccan Jewish children reached Israel via Switzerland in the summer of 1961 as a result of "Operation Mural," thus inaugurating a process that soon led to the Aliyah of 100'000 Moroccan Jews within three years ["Operation Yakhin"].

Fig. 78 Speech delivered by D.G. Littman at the Sacher Park, May 1, 1986

Speech delivered on May 1, 1986 on the occasion of the Mimouna Festival held in the Sacher Park in Jerusalem with many important dignitaries and thousands attending the event. In this speech D.G. Littman expresses his gratitude for receiving together with his wife (the author Bat Ye'or) a certificate of recognition handed by Prime Minister Shimon Peres on behalf of the organisation the Ideological Movement of Jews of North African Origin (Beyahad). On this occasion he praises the work of Alex Gattmon, Gad Shahar and the Misgeret (the Framework) and the courage of the parents and the children.

We owe this honour to the innumerable Jewish men, women and children of North Africa who inspired us with their example of courage and dignity in the face of adversity. We owe it no less to the spiritual values of the people of Israel who — first in recorded history, by their exodus from Egypt — exemplified for humanity the significance of the word "liberty," a people whose spirituality and striving thus freed mankind from the shackles of bondage 3,200 years ago — the Pessach — Passover celebrations of which have just ended.

The notion of faith and "togetherness" (*Yahad*), so appropriate to the spirit of the Mimouna celebration, also implies the notion of *Yahid* — that of uniqueness and diversity: to be together, however diverse our traditions and to esteem one another in spite of all our differences. This is the essence of '*Yahad*' and '*Yahid*', whether we are Ashkenazim or Sephardim, whether we are religious or secular, whether we are Jews, Christians or Muslims.

This spirit of unity and uniqueness which we see in Jerusalem continues to inspire Mayor Teddy Kollek and Israel's leaders: this small, but great country — the pride of free peoples worldwide. May the words of David the psalmist, king of this unique city, be heard throughout the land, and in the world beyond: ***"Behold, how good and how pleasant it is for brethren to dwell together in unity."***

Fig. 79a Certificate of Gratitude in Hebrew, May 1986

Certificate of Gratitude in Hebrew awarded in May 1986 by The ideological Movement
of Jews of North African Origin (The Beyahad organization) to David Littman and Gisèle
Littman (Bat Ye'or).

```
                              Le mouvement Beyahad
                              Mouvement idéologique
                              fondé par des ressortissants
                              d'Afrique du Nord


          Célébration de la Mimouna 1986 sous l'égide "ton frère
          vivra avec toi"

          Attestation que David et Gisèle (Bat Ye'or)

                    LITTMAN

          de Suisse

          furent décernés par le mouvement Beyahad du titre de

          membres honorifiques de Beyahad pour l'année 1986
```

Ce titre est décerné au couple Littman en raison de leurs activités
clandestines au service de l'Etat d'Israël, lorsque, tout en mettant
leur vie en danger, ils firent sortir clandestinement en 1961, par
voie de mer et d'air, 530 enfants juifs du Maroc en Israël, en tran-
sitant par la Suisse.
D'autre part, Bat Ye'or s'est signalée par ses publications concernant
les persécutions des Juifs dans les pays arabes et en rendant l'opinion internationale sensible à leur situation.
Le titre de membre honorifique de Beyahad pour l'année 1986 est offert
en reconnaissance du dévouement du couple dans la réalisation de la
devise "Et ton frère vivra avec toi", sous laquelle les événements
de cette année sont placés.
En foi de quoi, nous signons.

```
    Shimon Peres              Yitzhak Shamir        Sam Benchetrit
    Premier Ministre          Vice-premier
                              ministre et ministre      Président du
                              des affaires étrangères    Mouvement Beyahad
```

Fig. 79b Certificate of Gratitude translated in French, May 1986

Translation in French of the title bestowed on the Littman couple for their clandestine
activities in Morocco which resulted in 530 Moroccan children arriving in Israel via
Switzerland, and also for Bat Ye'or (Gisèle Littman) historical research on the Jews in Arab
countries. The title is signed by Prime Minister Shimon Peres, Vice-Premier and Foreign
Minister Yitzhak Shamir and Sam Benchetrit, Head of Beyahad movement.

Address by David G. Littman

Chers amis,

Il y a 25 ans, nous étions ensemble à Casablanca. Je me rappelle de vous. Vous étiez des enfants. Je voulais vous parler au bureau, quand vous preniez le bus, ou quand vous embarquiez à l'aéroport de Casablanca, ainsi qu'aux ports de Casablanca et de Tanger, mais je ne pus le faire. Ma femme comprenait l'inquiétude de vos parents et leur courage. Vous étiez tellement contents de partir, mais les plus jeunes ne savaient pas que leur destination était la terre d'Israël.

Aujourd'hui, ma femme et moi sommes très émus de vous retrouver ici en Israël, des adultes, pères et mères de famille avec des situations importantes. Vous êtes arrivés démunis mais maintenant vous êtes établis.

KOL HAKAVOD LE ERETZ ISRAEL VE KOL HAKOVOD LEHEM.

Au nom de ma femme et de moi-même, je remercie le président du mouvement BEYAHAD, M. Sam Benchetrit et tous ses collaborateurs pour avoir organisé cette extraordinaire rencontre dans l'esprit de Beyahad : ensemble un peuple uni.

Fig. 80 Speech in French by D. Littman to the "Children" and their families delivered in Tel Aviv, May 14, 1986

D. Littman delivers his speech to the 'children' he still remembers from the mission in Casablanca twenty-five years ago. Although he could not do so, he yearned to speak to them, then, at his office, as they boarded the buses, the planes, the boats taking them to Israel via Switzerland. Today together with his wife, he pays honour to their courage as well as the courage of to Alex Gattmon, Gad Shahar and the Misgeret, to OSE-Suisse and the Youth Aliyah. Touched to see them today accompanied by their children, he thanks Beyahad for having organized this extraordinary meeting on the Independence Day of the State of Israel.

Le mouvement Beyahad signifie : tous ensemble, être solidaires, joindre nos efforts pour une action commune.

Il est écrit dans le prophète Esaie (Yeshayahoo) : VAESHMA ET-KOL ADONAI OMER ET-MI ESHLAH OOMI YELEH VA-OMAR HINNIY SHELAHNIY (J'entendis la voix du Seigneur, disant : Qui enverrai-je, et qui marchera pour nous? Je répondis : Me voici, envoie-moi (6 :8)).

Voici 25 ans au Maroc, avec la collaboration d'Alex Gattmon (décédé en 1981), chef des opérations, avec Gad Shahar (ici présent) et avec tout leur groupe dévoué dont certains sont aussi ici avec nous, avec l'aide d'OSE-Suisse et Aliyah les Jeunes, tous ensemble nous pûmes accomplir notre mission.

Cet honneur qui nous est fait aujourd'hui, nous le devons aux Juifs d'Afrique du Nord, hommes, femmes et enfants, dont le courage et la dignité face à l'adversité, nous servirent d'exemple. Nous le devons aux valeurs spirituelles du peuple d'Israël qui le premier dans l'histoire par leur exode d'Egypte, donne une signification au mot "liberté". Nous le devons à vous, chers amis du Maroc, qui êtes montés en Israël il y a 25 ans.

Les notions de foi et de solidarité (Yahad) impliquent aussi la notion de Yehid, c'est-à-dire celle de spécificité et de diversité. Etre ensemble, quelque diverses que soient nos traditions et s'estimer les uns les autres en dépit de toutes nos différences, tel est le sens de Yahad et de Yehid.

C'est cet esprit de solidarité que nous fêtons aujourd'hui, jour de l'Indépendance, sur la terre d'Israël, où se réunissent des Juifs venus du monde entier.

Puisse être entendu dans tout le Pays et à l'étranger le message du psalmist, le roi David : "Qu'il est agréable, qu'il est doux pour des frères de demeurer ensemble." (Psaume 133 :1)

HINE MA TOV OOMA NAIM SHEVET AHIM GAM YAHAD. (Chantons ensemble)

Fig. 81 "A Thousand and One Nights" by Zvi Gilat, *Hadashot*, May 9, 1986, interviews in Hebrew with David and Gisèle Littman, Gad Shahar, and David Bar Sheshat, pp. 25–29.

In this detailed article Zvi Gilat interviews David Littman, his contact in Morocco, Gad Shahar (Georges) from the Kibbut Regavim and David Bar Sheshat from Ashdod, one of the

9.5.1986 ● יום ו' ● כ' ניסן תשמ"ו

"אִמָּא אמרה לי: 'תשגיח על האחים
שלך. שלא תפרדו אף־פעם. יצחק יש לו
בעיות באוזניים, תדאג שיקבל טיפול. ואל
תשכחו שאתם נוסעים לטקסס. תראו
שם קאובויס וחיות, ותחכו לנו...
ניסע ביחד לישראל...'"

דוד בר־ששת היום עם שני ילדיו מתגורר באשדוד. ב"61, עם שני אחיו, לבד
בארץ, מיקי קרצמן

כתובת החייל אברה

בן, אני יליד '49

לכו מכאן, ציונים

ביקור קצר בישראל

ג'ורג' מוסתל במרוקו

"children" who left Casablanca on the second convoy (July 10, 1961) with his two younger
siblings. Bar-Sheshat who was eleven years old at the time, recounts how he and his brothers
believed they were going to Texas to see cowboys.

Fig. 81b "A Thousand and One Nights," p. 27

9.5.1986 ● ל' ניסן תשמ"ו ● יום ו'

אבא היה מבסוט

בגישה מחודשת

"בבוקר מצאנו את עצמנו בין עצים בבית עץ גדול. אמרו לנו שלמקום קוראים שווייץ. איפה טקסס? איפה קאובויס?... היו ילדים שבכו וצעקו, אמרו שרימו אותם..."

ליטמן מבריח את אישתו

Fig. 81c "A Thousand and One Nights," p. 29

Maariv 15.5.1986

25 שנה אחרי שהתחזה לנוצרי התראה ליטמן עם הילדים שהבריח ממרוקו

מאת נורית דברת

מפגש ראשון של מאות ילדים שהוברחו לפני 25 שנה ממרוקו, נערך אתמול ב„גני אורנים" בתל-אביב, ביוזמת תנועת „ביחד" של יוצאי צפון אפריקה.

אך לא הילדים שעלו לארץ ב-1961 – במסגרת מבצע „מולאר" – היוו את מרכז תשומת הלב. היו אלה דוד וג'יזל ליטמן, יהודים המתגוררים בשוויץ, שהיוו את האטרקציה המרכזית. לפני 25 שנה חיפש דוד, יהודי-אנגלי, בעל נכסים, לעשות משהו מועיל בהתנדבות.

הארגונים היהודיים אליהם פנה לא התרגשו מהצעתו, שסיפר כי נדרש לפעולה לאחר קריאת הספר „עלייתו ונפילתו של הרייך השלישי". כשכמעט התיאש וחזר לאנגליה, פגש בשוויץ את מנהלי של גוף שעסק בפרויקטים למען ילדים יהודים. יחד עם אשתו ג'יזל, יהודיה ממוצא מצרי, הגיע ליטמן ב-1961 למרוקו והתחזה לנוצרי.

ליטמן הבריח את הילדים באמצעות מוסדר, כביכול, לרישום ילדים לקייטנות בשוויץ.

פרופסור אלפסי היה אז בן 13, ואחיו כן 9. אתמול הוא נזכר באותה נסיעה בהתרגשות: „הגענו לשדה התעופה לבושים יפה ומנפים דגלים של מרוקו ואיש לא חשד בכלום. רק בשוויץ הבנו מהמרוקאים כי התחנה היא ישראל".

„לפני העלאת הילדים המתים בסוף קיץ '61 ובני הזוג ליטמן שמשו שלשלטונות מארוקו החלו לרדוף סביבם, מיהרו לסגור את המשרד ולעזוב את המדינה. מעשה זה שלהם לא היה נודע כרבים לולא חשיפת הפרשה ב„מעריב" על ידי העתונאי שמואל שגב, שפירסם פרקים מסיפרו „מבצע יכין" על העלאת יהודי מארוקו לישראל.

HADACHOT – 15-5-86

ססו ילדים במוראל גבוה

כ100% מבין 530 הילדים שהוצבאו ארצה ממרוקו בקיץ 1961, במסגרת מבצע מורׁאל.

נמפגש אתמול שוב בתל-אביב. עברו רבים מהם היתה זו הזדמנות ראשונה לגלות איך אורגנה עלייתם ארצה. אז. לפני 25 שנה, היו כולם בני 16"10. אתמול הם הסתובבו בגדירושים עם תמונות מהימים ההם. זיהו את עצבם, זיהו אחרים, ושמחה לגלות כי כולם הסתדרו בחיים אחוז או יותר. הבכם. שאורגן עליהדי תנועת „ביחד" ל„חדשות", במעמד שרי-הקואליצה, עמד בסימן הוקרה לבני הזוג דוד וג'יזל ליטמן הׁשוויצרים. שמולטו את הילדים לארין. הסיפור המלא של המפגש מחר, ב„חדשות" של שבת. (כתב: צבי גילת, צילום: משה שי).

Fig. 82 Articles in *Maariv* and *Hadashot* (May 15, 1986) describing the meeting of the Littman couple with the "children" twenty-five years later

THE JERUSALEM POST

POST
INTERNATIONAL EDITION
Published in Jerusalem יצא לאור בירושלים

THE LATEST NEWS FROM ISRAEL →

Independence Day 4
The Galilee's demography 6
Bringing the Moroccan children 12
Spokesman for the young 13
Jewish life in Yugoslavia 15

THE JERUSALEM POST INTERNATIONAL EDITION

PEOPLE   No. 1,333 ● WEEK ENDING MAY 24, 1986 ● 1 YAR 15, 5746 ● RAMADAN 16, 1406.

The mission

By ABRAHAM RABINOVICH

THE TALL Englishman may have been prominent in singing hymns at Sunday services of the Anglican church in Casablanca but to the local Mossad operative in 1961 he looked far too Jewish for his mission.

At the Mimouna celebrations in Jerusalem last year, the hymn singer, David Littman, and his Egyptian-born wife, Giselle, were honoured for the risky role they had played 25 years ago in bringing 530 Jewish children to Israel at a time when the emigration of Jews from Morocco seemed blocked.

The son of an American Jew who had acquired British citizenship in the course of operating a successful real estate business in England, David was motivated to undertake the mission by reading William Shirer's book on the Third Reich. What has been done then to help Jews in distress, he asked himself; what was being done now? He had just moved to Switzerland from England with his young wife and their infant daughter and began making the rounds of international Jewish organizations in Geneva to ask whether he could be of service. He made it clear that he had an independent income from his father's estate and was not seeking remuneration. By the time he reached his last address, the Hilfsfund, he had grown accustomed to the polite rejections his offer elicited. Here, however, he would be offered even more than he had hoped for.

The Hilfsfund was an organization devoted to assisting Jews abroad. Just a few days before Littman's appearance, its elderly director, Prof. Jacques Bloch, had been approached by a Jewish Agency official requesting assistance in a plan for the rescue of Jewish Moroccan

children. The plan called for several hundred children to be brought to the hostels operated by Hilfsfund in Switzerland for "health vacations" and for their subsequent transfer to Israel. Bloch had agreed in principle but said that everything hinged on finding a suitable person to organize the Moroccan end of the operation. The appearance of Littman in his doorway was a prayer answered.

WHEN THE mission was explained to the 27-year-old Englishman, he readily assented. He would be provided with letters of recommendation from legitimate Swiss relief organizations whose officials knew

David and Giselle Littman with their daughter, photographed in 1961.

only that he intended to bring sickly Moroccan children to Switzerland for three-week vacations. Littman would go in under his own name but pose as an Anglican – his education in an Anglican public school, including hymn singing, well equipped him for the role.

Giselle was far more alert to the dangers of the mission than her husband. She and her family had been expelled from Egypt in 1957 after living through a period of anti-Jewish violence in Cairo. However, when her husband insisted that he must go, she agreed to join him with their baby.

In Casablanca, the Littmans

rented an apartment, registered at the British consulate and regularly attended Sunday services at the Anglican Church. David, who had been a tennis champion in his youth, played an occasional early morning set with the British consul. The couple even were mentioned in a social gossip column of a Moroccan daily when they attended celebrations at the consul's residence for Queen Elizabeth's birthday.

Littman, meanwhile, was establishing his credentials with Moroccan officials who expressed enthusiasm about his proposal for Swiss vacations for sickly Moroccan youngsters. He also met in a local cafe with his Mossad contact, a Tunisian-born kibbutznik with the cover name of George. The latter was taken aback at Littman's conspicuous height, Semitic appearance, broken French, and naivety. He gave Littman some basic pointers – making contact with him only from a public phone, and using a veiled but seemingly logical language.

The enthusiastic young volunteer soon found himself at odds with his controllers in France and Switzerland. He had arrived in March, and, after studying the situation on the ground, concluded that the plan to begin bringing groups of children out before summer would not work because parents would object to pulling children out of school in midterm. He also attempted to cloak the Jewish nature of the operation by persuading Moroccan authorities to include Moslem children – an initiative which angered Agency officials who feared that the hostels would be flooded with Moslem children. Littman offered to pay the expense for the Moslem children himself. In the end, the Moroccan bureaucracy caused this aspect of the plan to fall

through, but Littman's offer provided invaluable cover when police officials, scanning the names of the children for whom passports were being requested, found them all to be Jewish.

George's team had organized the parents and provided them with the necessary medical documents and the money they ostensibly paid Littman for their children's trip. In order to encourage them to keep silent about the children's ultimate destination, they were told that Littman was Christian and was unaware that the children were going to end up in Israel.

The first group of children left for Geneva on June 26. Four more groups would leave within the next month by chartered plane and by ship. Giselle and the baby left two days before the final group. The night before Littman himself was to leave with that group, he was summoned to his first meeting with the head of the Mossad in Morocco. He was driven to a pre-arranged street corner where "Alex" got in. The Mossad officer said he wanted to personally thank Littman for his efforts. These words of appreciation would be warmly recalled by Littman in the decades that would follow.

There would be no more cloak-and-dagger for Littman after he had safely landed in Geneva and rejoined his family. He would, however, figure in an academic detective story more than two decades later when, acting on behalf of Hebrew University, he located crates in a Geneva storage room containing a large-scale model of Jerusalem executed more than a century ago. That model is now a central feature of the museum in Jerusalem's Citadel.

Fig. 83 "An Englishman to the Rescue" by Abraham Rabinovitch, *The Jerusalem Post*, May 9, 1986 republished in *The Jerusalem Post Int. Edition* as "The Mission," May 24, 1986.

HOME NEWS

Thursday, May 15, 1986   The Jerusalem Post   Page Two

First reunion for children smuggled out of Morocco in 1961

By MICHAL YUDELMAN
Jerusalem Post Reporter

"We were 120 children in the group wearing scout uniforms and waving Moroccan flags, excited to be flying in an airplane for the first time. I knew we were bound for Israel, but we weren't allowed to talk about it or sing any songs in Hebrew. My little nine-year-old brother thought we were just going on a summer trip. I knew I was responsible for him until our family was reunited in Israel. British Consulate receptions use two years later."

This is the testimony of Prosper Alfasi, 38, one of the 530 Jewish children aged nine to 17 who were smuggled out of Morocco to Israel in 1961, as part of the Yakhin Operation to get Morocco's 110,000 Jews

to Israel. The project was veiled in secrecy until two years ago.

About 100 of the children who arrived in that operation convened with their families at the Gan Oranim halls yesterday morning for their first reunion with each other and with David Littman, the man who made it all possible.

Littman, at the time a 24-year-old post-graduate student at the London Institute of Archeology, had been recruited in Geneva in 1961 and sent to Casablanca, to register children for a "summer school" in Switzerland. He was accompanied by his young Egyptian-born wife, Giselle. The two joined the local Anglican community, attending church services,

and weekend tennis matches.

The price for the summer school was high, to dissuade Moslem children from joining without arousing suspicion. The Jewish families "paid" Littman, who later returned their money secretly, for most of the families were very poor.

Littman, who now lives in Geneva, was contacted by the Bayabad movement and asked to attend yesterday's reunion. A few weeks ago he received the Mimouna Award from Prime Minister Peres for his part in the operation.

The children were flown in groups from Morocco to France, taken by bus to a makeshift camp in Switzerland and then flown to Israel. "Every time a group was to leave for Israel, we told the authorities we

were going on a two-day trip. At the airport, we sent the group of children received a new group of children to leave from Morocco, on a collective passport," Avraham Goldfischer, a student in Switzerland aged 25 years ago, who was recruited as a counsellor for the Moroccan children, recalled.

"Once we discovered that we were being followed, probably by someone from the Moroccan government, and we dispersed the children to other places. Once we were followed on the way to the airport and had to take side paths until we shook our tail," Goldfischer said.

When the operation was well underway, the absence of some 500 Casablanca Jewish community, and the authorities became suspicious.

Littman sent his wife and baby daughter back to Europe and joined the larger group of children to leave Morocco. His hastily closed office, in which many documents of Moroccan Jewish families were stored, later created problems for these families when they tried to join their children in Israel.

"I kept writing to my parents asking them when they would join me, and my father replied that the 'summer school' office had suddenly closed and that they had been left without papers. (Moroccan families had one joint identity card.) Many families managed to leave illegally, without papers, explained Alfasi, who today lives in Tel Aviv with his wife and three children.

At yesterday's reunion, the "chil-

dren," today parents surrounded by their own children, crowded around Littman and his wife. "He is our collective father," one of them told *The Jerusalem Post.*

The idea of bringing Littman to Israel to meet his "children" came from Bayabad member Dr. Raphael Israeli, a lecturer in Chinese History and Islamic Civilization at the Hebrew University.

After his mission to Morocco, Littman and his wife created the Geneva Centre of Information and Documentation on the Middle East. Littman was nominated as representative at the UN in Geneva by the conference of the World Union for Progressive Judaism, and earlier this year participated at the session of the UN Commission on Human Rights.

Fig. 84 "First reunion for children smuggled out of Morocco in 1961" by Michal Yudelman, *The Jerusalem Post*, May 15, 1986

TÉLÉPHONE

(VAUD) SUISSE

The Editor
Jerusalem Post
POB 81   9 June 1986
91000 JERUSALEM / Israel

Operation "Mural" (1961)

As two extensive articles by Abraham Rabinovich ("An Englishman to the
rescue", of 9 May; republished in your 24 May international edition as,
"The mission") and Michal Yudelman ("First reunion for children smuggled
out of Morocco in 1961", of 15 May) concern me directly, may I be
allowed to make a few precisions.

1) The first annual "Beyahad" Awards (Diaspora) were presented *jointly*
to "David and Gisèle (Bat Ye'or) Littman" by the Prime Minister and the
Vice-Premier at the 1 May 1986 Mimouna festivities, held in the Sacher
Park, Jerusalem. Our testimonial refers not only to my wife's presence
at my side in Morocco, but also to her contribution to the historiography of Oriental Jewry, written under her pen name "Bat Ye'or".

2) The Jewish international organisation which served as the Geneva
cover for Operation "Mural" was OSE-Suisse (not "Hilsfund"), then run
by Prof. Jacques Bloch, aided by his wife and by secretary Aida
Schirmann, who three times flew to Casablanca to accompany groups of
children when volunteers were few and far between.

3) Michal Yudelman twice quotes Abraham Goldfischer (then a student and
holiday OSE monitor in Switzerland), now living in Israel. Regretfully,
I must contradict his statement. No bus convoys were "tailed" by anyone
— let alone Moroccan officials — in Morocco, France or Switzerland.
Fables should not replace reality, or as Shakespeare put it : "How easy
is a bush supposed a bear."

4) No family documents were left in my Casablanca office. I handed over
all of them the night before my precipitate 24 July departure with the
last convoy. Unfortunately, the person responsible for mailing them
panicked at the thought of being questioned at the post office and threw
them into a garbage bin. Prosper Alfasi is correct in stating that the
loss of these family identity papers (Livrets de famille) was the cause
of much anguish and problems for about fifty or more families, who
suddenly found themselves without identity papers and were obliged to
explain their inexplicable loss to the Moroccan authorities.

5) The extraordinary Independence Day First Reunion with 125 out of the
530 "children" (and their children !)organised by the Beyahad movement
was a profoundly emotional occasion for all of us. Unfortunately, Michal
Yudelman was unable to interview either of us on this occasion.

6) Operation "Mural" was first related by Shmuel Segev in a chapter of
his Operation Yakhin : the Secret Immigration of Moroccan Jews to Israel
(1984). My wife and I have described at length both the mission itself
and our personal background and experiences, in two articles (100 pages)
which will appear in a Hebrew volume, Roots in the East : an anthology
of documentation and research, by Yad Tabenkin (Hamayuhad).

David Littman

Fig. 85 Letter from D. Littman to the Editor of *The Jerusalem Post*, June 9, 1986

Littman refers here to the articles by A. Rabinovitch and M. Yudelman, stating that the
Beyahad Awards were presented jointly to David and Gisèle (Bat Ye'or) Littman by the Prime
Minister and the Vice-Premier at the May 1986 Mimouna festivities in the Sacher Park, Jerusalem. The testimonial refers not only to his wife's presence at his side in Morocco, but also to
her contribution to the historiography of Oriental Jewry. He goes on to stress that "Hilsfund"
is an invented name for OSE-Suisse, the Jewish international organization directed by Prof.
Jacques Bloch, which served as the cover for Operation Mural. Relating to Prosper Alfasi
and Avraham Goldfisher's testimonies, he specifies that no family documents were left in
his office but were thrown away by the person responsible for mailing them, nor were any
bus convoys followed by the Moroccan police.

Fig. 86 "Mission to Morocco," an interview with David and Gisèle Littman by Simon Griver, *The Jewish Chronicle*, October 9, 1987

ארגון פעילי המחתרת
ההעפלה ואסירי ציון
בצפון אפריקה

DAVID GERALD LITTMAN

אנו מעניקים לך תעודה זו על פעילותך המסורה
וחלקך בהבטחת פעילותה הסדירה של

״המסגרת״

בימי מאבקה בחירוף נפש של יהדות
צפון אפריקה במחתרת, בהעפלה ובהגנה
על הקהילות היהודיות

ועל כך הנך ראוי להערכה ולהוקרה

מאיר כנפו
יו״ר הארגון

Fig. 87 Certificate of recognition to David Gerald Littman signed by Meir Knafo, President of the Organization of the Clandestine Network of North Africa (The Misgeret)

Address by President Shimon Peres

Well, it is a belated ceremony, but it doesn't lose its value,
because what you did stands on its own legs and is not affected
by time. I think that the saving of 530 children is, I imagine,
the most moving experience a man can have. You say in Hebrew:
"The one who saves one life is like the one that saved the
life of the whole world." (*) But when you save 530 children
it's really unforgettable. I want to express, on behalf of
our people, our nation, our recognition of your courage,
your wisdom, of your determination under extremely difficult
conditions at a time when our connections were extremely weak.
   And I must say, whenever I read again the story, I am
moved to see the ingenuity and the courage that you have
shown, and the results. So, thanks to it we have 530 people,
families, children alive and it's unique because in North
Africa our connections were even weaker than in Europe, and
the ground was less known [President Shimon Peres was Deputy
Defence Minister in 1961] And, I think, if you wouldn't do
it, it wouldn't be done. In order to do it, you were in touch
with the Mossad and I wish to express the appreciation of
the Mossad for all the performance, your activities, under
cover, and successful result [a word or two inaudible]. It's
for me a pleasure to have your families, the children, the
grandchildren. They know the story? [turning to Littman]

David G. Littman: Yes . . .

President: All of you? [looking toward them, he spoke a
few words in Hebrew to Tair (in uniform) and to Daphnee and
Kalia, who were a bit timid and nodded.]

David G. Littman: . . . and I was asked to say a few words
about the story when it is convenient . . .

President: [smiling]: Now it's convenient. [general laughter].

David G. Littman [goes to podium to deliver his presentation
(**), followed by Swiss ambassador's speech]

**Fig. 88 Verbatim recording of President Shimon Peres Speech during the private reception
to commemorate Operation Mural at the Presidential Residence in Jerusalem, June 1, 2008**

President: [speaking in conclusion after speeches by DGL and Swiss Ambassador Walter Haffner]: I would like to thank the ambassador and would like to thank you and your family for coming over and really. . . [inaudible words] every praise and the thanks of our nation for this very unusual operation in a country where [inaudible words] King Hussein II, a great friend of Israel — and so was his father, Muhammad V [. . .]
  close to our hearts [inaudible passages]. That was the period when we could have lost the children, even the people. This act of salvation is an outstanding one. I thank you for coming and especially thank you for what you have performed and did. Thank you. [The president then greeted everyone and was the photographed with all of those present.]

---

* *The Mishnah*, Fourth Division, *The Sanhedrin*, 4:5 (trans. by Herbert Danby, Oxford University Press, 1933, p. 388]

** The presentation by David G. Littman followed, with daughter Diana humming a part of: *Yerushalayim shel-zahav* ("Jerusalem of Gold") at the close. Then, a five minute, moving speech by Swiss Ambassador Walter Haffner. (Before this, the president had received David and Gisèle Littman in his adjacent private study, where Bat Ye'or handed him an inscribed copy of her latest book *Eurabia* (Hebrew / Schocken), just published). A little later, he entered the official ceremonial room, shook hands with everyone, as DGL introduced each person; he then sat down and spoke impromptu.

  Except for the five minute private exchange beforehand in his private adjoining study, the whole event was graciously filmed by Rami Lital, cameraman of Israel Broadcasting Company Channel 1, who had filmed *"Operation Mural": Casablanca 1961* in Switzerland, Morocco and Israel (Sept.-Dec. 2006). A 14 minute DVD was later made by Ronit Dor, the producer and was put on a Swiss blog (drzz). Also present at this private ceremony in the presidential residence were: daughter Diana Littman (with Elizabeth Wider), Ariane Littman with her three children (Tair, Daphnee, Kalia), & former agents of the Mossad (1961–): Samuel Toledano (N° 2 to Isser Harel), Carmit Gattmon (widow of Alex Gattmon, N° 1 in Morocco), Gad Shahar & Pinhas Katsir ("contacts" for "Mural" in Casablanca) , Miriam Korshia, Col. Yamin Ka'anan (one of the 530 children), Tova Ronel (widow of Efraim Ronel, N° 1 in Paris) with daughter and son-in-law).

Address by David G. Littman

Mr. President, it is a great honour for all of us to be welcomed at Beth Hanassi, here in Jerusalem, by an illustrious Founding Father of the State of Israel and Nobel Peace Laureate.

On 16 March 1961, nine weeks after the 'Egoz' tragedy when 44 Moroccan Jews drowned — half of them children — I flew to Casablanca and my wife joined me two weeks later. Without the devoted presence and close collaboration of Gisèle — a true daughter of the Nile and the later Bat Ye'or - while caring for baby Diana, our mission would have failed.

What was later known as "Operation Mural" began with key letters of recommendation from René Steiner, the head of the Swiss Red Cross /Children's section in Bern, and from others there. It slowly gained momentum through my collaboration with those I met clandestinely in Casablanca, although I had no idea that they were Mossad agents. They knew me as "Gerald", my second name, which I used in rather than David, a name which is very Jewish-sounding in Morocco.

How appropriate that our dear, life-long friends are here on this very special occasion, 47 years later: Shmuel Toledano [87 years], Deputy for Diaspora Affairs to Isser Harel, renowned head of the Mossad; Carmit Gattmon, widow and companion in life and work of Alex Gattmon, the remarkably outstanding Mossad chief in Morocco, who died prematurely in 1981; Gad Shahar — "Georges" to me [85 years] — his close collaborator and my main 'contact' in Casablanca, with whose constant advice and support the operation slowly evolved; Pinhas Katsir — "Jacques" to me [70 years] who took over from him as my 'contact' for the last fortnight; and Miriam Korshia who, with her husband Abraham-Hubert Korshia, provided the logistics for those parents who wished to inscribe their children for Swiss holidays, en route for Zion — in some cases three or four children — although unsure of seeing them for many anxious months or more, until they could eventually join them in Israel.

This is also a time to recall the risks and recognise the devotion of all those unnamed and unsung volunteers of the

Fig. 89 Speech by D.G. Littman during the private reception to commemorate Operation Mural at the Presidential Residence, June 1, 2008

misgeret in Morocco — about 200 youngsters — and, of course, the late Efraim Ronel, Chief Mossad agent in Paris and head of the misgeret — the "frame", as it was called —and Tova, his widow [93 years] is also with us today. And, last but not least, the late Naftali Bar-Giora of the Jewish Agency who proposed the first 'Swiss holiday' idea, after the Egoz sank, and then found me by chance in Geneva, via Professor Jacques Bloch, director of OSE-Suisse whose friendly contacts in Bern were indispensable, facilitating a new name — OSSEAN: Oeuvre de Secours aux Enfants de l'Afrique du Nord. Prof. Bloch helped to save between 2000 and 3000 Jewish children in France during the Second World War before arriving in Switzerland.

The documentary film by Yehuda Kaveh and Ronit Dor, *"Operation Mural: Casablanca 1961"* — currently a Nominee for Best Documentary at the Israeli Film Academy Awards / Ophir 2008 — has been selected for more than four Jewish film festivals worldwide, gaining awards such as 'Best Jewish Film' at the DeREEL Film Festival in Melbourne, Australia. The film will be screened for the 2nd time soon on Israel's TV main Channel 1. Mr. President, you were aware of these 1961 activities and the subsequent mass aliya that followed in your senior Deputy Defence Ministry position — and you were present at Alex Gattmon's funeral 20 years later in 1981.

It was Shmuel Segev who first devoted an entire chapter to the 'Mural' story 25 years ago in his book, *Operation Yakhin* [1984 and a full chapter in *Maariv*, 20 April 1984]. His recent book, *Hakesher ha-Maroccani* ('The Moroccan Connection') covers this ground more fully, in chronicling a sequence of events in Israel's special relationship with Morocco from 1961, which had a dramatic aftermath 15 years later when Yitzaq Rabin flew to Morocco in October 1976 and Moshe Dayan followed him the next year. These fruitful contacts with King Hassan culminated in the historic Jerusalem visit of President Anwar as-Sadat to Jerusalem in November 1977. Unfortunately, Shmuel Segev could not join us as he is lecturing in Marrakesh on this newly revealed Israel-Morocco relationship.

Operation Mural succeeded "beyond all our expectations" — these were the words used by Alex Gattmon to me the very night before I left — mainly due to a simplified system of 'collective passports'. This 'feuille de route' method was first recommended to me — on the very day of my arrival in Casablanca — by the chief delegate of the League of Red Cross Societies in Morocco, A.E. Reinhard. Of course, he was only advising me with reference to "Swiss holidays" or convalescence for Moroccan children in general, but this proposed 'collective passport' system, which I then backed wholeheartedly — despite repeated counter-instructions from my superiors in Geneva — was also preferred by the Moroccan authorities as I soon learnt from senior officials in Rabat and Casablanca.

Finally, with Mossad backing for this special system, 530 Jewish children made their aliyah via Switzerland in summer 1961, soon followed by 100,000 more Jews — this time, entire families, via 'Operation Yakhin' [1962-64] — using this same method, under the cover of the HIAS organisation — but this time with the king's approval.

It is a symbolic testimony to these courageous children that Yamin Ouaknine, who reached Israel at seven, is here with us — Aluf-Mishne / Colonel Yamin Ka'anan.

Mr. President, allow me to quote from the prophet Jeremiah a pertinent passage:

"Behold I will bring them from the north country and gather them from the coasts of the earth, and with them the blind and the lame, the woman with child (. . .): a great company shall return thither. They shall come with weeping, and with supplications will I lead them (. . .) And there is hope in thine end, saith the Lord; that thy children shall come again to their own border" [31:8-9]

At this truly memorable moment, I also wish to state — in the presence of the distinguished Swiss Ambassador Walter Haffner — that this Moroccan page of Israel's heroic history occurred as a result of the diplomatic discretion of the Swiss authorities, who turned a blind eye to what might have become a potential exodus of Jewish children from Morocco to Israel via Switzerland, and implicitly accepted mass collective passport and Swiss visa facilities. This is now confirmed by the documents I received three months ago from the Federal Archives in Bern, thanks to the gracious initiative of the Tel Aviv Swiss Embassy.

Canford School, in Dorset, where I studied as a boy — while much preferring sports — had a Latin biblical logo motto under an oak tree: *Nisi Dominus Frustra / Without the Lord all is in vain*. I am tempted to add, regarding "Mural": *Nisi Helvetica Frustra* — since, without this positive Swiss attitude all would have been in vain for "Operation Mural", as with so many other humanitarian aliyah missions after Morocco's independence in 1956. This crucial green light in 1961 deserves full recognition as a page of Israel's history.

Yes, indeed, the ways of the Lord are often difficult to fathom. With this in mind, I now turn to our darling daughter Diana, who is very happy to be here with you, Mr President, and all of us today — especially with her parents, her artistic sister Ariane, her nieces, Tair — now in the army — Daphne and Kalia, and our dear friend Elizabeth Wider.

Without Diana's presence alongside her mother, I would never have remained in Morocco for 130 days. She also represented a solid asset to complete our Anglican 'cover'— a gorgeous, blue-eyed, blond baby. So again, I shall propose a last Latin motto: Nisi Diana Frustra — without Diana, all would have been in vain, and perhaps far worse. For 10 weeks she played a unique role, being a great joy and comfort for us as we lived our double family life in Casablanca. Here at Beth Hanassi, Diana would like to sing a delightful song she learnt 40 years ago soon after the Six-Day War.

With our fervent hopes for a future in the Middle East, in which "every man shall eat in safety under his own vine what he plants; and sing the merry songs of peace to all his neighbours", as Shakespeare wrote so eloquently. [King Henry VIII: Act III, v. 34]

I now call on Diana Littman to sing for His Excellency, the President of Israel, for the Swiss Ambassador, and for all of us, that blissful melody on the Eternal City of Jerusalem:

Yerushalayim-shel-zahav / Jerusalem of Gold.

Address by Ambassador Walter Haffner

```
Mr. President, Mr. & Mrs. Littman,
honored guests of this special gathering,
```

```
I first want to thank you from the bottom of my heart for
inviting me and making me a part of this private invitation at
the President's residence.
    I am truly touched by the documentary film "Operation Mural:
Casablanca, 1961" and by the story it tells. I am touched in
various ways.
    First of all I am touched by the bravery and the dedication
of the personalities, who made Operation Mural a success
beyond all expectations.
    David Littman, Shmuel Toledano, Carmit Gattmon, Gad Shahar,
Pinhas Katsir, Miriam Korshia and all the others, who cannot
be with us today, are a shining example of what individuals
can do for others, if they are guided by dedication, love and
bravery. People like you teach us a lesson in humanity.
    Secondly, as a father of four children, I am deeply touched
by the courage and dedication of the parents of these 530
children, who decided to send them on a dangerous journey to
Israel, not knowing if they would be able to join them in the
years to come.
    And thirdly, I am moved by the simple fact, that in 61, when
this operation was taking place, I was living the life of a
happy three year old child in Switzerland, having, of course,
no clue of what was going on in the world, and that at the same
time parents had to separate from their children, and that the
life and existence of those helping them were in danger.
    Mr President, Mr and Mrs Littman, distinguished guests,
during the terrible years, when Nazi Germany turned Europe
into a dark sea, Switzerland was an island in the middle of
this sea. An island or a boat.
    This boat, we know it all, was never full, and the Swiss
could have saved more Jewish refugees. This has to be and will
be part of our collective memory.
```

Fig. 90 Speech by the Swiss Ambassador Walter Haffner at President Peres' Residence at the private reception for Mr. & Mrs. Littman to commemorate Operation Mural, June 1, 2008

But to me, there is yet another important lesson to be learned.

It is the lesson, that in dark times, when authorities sometimes are over cautious and commit mistakes, individuals can still make a big difference.

Individuals like David Littman and everybody involved in Operation Mural, but individuals, also, like the 33 Swiss honored by Yad Vashem among the Just of the People for saving Jews during the Second World War.

As an Ambassador of Switzerland I also pay tribute to those in the Swiss administration, who turned a blind eye, as Mr. Littman rightly put it, to Operation Mural, implicitly understanding at a certain moment, that the true goal of the operation was not a vacation in Switzerland but emigration to Israel.

By issuing visas to some 500 children they contributed in their small way to the success of this wonderful operation.

While the main actors of Operation Mural — and I am happy and honoured to see many of those present — have my highest respect for their humanitarian mission, Ambassador Bernath and his colleagues in Switzerland and Morocco in the early sixties can also serve as a kind of role model for Swiss diplomats.

Thank you from the bottom of my heart for making me a part of this meeting. God bless you.

יקיר קהילת המודיעין

תעודת הוקרה והערכה ל:

דייוד ג' ליטמן

לוחם סתר אשר חרף נפשו
ותרם בכל מאודו לפעילות
חשאית למען מדינת ישראל

יו"ד הועדה   יו"ד העמותה

תא"ל (מיל') י' דסקל   מר אפרים הלוי

תשס"ט 2009

Fig. 91a Certificate of the Hero Of Silence Order from the Intelligence Heritage Community of the Mossad with its English translation

המרכז למורשת המודיעין (מל"מ) –
אתר הנצחה ממלכתי לחללי הקהילה (ע"ר)

"Hero of Silence" Order

An order of highest esteem and appreciation

Awarded to

Mr. David Gerald Littman

A clandestine warrior, who risked his life

And who served a sacred cause

Of the People and of the State of Israel

Yossi Daskal

Committee Chairman

Efraim Halevy

Chairman of the IICC

Maj. Gen. Aharon Yariv Blvd .P.O. Box 3555
Ramat Hasharon, 47134
Fax: 5497731-3-972 :פקס   Tel: 5497019-3-972 :טל

שד' אהרן יריב, ת"ד 3555
רמת השרון, 47134
mlm@intelligence.org.il   www.intelligence.org.il

Fig. 91b English translation of the Certificate of the Hero Of Silence Order from the Intelligence Heritage Community

Address by Efraim Halevy

Good evening David, Gisèle, veterans of the Mossad, veterans
who played a role in these Operations in Morocco, [the family]
Gattmon, Ronel, the family of David and Gisèle, and those
members of the MLM Intelligence Heritage Community, of the
Mossad. Guests, good evening,

The truth of the matter is that I think this occasion today
is unique. I cannot recall in the history of the MLM that
we ever held a separate ceremony for co-operation that took
place close to 50 years ago — 48 years ago. And this is an
operation like many other operations of the Mossad. It's very
difficult to find something similar, something comparative. It's
an operation which took place on the background of a crisis
which had its origin in the entire operation of bringing the
Jews out of Morocco. It was an operation which took place
at the time when tension in Morocco was rising, when the
Algerian-Moroccan war was beginning to take a very ominous
character. Within a couple of years of this operation, Morocco
was involved in a war with Algeria. As has now been published
[Shmuel Segev, *The Moroccan Connection*, preface by Efraim
Halevy (January, 2008)], Israel and Israelis played a role in
this war — far away from the shores of Israel — probably the
first time in the history of the State of Israel that Israel
began to function and to behave like a strategic power.
   But this operation related to the rescue of Jews, a
function which is unique in the history of the International
Intelligence Community. No other intelligence community —
no other intelligence organization in the world — has ever
been involved in rescue operations, mass rescue operations
of people, because basically the rescue of people, of masses
of people, of large numbers of peoples, contradicts the very
principle of intelligence activity, especially in enemy
country — especially in hostile environments. Normally, when
intelligence operations were carried out, it is essential, it

**Fig. 92 Verbatim transcript of the presentation by the Chairman of the MLM / I ICC – Head
of the Mossad 1998–2002, Mr. Efraim Halevy, recorded on July 1, 2009 at the Israel
Intelligence Heritage & Commemoration Center in Glilot**

is a rule that you do not expose yourself with your identity
to your environment. You don't make contacts, unnecessary
contacts with people around you. You certainly don't reveal
the nature of what your mission is — not only 10, 20, 50,
100, hundreds of people, but you don't reveal your mission to
anybody. When we come to rescue operations, you cannot operate
that way, you have to reveal your identity to people around
you, and when you're in enemy country you have to expose
yourself to hundreds of people at various points, at various
stages of your activities. This was the way it has been in
Iraq, this was the way it was in Morocco, this was the way it
was in Syria, and Iran, and Ethiopia, and in Sudan. And the
Israeli intelligence community operated for years in these
environments at great risk — at enormous risk for the people
involved in these operations. Moreover, we don't usually
recruit volunteers for these operations. Normally, these
operations were carried out by people who served in the Mossad
as intelligence officers, who had experience in intelligence
activities, who know how to create contacts, who know how
to use various types of equipment, who have a background,
and, who come from a family of activities which are directly
connected to the vision that they have to accomplish. In
the case of rescue operations, very often the people who
were recruited for these operations were not members of the
Mossad, were not officers of the Mossad, very often [they
were] volunteers. The risk in operating such an operation
was very great, it was a risk taken by the commander Sha..lon
[inaudible?] Mossad, but it was also a very, very grave risk
taken by the people who volunteered — and one such volunteer
was David Gerald Littman, who had no experience at all in
intelligence activities, who had no experience at all . . . in
. . . to the best of my knowledge — correct me if I'm wrong —
in private …[inaudible?] (laughter)

He had no kind of such activities in the school he went
to in Britain and he did not operate clandestinely on the
streets of London — to the best of my knowledge also . . .
his knowledge [inaudible?] (laughter). But, nevertheless,
when he came to Morocco he began to perform immediately like
a seasoned veteran of the [inaudible?] Mossad, creating
contacts, developing and cultivating contacts with key figures
and behaving in a manner which — had he wished to continue his
career in the Mossad — he could have come to Israel, become
a privileged member of the Mossad and not had to wait 48
years until his . . . [inaudible?] (laughter). But he choose
a different walk of life, together with his charming wife

Gisèle who was a part of this operation as you realised from
the short sequence movie that you have seen and who, to some
extent, maybe also deserves a credit, a partner to the award
we are giving today, but we decided to award the Award to
David — I think Gisèle agrees to that and I appreciate it . . .
[inaudible?] (laughter).

And I think that we have done something which is worthy and
very important, not only to them, but also to us. As people
who had taken ourselves the responsibility to do what we
can to preserve the heritage of the Mossad and the heritage
of the Intelligence Community as a whole, and to develop
and to maintain this Center as a center where hundreds of
thousands of children every year come and are exposed to
various activities of the intelligence community and where the
veterans meet to pass some time to speak about days gone by
and to feel a sense of pride, true pride, very, very dear and
sincere pride for the operations that have taken place over
the years.

I want to say something about the relations Israel had with
Morocco because one might believe that — given all that has
been published about the relations between Israel and Morocco,
and specifically the relations with the late King Hassan II
— one might have assumed, but wrongly, that there was little
danger of operating because, ultimately, there was a contact,
there was a line of communication with the sovereign, with the
man at the top — but supposedly, although we were operating in
a sense, in an environment, in an atmosphere of assurance.

Yes, there were connections with the King of Morocco… yes
there were, at that time as well with the King of Morocco…
but these relations were parallel relations and the truth
is not [inaudible?]. And I want this to be clear to you as
well — who are here this evening — that very often in the
history of the State of Israel we have been face with parallel
relations and we have operated to some extent in conflicting
ways and in conflicting lines of operation, maintaining the
relationships with the king — twice, maybe three times,
saving his sovereignty and saving his throne — and maybe more
times saving his throne without knowing it, or without him
knowing it — and at the same time conducting operations that
if the people were discovered, they would, indeed — as we've
seen in the movie — have faced very, very dire and serious
consequences.

There were other brave people who took part in these
operations — operatives of the Mossad who covered almost the
entire area of Morocco, who travelled far and wide, not only

in this operation, but in other operations over the years, who risked their lives, who risked their health and their future. And I believe this is also a moment in which we should recall the names of two people — Alex Gattmon and Efraim Ronel who had command positions at this particular time when David was operating.

I would like to end by saying this:

I believe that in awarding this award to David Gerald Littman, we are bestowing upon him a very, very distinct and a very, very unique honour. But, in his coming here, after so many years, to accept this award, I think he is bestowing something very unique upon us. The realisation, once again, of the solidarity of the people of Israel throughout the world is not an empty phrase. It's something very real, it's something very concrete and it's something which, in the end, continues an immense contribution to perpetuating the people of Israel and the State of Israel.

* * * * *

[After applause from over 200 present, the moderator invited Littman to come to the podium]

Address by David G. Littman

I am truly overwhelmed by what I have heard just now and wish
to express my profoundest thanks and deep gratitude to all
those in the MLM — the Israel Intelligence and Communications
Center — and particularly its Chairman Efraim Halevy and the
Head of the Committee of the 'Hero of Silence' Order, Brig.-
Gen. (res.) Joseph Daskal, for their decision to confer on me
this prestigious award and great honour for a humanitarian
mission in Morocco forty-eight years ago. We shall cherish
this precious moment forever.

On behalf of Gisèle, my one and only life companion; of
Ariane, our Israeli artist daughter, her children and our
grandchildren — 2nd Lt. Taïr, Daphnee and Kalia; and our
darling daughter Diana, who was with us in Casablanca as
a baby but could not join us today, I wish to express our
warmest thoughts and personal appreciation to you all. To our
relatives, to our dearest old and new friends, and to all of
you who have come to share with us this moving moment, here at
this unique Center — the symbol of Israel's determination and
inner strength.

Fifty years ago, almost to the day, a fellow student at the
London Institute of Archaeology left me only one choice: to
ask her to marry me. Barely two years earlier — after Nasser's
regime had created an intolerable situation for Egyptian
Jewry — she and her parents had been stateless refugees in
London. The rest is history, a particularly appropriate phrase
because Gisèle Orebi, whose grand-father had received the
title of Bey in 1908 from the Ottoman Sultan, was later to
become known worldwide as Bat Ye'or. It is nearly forty years
since the Daughter of the Nile began her pioneering research
on dhimmis and dhimmitude — both past and present. Since the
1980s she has written major studies which, despite opposition
from some academic and other circles, are regularly translated
into several languages, reprinted and considered as essential
reading in this field.

Why she accepted me as her "one and only" remains a mystery
for both of us, but it became a dream come true. I have always

Fig. 93 Address by D.G. Littman at the Israel Intelligence Heritage & Commemoration Center after being conferred the "Hero of Silence" Order, Glilot July 1, 2009

said that without Gisèle's presence and collaboration in Casablanca, while caring for Diana, I would probably have ended up in prison. The extraordinary thing was that she had the courage to remain by my side in an Arab country after fleeing Egypt. In fact, it was the birth of Diana that inspired her, a fervent Zionist, to do a good deed, a 'mitzva', for the Jewish people and for Israel. And that is why she agreed to join me in Morocco — despite her parents' opposition — aiding me for four months, even after she realised that she was expecting our second child, Ariane.

It is also fifty years since the famous Isser Harel, after visiting Morocco twice, became convinced that the Jews were ready to make aliyah en masse — as Ben Gurion and the early Zionist leaders had always envisioned. With Shmulik Toledano as his deputy for Diaspora Affairs, Harel appointed Efraim Ronel, based in Paris, as the head of the North African misgueret, and Alex Gattmon in Morocco, supported by his courageous wife Carmite, and also Gad Shahar and Pinhas Katsir who later became my two contacts. All praise is due to them for their remarkable achievements which have been officially recognised, and to Hubert and Miriam Korshia, and to all their colleagues in the network.

How wonderful that we are altogether again with our lifelong friends: Carmit, Shmulik, Gad, Pinhas — as well as Miriam and Tova, the widow of Efraim Ronel whom we met for the first time last year at the president's private reception.

This is a moment to pay homage to all those who have passed away: Alex Gattmon, Hubert Korshia, Isser Harel, Efraim Ronel, Moshe Kol and Naftali Bar-Giora, who I first met in Geneva three weeks after the 'Egoz' capsized with the tragic loss of 44 lives, half of them children; and sadly, only last month, Yehuda Dominitz, Naftali's Jewish Agency boss and deputy to Zalman Shragai, the head of Israel's Immigration Department. And a moment to remember as well Prof. Jacques Bloch, director of OSE-Suisse in Geneva, who helped save, via OSE-France, nearly 3000 Jewish children from deportation in Nazi-occupied France; and also those Swiss officials in Bern and Morocco who turned a blind eye to our 'holiday' project.

Remembrance and homage is due to those on the 'Egoz', and others, who lost their lives while dreaming of freedom, and also to all those unnamed and unsung members and volunteers of the misgueret in Morocco, nearly 200 youngsters, who dedicated themselves to the cause of North African Jewry in many dangerous operations — several of whom were tortured and one died soon after. I have vivid memories of their dedicated undercover work and I strongly recommend that their names and their stories be chronicled as pages in the early history of Israel's rebirth.

The story of Operation Mural was first recounted by Shmuel Segev in a full page 1984 article in *Maariv* and a chapter of his book. This led to a public recognition by President Chaim Herzog at an official presidential reception, followed in 1986 by the Mimouna award which Gisèle and I received in the Sachar Park in Jerusalem from the then Prime Minster Shimon Peres.

None of this would have happened without the initiative of Shmulik Toledano, a distinguished public figure and advisor in government and the Knesset over the years, a man deeply engaged in the Mossad at that early period. He had promised me that if ever our story could be told he would inform me.

After the tragic death of Alex Gattmon in 1981, an exceptional person, a decision was taken to allow a book to be written on a Mossad operation by which nearly 100,000 Moroccan Jews reached Israel under his mandate. Two years later, Shmulik put me in contact with Shmuel Segev, who was fascinated on reading my detailed 1962 Report. He decided then and there to add a chapter on the exodus of our 530 children in his book, Operation Yakhin, especially since no one had even mentioned it to him. Dear Shmuel let me express again my deep gratitude to you for your decision 25 years ago; without it, our children's Swiss holiday saga would have remained unknown.

Twenty years later, Meir Knafo generously decided that I should receive a special "Certificate of Recognition" at the 2004 Ashdod Day of Remembrance for Clandestine Networks of North Africa from Defence Minister General Shaul Mofaz. A warm welcome and reiterated thanks to Meir Knafo who is here tonight.

And last year, it was Shmulik who initiated that memorable private meeting with President Shimon Peres. We first met Shmulik forty-five years ago and I wish to express my warmest thoughts and deepest appreciation for all his constant efforts so that "Operation Mural" should receive the full recognition he felt it deserved.

*　*　*　*　*

I wish to say now a few words on the history of North African Jewry, which offers us a profound lesson in courage, perseverance and moral force, in spite of constant humiliation and discrimination that lasted well into the 20th century in Morocco. It only ended in 1912 with the French Protectorate, when the dhimmi system was abolished, whereby even the Chief Rabbi of Fez, Vidal Sarfaty, had to go barefoot on leaving the mellah as described in a 1911 document that I published in 1975.

I have written articles on the degrading dhimmi status of the Jews in Morocco over the centuries and am presently finishing a book on this subject with Professor Paul Fenton of the Sorbonne. This research has made me even more conscious of the courage and inner resistance of Moroccan Jewry, who remained determined to return to Zion, despite difficulties in leaving, and stringent restrictions in entering Ottoman Palestine.

After Israel's rebirth, about 92,000 Moroccan Jews made their aliyah before the gates were closed in 1956, soon after Morocco's independence. Clandestine departures continued, but somewhat haphazardly. Contacts by the Mossad with the new king's representatives were only beginning when I reached Casablanca on 16 March 1961, as delegate of an International children's organization [OSE], renamed OSSEAN.

Fortunately, Alex and Gad backed my determination on using a 'collective passport' system, which I knew the Moroccan authorities preferred, and thus 530 courageous children, some as young as seven, were able in this way to make their aliyah in five convoys between 26 June and 24 July 1961. "Operation Mural" was soon followed by "Operation Yakhin", whereby nearly 100,000 — entire families, the young and the old — reached Israel between 1962 and 1964, using the same agreed system of "collective passports", this time with the king's approval after negotiations with the Mossad.

The story of the courageous parents who entrusted up to four of their children to a non-Jewish organization, not knowing when they would ever see them again, has still to be told — and those who can best tell that story, and their own story, are the children themselves, some of whom are here with us today, having testified in the film to be shown soon: Yamin, Rosa, Yossi — and others here present today.

Allow me to welcome director Yehuda Kaveh, producer, Ronit Dor, Haim Oliel, musician, and cameraman Rami Lital — bravo for your professionalism in putting together such a fine documentary: "Operation Mural": Casablanca 1961. Shown twice on Channel 1, with a commentary by Efraim Halevy, it brought this story to the attention of the Israeli public and to thousands more worldwide, in a dozen festivals and on French Canadian TV, thanks to Michael Treves of JMT Films Distribution.

This is an exhilarating moment for the Littman family to be here at the MLM with you all, and for me to be honoured with the 'Hero of Silence' Order — almost 48 years after my precipitate departure from Casablanca & this three days prior to my 76th birthday on the 4th of July — and just two months before Gisèle and I will celebrate our golden wedding anniversary. Let me say, in very simple Hebrew, and with all my heart: Toda raba la Malam.

Looking back, I can truly say that the best decision I ever made in my life was to marry a very special Daughter of the Nile, and the second best was to volunteer to bring out Jewish children from Morocco to Israel, via Switzerland. Our Casablanca mission remains indelibly in our minds, as will this unforgettable moment here.

In conclusion, I wish to quote those inspiring words from the prophet Jeremiah: "Behold I will bring them from the north country and gather them from the coasts of the earth, and with them the blind and the lame, the woman with child (. . .): a great company shall return thither. They shall come with weeping, and with supplications will I lead them (. . .) And there is hope in thine end, saith the Lord; that thy children shall come again to their own border" [31:8-9].

Yes, the children of Israel have returned to "to their own border" — to the Land of Israel — and the long history of Moroccan Jewry is a special part of Israel's unique saga, achieved with much tears, pain, and suffering, but also with joy and hope, and great expectations over the ages.

*****

Appendix II
Lists of Children

The Five Convoys
(June–July 1961)

First Convoy

The first convoy with 127 Jewish Moroccan children left aboard the Greek ship *S.S. Ionia* sailing from Casablanca to Marseilles (France) on Monday June 26, 1961. The children arrived in Marseilles and from there left by bus for Morgins in the Swiss Valais.

One child, Amram Elbaz, at the bottom of the list has a star next to his name. Amram Elbaz was mentioned in a letter dated July 11, 1961 sent by Mr. J. Birchler, the Swiss Consul in Casablanca, to the Federal Police in Bern (see fig. 53). In his letter the Consul mentions that the boy Amram Elbaz, although listed on the first convoy in fact did not leave on June 26, 1961 because he was ill; instead he left on the second convoy (July 10, 1961). Sasportas Charles Simon, also listed on this first convoy must probably have left on the fourth convoy where his name is again mentioned. The children who left on June 26, 1961 were inscribed in four collective Moroccan passports except for Lisa and David Ohana who had individual passports (see fig. 47: letter from the Swiss Consul to the Federal Police in Bern, June 26, 1961). Aïda Schirmann alias N. Lehmann, OSSEAN's secretary-general, Dr. Claude Dreyfus and Michel Steuermann (director of the Home de la Forêt) accompanied this first convoy. On July 9, 1961 eighty-five children from this convoy left Morgins for Marseilles airport and were flown to Israel on an El Al plane. This reckless decision at the highest echelon could have compromised the whole mission.

Second Convoy

The second convoy with ninety-three children, registered on three collective passports, left Casablanca for Lyon (France) airport on a TAI "de-commercialised" and chartered plane on Monday July 10, 1961. The children then took buses from Lyon to Morgins.

David Barchechath from Mogador, age twelve, was one of the children who left on this convoy, together with his two brothers, Isaac and Nessim. His testimony was published in the article "A Thousand and One Nights" by Zvi Gilat, on May 9, 1986 in the Israeli newspaper *Hadashot*. The interview with Barchechath has been translated into English and appears in this book.

Aïda Schirmann, alias N. Lehmann, OSSEAN's secretary-general, arrived on July 8 and accompanied the children on this flight.

Third Convoy

The third convoy with eighty children left Casablanca for Lyon airport on a TAI (or UAT) "de-commercialised" and chartered plane on Monday July 19, 1961.

David Dahan (1947) from Mesfiona, although on the list did not leave on this convoy, instead he joined the fourth convoy. The eighty-one names on the list are thus reduced to eighty, which is the correct number of those who actually left on July 19, 1961.

Aïda Schirmann (N. Lehmann) who had arrived with the de-commercialised TAI plane on that same day, left with the eighty children on this flight.

Fourth Convoy

The fourth convoy with 147 children, registered on four collective passports, left Casablanca for Tangiers in five buses on Saturday July 22, 1961 and from there they sailed on the Pacquet line ship to Marseilles. One of the children called Isaac Fhima, was missing. Another boy who had come to say goodbye to a friend, upon hearing this name, stepped in saying that his name was David Fhima. That smiling boy left on this convoy under the name of Isaac Fhima, without any suitcase and without saying goodbye to his family. Joseph Sabbah, age twelve, today Yossi Shahar, left with this convoy and his testimony is published in this book. On this convoy was also a hunchback boy who had come on his own to register at the office, unscreened by the Misgeret; he had no deposit money yet D.G. Littman decided to let him go, thereby defying orders of selection he had received from his contacts in Geneva.

Miss Aïda Schirmann, Mr. Bruno Kern, Mrs. Runia Laski, Miss Andrée Guggenheim, and her friend Dr. Burgos accompanied the children on their journey to Marseilles. The ship anchored in Marseilles on July 25, 1961 and the children immediately re-embarked that same day for Israel aboard a ship that belonged to the national Israeli Zim line.

Fifth Convoy

The fifth convoy with eighty-three children left from Casablanca airport for Lyon on a TAI "de-commercialised" chartered plane on Monday July 24, 1961. D.G. Littman, code-name "Mural," left Casablanca on this plane under the excuse that no one had arrived with the incoming flight from Paris to accompany the children. A prearranged cable from N. Lehmann sent on July 17, 1961 was the official alibi for "Mural" to leave Casablanca with this last convoy; D.G. Littman was the only adult to escort the children (Fig. 57) The eighty-three children landed at Bron airport, outside of Lyon and left straight for Israel on a special El Al plane.

The present list is a preliminary list prepared before finalization; it contains sixty-eight names without places of birth or address. This preliminary list has fifteen names less than the final list with eighty-three names handed over by D.G. Littman to the Jewish Agency/Aliyah delegate at Lyon airport upon his arrival. Littman was reluctant to give it but he had no choice, he requested a copy to be sent to him for his records but he never received it.

OEUVRE SUISSE DE SECOURS

AUX ENFANTS DE L'AFRIQUE DU NORD.

SEXE	NOM	PRENOM	DATE ET LIEU DE NAISSANCE		DOMICILE
Masc	ABERGEL	ELIE	18/10/46	CASABLANCA	252, Rue des Anglais, Imp.6, Casablanca
"	"	BENJAMIN	7/ 1/49	"	" " " " " "
"	AMAR	HAIM	27/2/46	"	Hâb.El Hank, Bloc 3, Ap.46 "
"	"	SIMON	22/ 7/47	"	II, Rue Rachel "
Fem.	BARON	ESTHER	19/ 3/49	Marseille	chez M.Amar, 150, Avenue Mers-Sultan, "
"	BENBARUK	MARCELLE	14/9 /45	CASABLANCA	Hab.El Hank, bloc.3, Ap.34, Casablanca
"	"	ESTHER	24/ 7/49	"	" " " " " " "
Masc.	BENCHABAT	CHALOM	5/ 9/46	"	32, Rue Dar El Miloudi, "
"	"	MAKLOUF	1/ 1/49	"	" " " " " "
Fem.	BENESVY	ALIA	11/ 4/49	"	16, Rue des Anglais, Imp.4, Casablanca
Masc.	"	Isaac	20/ 6/50	"	" " " " " " "
Fem.	"	STELLA	24/ 1/52	"	" " " " " " "
Masc.	BENISTY	SALOMON	27/ 3/47	"	30, Rue Dar El Miloudi, Casablanca
"	BENSIMON	ISAAC	1946	AZZEMOUR	50, Rue des Anglais, Casablanca
"	"	ABRAHAM	6/ 6/48	"	" " " " "
"	"	JACOB	20/ 8/51	"	" " " " "
"	LITTON	DAVID	20/5/45	CASABLANCA	13, Rue Hoceria, Casablanca
"	"	SALOMON	9/ 4/47	"	" " " " "
Fem.	"	LUNA	30/ 4/49	"	" " " " "
Masc.	"	JOSEPH	16/ 8/46	"	58, Rue Dar El Miloudi, Casablanca
Fem.	"	Marie	14/ 9/48	"	" " " " " " "
"	"	SIMY	8/10/51	"	" " " " " " "
Masc	"	SALOMON	22/ 1/49	"	78, Rue Djamaâ Chleuh, "
"	"	SIMON AMRAM	22/ 5/51	"	" " " " " "
Fem.	BOUZAGLIO	RACHEL	11/11/47	"	10, Impasse El Miloudi, Casablanca
"	"	Jeanette	24/ 8/50	"	" " " " " "
"	BOUZAGLOU	ARETTE	30/ 4/47	"	12, Rue Méline, Casablanca
Masc.	"	PROSPER	11/ 5/51	"	" " " " " "
Fem.	CADOCHE	SYLVIA	2 / 5/47	"	63, Rue Jacquemin, Casablanca
Masc.	"	Armand-Joseph	1 / 6/48	"	" " " " "
Fem.	"	GILDA	7 /8/49	"	" " " " "
Masc.	CHAMT	NESSIM	5/ 5/45	TAHALA	69, Rue Moha ou Said, Casablanca
Fem.	CHRIQUI	CLOTILDE	17/10/49	RABAT	40, Rue de Mazagan, Casablanca
Masc.	"	Raphaël	13/ 3/46	CASABLANCA	" " " " "

Original (incomplete) list of names of the children sailing on the *S.S. Ionia* from Casablanca to Marseilles with the first convoy on Monday June 26, 1961

PAGE 2, Suite de la Liste

SEXE	NOM	PRENOM	DATE ET LIEU DE NAISSANCE		DOMICILE
Masc.	CHRIQUI	SIMON	30/ 4/50	Casablanca	40, Rue de Mazagan, Casablanca
"	"	ALBERT	25/ 8/51	"	" " " "
Fem.	COHEN	CHOCHANA(Senhat)	2/2/48	Berrechid	87, Rue Colbert "
"	"	Anette	4/ 7/51	"	" " " "
Masc.	DADOUH	DANIEL	I/ 7/46	Casablanca	24, Rue Worthington, Casablanca
"	"	Joseph	23/10/49	"	" " " "
"	"	Sion	22/ 8/52	"	" " " "
"	"	MESSOD	16/11/46	"	I7, Imp.I, Rue des Anglais, Casablanca
Fem.	"	BRORIA	16/12/48	"	" " " " " "
"	ELBAZ	ESTHER	en 1948	OULTAMA DEMNAT	40, Rue de Mazagan, Casablanca
Masc.	"	AMRAM	" 1951	" "	" " " "
Fem.	ELHARRAR	MAZAL	13/ 5/45	SETTAT	272 Bis, Rue Sidi Fatah, Casablanca
Masc.	"	Haim	13/ 4/46	"	" " " " " "
Fem.	"	YVONNE	en 1950	"	" " " " " "
Masc.	ELMALEH	CHARLES	24/12/46	CASABLANCA	66, Rue Gueroiaoui, Casablanca
"	"	SIMON	15/ 5/49	"	" " " "
"	"	DANIEL	8/ 2/52	"	" " " "
Fem.	"	VICTORIA	7/ 6/46	"	97, Rue des Synagogues, Casablanca
"	"	RENEE	18/ 5/48	"	" " " " "
"	"	YOTHA	24/12/48	"	63, Rue Dar El Miloudi, Casablanca
"	"	SOLA	18/ 8/50	"	" " " " "
Masc.	GABBAY	ISRAEL	2/12/44	"	II4, Impasse Dar El Miloudi, Casablanca
"	EZERZER	ARMAND	7/ 3/46	"	23, Impasse El Kerma, Casablanca
"	IFRAH	MIMOUN	3/ 4/45	"	I6, Rue Cap.Henri Ohayon, Casablanca
Fem.	"	Marie	25/ 5/49	"	" " " " " "
Masc.	"	Mardoché	25/3/5I	"	" " " " " "
"	KNAFOU	JOSEPH	4/12/45	"	Hab. El Hank, bloc 3, Appt.34, Casablanca
Fem.	"	JACQUELINE	7/2 /48	"	" " " " " " "
"	LAHIANY	RAYMONDE	I/12/47	"	Bld.Calmel, Bloc 4, Casablanca
Masc.	LOUSKI	DAVID	en 1948	"	56, Rue Sidi Regragui, Casablanca
"	LUGASSY	MESSAOUD	30/ 4/47	"	27, Rue Entre Jamâa, Casablanca
"	"	MAURICE	19/ 4/49	"	" " " " "
"	"	GABRIEL	I6/ 3/5I	"	" " " " "
Fem.	MALKA	ESTHER	28/2 /44	"	Hab. El Hank, bloc 3, Appt.35, Casablanca
"	"	RACHEL	20// /46	"	" " " " " " "
"	"	MARIE	7/II/47	"	" " " " " " "
"	"	MARIE	13/10/47	"	5I, Rue Centrale (Mellah), Casablanca
"	"	DENISE	23/10/49	"	" " " " "
"	"	ANNA	8/ 7/51	"	" " " " "

PAGE 3, Suite de la liste

SEXE	NOM	PRENOM	DATE ET LIEU DE NAISSANCE		DOMICILE
MASC.	MEDALSY	CHARLES	3 /II/47	Casablanca	Rue des Anglais,Imp.4, nO.I6,Casablanca
Fem.	MORYOUSSEF	MESSODI	en 1944	Settat	Hab. El Hank,bloc I2,Appt.2,Casablanca
Masc.	"	ABRAHAM	" 1946	"	" " " " " " " "
"	"	MESSAOUD	" 1949	"	" " " " " " " " "
Fem.	"	MARIE	15/IO/46	"	" " " " " 3 " 10 "
"	"	MESSODY	Mars 1959	Casablanca	" " " " " " " " "
Masc.	"	JUDAH	27/3/5I	"	" " " " " " " " "
Fem.	OHANA	THERESE	25/ 7/45	"	" " " " " 24 " I4 "
"	OHAYON	RACHEL	27/ 9/47	"	23,Rue du Hanam,Casablanca
Masc.	"	YEHICHE	I8/ 8/49	"	" " " " "
Fem.	"	ALIA	29/ 7/5I	"	" " " " "
Masc.	REVAH	SIMON	I8/ 2/49	"	Impasse Dalia,Rue Tbib,50,Casablanca
Fem.	"	SUZANNE	8/II/5I	"	" " " " " "
Masc.	SASPORTAS	CHARLES SIMON	5/I2/44	"	Rue Jean-Ja ques Roussou,22,Casablanca
"	"	MOISE	II/5/47	"	" " " " " "
"	SIBONI	HAIM	1946	ENTIFA(TANANT)	" de Marrakech,I20,Casablanca
"	"	SIMON	1949	" "	" " " " " "
"	SUISSA	DAVID	6/ 5/47	CASABLANCA	" des Coulanges,28,Casablanca
Fem.	"	TAMAR	9/ 4/48	"	" " " " " "
Masc.	"	ELIE	22/6/49	"	" " " " " "
Fem.	WAKRAT	JULIETTE	I6/IO/5I	"	Hab.El Hank,bloc 26,Appt.47,Casablanca
"	WAZANA	SOLICA	1948	"	Rue Jamâa Chleuh, Casablanca
"	ABERGEL	RACHEL	I/ 5/47	"	Rue Vignemale,9,Casablanca
Masc.	"	GABRIEL	I7/6/48	"	" " " "
Fem.	"	LOLA	I4/8/49	"	" " " "

Passeports individuels:

Fem.	OHANA	LISA	6/3 /45	"	" Cap.Henri Ohayon,Casablanca
Masc.	"	DAVID	IO/8/47	"	" " " " "

First Convoy: June 26, 1961

LAST NAME	FIRST NAME	SEX	DATE & PLACE BIRTH		ADDRESS (Casablanca)
ABERGEL	Rachel	F	5/1/1947	Casablanca	9 rue Vignemale
	Gabriel	M	6/17/1948	Casablanca	
	Lola	F	8/14/1949	Casablanca	
ABERGEL	Elie	M	10/18/1946	Casablanca	252 rue des Anglais, Impasse 6
	Benjamin	M	1/7/1949	Casablanca	
AMAR	Haim	M	2/27/1946	Casablanca	Hab. El Hank, Bloc 3, Appt. 46
AMAR	Simon	M	7/22/1947	Casablanca	11 rue Rachel
BANON	Esther	F	3/19/1949	Marseille	c/o M. Arnar, 150 av. Mers-Sultan
BENBARUK	Marcelle	F	9/14/1945	Casablanca	Hab. El Hank, Bloc 3, Appt. 34
	Esther	F	7/24/1949	Casablanca	
BENCHABAT	Chalom	M	9/5/1946	Casablanca	32 rue Dar El Miloudi
	Maklouf	M	1/1/1949	Casablanca	
BENESVY	Alia	F	4/11/1949	Casablanca	16 rue des Anglais, Impasse 4
	Isaac	M	6/20/1950	Casablanca	
	Stella	F	1/24/1952	Casablanca	
BEN HAIM	Charles	M	3/27/1945	Casablanca	48 bd. de la Gare AIN SEBAA
BENISTY	Salomon	M	3/27/1947	Casablanca	30 rue Dar El Miloudi
BENSIMON	Isaac	M	1946	Azzemour	50 rue des Anglais
	Abraham	M	6/6/1948	Azzemour	
	Jacob	M	8/20/1951	Azzemour	
BITTON	David	M	5/20/1945	Casablanca	13 rue Naceria
	Salomon	M	4/9/1947	Casablanca	
	Luna	F	4/30/1949	Casablanca	
BITTON	Joseph	M	8/16/1946	Casablanca	58 rue Dar El Miloudi
	Marie	F	9/14/1948	Casablanca	
	Simy	F	10/8/1951	Casablanca	
BITTON	Salomon	M	1/22/1949	Casablanca	78 rue Jamaâ Chleuh
	Simon Amram	M	5/22/1951	Casablanca	

LAST NAME	FIRST NAME	SEX	DATE & PLACE BIRTH		ADDRESS (Casablanca)
BOUZAGLIO	Rachel	F	11/11/1947	Casablanca	10 Impasse El Miloudi
	Jeanette	F	8/24/1950	Casablanca	
BOUZAGLOU	Annette	F	4/30/1947	Casablanca	12 rue Méline
	Prosper	M	5/11/1951	Casablanca	
CADOCHE	Sylvia	F	5/2/1947	Casablanca	63 rue Jacquemin
	Armand-Joseph	M	6/1/1948	Casablanca	
	Gilda	F	8/7/1949	Casablanca	
CHABAT	Nessim	M	5/5/1945	Tahala	69 rue Moha ou Said
CHETRIT	Alice	F	9/5/1946	Marrakech	43 rue Dar El Miloudi
	Jacques	M	2/1/1948	Marrakech	
	Deborah	F	11/15/1949	Marrakech	
	Sulamith	F	7/6/1951	Marrakech	
CHRIQUI	Raphaël	M	3/13/1946	Casablanca	40 rue de Mazagan
	Clotilde	F	10/17/1949	Rabat	
	Simon	M	4/30/1950	Casablanca	
	Albert	M	8/25/1951	Casablanca	
COHEN	Chochana (Sornhat)	F	2/2/1948	Berrechid	87 rue Colbert
	Anette	F	7/4/1951	Berrechid	
DADOUN	Daniel	M	7/1/1946	Casablanca	24 rue Worthington
	Joseph	M	10/23/1949	Casablanca	
	Sion	M	8/22/1952	Casablanca	
DADOUN	Messod	M	11/16/1946	Casablanca	17 rue des Anglais, impasse 1
	Broria	F	12/16/1948	Casablanca	
EDERY	Chalom	M	1944	Casablanca	78 rue de Marrakech
	Nissim	M	12/21/1949	Casablanca	
	Judah Pinhas	M	1/23/1952	Casablanca	
ELBAZ	Esther	F	1948	Oultama Demnat	40 rue de Mazagan
	Amram*	M	1951	Oultama Demnat	
ELHARRAR	Mazal	F	5/13/1945	Settat	272 bis rue Sidi Fatah
	Haim	M	4/13/1946	Settat	
	Yvonne	F	1950	Settat	
ELMALEH	Charles	M	12/24/1946	Casablanca	66 rue Gueroiaoui

LAST NAME	FIRST NAME	SEX	DATE & PLACE BIRTH		ADDRESS (Casablanca)
ELMALEH	Simon	M	5/15/1949	Casablanca	66 rue Gueroiaoui
	Daniel	M	2/8/1952	Casablanca	
ELMALEH	Victoria	F	6/7/1946	Casablanca	97 rue des Synagogues
	Renée	F	5/18/1948	Casablanca	
ELMALEH	Yotha	F	12/24/1948	Casablanca	63 rue Dar El Miloudi
	Sola	F	8/18/1950	Casablanca	
ELOUK	Fanny	F	1/17/1945	Casablanca	43 rue de Salé
	Viviane	F	12/7/1947	Casablanca	
	Simon	M	2/18/1950	Casablanca	
EZERZER	Armand	M	3/7/1946	Casablanca	23 Impasse El Kerma
EZERZER	Raphaël	M	5/4/1941	Casablanca	31 Impasse El Kerma
	Ziti	F	8/28/1951	Casablanca	
FHIMA	Yamine	F	12/2/1946	Casablanca	174 rue Dar El Miloudi
	Judah	M	6/15/1949	Casablanca	
GABBAY	Israel	M	12/2/1944	Casablanca	114 Impasse Der El Miloudi
HAMIAS	Hanna	F	11/18/1947	Casablanca	78 rue Jamaâ Chleuh
	Marcelle	F	2/17/1952	Casablanca	
IFRAH	Mimoun	M	4/3/1945	Casablanca	16 rue Cap. Henri Ohayon
	Marie	F	5/25/1949	Casablanca	
	Mardoché	M	3/25/1951	Casablanca	
KADOCHE	Moise	M	11/7/1946	Casablanca	11 rue Rachel
KNAFOU	Joseph	M	12/4/1945	Casablanca	Hab. El Hank, bloc 3, Appt. 34
	Jacqueline	F	2/7/1948	Casablanca	
LAHIANY	Raymonde	F	12/1/1947	Casablanca	Bd. Calmel, bloc 4
LOUSKI	David	M	1948	Casablanca	56 rue Sidi Regragui
LUGASSY	Messaoud	M	4/30/1947	Casablanca	27 rue Entre Jamaâ
	Maurice	M	4/19/1949	Casablanca	
	Gabriel	M	3/16/1951	Casablanca	
LUGASSY	Suzanne	F	10/12/1949	Casablanca	219 Bd. Tahar El Alaoui
	Liliane	F	5/28/1951	Casablanca	
	Fanny	F	1/20/1953	Casablanca	
MALKA	Esther	F	4/28/1944	Casablanca	Hab. El Hank, bloc 3, Appt. 35

LAST NAME	FIRST NAME	SEX	DATE & PLACE BIRTH		ADDRESS (Casablanca)
MALKA	Rachel	F	1946	Casablanca	Hab. El Hank, bloc 3, Appt. 35
	Marie	F	11/7/1947	Casablanca	
MALKA	Marie	F	10/13/1947	Casablanca	51 rue Centrale (Mellah)
	Denise	F	10/23/1949	Casablanca	
	Anna	F	7/9/1951	Casablanca	
MEDALSY	Charles	M	11/3/1947	Casablanca	16 rue des Anglais, Impasse 4
MORYOUSSEF	Messodi	F	1994	Settat	Hab. El Hank, bloc 12, Appt. 2
	Abraham	M	1946	Settat	
	Messouad	M	1949	Settat	
MORYOUSSEF	Marie	F	10/15/1946	Casablanca	Hab. El Hank, bloc 3, Appt. 10
	Messody	F	mars-49	Casablanca	
	Judah	M	3/27/1951	Casablanca	
MORYOUSSEF	David	M	7/7/1944	Casablanca	11 rue Sidi Embarek
	Rachel	F	7/6/1947	Casablanca	
OHANA	Thérèse	F	7/25/1945	Casablanca	Hab. El Hank, bloc 24, Appt. 14
OHAYON	Rachel	F	9/27/1947	Casablanca	23 rue du Hamam
	Yehiche	M	8/18/1949	Casablanca	
	Alia	F	7/29/1951	Casablanca	
OHAYON	Rachel Marie	F	8/4/1946	Casablanca	16 Impasse El Miloudi
REVAH	Suzanne	F	11/8/1951	Casablanca	50 rue Tbib, Impasse Dalia
	Simon	M	2/18/1949	Casablanca	
SASPORTAS	Charles Simon**	M	12/5/1944	Casablanca	22 rue Jean-Jacques Rousseau
	Moïse	M	5/11/1947	Casablanca	
SIBONI	Haim	M	1946	Entifa (Tanant)	120 rue de Marrakech
	Simon	M	1949	Entifa (Tanant)	
SIMONY	Hanania	F	1947	Casablanca	23 Bd. Lalla Yaccout
SOUSSAN	Raphaël	M	8/1/1944	Casablanca	170 rue El Miloudi
SUISSA	David	M	5/6/1947	Casablanca	28 rue des Coulanges
	Tamar	F	4/9/48	Casablanca	
	Elie	M	6/22/49	Casablanca	
SUISSA	Moise	M	3/1/1947	Casablanca	31 Impasse El Kerma
	Chalom	M	12/20/1948	Casablanca	

LAST NAME	FIRST NAME	SEX	DATE & PLACE BIRTH		ADDRESS (Casablanca)
SUISSA	Hélène	F	6/14/1950	Casablanca	31 Impasse El Kerma
WAKRAT	Juliette	F	10/16/1951	Casablanca	Hab. El Hank, bloc 26, Appt. 47
WAZANA	Solica	F	1948	Casablanca	Rue Jamaâ Chleuh
ZRIHEN	Abraham	M	1/6/1950	Casablanca	78 Bab Harrakech

INDIVIDUAL PASSPORTS

OHANA	Lisa	F	3/6/1945	Casablanca	Rue Cap. Henri Ohayon
	David	M	8/10/1947	Casablanca	

Second Convoy: July 10, 1961

LAST NAME	FIRST NAME	SEX	DATE & PLACE BIRTH		ADDRESS (Casablanca)
ABERGEL	Hanna	F	1945	Casablanca	8 impasse Hebacha, R. Sidi Fatah
ABITTAN	Joseph	M	30-10-46	Casablanca	50 rue des Anglais
ABITTAN	Solange	F	2-8-47	Casablanca	14 rue du Consulat d'Espagne
	Samy	M	14-8-49	Casablanca	
AKIBA	Joseph	M	17-5-46	Casablanca	122 Derb El Haddaoui
	Haim	M	15-2-49	Casablanca	
AMAR	Gabriel	M	3-9-49	Casablanca	191 bd d'Alsace
	Max	M	31-7-51	Casablanca	
AMAR	Rachel	F	5-12-45	Casablanca	9 rue des Anglais, impasse 2
	Rosa	F	9-8-48	Casablanca	
AMZALLAG	Maklouf	M	11-9-50	Casablanca	9 rue de la Marine
AMZALLAG	Zohra	F	12-1-44	Casablanca	31 rue Saint Brix (Bourgogne)
	Amram	M	10-1-48	Casablanca	
ARZOUANE	Rachel	F	21-7-44	Casablanca	37 rue Guerrouaoui
	Isaac	M	3-1-47	Casablanca	
	Titi	F	1-1-49	Casablanca	
	David	M	17-1-51	Casablanca	
AYACHE	Rachel	F	8-5-46	Casablanca	80 rue des Anglais, impasse 6
	Michael	M	12-4-49	Casablanca	
BARCHECHATH	Nessim	M	26-12-45	Mogador	Rue Moha ou Said, impasse Dahlia 138
	Isaac	M	11-3-48	Mogador	
	David	M	24-7-49	Mogador	
BENZECRI	Rachel	F	1947	Tiznit	20 rue du Hammam
	Albert	M	1949	Tiznit	
BITTON	David	M	17-2-47	Casablanca	235 rue Jamaâ Chleuh
	Fanny	F	3-2-49	Casablanca	
	Albert	M	20-8-50	Casablanca	
BITTON	Liahou	M	19-12-50	Casablanca	13 rue Nacéria, 2 étage

LAST NAME	FIRST NAME	SEX	DATE & PLACE BIRTH		ADDRESS (Casablanca)
COHEN	Jacob	M	23-9-47	Imintanout	30 rue du Hammam
	Hanina	F	1949	Imintanout	
	Fiby	F	20-9-50	Imintanout	
COHEN	Victor	M	5-4-46	Casablanca	11 rue des Chleuh
DAHAN	Simy	F	28-5-47	Casablanca	78 rue de Marrakech
	Raphaël	M	3-6-49	Casablanca	
	David	M	12-6-45	Casablanca	
EDERY	Abighaël	F	11-7-47	Casablanca	169 rue des Anglais
	Amram	M	11-4-48	Casablanca	
EDERY	David	M	24-10-49	Casablanca	60 rue de Safi
	Freha	F	1951	Casablanca	
ELBAZ	Amram	M	26-11-45	Oultama Demnat	40 rue de Hazagan
ELKAIM	Perla	F	31-1-48	Casablanca	6 Impasse des Tolbas
	Haim	M	26-10-45	Casablanca	
ELMALEM	Jacqueline	F	6-7-50	Casablanca	10 rue Sidi Embarah
	Judah	M	19-2-47	Casablanca	
GABBAY	Amram	M	21-1-46	Casablanca	Rue Hauche, c/o Amar, Cinéma Lynx
GABBAY	Haim	M	26-10-48	Casablanca	Bd. Abdella ben Hohamed, bloc 4
	Rosa	F	14-7-47	Casablanca	Ex. Boulevard Calmel
HAZAN	Alice	F	28-10-48	Casablanca	155 rue de l'Horloge
	Juliette	F	4-1-50	Casablanca	
	Fanny	F	22-2-49	Casablanca	
IFERGAN	Rosa	F	22-6-51	Casablanca	308 rue Jamaâ Chleuh
	Raphaël	M		Casablanca	
IFRAH	Solange	F	22-11-50	Casablanca	16 rue Cap. Henri Ohayon
	Elie	M	17-12-49	Casablanca	
	Jacob	M	10-9-51	Casablanca	
KAKONE	Jacqueline	F	25-1-48	Casablanca	287 rue Sidi Fatah
	Sylvia	F	6-8-50	Casablanca	
LAHIANY	Salomon	M	2-7-45	Casablanca	Bd. Calmel, bloc 4

LAST NAME	FIRST NAME	SEX	DATE & PLACE BIRTH		ADDRESS (Casablanca)
LEVY	Jacqueline	F	25-12-44	Casablanca	5 rue Abd Al Chrim Diouri
	Florie	F	8-8-46	Casablanca	
	Haim	M	10-6-49	Casablanca	
	Salomon	M	23-7-51	Casablanca	
LEZMI	Saadia	F	13-8-47	Casablanca	219 bd. Tahar El Alaoui
	Fortunee	F	23-12-49	Casablanca	
	Samy	M	2-12-51	Casablanca	
MOUYAL	Jacqueline	F	4-5-48	Casablanca	C1 Rue Jamaâ
					Impasse El Medra 2
	Sarah	F	21-1-51	Casablanca	
OHAYON	Joseph	M	25-5-45	Casablanca	78 rue de Marrakech
OHAYON	Saada	F	9-7-46	Casablanca	3 rue des Anglais, Impasse 1
	Marcelle	F	1949	Casablanca	
	Gotta	F	24-1-48	Casablanca	
OHAYON-BENDAVID	Joseph	M	29-8-48	Casablanca	50 rue Dar El Miloudi
	Abraham	M	26-7-50	Casablanca	
	Thérèse	F	4-6-52	Casablanca	
OUANONOU	Elie	M	6-2-48	Casablanca	6 rue Sarah Bernhard
	Berto	M	9-4-49	Casablanca	
PORTAL	Emile	M	28-5-45	Casablanca	118 rue Dar El Miloudi
PEREZ	Naim	M	28-11-46	Casablanca	46 rue Sidi Regragui
	Aaron	M	4-3-49	Casablanca	
	Meyer	M	25-10-51	Casablanca	
	Simy	F	1948	Casablanca	
PEREZ	Jacqueline	F	10-6-45	Casablanca	58 rue des Anglais
	David	M	13-2-47	Casablanca	
	Rachel	F	21-1-49	Casablanca	
	Amram	M	10-11-50	Casablanca	
RBIBO	Liliane	F	13-7-45	Casablanca	El Hank, bloc 3, Appt. 26
	Prosper-Simon	M	8-11-46	Casablanca	
	Maurice	M	20-10-48	Casablanca	

LAST NAME	FIRST NAME	SEX	DATE & PLACE BIRTH		ADDRESS (Casablanca)
RBIBO	Salomon	M	26-11-49	Casablanca	El Hank, bloc 3, Appt. 26
SIBONY	Haim	M	1946	Casablanca	120 rue de Marrakech
	Simon	M	1949	Casablanca	
SUISSA	Jacob	M	18-1-46	Casablanca	206 rue Tahar El Alaoui, impasse Bas
	Elie	M	11-12-48	Casablanca	

Third Convoy: July 19, 1961

LAST NAME	FIRST NAME	SEX	DATE & PLACE BIRTH		ADDRESS (Casablanca)
ABERGEL	Aziza	F	19-4-44	Casablanca	66 rue Goulmima, impasse 4
	Tamar	F	21-2-48	Casablanca	
ABISROR	Naphtalie	F	1947	Casablanca	28 rue de Salé
ABITAN	Charles	M	15-5-44	Casablanca	3 rue de Mogador
ABIZIZ	Tamar	F	16-12-49	Casablanca	34 rue du Four
ASSOULINE	Yvette	F	23-3-46	Casablanca	41 rue Cuvier
	Salomon	M	5-11-48	Casablanca	
	Elie	M	23-1-51	Casablanca	
AZOULAN	Mardockhai	M	1945	Imadiden-Zaliouine	112 rue des Anglais, Impasse 5
	Rachel	F	1947	Imadiden-Zaliouine	
BENBARUK	Liliane	F	12-4-49	Casablanca	El Hank, bloc municipal
	Sylvia	F	10-4-50	Casablanca	
	Monique	F	22-1-52	Casablanca	
BENDAVID	Simon	M	23-6-45	Casablanca	El Hank, bloc 6, appt. 10
	Marcelle	F	26-1-47	Casablanca	
	Jacob	M	20-9-48	Casablanca	
	Albert	M	2-4-50	Casablanca	
BENHAYON	Zébolan	M	10-9-46	Casablanca	14 rue de la Mer
	Elie	M	30-1-49	Casablanca	
	Françoise	F	4-7-50	Casablanca	
BENSADOUR	David	M	4-4-44	Casablanca	17 rue des Anglais, impasse 2
	Rachel	F	20-8-48	Casablanca	
BITTON	Bloria	F	22-3-49	Casablanca	72 rue des Chleuh
BITTON	Marie	F	1949	Casablanca	12 rue de Rabat
	Lisa	F	1950	Casablanca	
	Salomon-Joseph	M	17-8-52	Casablanca	
BOHBOT	Lidicia	F	18-9-45	Casablanca	4 rue du Lieut. Roger Farache
BOHBOT	Fiby	F	24-11-50	Casablanca	4 rue du Lieut. Roger Farache
DAHAN	Salom	M	1945	Ben Ahmed (Chaouia)	10 rue des Anglais, impasse 6

LAST NAME	FIRST NAME	SEX	DATE & PLACE BIRTH		ADDRESS (Casablanca)
DAHAN	Ruth	F	1947	Ben Ahmed (Chaouia)	10 rue des Anglais, impasse 6
	Joseph	M	1948	Ben Ahmed (Chaouia)	
DAHAN	Aicha	F	1948	Mesfiona	10 rue Sidi Mbarek
	Orvida	F	1950	Mesfiona	
	David	M	1947	Mesfiona	
DAHAN	Nicole	F	18-4-46	Casablanca	19 rue d'Artois
	Madeleine	F	27-8-47	Casablanca	
	Richard	M	3-4-49	Casablanca	
EDERY	Salomon	M	31-8-46	Casablanca	17 rue du Hammam
EDERY	Michel-Prosper	M	14-9-46	Casablanca	7 bd. Jeoffroy
	Nissim-Jacques	M	24-3-48	Casablanca	
	Albert-David	M	4-7-50	Casablanca	
EHARAR	Sultana	F	1949	Casablanca	El Hank, bloc 5, appt. 5
	Joseph	M	1951	Casablanca	
ELKAIM	Chalom	M	11-3-44	Casablanca	79 bd.de Bordeaux
	David	M	29-3-48	Casablanca	
	Simi	F	31-12-49	Casablanca	
ELMALEH	Gisette	F	27-7-49	Casablanca	Rue du Cap H. Ohayon
	Annette	F	10-10-48	Casablanca	
ETTEDOUI	Maurice	M	20-4-52	Casablanca	27 rue Seguin
HAZAN	Albert	M	16-3-47	Casablanca	9 rue Sidi Mbarek
HAZAN	Yechoua	M	Jun-49	Imadiden-Zaliouine	31 rue Sidi Regragui
	Messoda	F	Apr-48	Imadiden-Zaliouine	
ILLOUZ	Joseph	M	26-9-46	Casablanca	El Hank, bloc municipal, appt. 25
LEVY	Marie	F	7-5-49	Casablanca	196 rue Jamaâ Chleuh
LEVY	Saada	F	12-5-46	Casablanca	510 rue Goulmima, appt. 2
	Fortunée	F	2-7-49	Casablanca	
	Meyer	M	5-10-50	Casablanca	
MEDINA	Fanny	F	10-3-46	Casablanca	15 rue du Cap. H. Ohayon
	Albert	M	4-10-47	Casablanca	
	Yvonne	F	9-7-50	Casablanca	
MERRAN	Salomon	M	1-11-47	Casablanca	39 Impasse El Kerma

LAST NAME	FIRST NAME	SEX	DATE & PLACE BIRTH		ADDRESS (Casablanca)
MORENO-HALEVY	David	M	24-3-44	Fès	Rue d'Ajjaccio
	Suzanne	F	1-7-46	Fès	
	Armand	M	28-1-50	Casablanca	
OHAYON	Suzanne	F	31-5-48	Casablanca	28bis rue El Miloudi
	Rachel	F	24-1-50	Casablanca	
OUAKNINE	Raphaël	M	3-6-47	Casablanca	14 rue Maréchal Fayolle
	Simy	F	18-12-47	Casablanca	
OUAKNINE	Yahia	M	7-1-46	Casablanca	69 rue Moha ou Said
OUANONOU	Salomon	M	25-5-46	Casablanca	El Hank, bloc municipal
	Nissim	M	10-12-49	Casablanca	
	Meyer	M	17-6-51	Casablanca	
PEREZ	Khalifa	F	7-10-48	Casablanca	98 rue de Mogador
	Albert	M	5-10-50	Casablanca	
	Rachel	F		Casablanca	
PEREZ	Dina	F	12-12-45	Casablanca	41 rue Sidi Regragui
PORTAL	Simy	F	1946	Rahhala Tafingoult	19 rue de Marrakech
ZOHAR	Maklouf	M	25-1-45	Casablanca	38 Impasse El Hebacha
ZRIHEM	Raymonde	F	31-1-48	Casablanca	Bd. Calmel, Bloc 4
ZUANONOU	Simy-Simone	F	1-1-47	Casablanca	2 rue Rachel
	David	M	5-4-49	Casablanca	

Fourth Convoy: July 22, 1961

LAST NAME	FIRST NAME	SEX	DATE & PLACE BIRTH		ADDRESS (Casablanca)
ABERGEL	Berouria	F	10-2-45	Marrakech	168 rue Jamaâ Chleuh
	Suzanne	F	10-3-47	Marrakech	
	Sepoura	F	22-9-49	Marrakech	
ABITBOL	Baruk	M	15-2-43	El Jadida	34 rue du Hammam
ABITBOL	Hassiba	F	31-7-47	Casablanca	14 rue Worthington
ABITBOL	Meyer	M	9-3-43	Casablanca	298 bd. Mohammed
	Salomon	M	19-6-47	Casablanca	
AFLALO	Isaac	M	29-9-44	Casablanca	20 rue Hammam
AMAR	Isaac-Chalom	M	30-5-51	Casablanca	40 rue Edjeimal
	Paulette	F	7-6-52	Casablanca	
AMAR	Jacqueline	F	15-9-46	Casablanca	62 bd. Moulay Youssef
	Albert	M	2-10-48	Casablanca	
ASSOE	Malia	F	12-1-45	Casablanca	35 rue Macon
	David	M	29-9-45	Casablanca	
	Victoria	F	29-5-51	Casablanca	
ASSOULINE	Baruk	M	22-3-44	Casablanca	32 rue Hammam
	Nissim	M	28-10-48	Casablanca	
BENHAMOU	Fiby	F	1947	Marrakech	41b rue Aoudja
	Annette	F	1948	Marrakech	
BENISTY	Raymonde	F	11-10-49	Casablanca	7 bd. Mohammed V
	Rachel	F	20-12-46	Casablanca	
BENSIMON	Camille	F	28-2-48	Rabat	51 rue J. Cartier
	Janine	F	23-5-50	Rabat	
	Suissa	F	16-1-52	Rabat	
BENSIMON	Henri	M	28-12-48	El Jadida	Bd. Calmel, bloc 8
	Joseph	M	17-12-50	El Jadida	
BENZAQUEN	Maurice	M	25-6-45	Casablanca	99 bd. d'Anfa
	Jacques	M	26-10-47	Casablanca	
	Daniel	M	13-4-50	Casablanca	

LAST NAME	FIRST NAME	SEX	DATE & PLACE BIRTH		ADDRESS (Casablanca)
BOUSKILA	Moise	M	15-12-46	Casablanca	13 rue de Bourgogne
	Meyer	M	1-9-48	Casablanca	
CABESSA	David	M	17-12-45	Casablanca	28 rue de Bourg
COHEN	Evelyne	F	12-5-51	Casablanca	1 rue du Sol. André Ahmed
COHEN	Jacqueline	F	21-3-53	Casablanca	86 rue de Briey
COHEN	Raphaël	M	5-6-47	Casablanca	190 rue Jamaâ Chleuh
COHEN	Renée	F	27-12-47	Casablanca	4 rue Mauret
	Sol	M	26-1-49	Casablanca	
	Simon	M	13-3-50	Casablanca	
DAHAN	David	M	1947	Mesfiona	10 rue Sidi Embarek
DRAY	David	M	1948	Au Guich	20 rue Hammam
	Meyer	M	1950	Au Guich	
EDERY	Anna	F	2-12-44	Casablanca	60 bis rue Safi
EDERY	David	M	1946	Casablanca	16 rue du Hammam
	Amram	M	1950	Casablanca	
EDERY	Haim	M	1-8-47	Casablanca	13 rue du Commissaire Ladeui
	Moise	M	9-11-49	Casablanca	
EDERY	Jacob-Sion	M	24-7-50	Casablanca	10 rue des Anglais, impasse 6
EDERY	Joseph	M	27-12-44	Casablanca	49 rue Jamaâ Chleuh
ELBAZ	Isaac	M	28-6-48	Casablanca	13 rue du Jardin Ftieh
	David	M	8-7-50	Casablanca	
ELMALEH	Jacqueline	F	Jan-49	Casablanca	236 rue Jamaâ Chleuh
	Salomon	M	Oct-51	Casablanca	
	Flory	F	1950	Casablanca	
ELMALEH	Mardochée	M	26-9-48	Marrakech	132 Av. Moinier
ELMKIES	Simy	F	1950	Aît-Tididi	106 rue des Anglais, impasse 6
EZERZER	Alice	F	5-7-50	Casablanca	492 rue de Goulmina
	Monique	F	23-4-46	Casablanca	
	David	M	26-5-48	Casablanca	
FHIMA	Meyer	M	8-2-46	Casablanca	105 bd. Moulay Youssef
	Isaac	M	13-10-48	Casablanca	
HACHUEL	Chalom	M	10-5-45	Casablanca	34 rue Ferd. De Lesseps

LAST NAME	FIRST NAME	SEX	DATE & PLACE BIRTH		ADDRESS (Casablanca)
LEVY	Denise	F	1951	Casablanca	45 rue Musée
	Haim	M	1950	Casablanca	
	Jeanette	F	1945	Casablanca	
	Rachel	F	1948	Casablanca	
LIBRATY	David	M	11-10-44	Casablanca	El Hank, bloc 3, appt. 39
	Rebecca	F	1-11-49	Casablanca	
	Daniel	M	7-6-51	Casablanca	
MALKA	David	M	5-9-48	Casablanca	6 rue des Anglais
MELLUL	Raphaël	M	1-4-45	Casablanca	6 rue Sarah Bernhard
	Saoulange	F	26-3-47	Casablanca	
	Simy	F	18-1-49	Casablanca	
	Messody	M	5-3-51	Casablanca	
OHAYON	Salomon	M	12-1-45	Casablanca	28 rue du Cimetière
OHNONA	Liliane	F	28-1-47	Casablanca	6 rue Sarah Bernhard
	Moise	M	26-1-49	Casablanca	
	Maxime	M	26-12-50	Casablanca	
OHNANA	Solange	F	2-1-46	Casablanca	31 rue de Libourne
	Elise	F	28-12-47	Casablanca	
	Jacob-Henri	M	25-11-49	Casablanca	
OSSADON	Nissim	M	30-3-52	Casablanca	36 rue Sidi M'Barek
	Isaac	M		Casablanca	
OUAKNINE	Abraham	M	19-5-48	Casablanca	28 rue Hamman
	Yamine	M	24-9-52	Casablanca	
	Fréha	F	11/45	Casablanca	
OUAKNINE	Eliahou	M	21-6-47	Casablanca	3 rue des Chleuhs
	Raphaël	M	11-2-50	Casablanca	
OUTEGUERGOUST	Emmanuel	M	15-9-46	Casablanca	270 rue Jamâa Chleuh
	Habiba	F	29-3-49	Casablanca	
PEREZ	Abraham	M	28-5-47	Casablanca	11 rue Maréchal Fayolle
	Rosa	F	1-7-49	Casablanca	
PEREZ	Sulamite	F	2-7-50	Casablanca	Bab El Hank, bloc 2, appt. 40
	Sylvia	F	27-9-51	Casablanca	

LAST NAME	FIRST NAME	SEX	DATE & PLACE BIRTH		ADDRESS (Casablanca)
PEREZ	Perla	F	17-8-47	Casablanca	Rab El Hank, Blc 2, appt. 40
PEREZ	Gaby	M	8-11-48	Casablanca	348 rue Jamaâ Chleuh
	Marcelle	F	31-8-50	Casablanca	
	Hélène	F	1-5-52	Casablanca	
PEREZ	Hélène-Pénina	F	2-8-51	Casablanca	9 rue de l'atelier
	Jacqueline	F	17-4-49	Casablanca	
	Charles	M	29-1-47	Casablanca	
PEREZ	Perla	F	1950	Casablanca	262 rue Sidi Fatah
PORTAL	Charles	M	28-6-47	Casablanca	118 Dar el Miloudi
PORTAL	Aziza	F	13-8-51	Casablanca	32 rue El Hadjajmâa
	Nissim	M	13-12-46	Casablanca	
	Isaac	M	21-5-49	Casablanca	
REVAH	Raphaël	M	21-5-48	Casablanca	15 rue du Cap. H. Ohayon
	Moise	M	1-11-50	Casablanca	
ROSILIO	Albert	M	15-5-50	Casablanca	20 rue Fayolle
RUIMY	Aaron-Nissim	M	1944	El Jadida	20 rue du Hammam
SABBAH	Messod	M	21-4-48	Casablanca	20 rue Miloudi
SABBAH	Joseph	M	11-10-49	Casablanca	348 rue Djamaâ Chleuh
SASPORTAS	Charles Simon	M	5-12-44	Casablanca	22 rue Jean-Jacques Rousseau
SAYA	Rachel	F	1-1-51	Fès	335 rue Ziraoui
	Haciba	F	27-6-46	Fès	
SEBBAG	Hassiba	F	14-1-47	Casablanca	191 rue Jamaâ Chleuh
	Salomon	M	1949	Casablanca	
SERFATY	Hélène	F	1-7-47	Casablanca	12 bd d'Anfa
	Josiane	F	26-9-46	Casablanca	
SOUSSAN	Maklouf	M	15-8-47	Casablanca	27 rue Seguin
SOUSSANA	Raphaël	M	10-3-45	Casablanca	119 bd. Moulay-Youssef
	Flora	F	8-8-52	Casablanca	
	Aicha-Zora	F	3-4-46	Casablanca	
	Jacob	M	3-5-49	Casablanca	
SUISSA	Laurette	F	11-3-47	Casablanca	4 rue des Anglais, impasse 6
SUISSA	Elie	M	12-10-45	Casablanca	114 Dar El Miloudi

LAST NAME	FIRST NAME	SEX	DATE & PLACE BIRTH		ADDRESS (Casablanca)
SUISSA	Samuel	M	24-10-44	Casablanca	14 rue Cap. Hen Oyahom
SUISSA	Joseph Chalom	M	19-6-48	Casablanca	22 rue Lusitania
TORDJMAN	Meyer	M	15-4-45	Casablanca	3 rue de Mogador
TORDJMAN	Marie	F	29-7-50	Casablanca	49 rue du Com. Provost
WEIZMANN	Daniel	M	9-12-50	Casablanca	48 rue Guerrouaoui
	Isaac	M	18-12-47	Casablanca	
	Thérèse	F	24-3-49	Casablanca	
WIZMAN	Simy	F	22-3-51	Casablanca	24 rue de Mogador
	Simon	M	16-10-45	Casablanca	
	Victoria	F	20-5-49	Casablanca	
WIZMAN	Simy	F	13-4-45	Casablanca	39 rue Sidi Regragui
	Joseph	M	7-10-47	Casablanca	
	Haim	M	31-12-49	Casablanca	
WIZMAN	Eliahou	M	17-1-47	Casablanca	28 rue des Anglais, Impasse 13
	Ziti	F	2-5-49	Casablanca	
ZAFRANI	Simy	F	Oct-44	Essaouira	88 Impasse El Miloudi
	Berouria	F	19-6-47	Essaouira	
	Etoile	F	20-8-51	Mogador	
ZNATI	Haim	M	1944	Ouezzane	70 rue des Anglais, Impasse 5
ZRIHEN	Raymonde	F	29-7-46	Marrakech	49 rue Ferd. De Lesseps
	Thérèse	F	1948	Marrakech	
	David	M	1951	Marrakech	

Fifth Convoy: July 24, 1961

LAST NAME	FIRST NAME	SEX	DATE & PLACE BIRTH		ADDRESS (Casablanca)
AMIEL	Albert	M	14-10-44	?	?
AMZALLAG	Moshe	M	4-10-45	?	?
AMZALLAG	Solange	F	1949	?	?
AZOULAY	Mordechai	M	10-2-47	?	?
AZOULAY	Rachel	F	24-10-47	?	?
AZOULAY	Eliane	F	29-7-46	?	?
AZOULAY	Ninette	F	8-8-48	?	?
BARBIBAI	Tamar	F	6-5-50	?	?
BARBIBAI	Suzanne	F	26-10-48	?	?
BARKALIFA	Makhlouf	M	15-10-46	?	?
BARKALIFA	Marie	F	30-7-51	?	?
BARKALIFA	Jacote	F	16-1-44	?	?
BENACHA	Zora	F	1-9-45	?	?
BENCHETON	Mercedes	F	14-10-44	?	?
BENCHETON	Joseph	M	5-4-41	?	?
BENCHETON	Chalom	M	16-4-49	?	?
BENSAADOUN	Simon	M	4-4-44	?	?
BENSAADOUN	Rachel	F	24-9-48	?	?
BENSIMON	Haim	M	23-6-47	?	?
BENSIMON	Huguette	F	2-12-49	?	?
BITTON	Messody	F	10-3-45	?	?
DAHAN	Jacob	M	8-6-46	?	?
ELFASSY	Prosper	M	22-1-48	?	?
ELFASSY	Robert	M	27-9-50	?	?
ELMALEH	Simon	M	1-1-45	?	?
ELMALEM	Alice	F	28-4-47	?	?
ELMALEH	Renée	F	23-3-49	?	?
ELMALEH	Messody	F	21-7-51	?	?
EZERZER	Viviane	F	13-9-46	?	?

LAST NAME	FIRST NAME	SEX	DATE & PLACE BIRTH		ADDRESS (Casablanca)
EZERZER	Flora	F	20-5-49	?	?
EZERZER	Sylvia	F	7-1-51	?	?
EZERZER	Maxime	M	24-12-51	?	?
HAYOT	Albert	M	3-10-44	?	?
HAYOT	Liliane	F	14-12-46	?	?
HAYOT	Amram	M	7-3-49	?	?
HAYOT	Tsipora	F	27-2-51	?	?
HAZAN	Haim	M	1946	?	?
HAZAN	Esther	F	1-5-05	?	?
IBGHI	Esther	F	21-1-49	?	?
IBGHI	Simy	F	12-8-45	?	?
LEVY	Esther	F	27-1-45	?	?
LEVY	Jacob	M	22-8-47	?	?
LEVY	Marie	F	30-12-48	?	?
LUGASSY	Moshe	M	12-7-44	?	?
LUGASSY	Mazal	F	11-3-49	?	?
LUGASSY	Daniel	M	19-2-51	?	?
LUGASSY	Chalom	M	4-2-47	?	?
MALKA	Jacques	M	13-7-49	?	?
NAHMIAS	Haim	M	1944	?	?
NAHMIAS	Hana	F	1948	?	?
NAHMIAS	David	M	1950	?	?
OHNONA	Itshak	M	24-12-49	?	?
OHNONA	Nissim	M	1945	?	?
OUANOUNOU	Haim	M	11-6-45	?	?
OUANOUNOU	Simone	F	1-1-47	?	?
OUANOUNOU	David	M	5-4-49	?	?
PARIENTE	Raphaël	M	13-10-47	?	?
PEREZ	Marcelle	F	4-4-47	?	?
PEREZ	Bloria	F	20-6-49	?	?
SOUSSAN	Gabriel	M	1944	?	?
SOUSSAN	Raphaël	M	9-2-46	?	?

LAST NAME	FIRST NAME	SEX	DATE & PLACE BIRTH		ADDRESS (Casablanca)
SOUSSAN	Hanania	M	20-1-48	?	?
TORDJMAN	Habiba	F	1946	?	?
TORDJMAN	Kaphael	M	17-1-49	?	?
WILMAN	Dina	F	23-4-48	?	?
WIZMAN	Haim	M	26-11-46	?	?
WIZMAN	David	M	14-7-49	?	?
WIZMAN	Avram	M	20-12-51	?	?

Appendix III
Chronology

General chronological facts, figures, and details on legal and clandestine Jewish emigration from Morocco to Israel (1948–1963)[1]

1948

In 1948 there were about 300,000 Jews in the French and Spanish Moroccan Protectorates. The natural annual increase from 1948–1961 makes this figure realistic.

May 15, 1948 to September 27, 1956

About 92,000 Jews emigrated to Israel via the Jewish Agency's transit camp at Mazagan, called "Quadima," twenty-six kilometers south of Casablanca. Of those immigrants, 56,000 departed between the years 1955–1956. In October 1956, after Moroccan independence (March 3, 1956), the Istiqlal Party (Independence) requested the closure of the camp and the departure of all Zionist organizations from Morocco. Henceforth the Jews became virtual hostages in Morocco.

September 1952

In Israel the entire intelligence apparatus was reorganized by Isser Harel, a close associate of Prime Minister David Ben-Gurion. Harel was given full authority over both the Shin Bet (interior) and the Mossad (exterior) secret services (the only time this occurred). Ben-Gurion retired as prime minister in December 1953.

Early 1955

Harel named Paris-based Shlomo Havilio as chief of the Moroccan Mis-geret ("network"); he had travelled extensively in Morocco in November 1954. A year later, the "network" was ready to function. Havilio collaborated closely in Paris with Zalman Shragai, head of Israel's Immigration Department. Harel wanted the legal and clandestine emigration wings to overlap and collaborate in their work, and this was finalized with Shragai on September 16, 1956.

February 1955

Defence Minister Pinhas Lavon resigned after the collapse of an Israeli "spy ring" in Egypt. Ben-Gurion replaced him by Prime Minister Moshe Sharett. After the November 1955 elections, Ben-Gurion became prime minister again, even retaining the defense ministry. He acted immediately against increased terror raids inside Israel by systematic reprisal actions beyond the 1949 armistice borders.

April 1955

Key Bandung Conference (Afro-Asian states) where Egyptian President Gamal Abdel Nasser triumphed. In September 1955, after the nationalization of the Suez Canal by Nasser, the Czech/Soviet-Egyptian arms deal was signed.

November 16, 1955

Exiled Sultan Sidi Muhammad Ben Youssef returned to Morocco which gained its independence on March 3, 1956. He became King Muhammad V on August 15, 1957.

September 27, 1956

The Moroccan National Security Director, Mohammed Laghzaoui, obtained the monarch's ratification of decree 424 which expressly "forbade Moroccan Jews to visit Palestine," and called on those who had left to return. Jews were no longer to receive passports. However, with the closing of the Quadima transit camp, as many as 12,600 Jews left for Israel during the

1956 New Year/Yom Kippur period, double the number previously agreed with the emissaries of the World Jewish Congress (WJC), Alexander Easterman and Joe Golan, for WJC President Nahum Goldmann. The Moroccan clandestine emigration operations had begun and could now continue.

October 1956
Ben-Gurion flew to France and met secretly with French and British ministers. Egyptian sabotages, blockades and threats against Israel, as well as the increased of Arab military forces and Nasser's nationalization of the Suez Canal, triggered the Sinai campaign (October 29, 1956). Israel invaded the Sinai while Anglo-French troops landed in Suez.

Late November 1957
Just before Moroccan King Muhammad V's visit to Washington and New York, a meeting took place in Jerusalem between David Ben-Gurion, Golda Meir, Nahum Goldmann, Isser Harel, Zalman Shragai and Shlomo Havilio. It resulted in disagreement with WJC regarding the seriousness of the WJC's arrangement for only 500 passports to be granted officially each month by Morocco.

1957–1958
Clandestine Moroccan Jewish emigration to Israel slowed down considerably. In 1957 it numbered 8,758, but only 1,803 in 1958 and 3,325 in 1959. With scarcely 4,000 departures in 1960, it would have take fifty years for all the Jews to leave the country. This was considered inacceptable by Harel who, dissatisfied with Havilio, named Ephraïm Ronel to take over from Havilio in Paris, in supervising the three Mossad networks in Algeria, Tunisia and Morocco.

October 1958
Admission of Morocco and Tunisia to the Arab League, followed by the September 1959 Arab League Summit in Casablanca, when Morocco, specifically at the request of Nasser, agreed to cut postal, telephone and telegraphic relations with Israel. A parallel service was created in early 1960 between Tel Aviv, Paris and Rabat.

October 1959
Isser Harel returned to Morocco and reported to Ben-Gurion and Golda Meir that the Jews were not afraid to leave illegally en masse. At a key meeting on November 4, Nahum Goldmann remained hostile to any clandestine emigration. Golda Meir supported Harel, who opened a gallery in Casablanca for Shalom-Weiss of "Exodus" fame ("Dany"), a painter and expert at fabricating false passports; about 3,000 passports were made before he returned to help in preparing for Eichmann's capture.

May 2, 1960
Isser Harel was directly responsible for Adolf Eichmann's capture in Argentina; the dramatic Jerusalem trial took place from April 1961.

Summer 1960
Lt. Col. Alex Gatmon resigned from Israel's air force and prepared for his mission. He arrived in Casablanca on a Belgium passport, with his wife Carmit, in late November and took over as head ("Armin") of the network in Morocco. Gad Shahar ("Camus") was his right hand man in charge of all branches of the "Mak'hela."

March 1, 1960
An earthquake in Agadir (Morocco) took 22,000 victims, of whom there were about 800 local Jews and 1,000 Europeans. The Swiss Red Cross Societies were very active in Morocco.

January 3, 1961
Egyptian President Gamal Abdel Nasser received a triumphal reception on his arrival for the Conference of Casablanca (January 3–7); Israel was much condemned. Many anti-Zionist manifestations took place and several Jews were arrested while Judeophobia gained momentum.

January 3, 1961

First success of the network: Sixty-four young Jews disguised as Moroccan scouts en route for a holiday camp in Tangiers, went by boat clandestinely to Gibraltar, and from there helped by the Jewish Agency, reached Marseilles, and then Israel.

January 11, 1961

The Spanish *Piscès* (*Egoz*) sank with the loss of forty-three clandestine emigrants (twenty-four children), the Israeli Haim Sarfati (radio contact), and one of the four Spanish crewmen. There was much media coverage (e.g., "Toujours la tragédie de l'Exodus," *Paris Match*, January 28, 1961). It greatly embarrassed Morocco and Israel, where an official enquiry was ordered but its results remained secret.

End January 1961

Ben-Gurion offered his resignation over the "Lavon Affair" (October 1960 report), but was re-nominated by the Labour party (a public report on the *Egoz* tragedy at that time might have been fatal for him).

January 15, 1961

Alex Gatmon—fearing an isolated action of reprisal by the Moroccan Jewish Youth Movement—proposed Operation Bazac ("Eclair") to Ronel in Paris, who had just asked him to cease all initiatives, and modify his tactics. Ten thousand tracts would be distributed throughout Morocco on February 9, commemorating the 30th day after the loss of those who had drowned when the *Egoz* capsized.

February 9, 1961

Operation Bazac succeeded, but mistakes were made and harsh results followed. Mohammed Oufkir, the newly appointed director of National Security, decided to dismantle the network and twenty of its members (including Michel Knafo) were arrested, kept in prison for twenty-one days and tortured; on his release, Raphael Ouaknine died later in a Parisian hospital.

February 17, 1961

The minister of the interior announced that Jews could obtain passports like any other Moroccans, as had been stated by his predecessor in 1957 and this was confirmed to *The New York Times* soon after (the news was relayed by Moroccan newspapers).

February 20, 1961

In a letter to Ephraim Ronel in Paris, Isser Harel explains how negotiations with the king and the minister of the interior were now engaged as a result of the recent media and other campaign strongly criticising Morocco's policy, and that demands for passports should be increased everywhere.

February 26, 1961

Muhammad V died unexpectedly during a benign operation and his son succeeded him as King Hassan II on March 3.

February 27, 1961

Isser Harel's letter to Ronel suggested rapid contacts with the new king and those close to him. This was immediately initiated, but no concrete steps resulted for the first four months of his reign. However, the clandestine emigration continued, with another ship, the *Cocus*, which replaced the *Egoz*, taking from 100 to 120 passengers regularly from a private beach on the Atlantic.

April 22, 1961

A Putsch by French generals took place in Algiers. The Mossad had warned General de Gaulle of an imminent attack on him just before; he now increased French support for Jewish emigration from Morocco, as did Britain, encouraging the new King Hassan II to act.

May 10, 1961

On this question, the opposition's Istiqlal's journal had this to say: "The emigration of Moroccan Jews to Israel should be punished by death, as it is the equivalent of an act of treason. The penalty imposed on twenty Jews arrested as they tried to leave the country illegally, and recently condemned to three months in prison by the tribunal of Nador is insufficient."

March 16–July 24, 1961
In Operation Mural 127 children leave with collective passports on June 26 from Casablanca on the *S.S. Ionia* to Marseilles for holidays in Switzerland; 403 more in four convoys on July 10, 19, 22, and 24. These were uncertain times before the success of the main negotiations became apparent. When this occurred the "collective passports" were used for all.

November 27, 1961
First collective passport signed by Mohamed Oufkir on instructions from King Hassan II.

1962–1964
Operation Yakhin—over 100,000 Jews left Morocco for Israel with collective passports.

Summer 1963
Alex and Carmit Gattmon leave Morocco; Gad Shahar and Pinhas Katsir would depart a year later.

---

1   Many of the facts and dates regarding Morocco have been gleaned from Agnès Bensimon's book, *Hassan II et Les Juifs. Histoire d'une émigration secrète* (Paris: Seuil. L'Histoire Immédiate, October 1991).

Credits

Most of the illustrations in this book are from David and Gisèle Littman's personal archive. Other sources that provided illustrations are listed below.

Dr. Claude Dreyfus: p. xii, pp. 65, 67–68
Carmit Gatmon, private collection: p. 204, p. 206, p. 208
Pinhas Katsir, private collection: p. 211
Ariane Littman: pp. xxiv–xxv, pp. 151–155, pp. 157–159
Raphael Rebibo, private collection: p. 198
Gad Shahar, private collection: pp. 199–201
Yossi Shahar, private collection: p. 185, p. 189, pp. 192–194.
Shmuel Toledano, private collection: p. 212
Swiss Archives, p. 51

For the illustrations used in the book every effort has been made to trace the holders of copyright and to acknowledge the permission of authors and publishers where necessary. If we have inadvertently failed in this aim, we will be pleased to correct any omissions in future editions of this book.